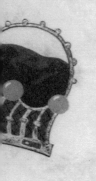

ירושלים הבנויה

...ation to

BARON JAKOBOVITS OF

LONDON, CHIEF RABBI OF

...ONS OF THE COMMONWEALTH

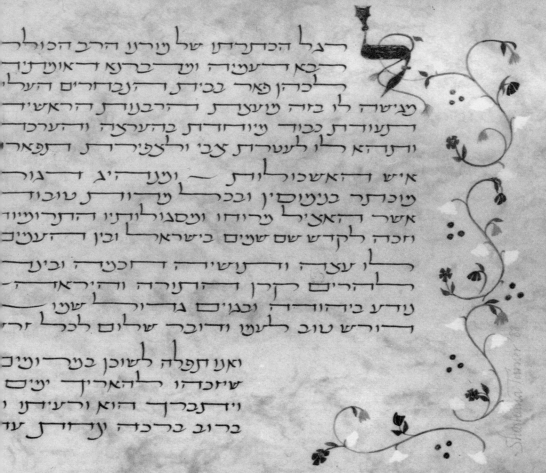

IMMANUEL JAKOBOVITS:
A PROPHET IN ISRAEL

Lord Jakobovits on his introduction in the House of Lords, 9 February 1988

IMMANUEL JAKOBOVITS:
A PROPHET IN ISRAEL

Compiled and edited

by

Meir Persoff

VALLENTINE MITCHELL
LONDON • PORTLAND, OR

First Published in 2002 in Great Britain by
VALLENTINE MITCHELL
Crown House, 47 Chase Side
Southgate, London N14 5BP

and in the United States of America by
VALLENTINE MITCHELL
c/o ISBS, 5824 N. E. Hassalo Street
Portland, Oregon 97213-3644

Website: http://www.vmbooks.com

British Library Cataloguing-in-Publication Data

Immanuel Jakobovits: a prophet in Israel
  1. Jakobovits, Immanuel   2. Rabbis – Great Britain – Biography
I. Persoff, Meir
296'.092

ISBN 0-85303-444-3

Library of Congress Cataloguing-in-Publication Data

Immanuel Jakobovits: a prophet in Israel/compiled and edited
by Meir Persoff.
    p.cm.
  Includes bibliographical references and index
  ISBN 0-85303-444-3 (cloth)
  1. Jakobovits, Immanuel, Sir, 1921   2. Rabbis – Great Britain – Biography.
  3. Zionists – Great Britain – Biography.   4. Chief Rabbinate – Great Britain
I. Persoff, Meir.
BM755.J28 L54 2002
296'.092–dc21
[B]
                                                                2002023503

Typeset in Palatino by Cambridge Photosetting Services
Printed in Great Britain by Bookcraft (Limited), Midsomer Norton

For my parents,
Mark and Sarah Persoff,
of blessed memory

*'Let him come now to me, and he shall know
that there is a prophet in Israel.'*
II Kings 5:8

Contents

Illustrations

Endpapers: Illuminated citation by Shoshana Turner.
p. ii: Lord Jakobovits on his introduction in the House of Lords, 9 February 1988.
p. xiv: Lord Jakobovits with Nobel Peace Laureate Elie Wiesel.
p. xxii: Lord Jakobovits with Chief Rabbi Professor Jonathan Sacks.

Between pages 38 and 39

1. Rabbi Dr Julius Jakobovits in Königsberg with his three eldest children – Immanuel, Lotti and George.

2 and 3. The newly appointed Dayan Dr Julius Jakobovits in Berlin in 1928, and the newly ordained Rabbi Immanuel Jakobovits at the Great Synagogue, Duke's Place, in 1948.

4 and 5. Engagement portraits of Immanuel and Amélie soon after he took up his appointment as Chief Rabbi of Ireland in 1949.

6. Amélie's parents, Rabbi Dr Elie Munk and Fanny Munk (née Goldberger), at home in Paris.

7. The marriage of Ireland's Chief Rabbi and Amélie at the rue Cadet Synagogue in Paris on 5 July, 1949.

8. Paula Jakobovits (née Wreschner) and her son enjoy a rare moment of relaxation together during the summer of 1954

9. Chief Rabbi and Mrs Jakobovits on horseback in Ireland in 1950.

10. With Colonel and Mrs Chaim Herzog at a Dublin banquet in 1958 to mark the inauguration of the Jewish National Fund's Herzog Forest in Israel.

11. Dublin, 1949: Talmudical studies vie with pressing diary engagements.

12. Dublin, 1957: Professor Leonard Abrahamson presents a gift to Ireland's departing Chief Rabbi.

13. The Jakobovits family on the eve of their move to New York.

Between pages 70 and 71

14. Fifth Avenue Synagogue's founding rabbi on his appointment to the congregation in 1958.

15 and 16. The designer's drawings of the main prayer hall and the beth hamidrash at Fifth Avenue Synagogue, described by its founders as 'truly unique in the inspiring beauty of its architecture'.

17. Fifth Avenue's Judge Sol Rosenberg and Hermann Merkin present Rabbi Jakobovits with a mantle to accompany the Sefer Torah he received before taking up the post of British Chief Rabbi in 1967.

18. 'This resplendent occasion, usually witnessed but once in a generation': the newly installed Chief Rabbi at his induction service in London's St John's Wood Synagogue in April 1967.

19. A call to action as thousands gather for an Israel solidarity rally at the Royal Albert Hall, London, on 5 June 1967, the first day of the Six-Day War.

20. Conversing with excited Israelis paying their first visit to the Western Wall in Jerusalem, days after the liberation of the Old City during the Six-Day War.

21. Israeli statesman Abba Eban joins the Chief Rabbi and other communal leaders at a Board of Deputies meeting in London in March 1979 to mark the signing of the Israel–Egypt peace treaty.

22. Chief Rabbi Jakobovits looks on as Board of Deputies president Greville Janner, QC, MP, signs a declaration in 1980 opposing PLO policies.

Between pages 134 and 135

23. With Israeli Prime Minister Yitzhak Rabin at a meeting of world Jewish leaders in Jerusalem in November 1976.

24. Congratulating Israeli Prime Minister Menachem Begin on the completion of the peace talks with Egypt.

25. With Israeli Foreign Minister and Deputy Premier Shimon Peres at a London meeting in 1987.

26. Welcoming Israeli Prime Minister Yitzhak Shamir at a communal gathering in London in 1990.

27. Inter-faith encounter: Chief Rabbi Jakobovits and Israeli Chief Rabbi Shlomo Goren with the Archbishop of Canterbury, Dr Michael Ramsey; the Archbishop of Westminster, Cardinal John Heenan; and the Rev A. S. Cooper, Moderator of the Free Church Federal Council.

28. Queen Elizabeth the Queen Mother conversing with the Chief Rabbi and violinist Yehudi Menuhin at a Westminster Abbey concert in aid of the Council of Christians and Jews and the Royal Silver Jubilee Fund, 1977.

29. The Duchess of Kent with Sir Sigmund Sternberg, Lord Coggan and Chief Rabbi Jakobovits at a reception in London.

30. With the Archbishop of Canterbury, Dr Robert Runcie, after receiving a Lambeth degree in 1987.

50. In conversation with Chief Rabbi Moses Rosen of Romania at a 1982 education conference in London.

51. With United Synagogue honorary officers at the launch of the Year of Jewish Education in 1987.

52. Lighting the menorah on the fifth night of Chanukah for MPs and peers in the crypt of the House of Commons.

Between pages 262 and 263

53. The Chief Rabbi at an intra-communal gathering with Eric Moonman, MP, Professor Emil Fackenheim, Greville Janner, QC, MP, and Rabbi Sidney Brichto.

54. Watched by Rabbi Hugo Gryn, Sir Sigmund Sternberg presents the Chief Rabbi with a 'Peace Through Dialogue' award for his contribution to inter-faith co-operation.

55. Chief Rabbi Jakobovits welcomes the Queen to the 1971 centenary celebrations of the United Synagogue. With them are Board of Deputies president Michael Fidler, MP, and US president Sir Isaac Wolfson.

56. Accompanied by his wife, Chief Rabbi Sir Immanuel Jakobovits displays the insignia of his knighthood conferred in the 1981 Queen's Birthday Honours.

57 and 58. With Lady Jakobovits after receiving the freedom of the City of London in 1983; and with chairman Norman Tebbit, MP, at the 1991 'Men of the Year' awards.

59. In the Chinese Room at Buckingham Palace with the Duke of Edinburgh following the 1991 award of the Templeton Prize for Progress in Religion.

60. In the Moses Room of the House of Lords on 9 February 1988, before being introduced by Baron Mishcon of Lambeth and Baron Young of Graffham, the Secretary of State for Trade and Industry.

61. Guest speaker Margaret Thatcher, MP, with Lord and Lady Jakobovits and Chief Rabbi-elect Dr Jonathan Sacks at a Jewish Educational Development Trust dinner in March 1991 to mark the Chief Rabbi's retirement.

62 and 63. Chief Rabbi Jakobovits with Israeli Chief Rabbi Shlomo Goren following the inauguration of the Immanuel Jakobovits Chair in Jewish Law at Bar-Ilan University, Ramat Gan, in 1974; and in the company of fellow recipient Mikhail Gorbachev, Lord Jakobovits receives the honorary degree of Doctor of Philosophy at a ceremony at Bar-Ilan in 1992.

Photo credits: Universal Pictorial Press and Agency Ltd, ii; Basil Henry, Dublin, 12; K. Weiss, Jerusalem, 20; Rachamim Israeli, Jerusalem, 23; John R. Rifkin, 26, 47; Peter Fisher, 21, 22, 27, 30, 38, 39, 41, 53, 58, 60, 61; Sidney Harris, 24, 25, 29, 31, 32, 33, 40, 42, 43, 44, 46, 48, 49, 50, 51, 54, 56; John Nathan, 52; *Jewish Chronicle*, 10, 18, 19, 45; United Press International, 55; Professional Photographic Services, 57; Jonathan Reif, Tel Aviv, 63. All other photographs are from the Jakobovits family collection, courtesy of Lady Jakobovits.

Lord Jakobovits with Nobel Peace Laureate Elie Wiesel

Foreword

PROFESSOR ELIE WIESEL
Winner of the Nobel Peace Prize, 1986

To his numerous admirers in America and Britain, Lord Jakobovits was a Renaissance man in the original sense of the term. He gave new life to concepts, ideas and principles forgotten by some and repudiated by others.

Indeed, one could not but be impressed by the immensity of his knowledge in the field of halachah, nor by his sensitivity when relating to those who turned to him for a direction in their lives. A true *talmid chacham*, he knew how to inspire the joy of learning and respect for the texts as much as for the teachers who transmitted them.

Wherever he travelled, whether to the communities he led or the conferences he chaired, he awakened a Jewish consciousness – an involvement, ethical rather than political, in the society in which we find ourselves.

For him, Judaism was exactly that: perfecting the Creation by helping others to attain fulfilment, as a Jew or as a human being, in a permanent quest for truth, justice and dignity.

Hence his seminal work in the field of bioethics. The protection of life, as also of the meaning of life, was the goal he seems to have set himself when exploring the limits of medical and scientific intervention.

Nor is it surprising that he was frequently invited to international conferences on such matters, a recognition of the unique insights he was able to shed.

He spoke always as a Jew, as a rabbi, and as a disciple of the Sages. His speeches and essays are essential reading: one can find in them his singular contribution which, through shrewd analysis and understanding, marks the flowering of contemporary Jewish thought. This was acknowledged with his award, in 1991, of the Templeton Prize for Progress in Religion.

For my part, I admired also his willingness to express, with characteristic elegance, what he had to say – on all possible topics – without fear or flattery. He said what he thought; he thought what he believed. Hence his courageous attitude towards Judaeo–Christian dialogue – and equally, towards the various extremists in his own camp.

Known for his religious liberalism, he neither separated nor distanced himself from the tradition of our ancestors. On the contrary, the more he made it accessible to modern Jewry, by enriching it, the more faithful he remained to it. Thinking about him, and celebrating his life and work, means emphasising one's pride in being a Jew in a turbulent century strewn with pitfalls and ambiguities that are dangerous for the comfort they seem to afford.

New York, 2002

Preface

In the sweep and swathe of modern Jewish history, Immanuel Jakobovits was a generation ahead of his time. Whether on the international stage or on the home front, he evinced a shrewdness of mind and sureness of touch that went to the heart of any matter he chose to explore. Professor Sir Isaiah Berlin reflected on the Chief Rabbi's 'unswerving integrity, moving faith and exemplary courage' – qualities which evoke images of the biblical prophets who, throughout eras of upheaval and uncertainty, courted neither popularity nor preferment in their bid to convey God's message to man. Few other Jewish leaders of the twentieth century displayed Lord Jakobovits' ability not only to predict unfolding events and currents across a range of canvases – from Soviet Jewry and the Middle East to Jewish education and inter-faith relations – but to apply the tints and textures that would mould the finished picture and create its character.

It is this range of issues, and his impact upon them, that mark out Immanuel Jakobovits from his contemporaries and peers. As a pulpit and pastoral rabbi in the early years of his ministry, he laid the foundations for educational excellence, marriage guidance, youth leadership, literary endeavour and Torah scholarship in a number of congregations. As Chief Rabbi of Ireland, he fashioned an entire community in the round, and introduced to the rabbinate and academia the hitherto untouched study of Jewish medical ethics. And as founding rabbi of New York's Fifth Avenue Synagogue, he advanced the concept of Modern Orthodoxy in a challenging and innovative manner. But it was during his Adler House incumbency – following a period of unprecedented turbulence within Anglo-Jewry – that his gifts of leadership, diplomacy, grace and wisdom bore greatest fruit, smoothing the ruffled feathers of a torn and troubled flock, and accelerating the emergence of a vibrant and revitalised Orthodoxy in the centrist community.

Decades before Madrid, Oslo and Camp David became the cradles of peace, years before *perestroika* presaged the downfall of Communism and freedom for Soviet Jewry, HaRav Jakobovits was at the hustings, calling for talks with the Palestinians and for a programme of enlightenment – labelled 'Let My People Live' – for his coreligionists behind the Iron Curtain. Standing his ground against widespread scepticism, he travelled widely, and corresponded more widely still, to garner support for policies then unpopular but later shown to be of enduring merit. In many of these campaigns, he suffered the slings and barbs of vested interests, the taunts and contempt of so-called constituents, as he echoed the words of the prophet Micah (3:1): 'Hear, I pray you, ye heads of Jacob, and rulers of the house of Israel: is it not for you to know justice?'

The Chief Rabbi's frustrations found expression in constant references to the prophetical mission. Discussing – in the aftermath of the Yom Kippur War – the Jewish destiny, the pursuit of peace, and 'sensitivity to the plight of Arab refugees, whatever the cause of the problem', he told a 1974 gathering in London: 'Only through an intensely religious conscience can such high moral standards be attained as will eventually reassure our adversaries that they can dwell securely and without fear. Real peace is a state of mind, rather than an expedient accommodation.' And, anticipating the kind of critical response that was soon to dog him at every turn, he added: 'We may be bitterly opposed, if not abused, by those who do not share our commitment and who will not easily submit to an exacting way of life or abandon the little gods and supermen they have fashioned to replace the God of Israel, however disastrous the course they have chosen may be. But, as heirs to the Hebrew prophets – and like them – we must be prepared to expose ourselves to the risk of loneliness, unpopularity and sometimes even derision. They, too, were often ignored and harassed by their contemporaries. Yet their work has remained immortal, and thanks to their reproof and consolation, we are alive while others have disappeared.

'Today, some 25 centuries later, our task is, thank God, far easier than theirs. We can build on the foundations of immense goodwill, on a vast fund of high idealism, self-sacrifice and passionate dedication, as displayed so heroically by the builders and defenders of our Homeland, and by the supporters of Zion's cause throughout the world. The will is there, if only we provide the direction and inspiration for its expression.'

Seven years earlier, within sight of the Six-Day War, he had spelled out that mission in similar terms. 'I am summoned', he declared in his installation address, 'to provide the vision and inspiration of the prophet, whose mantle, according to the Talmud, was bequeathed to the rabbis from the day the Temple was destroyed. Unlike the priests, who expected the people to come to them in the sanctuary, the prophets went out to the people to proclaim their message. I shall likewise seek out my brethren wherever they are …

'As successor to the prophets, the rabbi today must demonstrate the relevance of Judaism to the contemporary experience. He must also spiritualise the mechanics of Jewish observance, showing the moral grandeur of religious discipline, the stirring uplift of true prayer, and the holiness of lives daily consecrated to God's service. He must interpret the interplay between faith and reality, between ritual and ethics, between Israel and the nations. He must make manifest the gap between the laws of nature and the moral law, between impersonal science complacently dealing with things as they are and personal religion impatiently dealing with things as they ought to be. He must demand commitment, denounce indifference, and ennoble the aim of life as a quest for living in the image of God, instead of the selfish pursuit of happiness and personal success.'

There are resonances here of Amos' admonition to the inhabitants of the Northern Kingdom of Israel for having spurned the ethical laws of God in

everyday life. Inveighing against the vacuous nature of their religious observance, the prophet declared (5:23–24): 'Take away from me the noise of your
songs; to the melody of your harps I will not listen. But let justice roll down like
waters, and righteousness like an ever-flowing stream.'

Lord Jakobovits personified Maimonides' doctrine of prophecy in relation to
the individual, and the medieval philosopher's concept of the type of leader
that God sends to mankind. Hebrew University Professor Haim Hillel Ben-
Sasson cites 'greatness of intellect and learning' as the Rambam's 'essential
prerequisites for prophecy. Yet, while intellectual as well as moral accomplishments are necessary conditions, they are not in themselves sufficient qualities
for prophecy. Unlike his predecessors among the Arab philosophers, Maimonides
left to divinity the right of "veto": the man who has reached these heights of
human achievement is potentially capable of prophecy, but whether or not he
does prophesy depends on the Divine Will. In his view, it is also possible for a
man to be a "prophet unto himself ... able to prophesy for himself in his heart,
expanding ... and extending his knowledge and thought until he knows what
he never knew previously of those great matters".'

This book, which marks the establishment at Bar-Ilan University, Ramat Gan,
of Beit HaRav Jakobovits for the Study of Philosophy, Ethics and Jewish
Thought, owes its existence to the initiative, encouragement and sponsorship
of the British Friends of Bar-Ilan, under the inspired chairmanship of Conrad
Morris. From conception to fruition, the Friends have shown a keen interest in
its development, and I am deeply grateful for the support I have received at all
stages of production. Beit HaRav Jakobovits, due to open in 2004, is the British
Friends' permanent tribute to the late Chief Rabbi's outstanding record of
service to both Anglo-Jewry and world Jewry and his drive to project the teachings of Judaism 'in terms of the scientific thinking and intellectual stirrings of
our times'. The relationship between HaRav Jakobovits and Bar-Ilan was one of
shared values and a common ideology. Despite the numerous demands on his
time, he served for some 30 years as a trustee of the university and a firm
supporter of its British Friends. In keeping with his profound example, Beit
HaRav Jakobovits aims to become a vibrant resource for influential and inspiring analysis and guidance in the fields he pioneered and championed, a living
legacy dedicated to Jewish learning from which future generations in Israel and
throughout the Jewish world will continue to benefit.

The title of this book is derived from the Second Book of Kings (5:8), wherein the
prophet Elisha sends word to Naaman, the leprosy-stricken captain of the host
of the king of Aram, assuring him of a cure: 'Let him come now to me, and he
shall know that there is a prophet in Israel.' The prophetical passage, replete with
medical advice, serves as the haftarah of the sidrah Tazria (Leviticus 12:1–13:59),
which likewise deals with sickness, disease and healing. In our day, no individual
has devoted his life to morality, medicine and medical ethics in a Jewish context
with greater commitment than Immanuel Jakobovits, whose Hebrew name affirms
that in this Israel – HaRav Yisrael ben HaRav Yoel – there truly was a prophet.

My late father, Mark Persoff, of blessed memory, was a joint worker with HaRav Jakobovits on the Jewish Marriage Education Committee in its formative years. In due course, it was my privilege, too, to have worked with the Rav throughout his Chief Rabbinate. As a member of the *Jewish Chronicle* staff, I met with him on countless occasions, gaining an insight into the breadth of his vision, and benefiting from his unbounded counsel and consideration. In various capacities, I benefited also from the friendship of three other personalities – one sadly no longer with us – with whom I was in constant touch over many years. Nobel Peace Laureate Elie Wiesel, who contributed regularly to the *JC* while I was features editor, has kindly written the Foreword to this book; Chief Rabbi Professor Jonathan Sacks, another long-standing *JC* contributor, has penned the Prologue; and the spirit of Chaim Bermant, whose *JC* column (and other pieces) I edited for longer than I can remember, hovers over several of these pages.

Chaim was Lord Jakobovits' authorised biographer, to be followed, in the same genre if in different contexts, by Gloria Tessler and Michael Shashar. *Immanuel Jakobovits: a Prophet in Israel* does not profess to be a biography, but concentrates on the Rav's own writings and speeches, as well as on contemporary accounts, to convey the magnitude of his achievement. In its variety and effervescence, the kaleidoscope illustrates the richness of his life, the depth of his contribution, and its dramatic impact on the Jewish world. Controversial it may have been, but the very nature of that contribution – in line with that of his forebears – adds to the colour and luminosity of his prophetic light.

My greatest debt of gratitude is owed to Lady Jakobovits, who led me to this task and whose warmth, hospitality, co-operation and kindness have added to my joy in bringing it to fruition. As the pages unfold, it becomes clear (to those who do not already know) that 'Lady J' is an integral part of the story, perpetuated through her ongoing devotion to the community, and, in large measure, through her children, grandchildren and great-grandchildren – the Jewish family *par excellence*. The family plays a prominent role in the sections of this book entitled 'Flashback', the fledgling fragments of an unfinished autobiography – written by Lord Jakobovits in the early 1990s – that until now have never seen the light of day.

I am also indebted to former colleagues at the *JC*, including librarians Anna Charin and Keith Feldman, for their valuable assistance, particularly when the avalanche of material threatened to overwhelm me. That the paper remains the pre-eminent medium of Jewish news, and an unparalleled resource for academics, researchers and students of Anglo-Jewry and beyond, is amply demonstrated throughout this book.

Thanks are extended to the following newspapers and magazines for permission to reproduce copyright material: *Daily Mail, Daily Telegraph, Evening Standard, Financial Times, The Guardian*, the *Irish Times*, the *New York Times, Time, The Times*, and the *Yorkshire Post*.

I am grateful to the following Jewish publications (some no longer extant) for material used: *Chayenu, HaChaim, Hamesilah, Jewish Chronicle, Jewish Echo, Jewish Tribune, Living Judaism, Pointer, Rivon*, and *Tradition*.

Parliamentary copyright material from *Hansard* is reproduced with the permission of the Controller of Her Majesty's Stationery Office on behalf of Parliament.

Lord Jakobovits' 'The Status of the Embryo in the Jewish Tradition' (Chapter 7 of *The Status of the Human Embryo: Perspectives From Moral Tradition*, edited by G. R. Dunstan and Mary J. Seller, 1988), is reprinted by permission of the King's Fund.

Extracts from Dr Yoel Jakobovits' 'The Father of Jewish Medical Ethics' (in *Pioneers in Jewish Medical Ethics*, edited by Fred Rosner), are reproduced by permission of the publisher, Jason Aronson, Inc., Northvale, New Jersey, © 1997.

Immanuel Jakobovits belies the assertion of New York theologian Peter Zaas that 'modern Judaism cannot look to contemporary prophets for consolation or moral guidance'. As the citation to his Templeton Prize reminds us, the Chief Rabbi was 'a man whose steadfast principles and unwavering integrity have extended his moral authority far beyond the Jewish community. In 50 years of rabbinical leadership, Lord Jakobovits has developed a reputation as a rock of unyielding ethics. His efforts to advance Judaism have set him on an often-lonely path, sometimes putting himself at odds with many of his own faith.'

Lamenting the fact that 'prophetical courage and vision are in preciously short supply today', HaRav Jakobovits articulated that voice in the wilderness to which he frequently referred throughout his rabbinate. In this, he gave substance to Ahad Ha'am's depiction of the Hebrew prophet as 'the man of truth', the 'moral extremist who places righteousness ("truth in action") at the centre of human life'.

Justice, peace, righteousness, bridge-building – these remain the key elements of the prophetical, moral and ethical utterances of Lord Jakobovits as revealed in the ensuing chapters. In sum, they constitute a testament to his sagacity and perspicacity, his vision and courage, his forthrightness and frankness, and, above all, his love of – and dedication to – his God, his people and his land. Ours is a generation, like so many others, that appreciates greatness only when the great have departed, but it is within our grasp to carry forth the noble Rav's legacy beyond the confines of his life.

Meir Persoff
London, 2002

Lord Jakobovits with Chief Rabbi Professor Jonathan Sacks

Prologue

CHIEF RABBI PROFESSOR JONATHAN SACKS
Chief Rabbi of the United Hebrew Congregations of the
Commonwealth

The life of Lord Jakobovits, of blessed memory, came to an end with an almost poetic sense of closure. He died having made havdalah and entered the week in which we read the portion of Chayei Sarah, the section of the Torah that describes the death of Sarah and Abraham, the founders of the covenant and of Jewish history. At the beginning of that sidrah, there is a striking phrase. It occurs early in Abraham's negotiations with the Hittites for the purchase of a burial site for his wife. They say to him: *nesi Elokim atah betochenu*, 'You are a prince of God in our midst.' If one were to search for the simplest tribute to Lord Jakobovits' life – his epitaph – it would be those words.

He was a man who epitomised the dignity and majesty of Torah – its moral vision, its high ideals, its summons to righteousness and justice. These things shaped his teachings and activities as a leader, even his physical and psychological bearing. He walked tall as a Jew, and because of him, we walked a little taller also. He won great respect and admiration, not only throughout the Jewish world but far beyond. His life was a *kiddush hashem*, a sanctification of the name of God. He was a prince of God in our midst.

Great lives have about them a narrative unity, a theme. They are more than the sum of their parts. Through their multiple episodes and engagements, there runs a connecting thread of purpose and principle. In the case of Lord Jakobovits, this was disclosed in the address he gave on his installation as Chief Rabbi of Britain and the Commonwealth in April 1967. In it, he did more than set out his plans for the future. In a bold and imaginative speech, he articulated his understanding of the rabbinate, and thereby of the nature of Jewish spiritual and moral leadership.

He took his cue from the date of the ceremony itself – Rosh Chodesh Nisan. This was, he reminded his audience, the anniversary of all three of Judaism's 'crowns' – the crowns of kingship, priesthood and Torah. There never was, in Judaism, a single model of leadership. Instead, in the biblical era, there were kings, priests and prophets. Each had a particular task, and each carried its own orientation and sensibility. What made Lord Jakobovits' argument unusual is that he saw each as integral to the task of the rabbinate. A rabbi must aspire to all three crowns. He must be king, priest and prophet. That is what, at the outset of his Chief Rabbinate, he set himself to be, and it is what, to an unusual degree, he became.

The crown of kingship meant, he said, that Jewish leaders were 'invested with certain royal prerogatives in guiding the destinies of our people'. This meant leadership on a bold scale, not only within, but also beyond, the boundaries of the Jewish community. His ambition was nothing less than 'the moral regeneration of society'.

I am not sure whether his audience back in 1967 realised how literally he meant this. He became perhaps the first Chief Rabbi to aspire to, and achieve, an influence far beyond his Jewish constituency. The timing, especially in the 1980s, was fortuitous. In Margaret Thatcher, he found a politician very much in tune with his views. She, in turn, saw in him a vigorous defender of traditional ethics at a time when its committed advocates were few. There developed between them a strong mutual admiration. Not only did she grant him the distinction of becoming the first Chief Rabbi to have a seat in the House of Lords. He also became, in his own right, the strongest exponent of biblical morality in an all-too-secular age.

It was a role he fulfilled with distinction. Before he became Chief Rabbi, he was already an acknowledged expert in medical ethics. To this, he added a wide-ranging series of affirmations on social issues. He spoke with passion and persuasion about the sanctity of the family. He insisted on the importance of responsibilities as well as rights. He defended objective standards of right and wrong. At any other time, these would have been conventional stances for a religious leader, but the so-called 'moral revolution' of the 1960s had left public debate confused and relativistic. Refusing to bow to the mood of the age, his voice was bold and unusually clear. It did, indeed, have a royal reach.

The crown of priesthood meant a responsibility for Jewish education. Moses had charged the priesthood with these words: 'They shall teach Thy laws unto Jacob, and Thy Torah to Israel.' Lord Jakobovits took this injunction with great seriousness. He knew that, for various historical reasons, the Jewish educational system – especially day-schools – had been neglected in Britain. He was deter-mined to remedy this. The health of a Jewish community, he was convinced, was measured not by the magnificence of its synagogues but by the breadth and depth of the Jewish knowledge it gave its children. As I once put it: to defend a country, you need an army; but to defend a civilisation, you need schools. It was a view he shared.

The greatest of his practical initiatives in Anglo-Jewry was the launch, in 1971, of the Jewish Educational Development Trust, under the slogan, 'Let My People Know.' Its aim was to generate resources for the improvement of Jewish education generally, and specifically to build more Jewish day-schools. One of its lasting achievements was the opening, at the end of his Chief Rabbinate, of an impressive secondary school, Immanuel College, that bears his name. I think of it with particular emotion, since it was a project on which we worked together – I wrote the document upon which its educational philosophy and curricular principles were based, and our youngest daughter went there. Of all his memorials, it is the one that best symbolises his hopes for British Jewry.

The last of the crowns – that of Torah – represents the heritage of the prophets of Israel, of whom the first was Abraham himself. Abraham was many things: a shepherd, a tribal chief, a leader, a man prepared, if necessary, to go to war. But the Torah adds a further description. God appears to Abimelech, king of Gerar, and tells him to honour Abraham 'for he is a prophet'. On this phrase, Rabbi Samson Raphael Hirsch comments that it means that he 'judges conditions, and the behaviour of people, not in accordance with the views which arise from the customs and opinions of any particular age or country, but in accordance with the eternal, unchangeable law of morality'. A prophet is the voice of eternity in the midst of time. That calls for vision and courage – the vision to see beyond the moment, and the courage to challenge the idols of the age. This was Lord Jakobovits' most striking attribute.

Whether speaking about ethics or politics – in particular about Israel, land and peace – he was prepared to take unpopular stands on the basis of moral conviction. He was not a man who relished conflict. On the contrary, he was, if anything, a man of peace. Yet once he had formed a view on the basis of his understanding of Torah, he was unshakeable. Several were the occasions on which it could have been said of him, as it was of Abraham, that 'all the world was on one side and he was on the other'. Yet he never faltered or weakened, and in several cases history vindicated his judgement. Often, as I witnessed his lonely courage, I thought of the words of God to Ezekiel: 'Whether they listen or fail to listen … they will know that a prophet has been among them.'

This was, then, a man who exercised leadership on a grand scale, in many arenas and across the broadest of canvases. Whether as spiritual leader of Commonwealth Jewry, president of the Conference of European Rabbis, exponent of Jewish medical ethics, or defender of biblical values within British society as a whole, there was a consistency and integrity to his work that compelled admiration, even among those who disagreed with him.

He acknowledged many debts. He was always conscious of what he owed Britain, the country that had given his family refuge from Nazi Germany and which he never ceased to describe as a *malchut shel chessed*, a 'kingdom of kindness'. He was profoundly influenced by his late father, a rabbi and dayan, whose Torah interpretations he often quoted. Above all, he knew how much he owed his beloved wife and companion, Amélie, his constant source of support and strength. Together, they achieved that most difficult of dual achievements: a glittering public career and a no less successful family life. He lived to see their children, grandchildren and great-grandchildren continue along the path he had followed all his life, and his last years were framed by their loving presence. Much of him lives on in them.

How shall we sum up a life of such multifaceted grandeur? A remark of Rabbi Samson Raphael Hirsch – the thinker to whom he was closest – is singularly appropriate. In one of the most haunting passages of the Torah, Abraham challenges God on the justice of the fate awaiting Sodom and the cities of the plain. 'What if', he says, 'there are 50 righteous people in the midst of the city?' Shall their merit not save their fellow townspeople from destruction?

Hirsch meditates on the significance of the phrase *tzaddikim betoch ha'ir*, 'righteous people in the midst of the city'. There are, he says, two kinds of righteousness. There is the person for whom righteousness takes the form of private perfection, a sanctity of the soul. Such an individual keeps to himself. Not for him the cut and thrust of ordinary life, the battle for justice and spiritual truth in the public square. There is much to be said for this kind of righteousness, but it does not change the fate of nations. It does not save the city. Abraham did not predicate his prayer on the existence of this kind of solitary virtue.

Instead, he spoke of 'the righteous in the midst of the city' – the person who, in Hirsch's words, 'never leaves off admonishing, teaching, warning, bettering, wherever and however he can'. He lives 'in lively connection with everything and everyone'. He 'never despairs and is never tired of trying, however distant the hopes of success may be'. This kind of person makes a difference to his environment and age. For him, religion is about the kind of society we make, the values for which we live, the way we construct a set of relationships with others, the uses to which we put science and technology, wealth and power. Faith is more than a transaction in the soul. It is the architecture of a civilisation, the shape of our common life as citizens under the sovereignty of God.

Lord Jakobovits was a *tzaddik betoch ha'ir*, a righteous man in the midst of the city, whose moral courage and spiritual vision enlarged the horizons of his contemporaries and left us his grateful heirs.

Part One

LIFE

Childhood and Youth

I was born in 1921 in the city of Königsberg, situated in what was then East Prussia. From 1945 until the fall of Communism, it was part of the Soviet Union and known officially as Kaliningrad. But whatever its name, it tugs at no heart-strings of mine.

The efforts so often made in biographical studies to relate character traits to ancestral estates or the geographical surroundings of youthful experiences would be quite irrelevant in my case. Had I been born seven years later, when my parents moved to Berlin, or in Paris, my wife's birthplace, or in London, where I was to spend the greater part of my life, or, indeed, in any other centre with an organised Jewish religious life, my early background would have been just the same. The spoken word might have been different, but the pieties, observances and studies of traditional Judaism would have been identical.

Both my parents came from long rabbinical lines and, to them, the slightest deviation from strict Orthodoxy would have been unthinkable. The mould was never broken, even though they and their children were to experience vicissitudes they could never have foreseen, and despite the many homes they were to set up in vastly different countries and continents.

My father, Julius, was born in 1886 in the small, but distinguished, Austro-Hungarian village of Lackenbach. Hungarian was, however, only his second language, as German was the vernacular of the Jewish community.

The religious standards of the place may be gauged from the fact that my father had never seen the slightest vestige of Sabbath desecration until he visited Vienna at the age of 13, when he came across a coreligionist apparently smoking in the street. His first reaction was one of complete incredulity and he could not believe the evidence of his own eyes until he had walked round the offender and verified the existence of the light and the smoke.

By that time, he had already spent two years in a yeshivah, having been sent away from home to study in the town of Deutschkreuz. That, at least, was its official name, but the local Jews always referred to it as Tzelem, the Hebrew for 'image' or 'cross'.

Father progressed to larger institutions and ultimately studied at the most prestigious of them all, that of Pressburg. This had been established about a century earlier by one of the giants of the rabbinical world, Rabbi Moses Schreiber (Sofer), and was still strongly influenced by the personality, methods and outlook of its founder, universally known as the Chatam Sofer. The greatest compliment a rabbinical scholar can receive is to be known by the title of his most illustrious literary work rather than by his name.

My father represented the Hungarian pattern of rabbinical Judaism rather than that projected by the Lithuanian or Polish yeshivot. These differences were very real in the rabbinical world, though not so obvious outside. He did not, however, subscribe to the complete ban imposed by the Schreiber dynasty on contact with the Reform movement. While totally rejecting its ideology, of course, he was able to establish cordial personal relationships with some of the Reform or Liberal religious leaders with whom he came in contact at various stages of his career.

His secular studies could have received only minimal attention during his yeshivah years, yet he must have been able to make good his deficiencies, since he was accepted as a student at the University of Würzburg. There was nothing unusual about this. Many rabbinical students from Eastern Europe, their intellects sharpened by their prodigious talmudical scholarship, were able quickly to gain the levels of secular knowledge required by the universities.

I never knew why my father chose Würzburg, though I have an idea that its academic standards may have been a little less onerous than those of some other institutions he might have attended. Nor do I know what subjects he studied; but they must have included philosophy, since his doctorate, later published, was earned for a thesis on *Die Luege im Urteil der neuesten deutschen Ethiker* ('The Lie in the Judgement of the Latest German Ethicists').

Würzburg had a sizeable Jewish community. One of its rabbis, Samuel Bamberger, had engaged in a public dispute with Samson Raphael Hirsch, of Frankfurt-am-Main – to whom I refer later – on the religious legitimacy of *austritt*, whereby the Orthodox elements of a Jewish community seceded from the wider community if they felt that it was becoming so influenced by Reform as to endanger the interests of Orthodoxy.

It must be remembered that the Jews of Germany were organised in confessional communities; they were not the collection of separate synagogues known in most other countries. Bamberger was totally opposed to *austritt*, and I believe that my father's indifference to the idea, which was not likely to have been fostered at Pressburg, may have originated at this period.

From Würzburg, the young Dr Jakobovits moved to Berlin's Seminary for the Training of Orthodox Rabbis. Rabbinical seminaries were first established in the nineteenth century, in order to provide a grounding in both religious and secular subjects, as demanded – to a greater or lesser extent – by the students, the congregations, and sometimes even the State. The Berlin seminary had an international reputation, unlike its London counterpart, Jews' College.

Its principal since 1899 had been Rabbi Dr David Hoffman, an outstanding example of the synthesis of rabbinical expertise with modern scholarship. A select few achieved this fully, but for most it was an ideal, and my father never subscribed to later suspicions of secular attainments. The attitude he espoused belonged very much to the pre-Holocaust age, with respect for the cultural heritage of the Western World dying – for many – in the fires of the crematoria.

By 1913, my father had received rabbinical ordination in Berlin – he had already gained semichah from the authorities in Pressburg – and obtained his first post in Randegg, a town in the south-western corner of Baden. Four years later, he became rabbi to the Orthodox Jews of Königsberg. Overall, this was not a large congregation, and he felt that the price of separation, both financial and spiritual, was too high if it led to a fractured community. So he led his flock back into the general communal framework, a process he was to repeat when he moved to Berlin.

By then, he was well into his thirties, and his unmarried status must have been of concern to both himself and his community. Traditional Judaism always strives to hallow the licit, never to deny it, as there is little patience with asceticism and none with celibacy. A young, unmarried rabbi will be tolerated for a while, but the situation cannot be allowed to last too long. Quite exceptionally, Dr Israel Brodie, my predecessor as British Chief Rabbi, jogged along into middle age without either a wife or a beard. When he acquired both, no one doubted that he had secured the succession. And both, incidentally, suited him admirably.

My mother, Paula Wreschner, was 11 years younger than my father. At the time of their marriage, her father, Dr Leopold Wreschner, was rabbi of Samter, in the German province of Posen.

The family came originally from Posen, and one of my forebears on my mother's side – Rabbi Joshua Falk ben Alexander Hacohen, who died in 1614 – was an illustrious figure. Like the Chatam Sofer after him, he was accorded the ultimate accolade of being known by the name of his most famous work, the *P'nei Yeshivah*, a multi-volume collection of homilies; and his double commentary, *Derushah im Perushah* – on one of the standard codifications of Jewish law, the *Arba Turim* – is printed in every edition of that work.

I have never had much time for family gossip, so I cannot recall who brought my parents together, but he – or she – deserves every commendation. They were married in 1920, and I was born a year later, followed closely by Charlotte (Lotti) in 1922, George in 1923, and Joseph in 1925. The last three – Shulamith (1929), Solomon (1933), and Manfred (1934) – were born in Berlin. By then, I had begun to sense that our family was becoming unfashionably large, and I found the later arrivals a trifle embarrassing.

As a rabbi, my father had a strong sense of duty, was devoted to his work, and meticulous in its performance. This, apparently, was no less than was expected of him, for he went to great trouble to memorise his sermons – which meant that he had to closet himself in his study for hours on end while he rehearsed them laboriously.

He expected everyone else in the family to manifest a similar spirit of conscientiousness, and I, as the eldest, had to show an appropriate example to my younger siblings. They, in turn, readily accepted my role and allowed – perhaps even wished – me to exercise my special responsibilities as a natural aspect of my birthright. For myself, I was less sure that this leadership role was either desirable or essential. As a result, a measure of shyness – inherited from my mother – never left me.

The single, most potent, influence on my childhood was – and remains – the centrality of the family. Both my parents grew up in large families and I, in turn, found a large family (embarrassed as I may have been at the time) an excellent training ground in social virtues – in caring for others and sharing with others. Whenever, as the eldest of seven children, I received a bar of chocolate, I had to give away six parts before I could eat my own. Selfishness has little room in a large family, where everything cannot revolve around only one or two children.

My interest in the promotion of the family is thus deeply ingrained. I was partial to large families long before I myself became the father of six children and, in due course, the progenitor of over seven times that number of grandchildren.

I have never countenanced the argument that smaller families do greater justice to each child because he or she can receive more exclusive attention and support. Such children may enjoy more comforts and face fewer hardships, but we do them no favours in making life easy. What one gets for nothing is worth nothing, and, in the end, the real thrills of life are enjoyed only with the triumph of success born of struggle.

Our home, like the society in which I grew up, found nothing incompatible between rigid adherence to principle, especially in religious matters, and tolerance in human relations, transcending differences of conviction.

My father's unification of the Königsberg community, to which I have already referred, was a case in point. He had originally been called to the city as rabbi of the separatist Orthodox congregation in succession to Dr Ezra Munk (a relative of the family into which I was to marry), who later maintained the independent Orthodox line as the distinguished rabbi of the Berlin Adath community. But my father soon succeeded in merging the two Königsberg Orthodox congregations – the one inside and the other outside the general communal structure – into a single Orthodox grouping within the wider community, which included a major Reform component.

From my earliest years, working with communal and religious leaders who were not necessarily Orthodox in thought or practice was perfectly natural – a philosophy that was to leave a permanent mark on my attitudes and convictions in later communal life. In this as in so many other respects, my father's impact on me was dominant from my childhood to the present day.

Intense and sometimes demonstrative as his love was, he was stern, industrious and intensely ambitious. I believe I inherited none of these characteristics to the same degree, replicating rather the more mellow, yet distinctly resolute, disposition of my mother. My father was more of an extrovert, immaculately dressed and conscious that his bearing, his manner of speaking, even his gait, had to be in keeping with the dignity of his rabbinical vocation.

Mellow as she was, my mother was hardly carefree and, on the whole, tended to humour or jollity little more than my father. But she was softer, more easily content, and certainly more reticent in public.

She was one person who needed no exhortation to work hard. With a growing family, a third-floor flat on the Lindenstrasse, few modern labour-saving devices, and all the responsibilities of a rabbi's wife, she had little time for leisure – nor, perhaps, much taste for it. She displayed the meticulous care associated with the ideal *hausfrau* and, although she had domestic help, I cannot remember a time when she did not take charge of everything herself.

By contemporary standards, I suppose, our home atmosphere was none too easy-going. Yet we were treated to month-long holidays every summer, some necessitating long train journeys to far-flung destinations.

Throughout my childhood and youth, I had virtually no contacts with non-Jews. For a year or two in Königsberg, I attended a non-Jewish school, but I cannot remember ever having visited a Gentile home or having had Gentile friends. (I amply made up for this in later years.) Withal, the intensely Jewish environment in which I was nurtured prevented me from feeling self-conscious as a Jew, perhaps even from sensing the first manifestations of anti-Semitism. There was no dichotomy between being a Jew and being a German, and I accepted minority status as a natural condition.

My father tacitly assumed that I would follow the rabbinical tradition inherited from both sides of the family. As a child, I was taken to the slaughter-yard to watch the process of shechitah and was shown how to run my fingernail along the edge of the shochet's knife to ensure that there were no indentations. The supervision of shechitah standards is of paramount importance to a communal rabbi, and my father enjoyed high esteem for his expertise in the subject. Although I suffered no trauma from my visit, I did not repeat the exercise when my own sons were small.

Despite his uncertainty over my rabbinical future, my father in no way forced me to acquire talmudical knowledge. In Königsberg, I attended the religion classes run by the community, and later, in Berlin, I was to follow the ordinary syllabus of the Adath Israel *gymnasium* (secondary school), where the time allocated to religious studies was somewhat less than would be acceptable today in an Orthodox school. No doubt, I would have been sent to a yeshivah in due course, but we never got round to discussing this, and it was not until I was in London that my rabbinical studies began in earnest.

Two associations with Königsberg were never broken. The first was my name. My Hebrew name is Israel, but biblical forenames for secular purposes were usually avoided, at least in our circles. My father was Joel in the synagogue, and he sought a similar resonance for me. He found it in the first name of Immanuel Kant, the most famous scholar to be associated with the city.

Whether the choice was in honour of the locality or because my father had some special liking for Kant's philosophy, I never discovered. Immanuel is, of course, also biblical, but it was acceptable in non-Jewish society possibly because of its messianic overtones. For all that, I did not inherit my father's interest in philosophy, nor studied anything from the pen of my distinguished eponym.

The second association involved one of my teachers – Martin Miloslawer (Mordechai in the synagogue). He later came as a refugee to Britain and passed most of his life ministering to minor congregations where the levels of knowledge and observance were frequently lamentable. He remained remarkably unsoured by this experience and was proud that, at best, one of his pupils emerged to reflect credit on him.

He was also grateful to my father for having introduced him to his future wife – although, since she was a congregational employee (my father's secretary, I believe), the introduction could scarcely have required great matchmaking skills. In any event, I doubt that my father had much aptitude for this sort of activity.

In 1928 we moved to Berlin, where my father had been appointed dayan to the general community. He progressed to the position of communal rabbi in 1933, and from 1937 he was chairman of the rabbinical court.

Originally, he also acted as rabbi to the Matzmiach Yeshuah congregation in East Berlin, and later he assumed the responsibility of the Rothbuser-Ufar Synagogue in Neuköln, the south-eastern area of Berlin. This last was, in fact, a complex of synagogue buildings; the imposing main synagogue, accommodating 2,000 worshippers, was used only on festivals; the second, of moderate size, was used on ordinary Sabbaths; and the small one was reserved for weekday services.

The members of Matzmiach Yeshuah were mainly of East European origin, whereas the larger congregation was in the usual German mould and boasted a male choir. Father officiated in canonicals, which were then regarded as being fully in accord with Orthodox standards (no less a personage than Samson Raphael Hirsch had worn them).

His duties lay entirely within the ambit of the general community, while the separatist body pursued its own self-contained religious path. The traditional rabbis of both groups were equally scholarly and observant, but while the separatists were known as 'Orthodox', the integrationists were termed 'Conservative'.

It was in the Orthodox section, however, that I was educated, spending all my student years at the Adath Israel school. I began in the juniors, proceeded in due course to the boys' *gymnasium* and, when I left at the age of nearly 16, had reached the form known as the *Obersekunda*.

Ezra Munk, rabbi of the separatist community – whom my father had succeeded as rabbi of Königsberg – was our spiritual guide, while among my other distinguished teachers was Rabbi Meir Hildesheimer, a son of the founder of the Berlin Rabbinical Seminary, at which my father (and much later my father-in-law) had studied. Dr Eduard Bieberfeld, who taught Talmud, was a teacher whose great wit and wisdom I still vividly recall.

Oddly enough, the teachers of secular subjects had more influence on my religious outlook than those who taught specifically Jewish subjects. I often felt that the latter were, so to speak, financially compensated for their Orthodoxy, while the others were clearly observant from genuine conviction. But since only strictly Orthodox people were allowed to teach at the school, the distinction was clearly more apparent than real. At the time, however, it was impressive enough.

Behind all my teachers and their teaching stood a much greater figure, whose writings and attitudes had determined the whole ideology of the separatist movement. This was the aforementioned Samson Raphael Hirsch (1808–88), who, as leader of the *Religionsgesellschaft* of Frankfurt-am-Main, had created one of world Jewry's most outstanding Orthodox communities in a city where, before his arrival, Reform of the most radical kind had seemed to be carrying everything before it.

Hirsch had bequeathed a great literary heritage on Jewish observances and religious philosophy, together with biblical and liturgical commentaries. Even more importantly, he had left a myth, according to which, in 1851 – when he had achieved a status of authority as Chief Rabbi of Moravia – he had unhesitatingly abandoned all his honours to come to the aid of the struggling handful of Orthodox Jews in Frankfurt. Much later, I was to realise that the truth was less supernormal: Hirsch had been unsuccessful and unhappy in Nikolsburg, while the alleged pathetic minority in Frankfurt included a Rothschild millionaire.

I later wrote and published several critical essays on Hirsch – critical of the man rather than of his teachings. For instance, he left no disciples of whom one could say that they were fashioned by him in his image, nor did he retain any personal friends on whom he exerted a lasting influence. Early friends had included Heinrich Graetz (1817–91), the famous Jewish historian, and Abraham Geiger (1810–74), the arch-apostle of extreme Reform, but both soon became estranged.

Nevertheless, Hirsch's achievement was phenomenal, and his spirit was instilled into us by the study of his works and the inculcation of his modes of thought. I have never ceased to be influenced by his attitudes, nor ever wanted to abandon them. They can still be traced, half a century later, in my notes to the *Centenary Edition of the Authorised Daily Prayer Book* (1990).

His German style, heavy and lachrymose, did my English writing no good, until I came to realise that the emotional intensity tolerable in German had to be cooled down considerably to sound reasonable in English. One of his main tenets – that Judaism needs to be studied and practised alongside secular knowledge and pursuits (*Torah im derech eretz*) – is one that I still cherish, together with his insistence on studying Judaism from within, rather than analysing faith out of existence with external criteria.

But I absorbed his ideas as a student at a period when my principal interest was in the sciences; I was less successful in the arts, such as languages and history. My school reports also testify to my unsatisfactory results in Jewish religious – as well as some secular – studies, much to my father's frequent annoyance. At school, I was simply an indifferent pupil.

My social life – it was not extensive, for everything centred on the family – existed mainly in the Ezra youth movement, where, in contrast to the school, mixed activities were the norm. Nothing demonstrates more clearly the change in Orthodox outlook than the fact that my youth leader was Joseph Dunner, who later became rabbi in my father's former community of Königsberg, before moving to England. He ultimately succeeded Dr Solomon Schonfeld as presiding rabbi of the Union of Orthodox Hebrew Congregations, in which capacity he would certainly never tolerate such socialising between the sexes.

If I showed little aptitude or yearning for rabbinical studies, I did manifest some signs of religious interests and accomplishments. I read a haftarah in public for the first time at the age of 11. After my barmitzvah, in 1934, I was fully involved in the conduct of youth services and even delivered occasional lectures.

As befitted a student interested in the sciences, one of my main pursuits was an attempt to reconcile the biblical account of Creation with modern theories on the origins of the universe. Cosmology, astronomy, the origin of life and matter – in fact, the philosophy of science generally – have always fascinated me, today no less than then.

Ominously, all these activities were played against a background that became increasingly overcast as the Nazis swept their way to power – soon ruthlessly crushing all opposition and whipping up a vicious campaign against all Jews.

School life was at first little affected; if anything, we felt a greater degree of cohesion and stability because of the outside threats. But at every street corner, display cases of *Der Stürmer* vomited out their unceasing and obscene Jew-hatred. There were sporadic outbreaks of violence, endless street marches, an atmosphere of rising tension and fear.

I have an indelible memory of seeing Hitler in the Olympic procession of 1936, through West Berlin to the stadium. Millions lined the route. I had gone to watch and found myself hemmed in by hordes whose delirious acclaim of their leader was terrifying.

I had an overwhelming impression of the ease with which human minds can be manipulated into a state of frenzy, stripping off the veneer of civilisation and leaving exposed the brutal, uncontrolled savagery that lurked in the soul of what was once a civilised people. All it needs is one rabble-rouser with access to the media (then the press, and especially the radio) to mesmerise these masses, in time turning them into millions of murderers and their accomplices.

The earliest anti-Jewish legislation of the Nazis created two particularly difficult problems for the rabbinate. Ostensibly in the name of animal welfare, the practice of shechitah was banned soon after the Nazis came to power early in 1933, and thereafter kosher meat had to be imported.

With Rabbi Michael Munk, who later emigrated to New York via London, my father investigated the effects of prior electrical stunning. Scientific experiments soon revealed that this damages the brain tissue, causing the animal to become religiously unfit for Jewish consumption, or that it might be dead or dying before the act of religious slaughter took place. (The human hatreds that lurk beneath the cloak of animal welfare are a sadly abiding factor of anti-shechitah agitation: 'They who slaughter men kiss the calves' [Hosea 13:2] is its recurring text.)

My father was also increasingly involved in the heartbreaking problem of the *agunah*, including the woman whose husband has disappeared without trace.

Judaism sanctions presumption of death only when the inference is conclusive – as where, for example (subject to rigorous conditions of evidence), a ship has foundered, with no survivors. Mere prolonged absence does not suffice to permit remarriage. When whole communities are uprooted and people are driven across the world as refugees, the break-up of family units can lead to heartbreaking situations.

The *agunah* problem – particularly in the context of the husband who withholds a *get* – has become the subject of much anti-Orthodox agitation, with the implicit charge that rabbis administering the law do not care enough to release such 'chained women' and free them for remarriage.

I can testify otherwise. Years later in London, after my father was stricken by a heart attack, he spent the last night of his life restlessly, telling me in the morning that the *agunah* women who had appeared before him over the years would not let him sleep.

I related this experience in the early 1980s at a reception given by Yitzhak Navon, then President of Israel, to a delegation of the Conference of European Rabbis which I headed. He produced a letter from one such woman, pleading for his intervention with the rabbinical authorities, and challenged us to do something about it.

I answered that the rabbis were hardly indifferent to the problem, and I told him the story of my father. I added that we appreciated the ordeal which our sages called 'the tears of the oppressed'. We did our utmost to help, but sometimes were unable to do so. We felt the anguish no less than did politicians or army commanders who sent their troops into battle for the defence of their country, knowing that some would never return to their loved ones. Without occasional sacrifices for a higher ideal, a nation cannot survive.

True, I told President Navon, because of our strict marriage laws, some women occasionally suffered grievously. But for every such case, there were thousands who, because these laws were so demanding, sanctified their marriages, lived happily with their spouses in faithfulness, and built hallowed homes such as have preserved our people over the ages more than any valour in battle. I think he understood.

One Berlin colleague whom my father esteemed highly was Dr Leo Baeck, the religious leader of the Progressive community. Despite their great differences in belief and practice, he respected Baeck as a spiritual guide of rare stature and integrity – as was to be amply demonstrated by the greatness he showed while in Theresienstadt.

In West European communities, the symbol of the great divide between Orthodoxy and Reform was the organ at synagogue services. Elsewhere, the *casus belli* was the mixed choir, or mixed seating. In fact, the ordination certificate of the Hildesheimer Seminary specifically stated that the rabbinical authority of the recipient was automatically withdrawn if he accepted office in a non-Orthodox synagogue.

As Chief Rabbi in Britain, decades later, I introduced a similar document to qualify any rabbinical authorisation which I conferred as president of Jews' College.

Ordination is not to be compared with a university degree, for, in addition to knowledge, it demands a lifelong commitment to live and instruct in strict accord with Jewish law. Nowadays, even more weighty divisions than mixed choirs and mixed seating occupy our attention: they concern the very question of Jewish status, revolving round the religious standards which the Progressive rabbinates consider adequate for conversions or divorces, or the performance of marriages forbidden by traditional law.

Despite the menacing outside world, life continued happily at home. We were by now a large family and, if I had less parental attention and individual pampering than might have come my way in a smaller unit, this was more than outweighed by the compensation of sharing with, and caring for, others.

We joined in each other's hopes, trials and experiences, and everyone had an opportunity to develop a personality that was rooted in belonging, not in selfishness. If, inevitably, there are problems in raising a large family, there are also ample compensations, and many joys beyond price.

All this time, the German-Jewish community was beginning the process that was to bring it from its lofty position in the Jewish world to impending extinction. In 1938, my father's brother Moshe – then still known to us as 'Onkel Moritz' – became the first of the immediate family to leave, moving from his rabbinate in Cologne to Strasbourg, and later to New York, as dayan of the Breuer community.

Once a week, a train leaving Berlin for the Italian port of Trieste carried a group of Jews who had obtained certificates for immigration into Palestine, and they were given an emotional send-off by their family and friends. I was there from time to time to bid farewell to a classmate or some other close acquaintance.

My father regularly paid in money to the *Hilfsverein* on which any family members could draw if they came to London – which was accepted as my destination on leaving Berlin in due course.

In common with so many others, I recall with profound gratitude the name of Rabbi Dr Solomon Schonfeld, who was so tireless and effective in arranging for the emigration of German Jews. In November 1936, travelling alone, I set off for London, having been accepted as a boarder at the Jewish Secondary School in Stamford Hill of which Dr Schonfeld was principal in name, and presiding genius in fact.

A few months into 1937, my brother George joined me in London, and we boarded together for a while with a family in Stamford Hill. The following year, after the infamous Kristallnacht of 9 November 1938, the rest of the family came to London, also assisted by Rabbi Schonfeld. Father brought with him a pathetic relic of past greatness – a charred piece of the pulpit from his main synagogue, burned down by the Nazis on that horrendous night.

Along with a small group of boys from Germany, I was soon accepted into Rabbi Schonfeld's Jewish Secondary School in North London. Although I had studied English in Germany, I spoke it badly, but within a few months had attained sufficient competence to gain my matriculation certificate. At the same time, I attended courses at the Etz Chaim yeshivah and, later, at Jews' College and University College London, where I learned to integrate the worlds of religious and secular study. At Etz Chaim, the emphasis was on Talmud, but I was also greatly influenced by the *mussar* (ethical teachings) expounded by the head of the yeshivah, Rabbi Eliahu Lopian, in his time perhaps the greatest master of this field.

It was from him and his colleagues Rabbi Nachman Greenspan and Rabbi Leib Gurewitz that I was to receive my semichah some eight years later. I had planned a scientific career, and originally enrolled at Queen Mary College, London University. But after only one day there, I transferred to Jews' College at the behest of my father, who was determined that his eldest son should follow in the family's rabbinical tradition. I never questioned this decision, nor at any time looked back with regret.

I was the last student to be admitted to Jews' College by Dr Adolph Büchler – he had been its principal since 1907 and died soon after I joined – and was required to pass a stiff entrance examination. My main teachers were Dr Isidore Epstein (Büchler's successor), Dr Arthur Marmorstein, Rabbi Samuel Daiches, and Dr Cecil Roth – and later Rabbi Israel Brodie, who tutored at the college before becoming British Chief Rabbi in 1948.

I divided my days between the yeshivah and Jews' College, where I studied for, and eventually gained, my BA degree and ministerial diploma, before being appointed as temporary minister at the Brondesbury Synagogue. There, I soon encountered difficulties with one of the honorary officers, over my alleged Orthodox 'rigidity'. In growing despair, I plucked up courage and obtained an appointment with Chief Rabbi Hertz to pour out my heart and seek advice. Listening patiently to my tale of woe, he simply replied: 'Now, young man, if you multiply your *tsores* by 100, you will know what I am going through.' I was comforted – and later discovered how right he was.

Under growing pressure, I moved in 1944 from Brondesbury to the South-East London Synagogue, serving this war-battered congregation as minister, reader, headmaster, and secretary – keeping the books and sending out yahrzeit notices. In 1947, I was appointed to the Great Synagogue, Duke's Place, as its first minister for 105 years (and its last). While there, I founded the Jewish Marriage Education Committee, which eventually became the Jewish Marriage Council.

During my seven years with the United Synagogue, I was disenchanted with the limitations and chores of the London ministry. Twice, while still attending regularly at Jews' College and Etz Chaim, I applied for provincial positions – in Glasgow and Manchester – which I failed to obtain. (Significantly, I never stood as a candidate in any of the six positions I held in three countries.)

After my arrival in Britain, I was to return to Berlin one last time, for the barmitzvah of my brother Joseph, a few months before he came to London with the rest of the family.

Although German has long ceased to be my main language, I am still fluent in speaking, reading and writing it. But I find it almost impossible to give a public address in the language. Perhaps this is because I have not acquired the necessary idiom for all the concepts of medicine, ethics and, indeed, Judaism on which I usually lecture. I could, of course, achieve this with a little effort, but I suspect that the real cause is the psychological block in using before an audience a language which I associate with cruelties that brought a new Dark Age to humanity and destroyed six million of my brethren.

One incident, which occurred many years after I settled in Britain, provides me with a vivid recollection of the price I once paid for my refusal to return to Germany. I had been invited to speak at a colloquium organised by a Roman Catholic bishops' academy in the German city of Aachen, not far from the Dutch border, on some aspect of Jewish medical ethics. I initially declined the invitation, explaining that memories were still too fresh and painful for me to set foot on German soil, and hoping that they would understand. They replied that not only did they understand, but, because they understood, they would move the venue for my speech across the border, to Holland.

I now had no excuse to decline the invitation. I flew to a Dutch border town, from where I was taken to an enormous monastery. The other delegates arrived later by coach from Aachen. The lecture was delivered and the group departed, while I was left to spend the night in that decrepit building, once the educational establishment of a religious order but now almost deserted, with only five monks inhabiting the vast complex of cavernous and echoing rooms. It was a gloomy and depressing experience, and I felt as if the place was haunted. Nor did the presence of crucifixes on every wall do anything to reduce the eeriness of my situation.

Over the years, I have often had to miss pastoral visits, conferences and other events in Germany to which I was invited. My aversion was strengthened when, soon after the war, I found (and subsequently published) a passage from the protocols of the Portuguese–Jewish community in Hamburg, dating from about 1600.

The minutes of the community council recorded a meeting to discuss the visit of one of its members to Spain, and the penalty to be imposed. This was over 100 years after the expulsion of the Jews from Spain, yet the consequences of that event remained etched so deeply and painfully that a visit to the country still incurred communal sanctions. I thought – though it was never a view I imposed on others – how could we, so much sooner after the catastrophe of the Holocaust, tread on land soaked with the blood of martyrs many times more numerous than had ever suffered on Spanish soil?

Fragments from an unpublished autobiography

CHAPTER ONE

London Calling

THE INFLUENCE OF THE YESHIVAH ON THE JEWISH PUBLIC

This article does not lay claim to be an exhaustive study of the yeshivah's influence on the Jewish public, nor does it purport to advise on any course of policy to be taken, but it merely gives a few observations on the theme which may afford a stimulus for a more general and detailed discussion of the subject. Its importance can hardly be overestimated, and the necessity for such an influence to be favourable cannot be too strongly urged on yeshivah students who must needs realise that the responsibility for the survival of what they understand by Judaism rests largely on them.

My observations are confined chiefly to the yeshivah's external influences, which are effected in several ways. The most important means of influence in education is by example. The impression of a yeshivah student on the Jewish public at large invariably exerts an exemplary influence on them, instinctively or otherwise. Indeed, the actual influence by a mere superiority of knowledge – even if in only one specialised subject – which in itself may not be entirely appreciated by the majority of the community, must consequently never be lost sight of. To this must be added his clear and logical workings of the mind, his high standard of religious and moral life, and his elevated spirit of self-sacrifice.

One would, however, be subject to a serious misapprehension if one failed to conceive of the fact that the specialised education of the yeshivah student, and his segregation from those parts of the social life of the community which his conscience and lack of leisure forbids him to participate in, breeds antipathy towards him, which, in turn, cannot but have derogatory repercussions on the effects obtained by his bearing and conduct. It should, nevertheless, be clearly understood that an attempt to concede any compromise on this important part of the policy to be pursued by the yeshivah must finally be doomed to failure, since, by doing so, the fulfilment of the aims and ideals of the yeshivah – if it is to retain its original significance – is impeded and ultimately frustrated.

The second educational factor of the yeshivah is that of directly influencing the public by word of mouth. There are several media through which this may be achieved, of which I will mention only the pulpit of the synagogue, the teacher's desk, the platform of a society, and, last but not least, private conversation. Here the student's wit and knowledge certainly enable him to advocate his convictions and beliefs successfully, thus exercising a strong and beneficial influence, as well as counterpoising the repelling factor mentioned above.

Finally, the most important aspect of the yeshivah's influence lies in the fact that its existence furnishes Jewry with an institution of a high standard of Jewish scholarship that helps to raise the level of Jewish learning and observance in general, of which there is such dire need at present. The yeshivah establishes the most prominent link between the ancient – and yet ever-youthful and productive – school of learning and the modern – yet appallingly ignorant and indifferent – masses of the Jews, thus kindling an *esh dat* in a world of obscurity and ignorance, and preserving the fire of enthusiasm for the *Torah hakdushah* unquenched to lighten the path of darkness, sorrow and bitterness, and to vouchsafe a happy future for the Jewish youth of today and tomorrow.

HaChaim, *Students' Journal of the Etz Chaim Yeshivah, London, April 1940*

This contribution to *HaChaim* was 19-year-old Immanuel's first known published article, delineating the approach to yeshivah studies he was increasingly to adopt, and refine, as the years progressed. It also emphasised his mature attitude to communal responsibility, as was resoundingly exemplified only weeks later.

In June 1940, Immanuel was briefly interned with his father and brothers on the Isle of Man. At the end of their stay, the Jewish congregation of the camp presented him with an ornately inscribed certificate, signed by three rabbis and three lay leaders, which stated: 'This is to certify that Mr Immanuel Jakobovits has proved, in spite of his youth, a very good orator, reader and preacher, in excellent English, on the festivals and Sabbaths in the service of the Jewish community of the Onchan Internment Camp. The undersigned express to him their deepest gratitude for his idealistic activity on behalf of the Jewish religion and ideas.'

Despite his uncompromising faith in the yeshivah world, Immanuel was equally concerned to promote his academic studies and to play a full role in university life. The following year, he was elected assistant secretary of the Union Society at Jews' College, an affiliate of London University.

Five weeks later, he was appointed temporary minister of the Brondesbury Synagogue in North-West London, having acted for several months as teacher and reader of the Bedford Hebrew Congregation, where he conducted a number of youth study circles on various Jewish subjects. The Brondesbury appointment did not, however, pass without comment:

> Your readers must have read – as I did – with incredulity and indignation of the appointment which those responsible (I do not know whether it is the synagogue itself or the United Synagogue) have thought fit to make at Brondesbury Synagogue. A youth, barely 20, of German nationality, who only came to this country as a refugee five years ago, is appointed to the ministry of a synagogue by no means the least important in the metropolis. There is not even here the excuse that he is a rabbi famed for his learning and now exiled from a position of dignity and importance abroad, as so many are. The inference, of course, is clear – that there is no one among the recent graduates of Jews' College of English birth, no one holding a ministerial position in a less important London synagogue or provincial congregation, who is competent enough or fit to be 'translated' to the important Brondesbury Synagogue. When one recalls the

continual complaints that are made as to the standing and quality of the majority of the Anglo-Jewish clergy, one can fully realise why the community cannot obtain the best men for a profession which can be productive of so much good (or the contrary) to the community at large, and particularly to the rising generation. What encouragement is there for a young man to enter the clergy when he sees posts filled in this way? However eminent this young gentleman may be, even his best friends could not pretend that he was the only person who could lay claim to an appointment of this importance. The Anglo-Jewish community is at the moment in a state of flux. It has before it problems of the most difficult kind. It requires for its guidance men of experience, not only of these problems but with a background that would make them understand not only their own coreligionists but their English fellow-citizens of other creeds. However brilliant this young man may be, his experience has been limited to six months as a Reader in an evacuee community; he possesses no background as far as English life is concerned – he was, until comparatively recently, living in a country which will be, quite properly, abhorrent to all right-thinking people for generations to come; and, I repeat, he is barely 20 years of age, an age when, it seems to me, with the incessant and crying demand for manpower, he might have considered interrupting his career for some more active contribution to the war effort.

AJC
Jewish Chronicle, 2 January 1942

Nor was the young minister without his supporters:

With reference to the letter which appeared in your last issue, may I point out to your correspondent that he has entirely misstated the facts of the case. Firstly, he has entirely ignored the fact that the appointment is only a temporary one. Secondly, the young man selected, on merit, proved himself the most suitable candidate for the appointment. Thirdly, a young man receiving such an appointment will not deter others from entering Jews' College; in my opinion, this fact would tend rather to make them decide to enter the college, since it would prove to them that being young would not debar them from receiving good appointments provided they proved themselves worthy for selection. A final point: most of the young ministers who could have been suitable for the Brondesbury Synagogue are now serving with HM Forces.

M. Nisenbaum (Senior Warden), Ebbsfleet Road, Cricklewood, NW2

The letter about the Brondesbury Synagogue appointment in your esteemed paper on Friday, 2 January, caused me much amazement. A minister's qualifications ought not to include the flag under which he was born. If 'AJC's' proposals were enforced and only men with 'an English background' were allowed in high offices in British Jewry, I'm afraid that 'AJC' would be faced with the task of reappointing 75 per cent of the Beth Din. On the other hand, I appreciate 'AJC's' interest in this matter, and the thoroughness of his letter, which shows him to be a man well versed in Jewish matters. Therefore it is more than imperative that he should remember the Bible's references to 'the stranger that is within thy gates', and observe the appropriate commandments. I am very surprised that 'AJC' should have nothing better to do in such troubled times than to criticise a young man who, though he may have numerous shortcomings (for, after all, is anyone perfect?), will try his best to live up to the traditions of his important position. But I feel sure that as 'AJC' has the interests of the Brondesbury ministry so much at heart, he will show our young visitor a little more of Jewish charity coupled with British sportsmanship. I am a British-born Jew.

Charles Newberry
St John Street, EC1

The appointment of Mr Jakobovits was no precipitate act, the position having been vacant for the last couple of years. 'AJC' omits to mention that the appointment is, as yet, only for the duration, and that Mr Jakobovits is no less a graduate of Jews' College than those others who are depicted as balked and discouraged. If one graduate is to be preferred to another on the grounds of original nationality, it is a sorry prospect for Anglo-Jewry, which so far shows no sign of being religiously self-supporting. It is difficult to understand why this appointment should so depress the rising generation of ministers; if the position at Brondesbury were to be reserved for the ripest scholarship and the most impeccable lineage, such a feeling might be expected, but as it has been given to a young man on the grounds of ability, promise, and sincerity, regardless of his being a refugee, the effect can scarcely be that anticipated by 'AJC'. As to the likelihood that Mr Jakobovits will lack the ability to deal with non-Jews, he should not worry on that score. Intelligence can do as much in that direction as birth, which may mean very little. The remark on National Service was the unkindest as well as the stupidest of all. If 'AJC' is of the opinion that ministers of religion ought to be de-reserved, the Ministry of Labour is the correct quarter in which to ventilate that grievance. In the meantime, we may be grateful that the Government recognises that Mr Jakobovits is better employed as a minister than in labouring in the Pioneer Corps.

Norman M. Cohen, Chamberlayne Road, NW10
Jewish Chronicle, 9 January 1942

In order to 'gratify the ever-growing need and desire for a comprehensive exposition of Judaism', as he put it, the new minister drew up plans for a series of sermons devoted to Jewish laws and customs. He proposed 'dealing with their implications as viewed from the following aspects: historical, national, ethical, psychological, theological, educational. Scriptural readings on intervening Sabbaths will deal with texts bearing on the subject of the sermon to follow. Opportunities will be given for discussion at the shiurim on Sabbath afternoons.'

The series was clearly successful, enabling Mr Nisenbaum to report at the annual meeting that the congregation had had 'a year of progress' and that 'a great deal has been done to encourage social and educational activities among the young people. For this, the temporary minister, the Rev Immanuel Jakobovits, is largely responsible.'

In a statement foreshadowing by some 30 years his Chief Rabbinical aspirations, the Rev Jakobovits told a meeting of the Liverpool Mizrachi Organisation some months later: 'The only solution to the educational problems besetting our community is to embark on a large-scale Jewish day-school system, which would enable our children to become 24-hour-a-day Jews instead of six-to-eight-hour-a-week Jews.

'All communal, educational, and national institutions', he added, 'ought to be centrally directed in Eretz Yisrael to ensure a universal alliance between the different communities of the world. What is required is a United Synagogue of the world, rather than merely of Great Britain.'

The temporary nature of the Brondesbury appointment was brought home when, in June 1944, the young minister relinquished his post to occupy the pulpit of the South-East London Synagogue, Lewisham, enabling him to devote more time to his rabbinical studies.

Eight months later, and two years after his appointment as a dayan of the London Beth Din, Immanuel's father died at the age of 61. A memorial service was held at the Great Synagogue, Duke's Place, attended by the dayan's five sons and two daughters, and conducted by Dayan H. M. Lazarus (deputising for the Chief Rabbi), Dayan Yehezkiel Abramsky, Dayan Dr Isidor Grunfeld, Dayan Morris Swift, and the Rev Simchah Kusevitsky.

Shortly before his death, Dayan Jakobovits had been told of the imminent award of semichah to his first-born son and to another student, Shalom Gootnik. The diplomas, signed by Rabbi Nachman Greenspan and Rabbi Eliahu Lopian, were presented to the new rabbis, in the presence of a distinguished gathering, at the Yeshivat Etz Chaim in Thrawl Street, East London.

Taking issue with Rabbi Israel Brodie – who had initiated a communal debate after declaring, before a Leeds congregation, that 'no candidate should be granted a rabbinical diploma unless he has gained a degree from a recognised university, as well as passing an examination in general Jewish subjects equivalent to that of the minister's certificate of Jews' College' – Rabbi Lopian told the Etz Chaim gathering: 'There are two ways of obtaining semichah. One is by going to a rabbi for examination; the other is by studying at a yeshivah for years so that the teachers can get to know the applicant's character and capacity for learning.' It was in this latter manner, he said, that the two students had earned their semichah. [A year later, Dr Brodie was elected Chief Rabbi and gained greater control over the ordination of ministers within the United Synagogue orbit.]

In July 1947, at an extraordinary meeting of members of the Great Synagogue, Rabbi Jakobovits was unanimously elected minister of the congregation. There had been no incumbent since 1842, following the death of Rabbi Solomon Hirschell, the first formally recognised Chief Rabbi of the Ashkenazi community and predecessor of Chief Rabbi Nathan Marcus Adler. Since then, the pulpit had been occupied by visiting preachers.

Dr Israel Feldman, the presiding warden, told the meeting that Rabbi Jakobovits had been the only candidate recommended by the selection committee and the board of management. They had received 'very gratifying reports of the rabbi's character, scholarship, learning and abilities from the congregations he had served'.

At the time of this announcement, Rabbi Jakobovits was in Palestine, attending the World Conference of Hebrew Teachers organised by the Hebrew University. The visit provided the occasion for his first published views on Zionism and the Jewish State [see below], and for the following reminiscences nearly 40 years later:

MY FIRST VISIT TO PALESTINE

My conscious Zionism is about as old as the State of Israel. To be more precise, it is a year older, and dates back to my first visit to the Holy Land. I was then 26 years old, and had just been appointed to my third ministerial position in London as minister of the Great Synagogue, Duke's Place.

For me, Zionism was the object of intense interest and agitated debates, but I personally remained independent and non-conformist and found myself a critic of its Right and Left wings alike; even for the policies advocated by the religious faction, the Mizrachi, I had but qualified sympathies.

My visit in 1947 began to change all this. It was the first of over 100 visits, but that visit remains the incomparable experience of a lifetime. I had joined a teachers' group, sailing from London on the maiden voyage of the first Jewish boat, the *Kedmah*. Ten days later, we received a boisterous welcome on our arrival in Tel Aviv, given preference over Haifa to mark the Jewish significance of the event. The following three weeks were spent in a busy programme of travels and activities, largely with the group but often with members of my own family, of whom many had already settled there some years earlier.

While there was no love among the Jews for the British, there was widespread contempt for the Arabs. The prevailing opinion of Palestinian Jews everywhere, my relatives included, was that the British were the only real enemy; once they were driven out, the Arabs would present no problem, as they would soon and easily come to terms with Jewish rule. I found it difficult to follow and accept this line of thinking.

It was this experience which planted the seeds of the principal attitudes which I hold to the present day. My love at the first sight of the Holy Land deepened into an ever-growing commitment to the cause of Zionism. In the relative comfort and safety of my life in London, I felt humbled by the idealism, the valour, the hardship and the intense Jewish purpose of my brethren in the Land. A longing to join them one day was sparked in my heart.

But, at the same time, the visit reinforced my innate abhorrence of violence, and my profound belief in its futility. I could not share the unquestioning confidence of the Yishuv that the moment the struggle against the British was over, the Zionist dream would become a radiant reality, the State to be born thriving in peace as a haven for the Jewish people, so many of whom were still languishing in refugee camps in Europe and suffering various degrees of discrimination in Arab countries. To me, it appeared that the fierce hatred and bitterness of the Palestinian Arabs and their neighbours would not just go away, or be suppressed, with the departure of the British; and I could not dismiss from my mind the ceaseless Arab riots to which the Yishuv had been exposed in unremitting acts of terror and sabotage for decades past. I missed sustained efforts to replace, or at least to accompany, the show of strength by goodwill and reassurance. The cocksure manner in which my friends pooh-poohed the threat from the Arabs worried me. Yet any mention of my anxieties was curtly dismissed as defeatist and condemned as almost heretical. As I was to hear over and over again in the years and decades ahead – as an outsider I could not judge the situation, I did not understand the real character of the Arabs and their submissiveness in the face of force, and I had therefore neither the moral right nor the competence to express opinions in these matters, which were the sole province of Jews living in Palestine.

Under the pressure of such attitudes, if not their logic, my arguments were gradually reduced to a whisper, and in the end faded out altogether. The claim that only they knew the facts and what promoted their best interests was certainly plausible, and I accepted it, even though I remained unconvinced.

Another impression which left an indelible imprint upon me was the extraordinary social polarisation within the Yishuv, most markedly between the religious and non-religious segments. I had never seen such hermetically sealed divisions among Jews, inhibiting even some geographical cohesion between them. They lived mostly in separated – segregated may be a better word – quarters, and there was neither communication nor understanding between them. For instance, members of a non-religious kibbutz, or certainly their children, had never seen Jews at prayer, or a tallit, or a Torah scroll. For them, the Jewish belief in God was merely an archaic matter of ancient history, and they did not even know that there were still Jews who professed it. These were no longer the victims of assimilation, but rather of a new creed which deliberately sought to eradicate any trace of our religious heritage.

Equally, the comparatively small religious element also seemed completely insulated from the rest of society, relating to it with a mixture of indifference and hostility. Thus, the Land of Israel became the home of two Jewish peoples, divided almost like the ancient kingdoms of Judah and Israel. The only common denominator, apart from some joint self-defence activities, was the intolerance of each towards the other. Coming from England, with its flair for compromise and middle-of-the-road traditionalism, I found this acute form of polarisation particularly striking – and disturbing.

One further impression had a formative influence upon my subsequent thinking. Although the British were still in occupation, and the United Nations had not yet voted for the partition of the country authorising the establishment of the Jewish State, there was already a feeling of inevitability in the air. Underlying this feeling was the conviction, held and fostered especially by some religious leaders and their followers, that the convulsive events unfolding in the Holy Land were of messianic, or at least pre-messianic, dimensions. Of course, religious Zionism had always been inspired by messianic hopes and visions. Some had already hailed the Balfour Declaration as the imminent dawn of the messianic era. Later, the Holocaust catastrophe of the Final Solution inevitably intensified speculation that the Final Redemption was at hand. The whole drama of the Jewish return to the Land and the mighty struggle to regain Jewish national independence was seen as the realisation of biblical prophecies.

For me, such reliance on imminent deliverance always evoked haunting memories of the many pseudo-messianic disasters in our history, and I was troubled by the incipient signs of identifying contemporary events, however hopeful or even promising, with messianic certainties.

I came back from my visit with much exhilaration. It did indeed convert me to Zionism, but not to Zionist policies. I was entranced by the loveliness of the Land and the pioneering spirit of its builders. But I was estranged by some features, and disconcerted by others. Most of the fears then planted in my mind were only seminal and for long remained latent.

I returned, as a young rabbi, to minister in London's East End for the next two years, to become absorbed mostly in youth and social work. But, in retrospect, I can see that my stance in later years was moulded by this visit, and it has consistently guided my thinking and my public statements over the years to the present day.

If Only My People: Zionism In My Life, 1984

THE LAND OF EXTREMES

I had the great pleasure of visiting Eretz Israel this summer for the World Conference of Hebrew Teachers, held at the Hebrew University in Jerusalem. My all-too-brief but crowded stay gave me a somewhat different impression of life in Eretz Yisrael and its problems from the one with which I had set out. I cannot help feeling that we in Britain are not too well informed about the Holy Land, mainly because so much of the news emanating from it is tendentious. It is by no means easy to probe below the surface even in the Land itself; nearly everyone has some political or other axe to grind, and the superb material achievements of the Yishuv not unnaturally make it rather hard to see also the shades in the dazzling brilliance of accomplishments. Unless, therefore, one actually shares in the day-to-day life of the Yishuv and patiently listens to hundreds of accounts, experiences and arguments, as I did, if but for a few weeks, one cannot hope to obtain a tolerably sober and objective picture of conditions there.

The events of recent years have naturally raised passions high, and the schools, with the exception of a few, have, by their extreme nationalist emphasis in teaching, aggravated this tendency. The educational position and prospect are perhaps the most disquieting aspects of the Yishuv's internal problems. Not one school in Eretz Yisrael, I was told, teaches Latin or Greek. I mention this only because it is symptomatic of the narrow, chauvinist outlook which is being indoctrinated into the minds of the rising generation. The boundaries of Palestine and the world are for them more or less synonymous. This is serious, as we can hardly assert ourselves in a hostile – or, at best, lukewarm – world without understanding the national character and frame of mind of enemies and friends with whom we shall have to deal.

There is a regrettable rift between the youth and their parents – whom the former often call by their first names – and the tragic consequences, which will one day be all too apparent, of the spiritual and moral ruin wrought in the young by [Jewish] terrorism ought never to be forgotten in considering this vexed subject. These tendencies are no doubt only natural in a people that wishes to react to the repression of 2,000 years and to catch up with the still-rising tide of nationalism among the other nations, but far too little is being done, especially in the schools, to counter its more menacing manifestations.

In no sphere are the extremes more apparent than in the religious. Certain traditional associations pervade the entire Yishuv, of which the Sabbath as the official day of rest is, of course, the most notable example. But its popular conception and observance, except in Jerusalem, are in many ways much nearer to our Sunday than the original form and meaning of the Jewish Sabbath. Marriage and divorce are under the exclusive control of the Chief Rabbinate, obviating many of the difficulties now being experienced in Anglo-Jewry. There are regular broadcasts on Bible and Talmud on the Hebrew radio, which commences its daily programme with liturgical recitations.

Most private and public Jewish buildings have mezuzot, but unfortunately the religious interests of the masses do not go beyond the 'doorposts' of their houses and minds. Whatever traditional festivals are observed, they have been deprived of their religious content and meaning. In the widespread absence of filial piety, the last bonds with tradition have been snapped for many, and I have the impression that religion plays a much smaller part in their lives than it does among the average Gentile, and certainly Jew, in this country.

The Old Yishuv [is] still the invincible bastion of Orthodoxy in Eretz Yisrael, and perhaps in the world. Its tendency is strongly anti-secular; I frequently came across the trepidation with which parents looked to the establishment of a Jewish State lest secular school education be made compulsory! Under present conditions, the Old Yishuv derives its strength from its separation from the rest of the Yishuv, and the latter's material upbuilding of the Land. But that is also its weakness, especially *vis-à-vis* its youth, as the attractions of cultivating our spiritual heritage have always proved less fascinating than those of participating in reclaiming our material inheritance.

Between these extremes, we find a vast void. There is, for instance, not a single rabbinical seminary in the Holy Land. The Old Yishuv looks for rabbanim versed only in rabbinics, while the majority of the Yishuv has no use for religious leaders at all. Then there is the Mizrachi and the small chalutzic faction of the Agudat Yisrael. The Mizrachi, and especially its socialist sister-movement, Hapoel Hamizrachi, has a relatively large following, made up, however, of a great variety of religious elements, as those who are not completely irreligious can hardly join another party.

Its representatives exercise a considerable influence in the national and public institutions of the Yishuv, and the movement controls a third of all Jewish schools. Yet, despite the occasional successes achieved in the fight for Shabbat or kashrut observance and various other fields, I felt that the Yishuv looked upon the Mizrachi as a political force rather than as a specifically religious one. Standing essentially for a compromise between religion and nationalism in a country which so far knows only of extremes, the movement will yet have to synthesise its present dualism into a single and distinct unity of religious thought.

This inherent weakness may account for the deplorable failure of much of the Mizrachi school and teachers' training system, which its leaders themselves admit to be religiously in a poor state. On the whole, many of the Mizrachi's leaders, and most of its followers, seem to have resigned themselves to the creation of a political State within which the laws of Judaism shall be observed by, and possibly partly enforced for, the maximum number of citizens.

If the material and political development of Eretz Yisrael is still in its early stages, its spiritual and religious evolution has not, on the whole, reached even that stage. There are many obvious causes. The greatest tragedy, I think, is that the urge for *normalcy* – 'to be like unto all the nations' and to shake off the 'Galut-riven' shackles of Jewish particularism and 'peculiarity' – has itself become quite *abnormal*. That narrow-minded overemphasis on the desire to 'normalise' the Jewish people has its particularly unhappy consequences in the spiritual sphere. The Yishuv, including most of its Orthodox sections, takes more pride in the fact that it now also possesses bus companies and trade unions than in the specific and exclusive creations of the Jewish genius.

Political Zionism has now achieved the re-enthronement of the kings of Israel, but unfortunately even Orthodoxy within its ranks does not furnish the requisite balance of Hebrew prophets who would denounce fearlessly and passionately not the idea of a Jewish State but the deliberate suppression or negation of those ideals which have combined to make our people *unlike any other*, and who would advocate the realisation of our people's age-old dream for its return, in company with the *Shechinah*, to national and cultural self-sufficiency on our treasured soil.

Like the prophets, living at an equally critical juncture in our history, the traditional forces must now reorientate their attitude to the pagan cult of narrow nationalism and alien forms of life and government which threaten to turn us into an *am ha'aretz*, a mere 'people of the land'. That is the gigantic challenge which religious Zionism has yet to take up before the Battle of Judaism can be joined or won. On its outcome depends the Battle of the Jewish People.

Chayenu, *London, January 1948*

Rabbi Jakobovits was inducted as minister of the Great Synagogue on Shemini Atseret 5708. In a sermon given on Succot, he said that he would 'endeavour to live up to the traditions of an historic synagogue and the example of a great father whom the congregation had learned to love and respect'. He would judge his success as he measured that of the High Festivals, not by the momentary satisfaction his activities might produce but by the growing understanding and practice of Judaism among the community. On the day of the induction, Dayan Abramsky – who, with Dr Israel Feldman, led the Rav into the synagogue – delivered the address, during which he observed:

'It is a source of great happiness to me to bid welcome in your name to your minister and to call down the blessings of the Almighty on the work which he will perform in your midst for our faith and for our people. I am very happy for many reasons: first, because he is the son of my late revered friend and colleague, Dayan Dr Julius Jakobovits, whose labours for Jewry and Judaism meant so much to us all. All his life, he was a servant of the Lord until his untimely passing last year, and we pray for him in the words of the prayer which we recited just now. In reward of this, may he enjoy that the inspiration which he gave to this community shall be transplanted to his descendants.

Secondly, I am very happy because I myself lived and worked and worshipped for so long here at Duke's Place that I know something of your synagogue's great past, of its great problems and of its great possibilities. And, thirdly, I am very happy because I know your new minister intimately and I see in him a worthy son of a distinguished father, and a worthy leader of an historic congregation like yours.

Your minister has recently attained the status of rabbi, and awaits only the formality of Chief Rabbinic endorsement of that exalted status. He is a man with the energy of youth: with learning and the will to add constantly to his knowledge; with ability inherited from his lamented father; and with a sincerity that is transparent and infectious. I believe that those are the qualities that a spiritual leader requires today more than ever: learning that leads to ability; energy that leads to activity; sincerity that leads to devoted service.

And it is because I feel that Rabbi Jakobovits possesses these qualities that I gladly induct him into his high office today. He will need all those qualities, because his task will not be an easy one. He is to lead an ancient congregation which for a long time has not had a minister of its own. He will have to revive the religious life of a vast area which has undergone great changes in our time, but which still contains one of the most important Jewish communities in these islands. And he will have to attract young and old to our tradition at a time when many rival and often hostile distractions call them elsewhere. It will be a testing time for him, and I pray that God's blessing will always accompany him.'

Within weeks of his appointment, Rabbi Jakobovits was busy reviving some of the activities the Great Synagogue had undertaken before the war. In a letter to the 900 members of the congregation, he wrote: 'The appointment of a minister has opened a new era in the long history of the Great Synagogue [established in 1690]. It will be my duty and privilege to ensure that it will be an era of virile communal life and achievement in which all members, together with their wives and children, will be able to participate according to their needs and desires. The vast potential Jewish energies of the metropolis, and especially the East End, largely dormant at present, must be harnessed in an all-out effort to revive for our synagogue its former glory, and to continue to justify its historic claim to the special place of honour as the Mother Congregation in Anglo-Jewry.'

The Rav drew up plans which included *onegei Shabbat* and children's services for boys and girls, as well as regular social and cultural functions for youths and adults, and the establishment of a ladies' guild. The rationale for these plans became clear in the first annual Dayan Julius Jakobovits Memorial Lecture, delivered by his son at the Great Synagogue on 7 March 1948:

THE EAST END AND THE ANGLO-JEWISH COMMUNITY

'The individualistic structure of Anglo-Jewry – as the typical *gemilut chasadim* society of Jews – accounts, I think, for the fact that the pattern of Anglo-Jewish life has been far more decisively shaped by a few outstanding personalities than by the masses, to a greater extent than in any other centre of Jews in the world. That applies to the influence exerted by our distinguished lay as well as rabbinical leaders, which leads me to a remark on the occasion of this lecture.

The Anglo-Jewish rabbinate has been drawn predominantly from the Lithuanian and Polish schools of thought. Most of our rabbis, as far as they have not actually emigrated from those countries, received part of their training there or attended in this country yeshivot on the Lithuanian pattern. My father, to the perpetuation of whose memory these annual memorial lectures which we inaugurate tonight are dedicated, was essentially the product of the Hungarian-German concept of Jewish communal life. As an alumnus of some of the finest yeshivot and rabbinical seminaries in those countries, his ideal was the perfect community rather than the perfect academy of learning, and the learned and pious *ba'al habayit* rather than the professional scholar. His energies throughout his amazingly active life were devoted almost exclusively to the building of communities. Therein lay the distinguishing feature of his personality, outlook and activity. The agonising problem of the *agunah,* which tortured his mind literally to the last day of his life; the tremendous responsibility in organising and supervising of kashrut arrangements, which brought more grey hairs to his head than the advent of the Nazi régime; the keenest interest in Jewish schools and classes; the construction and maintenance of mikvaot; arbitration in civil disputes *(dinei Torah);* the crushing burden of ruling in matrimonial matters and practical religious problems: these and a host of other similar communal tasks were to him the duties to which a Rav should above all direct his attention. His personality, because of its divergence in training and outlook from that of many others, could, I believe, have given the communal aspect of Anglo-Jewry some distinctive impress, had it been allowed to unfold itself fully. This sadly accentuates the loss we sustained by his untimely departure from our scene when he had just begun to make his vast experience in these fields, especially of organising kashrut on a communal scale and of bringing social institutions under the religious orbit of the community, available to Anglo-Jewry.

Our desperate need for these values will become all the more apparent as I proceed to sketch some of the characteristic features of the East End in relation and comparison to the wider Jewish community in these isles. The East End – and for the sake of those who, for some reason, prefer borough boundaries to Jewish communal frontiers, I should say that I deliberately and proudly include this part of the City in the East End – can with justice claim to be called the cradle of Anglo-Jewry, and to this day it represents a microcosm of this country's Jewish community. It comes nearest to the communal self-sufficiency attained by most provincial centres, and it possesses many features which cannot be found in other London areas. In fact, communal development in the East End seems often to have proceeded on entirely different lines from that of other metropolitan districts. It will be the object of my paper to try to indicate these differences, to analyse their causes and to assess their effect on future prospects.

The most distinguishing feature of the East End of today is certainly its astounding multiplicity and variety of synagogal, social and educational institutions. Although more Jews are now living in North and North-West London than in the East, we still have here the greatest number of synagogues, the Beth Din, the burial societies of the United Synagogue and the Federation; many of the leading Jewish educational establishments, such as the Yeshivat Etz Chaim, the Brick Lane and Redmans Road Talmud Torahs and the Stepney Jewish Day School; most of London's Jewish social institutions, such as the Board of Guardians, the friendly societies, the Jewish Institute and Library, the Jewish Hospital, the Soup Kitchen and numerous kosher restaurants; and the largest clubs affiliated to the Association for Jewish Youth, which also has its headquarters in the East End. In fact, except for Woburn House and Great Russell Street, which from a Jewish point of view are situated in no-man's-land, almost all the major Jewish communal places of interest continue to be in the East End. Hardly any of these have joined the general human exodus to the Promised Land of North-West London. If, therefore, the Jewish East End has exported little, except human cargoes, of what was and is peculiar to it, it is even more remarkable that it has imported next to nothing of what other districts have created in the communal sphere. The intensive and extensive activities of Zionist, social and cultural groups and societies, which play such an important role in other congregations, have made only a nominal appeal, or less, to our local residents, who have provided very little for themselves in this direction. Again, I need hardly conceal my satisfaction at the fact that the East End is unique in having locked its old gate to the influx of Liberal or Reform Judaism, except at the St. George's Settlement. But I should add that this immunity to the Liberal infection is certainly not due to the strength of Orthodoxy in the East End, which proportionately fares today, I believe, worse here than in other parts of London.

The most striking absence of youth, social, political, cultural and ladies' guild activities attached to the local synagogues may be partly explained by the abnormal distribution of age groups among the Jewish population still in the East End. The most mobile group is, of course, those aged, say, 25 to 50, since they are old enough to be independent of their parents and young enough to start life afresh in a new district. The East End has, therefore, been most seriously drained of that group in the big and continuous exodus, while the younger and older groups are still well represented. Of the many marriages which I have solemnised at the Great Synagogue since my appointment, many of the partners lived as single individuals here, but all of them settled elsewhere after being married. That creates one of our most serious problems in the East End, since young married couples are obviously the most vital communal asset in every congregation, as the burden of stimulating all the activities which make up a healthy community rests primarily on them. We are thus left with a preponderance of rather old people on the one hand, and with children and especially youth on the other. Of these, only the youth will effectively look after themselves and work on their own initiative; that explains why the youth here are far more actively organised – in clubs and societies – than any other section of the population. But the steady removal of young married people is now also beginning to reduce the number of children which, owing to the higher birth-rate in the East End, has previously been little affected. The first barmitzvah at the Great Synagogue since my appointment took place yesterday! It seems to me, therefore, that the age groups are distributed in the following numerical order: old people, youth, children, and last, young married couples – an extraordinary development.

Before I return briefly to our children – and youth – problems, I must here mention what strikes me to be the second most serious cause for the phenomenal lack of communal activity among the Jewish residents. I have heard of members of this synagogue who have for 20 years or more worshipped here together week after week without knowing each other's names, or whether their neighbours in shul are single, married or divorced.

One factor explaining this truly amazing lack of social cohesion and attachment among people living in the same locality, which is quite characteristic of the whole East End, seems to be the often abominable and always inadequate housing conditions here. The East End has only few homes where it is physically possible to entertain visitors at a drawing-room meeting or other homely function bringing people together socially; and the opportunities for gossip in the queues and markets of the East End are no substitute for the frequent privately sponsored social meetings in other areas, meetings at private houses which represent, perhaps, the most important basis for communal contact and co-operation there. For I should say that most of Anglo-Jewry's noble as well as mischievous activities make their beginning over a pack of cards or a glass of whisky in some beautifully furnished, spacious home in Willesden or a similar district. If people there are not bedfellows nor necessarily bad fellows, at least they are not strangers to each other. That is why, even if they have not actually schemed the partition of Palestine in those pleasant mansions, they certainly have plotted the partition of Anglo-Jewry into those who like the New Look of the community and those who don't; but, truth to tell, it is also at those same parties where the unifying appointment of the new Chief Rabbi is being determined – at least in theory. It is self-evident how important such close social contact is in welding a community into a family of people who may fall apart in argument but who will stick together in sorrow and in joy.

The living conditions in the East End, however, are not alone to blame for the lamentable absence of this family spirit here. For what the landlords or borough councils did not provide by way of accommodation for social meetings should have been supplied by the local synagogues in fostering meetings other than divine services. In this, I am afraid, they have sadly failed. Now, if I exclude Bevis Marks and the East London United synagogues, which are really outside the scope of my review, there are two types of synagogue in the East End: there is the Great Synagogue, and there are the other synagogues: the Machzike Hadath, the Federation synagogues and the multitude of small *chevrot* and minyanim. I make this classification in no spirit of patriotic vanity or boastfulness, but merely because it suggests itself in what I have to say about these two types. The 'other' synagogues did once provide some very effective kind of social entertainment for their members; only it took the form of regular, often daily, shiurim and long Sabbath-afternoon sermons followed by very jolly and sociable *shalosh se'udot*. And then, of course, they had no such rigid discipline during the services as would prevent an occasional, whispered exchange of news and views between the worshippers. But now the shiurim have largely petered out, because the new generation are considered scholars if they can read the Kaddish faultlessly, and gossiping in shul is not nearly as interesting and socially profitable as it used to be, because the tiny number of regulars – making up the minyan in a score or more empty synagogues instead of filling one or two big amalgamated ones – already know all about each other.

On the other hand, here at this synagogue, conditions were and are quite different. This has always been known, with what I consider to be more good reason than good taste, as the 'Cathedral Synagogue' of Anglo-Jewry. As such, its divine services are to this day a model of dignity and decorum, their impressive splendour still being second to none. But, nominally, its only spiritual leader, apart from visiting dayanim, was until recently the Chief Rabbi. Yet neither the Chief Rabbi nor the dayanim were responsible for the internal organisation of the synagogue's activities or for stimulating its social life. The first function of a cathedral is to serve State occasions, and on such occasions the Chief Rabbi – or, to continue the metaphor, I should almost say the Jewish archbishop – was, of course, present. But for State occasions you want no children, which explains the absence of children and of Hebrew classes at this synagogue. It is true that certain large-scale social and literary functions used to be held here regularly, but they were designed to introduce some distinguished celebrity to the synagogue, or vice versa, rather than to introduce the ordinary local members to each other in social intercourse. And so it could happen that I found here an historic congregation of 900 members without any communal activities whatever other than divine services, during which – as befits a cathedral – the eagle's eyes of the watchful warden or beadle would rightly foil such attempts at social contact between neighbours as other synagogues permit at the expense of decorum. What is vitally needed, then, in the East End is the provision by the leading synagogues – which ought to be reinvigorated by further amalgamations with smaller units – of facilities for acquainting people with each other and each other's problems through functions which are homely rather than spectacular, and frequent rather than immense. And such functions will, in turn, sow the seeds of wider communal interests and activities.

I have already dealt with the numerical proportion of children and youth in the East End in relation to other districts. I must now devote a few minutes to an examination of the qualitative issues involved, to the chief Jewish educational and social establishments catering for our rising generation. Here, once more, the East End shows many unique features. Broadly speaking, Anglo-Jewry possesses two kinds of Jewish day-schools and two kinds of Jewish youth organisations. Among the day-schools, we can distinguish between those of a distinctly Orthodox character (such as belong to the increasingly popular Jewish Day School Movement in North and North-West London and in some provincial towns), and those which merely provide a more or less exclusively Jewish teaching staff to exclusively Jewish children but which supply no particularly intensive Jewish religious training (such as the late Jews' Free School and the Bayswater and Stepney Jewish Schools). There is a similar distinction between the youth societies with pronounced Orthodox or Zionist leanings – like the Habonim, Bnei Akiva, Bachad, Torah Va'Avodah and Federation of Zionist Youth organisations – and the clubs affiliated to the Association for Jewish Youth, whose primary object is the training for citizenship. In each case, the broad difference between the two types is really that, while the former desire to turn young assimilated Englishmen into good religious or national Jews, the latter originally aimed at turning young unassimilated Jews into good Englishmen. Now, it is peculiar, and significant, that the relation between these two types is the opposite in the East End to what it is in other parts of London or the provinces. The total membership residing locally of the AJY clubs – still the stronghold of organised Jewish youth in the East End – is estimated at well over 2,000, which is many times as high as the combined membership of all other local Jewish youth societies. In North-West London, for instance, the proportion is just the reverse. The same applies to the day-schools, which were once flourishing in the East End, but which were always of the merely denominational type. The sort of school which sets out to combine a first-class religious training in an intensively Orthodox atmosphere with a first-class secular education – so familiar to residents of Stamford Hill, Golders Green, Hampstead, Manchester and other centres – has never been known in the East End, though attempts to establish one such elementary school here are now being made.

One of the reasons for this curious development is, I think, that all great communal schemes in the East End have always been dependent on the inspiration and support of a few benevolent non-local Jews, who patronisingly looked upon the East End as a vast human clearing-house, whose individuals required some anglicising polish before they could be allowed to go forth into the big wide English world which would then be open to them. Those no doubt genuine, but all too short-sighted, benefactors wanted to be joined in their more respectable districts, not by a horde of foreigners who stuck to their alien Jewish habits and peculiarities, but by well-groomed patriotic Englishmen of the Jewish persuasion; but they forgot that after the polishing process even this Jewish persuasion was more often than not no persuasion at all except for three days a year and one final event in their lifetime, or rather death-time. Today we are reaping the bitter harvest of that narrow-minded policy of organised, mass-scale assimilation: the proportion of children receiving no Hebrew education whatever and of Jews who are entirely unattached to any synagogue is much higher in the East End than anywhere else.

This phenomenally rapid disintegration of the East End, which not so long ago was Anglo-Jewry's bastion of Orthodoxy and is now religiously and communally a shambles, cannot be explained merely by its numerical decrease; this debacle represents one of the few examples in Jewish history of the spiritual decline and fall of a community in so short a time. Had the Jews of the East End been able to govern their own affairs, and to direct the enormous sums of money which poured into schemes and institutions designed and controlled by themselves, the shape of things might have taken a different turn, and the East End might, to this day, have supplied the communities of these isles with creative, Orthodox workers, the human leaven to ferment Jewish religious growth everywhere. As it is, we are hard put to it to maintain our own religious life and to inspire our own communal vitality. Today, Jews from all over London come to the East End to obtain fish and chickens, not religious inspiration; and while the shuls struggle on with the help of mournful *Kaddish-zogers,* the 'Lane' is packed with gay bargain-hunters. We still have, of course, the sadly reduced Talmud Torahs and the yeshivah in our midst. Their contribution in the past to the production of many leading rabbis and Jewish educationalists must not be underestimated. Yet it is probably true to assert that the provinces, which only one or two decades ago numbered fewer Jews than the East End, have furnished Anglo-Jewry with far more outstanding communal figures, with more rabbis, ministers and lay-leaders, than the East End. To give only one statistical example: of the 36 ministers (excluding chazanim) serving with the United Synagogue at its constituent and district branches, 15 hail from the provinces, 11 from abroad, but only seven from the East End and three from other parts of London. This is just one amazing and significant result of a little research I have made on this subject.

But where the East End has been, and still is, really great and unchallenged is in its social institutions, the most important of which I have already enumerated. The staggering volume of welfare work undertaken by these institutions will eternally stand to the credit of those many Anglo-Jewish benefactors who have always regarded the Jewish East End as the first charge upon their generosity. Hence the superb and unequalled record of the East End in producing the finest social workers. Only it is somewhat depressing to reflect that most of the Jewish social welfare work in the East End grew up as a direct consequence of the poverty, often destitution, in this locality. The situation has, of course, vastly improved during the last few years, and there is today a greater measure of economic equality between East End Jews and others than ever before. But the East End has yet to emancipate itself fully from the stigma of a certain degree of social inferiority and the mentality of economic dependence which the former conditions have produced. The East End continues to be looked upon, by many local and other Jews alike, as a decreasing society receiving favours rather than as a creative community contributing its full share, spiritually, communally and financially, to the vigorous, healthy life of our people.

To stimulate this communal consciousness must now, I think, be our foremost duty and objective. The excellent series of articles on the East End which has been appearing in the *Jewish Chronicle* reads more like a glorified premature obituary than a description of a live community. The writer was 'In Search of the East End', and one does not search except for what is thought to be lost. The Jewish evacuation of the East End will, according to present portents, continue

to weaken our human potential for some years yet; but a hard core of a numerically strong community – at least as big as in Glasgow or Dublin and Liverpool
combined – will remain here, perhaps one day to enjoy the benefits of modern
town planning more thoroughly than our more impatient brethren in the now
fashionable but then out-of-date districts of the furthest reaches of North-West
London. With the growing solvency, if not prosperity, of our local population,
the eminence and importance of the social institutions that have made the East
End great and immortal in Jewish communal history will gradually recede into
the background; their place must progressively be taken by centres of culture
and communal life, if the Jewish East End is to survive as a potent factor in
Anglo-Jewry.

The East End may for a long time yet not be able to balance human exports
with imports, but its accessibility from all parts of the metropolis could make
possible the fusion of the London communities – now more or less separate units
– into one entity by attracting for regular Jewish social and cultural activities
and enlightenment the finest elements of this great city.

With the elimination of the great Jewries of Eastern and Central Europe,
Anglo-Jewry will, for the first time in its history, have to be self-sufficient; it will
now have to provide its own Torah and *avodah* as well as *gemilut chasadim*. This
will require a radical reorientation in our educational and communal planning.
In terms of Torah, it will mean, in the first place, that new and better means must
be found for popularising the study and practice of our wonderful religious and
cultural heritage. The impact of Jewish teachings upon the twentieth century
and its problems will have to be presented in a modern and attractive form to
the mass of our people whose warped view of Judaism is often restricted to the
synagogue, the kitchen and the cemetery, and whose knowledge of Jewish
literature is confined to a few pages in the *Singer's Prayer Book* and, of course,
the indispensable *Jewish Chronicle*. Such narrow and mutilated Judaism can
hardly be fascinating enough to fire the imagination of our sensation-hungry
age. Above all, our youth must be made Torah-conscious, proudly aware that
our religion is not just a ceremonial or ritual affair, too precious for everyday
use, some archaeological phantom of interest to historians and cranks, but a
unique way of life representing in all its domestic, religious, moral, social,
economic and political ramifications, a supreme and complete divine civilisation far in advance of any system embraced by other peoples.

Again, in the sphere of *avodah,* the required reorientation must mean the realisation of selfless service to the community, as the highest and noblest ambition
of every young Jew and Jewess. Today, many of our young people are brought
up to be pleasure-hunting, bread-earning machines, with little appreciation for
the higher values of life. We must give them a grand vision to strive for, a vision
not merely of packed synagogues, but of a dynamic community which draws
its inspiration from the age-old fountains of Jewish creativity and communal
achievement.'

On 5 November 1948, it was announced that Rabbi Jakobovits had accepted an invitation from the Representative Council of the Jewish Communities in Eire to become Chief

Rabbi of Eire. Early in January, he delivered his farewell sermon at the Great Synagogue, where he had ministered overall for just 18 months. It was his dearest wish, he said, that the congregation which had given him so much happiness should not turn its back on the teachings he had tried to impart. On behalf of the congregation, the Rev N. Fenakel presented Rabbi Jakobovits with an illuminated address recording that 'during his tenure of office, he won the esteem and regard of his congregants by his conscientiousness, his learning and his general communal activities'.

CHAPTER TWO

Jewish Marriage

Sir, Since my appointment as minister of the Great Synagogue a few months ago, I have insisted on seeing beforehand all bridal couples whom I was to marry, in order to explain to them the meaning of the wedding ceremony and to discuss with them the religious obligations of the Jewish wife. In each case, I have carefully probed into their attitude in principle towards the personal laws to be observed by Jewish married women, laws the desecration of which Judaism regards as a capital crime equal in status to eating on Yom Kippur or consuming bread on Passover.

The response has been remarkable in revealing the deep and widespread interest displayed in these vital regulations, and the lack of opportunity to discuss them in an enlightened atmosphere was generally regretted. I have the impression that, provided this subject can be approached with knowledge, tact, and broad-minded understanding of modern social conditions, its intelligent presentation would effectively appeal to many Jewish girls and women in whom there is still a spark of Jewish religious morality.

I am therefore arranging, under the auspices of the Carmel Youth Society (of the Great Synagogue), a Jewish marriage guidance course. Each complete series will last about three months and consists of fortnightly talks and discussions on the course, as well as on the principles of the Sabbath and kashrut laws as far as they affect the Jewish housewife. The course will be conducted by Mrs Ruth Royde, BA (Hons), whose exceptional Jewish and university qualifications should fit her ideally for this difficult – and almost revolutionary – task.

In order to make full and intimate discussions possible, admission must be strictly limited; it will be granted only to young ladies upon payment of a registration fee of two shillings [10p]. Applicants should write, within the next week, to Mrs Royde, Lauderdale Mansions, W9, stating which evening(s) of the week would be most suitable, and whether they are single or married.

I sincerely hope that this so far unique venture will contribute much towards restoring the sanctity of Jewish home life which has so nobly distinguished our people in the past, and towards a fuller appreciation of our matchless Jewish ideals in the world of today.

I. Jakobovits
Great Synagogue, Duke's Place, EC3

Following publication of this letter in the *Jewish Chronicle* of 23 January 1948, Rabbi Jakobovits drew up a prospectus of the Jewish Marriage Education Committee for circulation to Jewish clubs and societies, youth groups and individuals. It attracted widespread attention and immediate success.

JEWISH MARRIAGE EDUCATION COMMITTEE

What is the composition of the Committee?

The Committee is an independent body of rabbis, ministers, doctors and social workers (men and women) who are intensely interested in raising the level of Jewish home life. It includes members and representatives of numerous youth and other communal organisations, and is under the patronage of the Very Rev Chief Rabbi Israel Brodie.

What are the aims of the Committee?

'To enhance the sanctity and stability of Jewish home life by enlightening young men and women on Judaism's matrimonial and domestic teachings, and their relation to modern social conditions' (from the Constitution).

What are the educational spheres covered by the Committee?

The Jewish attitude to sexual morality, marriage, divorce and home life in the light of present-day conditions; the status of women; the laws – and their meaning – of sex, chupah, circumcision, Redemption of the Firstborn, Sabbath, festivals and kashrut; the biological and psychological aspects of marriage.

What are the Committee's activities?

Youth organisations. The Committee arranges for lecturers (male or female, according to requirements) to address Jewish youth clubs and societies. All speakers – usually young persons – are thoroughly briefed on the basis of a carefully designed outline, prepared by a special Speakers' Training Sub-Committee. These talks, which are followed by discussions, give a general survey of the Jewish approach to sex and marriage, and they serve to stimulate interest in it.

Marriage education courses. The Committee organises, in various districts (according to demand), detailed courses of instruction in series of seven weekly lectures. These courses, held for males and females separately, are conducted on personal and intimate lines, no more than 30 applicants being admitted at a time.

Synagogues. The Committee plans to raise marriages at synagogues – today purely formal, often mechanical, affairs – into functions, the full significance of which is realised by bridal couples. For this purpose, arrangements are being made for the minister and/or suitable persons to have a personal talk with those about to be married. The ultimate aim is to ensure that no one will go under the chupah until they have received adequate information by means of verbal and literary instruction on what the Jewish community expects from a Jewish home.

Literature. The Committee plans to issue literature, from small-scale pamphlets to comprehensive handbooks. The latter, which should be presented to all bridal couples by the community, are to consist of an intelligent, up-to-date presentation of all items of interest to a Jewish home, ranging from a kosher cookery section to the Jewish attitude towards the use of contraceptives.

Research. The Committee recognises that the contemporary breakdown of family life, among Jews and Gentiles alike, has its roots deeply embedded in the sociological, economic, moral and spiritual pattern of Western society today. Without a thorough analysis of these factors, the problem cannot be tackled. It is therefore planned to collect and interpret statistics, authoritative opinions and other relevant material, and to examine the impact of Jewish teachings on present-day conditions.

Within weeks, a panel of rabbis, doctors and social workers had been gathered to organise a series of lectures and publications on 'the Jewish aspect of life with regard to marriage'. Such was the popularity of the lectures that a group of participants felt impelled to remark on 'how much we enjoyed attending the first series', which had been approached with 'admirable tact and enlightenment'.

The essential nature of the courses was spelled out by Rabbi Jakobovits, by then Chief Rabbi of Eire, in a paper on 'Problems of Jewish Family Life' delivered in London in 1951 to the ninth Conference of Anglo-Jewish Preachers, over which Chief Rabbi Brodie presided.

Rabbi Jakobovits said that too little attention had been paid to the alarming rate at which Jewish home and family life was disintegrating. Young people entering marriage, he said, should be shown the interrelation between the happiness and stability of marital existence and the three pillars of Jewish home life: *taharah*, Shabbat and kashrut.

There was a growing lack of chastity outside marriage, and within it. Even if the rigid moral discipline of their rabbis could not be reimposed under present conditions, ministers should ensure that social and fund-raising activities promoted under Jewish – especially synagogue – auspices were never devoid of religious and cultural content. Support should be withheld from gatherings which offended against the Jewish code of morality by fostering vulgarity.

Years later, the Chief Rabbi again felt the need to address the problem:

THE FAMILY UNDER THREAT

In the same way as I plead in the Jewish community today that you cannot expect synagogues to exist tomorrow unless today you educate people to cherish their Judaism, and prepare them to face the commitments and disciplines that a synagogue stands for, so we are not going to have Jewish homes tomorrow unless we prepare young people to cherish, to love and to appreciate the splendours of Jewish home life.

This needs a vast campaign at various levels of activity and of education. It may well begin on a major scale in the higher classes of our day-schools, and some attempts have already been made, including brief courses on Jewish marriage education, in the broadest outline, to senior classes.

It certainly means regular lectures at the universities to Jewish students; it means adequate and competently conducted classes for engaged couples in preparation for marriage, both of which have proved highly successful under the auspices of the Jewish Marriage Education Council. It means that anyone who is going to enter into the sanctity of the marriage bond will have at least the same degree of preparation as they have had for barmitzvah.

One takes it for granted that one cannot become barmitzvah unless one has made the necessary preparations. Surely marriage – which is a much more serious step to take and requires much more information in order to live up to our ideals – needs an even more intensive kind of preparation to make our youngsters fit and worthy to become bearers of the traditions of the Jewish home.

All this means not merely that these various aspects of education must be manned, but one has to train people to be able to render this information; and therefore the Council has set up training courses whereby people can be given the background and the mode of presentation to make this instruction effective, and to attract young people, who are so highly critical, to see the rationale behind our Jewish marriage teachings.

As a result of the work carried out during these past 20 years, a number of volunteer counsellors have been trained and are now engaged in an increasingly impressive programme of individual counselling, in order to deal with marital and domestic problems as and when they arise. This is a tremendous service to numerous individuals. One also needs the specialist services of psychiatrists and sometimes doctors for referral, and we now have within the aegis of our Council an entire structure of such services available for those who turn to us for help.

The national authorities have now granted recognition to our Jewish Marriage Education Council, not merely for the purpose of referrals of Jewish cases that come before them and are then passed on for treatment to our own authorities, but also for consultations even on such matters as bear on legislation dealing with marriage and divorce.

Until now, there was no Jewish agency able to take its seat together with the Catholic and Protestant authorities in order to be consulted on the Jewish experience in this area, but now a number of instances have occurred on which the advice of our Council has been invited on a national level.

Rivon *magazine, Hampstead Synagogue, June 1969*

STEMMING INTERMARRIAGE: WHY AND HOW

The battle against intermarriage does not begin at the age of 16 or 17, when young people start to date seriously. By then, the battle is either won or lost. It begins at least ten years earlier, if not at a still younger age. A little anecdote may illustrate the point:

A young man once stood at a station platform, waiting for a train. 'Could you tell me the time, please?' he asked another traveller standing beside him. No answer. He asked again, only to be ignored. Impatient, he rebuked the elderly gentleman: 'If you have no watch, you might at least tell me so civilly.' The other man replied: 'I have a watch, and I could have told you the time. But had I done so, you would have thanked me, and on boarding the train you would have sat down next to me and engaged in conversation with me. Before the journey was over, you would have known where I was living. You would have come to look me up one day, found that I had a very attractive daughter, and eventually proposed to marry her – and I don't want a son-in-law who hasn't even got a watch!'

If one wants to prevent the wrong marriage, one cannot wait until the train has arrived. One must foresee the sequence of events while still waiting for the train, before the journey has begun. According to the Talmud, marriages are determined in heaven 40 days before a child is formed. It is certain that, on earth, intermarriages are made or unmade at about that time, determined by the attitude and ways of life parents have before the child is born.

The second barrier to intermarriage, now also widely breached, was the horror it evoked in the Jewish community. The very frequency with which inter-marriages now occur has vitiated this deterrent. Bashfulness and shame – once virtues particularly fostered among Jews as a safeguard against vice – are altogether in short supply in this age of immodesty.

It may be difficult to re-create the communal sense of outrage which often helped to rescue those who might waver, too weak to resist through their own personal resources of will-power and self-discipline. But the onus rests on the community to strive for its own survival and to secure it by any means, short of impinging on the individual's freedom of conscience. Yet this freedom does not curtail the community's right, and duty, to insist on reciprocity in its relations with its members. To belong to a community, to enjoy its privileges and honours, is the birthright of every Jew. In turn, he must meet his debt to the community and accept certain responsibilities.

On intermarriage, these responsibilities are renounced, and therefore any claim to communal honours and privileges lapses. By denying these, the community invokes sanctions designed to prevent the breach of faith from being taken for granted, and public honours being given in return for public dis-honour and damage. A community under such stress is also under a special obligation to ensure that societies, clubs and functions organised under its auspices, and supported to serve Jewish interests, will not encourage, or even permit, the kind of mixed membership which, far from stemming the tide of intermarriage, promotes it.

The obvious dilemma involved in advocating such policies nowadays may be considered in dealing with the third traditional barrier: the non-Jewish objec-tion to intermarriage which has now also all but disappeared. Not so long ago, it was generally accepted that religious groups kept together, and should keep

1. Rabbi Dr Julius Jakobovits in Königsberg with his three eldest children – Immanuel (right), Lotti and George.

2 and 3. The newly appointed Dayan Dr Julius Jakobovits (above) in Berlin in 1928, and the newly ordained Rabbi Immanuel Jakobovits at the Great Synagogue, Duke's Place, in 1948.

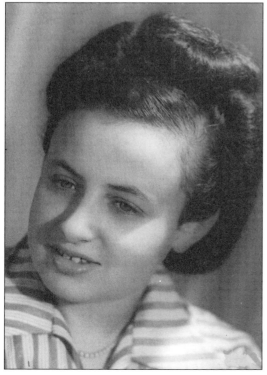

4 and 5. Engagement portraits of Immanuel and Amélie soon after he took up his appointment as Chief Rabbi of Ireland in 1949.

6. Amélie's parents, Rabbi Dr Elie Munk
   and Fanny Munk (née Goldberger),
   at home in Paris.

7. The marriage of Ireland's Chief Rabbi and Amélie at the rue Cadet Synagogue in Paris on 5 July 1949.

8. Paula Jakobovits (née Wreschner) and her son enjoy a rare moment of relaxation together during the summer of 1954.

9. Chief Rabbi and Mrs Jakobovits on horseback in Ireland in 1950. Lotti is in the centre.

10. With Colonel and Mrs Chaim Herzog at a Dublin banquet in 1958 to mark the inauguration of the Jewish National Fund's Herzog Forest in Israel.

11. Dublin, 1949: Talmudical studies vie with pressing diary engagements.

12. Dublin, 1958: Professor Leonard Abrahamson presents a gift to Ireland's departing Chief Rabbi.

13. The Jakobovits family on the eve of their move to New York. The children are (left to right) Shmuel, Shoshana, Esther and Yoel, with Paula Jakobovits holding the newly born Aviva.

together, without incurring the disapproval of social reformers or popular opinion. Such denominational cohesion was considered to be as natural and proper as the exclusiveness of family bonds – the relationship between husband and wife, or parents and children. Today, this restrictiveness is often branded as ghettoism. In our morally permissive and ethnically egalitarian society, it is becoming increasingly difficult to resist the common movement towards blurring all human differences and distinctions.

These present trends pose a double challenge to the Jewish people: how to maintain its identity as a tiny minority swimming against a mighty tide, and how to advocate religious particularism and so risk popular antagonism, if not hostility. Both challenges will demand sacrifice and courage of a high order. They call for a defiance of conformity, and nothing is harder in this age of conformity than to defy it. The post-Emancipation period has taught us that Jewish survival is no easier, and certainly no more assured, in conditions of freedom than under persecution. Indeed, while the Jewish people has demonstrated the capacity to survive oppression, it has yet to prove that it can survive liberty and equality.

What is now needed is nothing short of a new type of martyrdom – a martyrdom not to die for Judaism but, possibly harder still, to live for Judaism at the cost of unpopularity and the risk of rejection. Voluntarily to surrender some of the hard-won boon of social acceptance demands the highest form of idealism. The communal endorsement of policies to counter the ravages of inter-marriage will undoubtedly exact such a price. But it is no higher than the price Jewish communities in the Diaspora will have to pay for their readiness to identify themselves with Israel, even at the risk of incurring the charge of 'dual loyalties' and other grave embarrassments.

In the end, however, the choice on whether to marry in or out is a highly personal decision, little influenced by communal policies and attitudes. The real argument to be overcome is: 'As long as we are happy together …'

It is of little avail to counter such a philosophy of life with statistics. Experience may show, as in fact it does, that the rate of marriage failures and divorces is twice as high in mixed marriages as in endogamous unions. Sociological surveys may also indicate that children brought up in a spiritual no-man's-land are more prone than others to end up in misery and mischief. But no young couple in the flush of love thinks, or even fears, that its will be among the marriages to strike disaster, or that its children will turn out as misfits. Young people no more believe that they will land on the wrong side of the statistics than do inveterate smokers. The rate of casualties may be far higher, but love is an even more irresistible addiction than smoking.

The answer, therefore, will have to be found elsewhere. So long as our sons and daughters are brought up to believe the pernicious doctrine that all that matters in life is to be happy, to have 'a good time' – rather than to make the times good – they are bound to grow up as social parasites, doing no good to society or ultimately to themselves.

Happiness, like honour, as our sages said, eludes those who pursue it and pursues those who flee from it. Our children must be taught, if they are to be raised as solid and useful citizens, that we are not born simply in order to amuse ourselves. Life is too precious for that. It is also too sacred to be prostituted by any vice masquerading as a virtue by making the pursuit of happiness into an ideal, thinking that the selfish formula 'as long as it makes them happy' can legitimise and whitewash every breach of the moral and social order.

Some people are made happy by cheating – betraying their fellow-men's confidence; some by adultery – betraying their marriage; and others by marrying out – betraying their people. Only in a perverse society do the whims of personal happiness determine the norms of right and wrong, and only the most irresponsible parents tell their children to regulate their behaviour by whatever makes them happy. To Jews, this notion is particularly obnoxious. The cult of happiness could have saved the Jewish people 2,000 years of agony. Jews could have been as happy as anyone else for the asking. All they had to do to put an end to their suffering and martyrdom was to renounce their religious commitment, to betray their faith.

But the thought of purchasing happiness at the cost of their ideals never occurred to them. Jews simply were not brought up to think along those lines. They took it for granted that life served a higher purpose than just to enjoy oneself, and they cheerfully endured hardship and persecution for the sake of values which made life, and even death, worthwhile. And because they did not pursue happiness, it pursued them in the end. In all the misery of their circumstances, Jews were probably the happiest people in Western society. Inside their homes, they found ample compensation for their suffering outside. Cheered by their Sabbaths and festivals, and rejoicing in the delights of harmonious family bonds, untroubled by any generation gap and but rarely soured by divorce or infidelity, their domestic life and stability became the envy of even their oppressors.

Despite their ordeals, Jews loved life more passionately, they clung to life more tenaciously, and they mourned the dead with greater grief than anyone else. Jewish life, however grim externally, was infinitely precious, beautiful and full of joy. Only when Jewish young people are prepared and conditioned to cherish a similar outlook – placing law above love, and service above selfishness – can they and their people anticipate similar rewards of meaningful living combined with true happiness.

Chief Rabbi Jakobovits
Jewish Marriage Education Council, 1971

Early in 1973, an 'Intermarriage Anonymous' bureau was set up by the Chief Rabbi's Office in an effort to combat the growing rate of marrying-out. Operating it in the initial stages was a panel of eight London rabbis. The scheme was initiated by Rabbi Maurice Hool, minister of the Kingsbury Synagogue and head of the Chief Rabbi's department for the ministry, who explained that it was aimed at parents or young people reluctant to discuss intermarriage problems with their own minister and more ready to do so with someone they did not know.

Rabbi Hool said that the people most likely to be helped by the scheme were those who had no congregational ties, or others – Israeli students, for example – who might have no one to whom to turn. 'In any event, young people are more likely to approach an anonymous organisation.' Commenting on reports that the rate of intermarriage in Britain had reached one in four, and possibly one in three among Jewish students, he stated: 'It is difficult to say whether these figures are correct, but there is no doubt that the problem has reached alarming proportions.'

Some 20 years later, in response to growing calls for action to alleviate another major problem – the plight of so-called 'chained wives' – the Chief Rabbi published this background article on *get* amendments to the Family Law Act:

THE TORTUOUS PATH TO RELIEF FOR *AGUNOT*

For me, the amelioration of the *agunah* ['chained wife'] problem is a deeply personal commitment. On the last day of his life, nearly 50 years ago, my father told me that he had had a disturbed night. Visions of pleading *agunot*, whom he could not help, would not let him sleep. He was then a dayan of the London Beth Din, having previously been head of Berlin's communal Beth Din.

To show how rabbis agonise over the problem, I related this story to Lord Mackay when he became Lord Chancellor in 1987. The story registered. He reminded me of it in a discussion on the *get* [Jewish divorce] amendment to the Family Law Bill.

Agunot in the classic sense – of wives whose husbands are missing, at sea or in war or through the Holocaust, without firm evidence of their death – hardly exist now. The situation usually arises today with the refusal of either spouse to release the other by a *get* – often out of spite or to extort money. The numbers are very limited. Most cases are resolved by persuasion, through the Beth Din or its agents. I understand from the London Beth Din that the total of unresolved cases it has dealt with over the years is barely 100 – 60 women, plus 40 men whose wives refused to accept a *get*.

Notable among efforts to overcome the problem is the pre-nuptial agreement (PNA), whereby, prior to marriage, a couple signs an agreement to consult the Beth Din in the event of a divorce being contemplated. I considered this PNA option while still Chief Rabbi, but decided against it. A couple about to have their marriage sanctified would, I felt, hardly find it palatable to contemplate its breakdown.

In Canada and New York State, legislation has been introduced to counter the problem, and similar measures are now being promoted in South Africa and Australia. But in New York, the revised statute has met with rabbinical opposition, since it could be construed as coercion, which would nullify any *get*.

In Britain, many attempts, co-ordinated by the Board of Deputies and guided by rabbinical and legal authorities, were made over the past decade, but without success. Our opportunity finally came with the introduction of the Family Law Bill into the House of Lords at the end of 1995. During the second reading, I announced the intention of introducing an amendment that would overcome the special difficulties encountered by Jews.

A civil divorce, I said, 'while dissolving the civil contract … leaves the religious bond – equally recognised by the State – still intact, thus leading to a "limping marriage" liable to cause immense hardship'. 'The Lord Chancellor', I added, 'has been most helpful and has indicated that if I tabled an amendment … the Government would look seriously at it in committee.'

Lord Meston, whose help was indispensable, duly introduced such an amendment. He explained: 'I can tell the committee from experience, acting for Jewish clients, of long sojourns outside the door of the court … negotiating in effect the price to be paid for the husband to initiate the *get* procedure. It seemed necessary, therefore, for this Bill to take the opportunity to right what many regard as an injustice. It will enable a true, clean break to be achieved, and both the parties to have the right to remarry according to their religious beliefs. It gives the wife, in particular, the right to negotiate on equal terms.'

The amendment stated that, 'where one party's ability to remarry will be materially impeded as a result of the other party's failure to remove all barriers to remarriage, such failure shall be deemed to constitute grave hardship …' entitling the court to refuse making the decree absolute.

The Lord Chancellor commented on the proposed amendment: 'This is a difficult matter. I have been familiar with [it] almost from the time I became Lord Chancellor and Lord Jakobovits came to see me about it. I have received [other] representations … Many have suggested to me more specific amendments. This is a carefully and very generally drafted amendment which, in some ways, makes it easier to consider incorporating it in the Bill, because it does not refer to any specific difficulties.'

Then came a bombshell. In a letter dated 19 February 1996, Lord Mackay stated that our amendment 'raised several considerable difficulties'. He argued: 'The barrier with which you are concerned is to a marriage within the Jewish faith. I do not believe that the courts could properly take this into account unless they were specifically to do so by the Act.' [That was, of course, precisely the point of the amendment.] Lord Mackay continued: 'I am advised that it has been the practice of the Jewish authorities … never to grant a *get* unless and until the marriage had been dissolved by decree absolute … A husband could not therefore, under the new arrangements, remove the barrier to remarriage before the divorce was granted.'

Not so. The only reason for refusing to allow a *get* before the civil divorce is out of respect for the civil law. If a *get* were required before the civil divorce could become effective, then obviously there would be no objection to granting the *get* first.

Even more curious was a third argument: 'The court would, therefore, have to rely on a promise by the husband to remove the barrier after the divorce order was made … The prospect of courts being asked to commit Jewish husbands to prison for contempt of court … is not one I am happy to contemplate.'

No one has suggested imprisoning husbands for contempt of court, nor extracting a promise from the husband; imprisonment would arise only for bigamy. Clearly, ideas had been planted which were contrived, and based on a misconception of Jewish practice.

Before this letter, the only objection to the proposed amendment had come from Jewish quarters. It was argued that the rabbis who had created the problem should resolve it themselves. Some even called the recourse to the civil law a 'humiliation' for the Jewish community. The argument was plausible – but false. As I explained during the committee stage: '… the termination of the [Jewish] religious bond requires the consent of both [parties], just as the marriage contract can be established only with the agreement of both sides … The law in question is not ordained by rabbis but is biblical [Deuteronomy 24:1], and no rabbi is authorised to cancel or to override any biblical law. Nor can a contract in principle be terminated except by the parties who established it. The problem is not due to any anomaly in Jewish law. Were we to have exclusive jurisdiction in matrimonial matters, there would be no difficulty, since, in general, we would merely refuse to administer a divorce which does not enable both parties to remarry.'

Following further discussion with the Lord Chancellor, and through other contacts, a new version of the amendment was agreed on. It provided that, 'if the parties were married to each other in accordance with the usages of a kind mentioned in Section 26 (1) of the Marriage Act, 1949 … the court may, on the application of either party, direct that there must also be produced to the court a declaration by both parties that they have taken such steps as are required to dissolve the marriage in accordance with those usages'. The 1949 Act repeated the provisions of the 1836 Act, which expressly recognised synagogue marriages. There was a hint here that the anomaly had lain with the civil law, which accepted Jewish religious usages for marriages but not for dissolving them.

The amendment went through both Houses of Parliament without a word of dissent and became law on 4 July. This landmark legislation – which will no doubt serve as a model in other countries – will not solve all *agunah* situations, but will cover the great majority, excluding only those rare cases where the recalcitrant spouse is not interested in a civil divorce. For the rest, it should bring immense relief.

Jewish Chronicle, *26 July 1996*

[The House of Lords proceedings on the Family Law Bill are detailed on pages 296–8.]

FLASHBACK TWO

Dublin

On 28 October 1948, the then honorary secretary of the Jewish Representative Council of Ireland wrote to me: '… I would like to place on record the intense pleasure which we all feel at the thought that, in the very near future, you will be installed as our Spiritual Chief, and you can depend on this Council … for their wholehearted co-operation in the happy discharge of your onerous duties …'

Only a little more than a year earlier, I had been inducted as the first rabbi for 105 years of the Great Synagogue, Duke's Place, London – Anglo-Jewry's 'Cathedral Synagogue'. It had taken me several months to decide on accepting the call to assume the distinguished office left vacant for 13 years by Dr Isaac Herzog on his appointment as Chief Rabbi of the Holy Land.

On 1 February 1949, I took up residence in his former home and became heir to his great rabbinate. A fortnight later, Chief Rabbi Israel Brodie, my own former teacher, installed me into office at a memorable service in the Adelaide Road Synagogue, followed by a festive celebration dinner graced by the presence of Ireland's head of government, John Costello, the then Taoiseach.

Rabbi Brodie's participation in the service was accompanied by not a little soul-searching on the part of the community, always anxious to demonstrate that it was independent of the London Chief Rabbinate. But the precedent was in due course to be repeated, when I, as British Chief Rabbi, inducted into office two successive Irish Chief Rabbis.

In my own installation address, I said nothing startling, but I made a sincere attempt to speak honestly with my new flock. There was a strong echo of a famous passage in the writings of Samson Raphael Hirsch when I declared: 'Of late, our slogan has been "We must be a normal people". Heaven forfend that we, a nation destined to be "a kingdom of priests and a holy people", should become merely a normal people. For if we were just normal, we should have perished, like all other normal peoples of antiquity, thousands of years ago. If we were normal, we should have succumbed to the unparalleled martyrdom imposed upon us throughout the centuries, as any other nation on earth would have done. Our motto will now have to be "We must be an exceptional people."'

Inevitably, however, a 28-year-old Chief Rabbi could not be an entirely conventional figure, for, as I said, 'you have taken a daring step in appointing so young a man, and the eyes of the Jewish world will be upon us. You have put not only me, but Jewish youth in general, on trial.'

This led to perhaps an unusual emphasis in my statement of aims: 'Firstly, a Rav must serve the youth. They will be my principal allies – the spearhead of our advance to greatness. I want to arouse their passion for everything Jewish, their love of learning, and their devotion to the community and to Israel …'

In my mind, at the time I accepted the call, was the belief that this would be a ten-year assignment. In the event, those ten years proved to be the most momentous decade in post-exilic Jewish history. They also proved to be the most enjoyable and exciting period of my life thus far. Unlike the Hebrew slave who 'if he come in by himself shall go out by himself', I entered my service alone and left with the blessings of a dedicated wife and five happy children.

Initially, on moving into the former Herzog residence, my mother and my sister Shulamith shared it with me. George and Lotti were both married by this time, and living in America, while Joseph was pursuing his medical studies in London. Solomon and Manfred had been at Gateshead yeshivah. The former, after an unmemorable period of study at Jews' College, moved to New York; the latter went to the Bachad Farm in Thaxted, Essex, for *hachsharah* before leaving for Israel, where he became a founding member of Kibbutz Lavi. Shulamith soon married in Dublin and left for Zurich, where her husband was a leading international lawyer.

For my mother, this was her fifth home in 11 years. Life had not been easy for her, and she had enjoyed little of the assured security she might have expected from her marriage. Children always assume that mothers will infallibly cope with all domestic chores and crises; it was outsiders who were most impressed, and even moved, by the quiet resilience she evidenced under often very trying conditions. And, as she well knew, her situation as chatelaine in Dublin was only a temporary one, for the position of an unmarried Chief Rabbi was unacceptable from every point of view.

A cold-blooded arranged match had no appeal for me and I had resolved to seek a bride of my own volition, though inevitably in a rather restricted circle. A name in Switzerland had been suggested while I was still living in London but, during my preparations for the journey, a member of the Schreiber family – whose granddaughter, a generation later, was to marry my elder son – suggested that a call on Rabbi Elie Munk, the spiritual leader of Paris' rue Cadet synagogue, might prove of value. I learned later that he had had in mind the second daughter, but as the eldest was only 18, it is perhaps just as well that I did not act in accordance with his expectations.

It was Chanukah 1948 when I arrived in Paris, and nothing was more natural than that I should attend morning service at that most congenial of synagogues. Nor was it inappropriate, bachelor rabbis being a rare and endangered species, that I should be invited home for breakfast. And as the eldest daughter – Amélie by name – seemed to have time on her hands, would it not be a good idea for her to show the visitor round Paris?

The rabbi had quickly decided that I would prove a suitable son-in-law, but it took a little more time to convince Amélie that I would prove a suitable husband. She had never heard of Dublin and had to consult an atlas to discover its whereabouts. Nor was she all that enthusiastic about exchanging the attractions of Paris for the dubious advantages of the Irish capital.

She knew no English, but we conversed in German, since my French was limited to a few years' study at school. Later, we carried on a rather limping correspondence, and then she came to England, ostensibly to study at her uncle's girls' seminary in Gateshead, but in reality to learn English. We met up again in Manchester – at the home of a distant relative, the Rev (later Rabbi) Felix Carlebach – and by the time of my induction in Dublin, we were unofficially engaged. Amélie, however, did not feel it becoming to appear at the ceremony while her status was unfinalised.

We were married in Paris on 5 July 1949. Our marriage proved to be the greatest success of my life. A man may not be aware of all the changes a wife effects on his life; they come gradually, and seem only to be the rational outcome of matrimonial adjustment. Yet all who knew me well became certain that Amélie was changing me subtly, but to my great benefit.

My idea of the rabbinical position had been somewhat old-fashioned and I wore the frock-coats and large hats of my father's generation. Amélie cleared them out, and afterwards I appeared in the lounge suits and trilbies of a more modern style. My social manner eased, and my conversational range broadened from the theological and communal to the niceties of domestic life. My principles remained firm, but they no longer sounded rigid. I became, without quite realising how, a 1950s' model rabbi.

Amélie has frequently lamented her lack of regular schooling. At an age when ordinarily she would have inhabited a world bounded by examinations and school uniforms, she knew all the horrors of German occupation, of terror and deprivation. As the eldest of seven children, she had to shoulder responsibilities and tackle problems that might well have broken a more mature person. In her, they developed exceptional powers of initiative, understanding and perseverance.

On her father's side, Amélie came from a distinguished German rabbinical family, and the rabbi himself had achieved considerable repute, especially with his book, *The World of Prayer*. Her mother's father, Nathan Goldberger, had been a prosperous businessman and president of the Jewish community of Nuremberg.

Amélie was a resident of Paris, and that enchanting city could not fail to leave its mark on her development. She came to have an almost instinctive insight into people and situations. Her memory and energy are extraordinary. As our lives progressed, she was able to cope with the very different demands of three entirely disparate rabbinates, and when she achieved a state of official eminence never enjoyed by any previous rebbetzin in history, she never faltered for a moment in her sense of communal and social obligation.

I fail to see how more education could have enhanced her qualities. Had she been brought up in more normal times, she would doubtless have attended a religious girls' high school and, with her studies, possibly have acquired the rather self-effacing public persona often produced by such institutions. Possibly; but it would have had to be a very strong-minded institution.

This was not the sort of daughter-in-law my mother could have anticipated, or easily understood. Fortunately, she was not bound to Dublin. A loving grandmother, skilled in every domestic art, did not lack for occupation when all her seven children were producing their own families, and the mewling of new-born grandchildren provided the background for her travels in three continents.*

Rabbi Herzog's appointment as Chief Rabbi of the Holy Land was an honour which the Irish community cherished and, in the 13 years since his departure, the memory of his personality and attitudes had proved of abiding value in their maintenance of a full range of religious activities. Allied to these was their enthusiasm for aliyah, which was proportionately higher in Ireland than in other countries in the Western world.

Stories abounded of Dr Herzog's brilliant wit, but also of his unworldly absent-mindedness. When I first officiated at a Dublin wedding, I was surprised to find men and women sitting together, not just at the ceremony – then considered only a minor departure from tradition – but also at the preceding afternoon service, where it was totally inadmissible. When I remarked unfavourably about this, I was assured that it had been the undisputed norm in Rabbi Herzog's time. I discussed the point with one of the older members of the community and he confirmed that this was indeed the case. But, he added, Dr Herzog was so unobservant of the world around him that he had never noticed it!

During the long interval since his departure, and despite the effects of aliyah, the Irish-Jewish community had grown considerably – to well over 5,000 souls. The extent of my obligations soon grew far beyond the limits I had anticipated.

According to the terms of my contract, the Representative Council had promised to 'take steps ... within a reasonable time to appoint ... a Communal Minister to assist you in the discharge of your duties'. As this undertaking was, unfortunately, never carried out, and all the major synagogues remained without senior ministers most of the time, many ministerial and pastoral duties were added to my rabbinical responsibilities. Indeed, the community presented a scope of rabbinical activity as varied and challenging as any in the wide world.

The seven Dublin synagogues were far too numerous for a community of that size. But efforts to rationalise the situation always ran into the difficulties such schemes inevitably encounter. As the congregations subsequently dwindled, the wardens became ever-more intransigent, impervious to the wastage of

*Paula Jakobovits moved to the United States, but returned to London soon after her son became British Chief Rabbi. She died at his home on 10 April 1973, aged 75. In a tribute the same week (*Jewish Chronicle*, 13 April 1973), Dayan Dr I. Grunfeld wrote: 'Mrs Jakobovits was a "mother in Israel" in the true meaning of this honoured biblical term. A direct descendant of the famous talmudist Jacob Joshua Falk (1680–1756), she belonged to the Jewish intellectual and spiritual aristocracy. Born in Samter, Posen Province, a daughter of Rabbi Dr Leopold Wreschner, the Rav of her home town and later of Bad Homburg, near Frankfurt, Paula Jakobovits was a deeply religious woman, endowed with extraordinary intellectual gifts and possessed of a wide Jewish and general education. She had a dignified, almost regal appearance and bearing ... Mrs Jakobovits spent her time actively with her children all over the world and also leaves 31 grandchildren and 14 great-grandchildren.'

financial and human resources. All had a claim on my services, and sometimes even timed my sermons to ensure that I did not favour one congregation over another.

By having at least four more synagogues than our numbers warranted, or could properly maintain, our resources were frittered away by unduly high overheads, and our spiritual energies were split and dissipated. From the beginning, I advocated conserving our strength and enhancing our religious services by greater unity of effort. But the vested interests of sentiment and cheap charges proved too strong to be dislodged in one single sweep.

Only with the accumulation of ever-increasing debts did the idea gradually germinate, among more and more of the responsible leaders, that nothing less than a drastic reorganisation could avert a collapse. It became the declared policy of the Jewish Representative Council to make every effort in that direction, though I did not remain long enough to see the Promised Land of unity for which I had yearned.

Some statistics might give a graphic indication of the diversified work involved during my ten years as Chief Rabbi. I delivered no fewer than 3,000 sermons, lectures and addresses. I authorised, solemnised and spoke (twice on each occasion) at 213 marriages, and thus helped to lay the spiritual foundations of the homes of 426 young people as they entered into their new sanctuary.

The majority of the community's boys then aged ten years or less were initiated into the Covenant of Abraham while lying on my lap. Virtually all the boys between the ages of 13 and 23 years had once rehearsed their knowledge of Hebrew and of tefilin-laying in my study, and each of them had heard two barmitzvah addresses from me.

As honorary superintendent of the Talmud Torah, I set and marked some 500 examination papers and presided at scores of teachers' meetings. By virtue of the powers vested in my office, I sanctioned or made the appointments of eight new ministers in Dublin and Cork, and nine Hebrew teachers and one secular teacher at our national school.

I paid some 15 pastoral visits to the small but loyal and lively community in Cork, which numbered about 90 families. The smallest communities, at Waterford and Limerick – where only a handful of Jews remained – finally ceased all official existence during my term of office. In fact, I was instrumental in winding up the Limerick Hebrew Congregation through the sale of its synagogue. (In its time, it was the only place in Ireland that had ever witnessed serious anti-Jewish disturbances.)

The Dublin community was remarkably homogeneous, virtually all of its members deriving from a Lithuanian background. Their daily contact with highly assertive Irish nationalism gave an added edge to their Zionism. There had, after all, been no need to refrain from the harsh criticism of the Palestine mandatory power in a State itself revelling in its hard-won freedom from oppressors across the Irish Sea.

This Irish background also had a limiting effect on the activities of the rabbinical court, for we never handled any cases of divorce or conversion. These occupy a regrettably large part of the time of most batei din and also play a significant role in the propaganda and organisational life of Progressive congregations. Such activity being denied to the Progressives in Dublin, communal life was not embittered by the existence of individuals whose Jewish status, in Orthodox eyes, was unacceptable, irregular, or non-existent. Our relationship was polite, and devoid of the public rancour found elsewhere.

The emergence of a Progressive congregation in Dublin had been the most unfortunate consequence of the long interregnum preceding my appointment. Dublin never had effective *Lebensraum*, even for its many existing congregations. The setting up of a new and potentially growing splinter group was bound to weaken further the main religious institutions of the community and to bring many communal (and family) relations to breaking point.

Rightly or wrongly, I felt from the outset that the only sensible policy would be to avoid provocation and open campaigning, while at the same time exploring every possibility to narrow the divisions and to seek an understanding on the basis of a common loyalty to at least the most fundamental teachings of our faith. The vision of the dissidents' eventual return to the rest of the community perpetually guided me.

I never once made a public attack on the Progressives in my sermons or addresses. As a result, their influence as a catalyst of communal dissension gradually waned, their growth was contained, and the bitterness of the defections finally gave way to a constructive search for methods to repair the damage to the fabric of communal unity, even if it took years until my gestures of goodwill and suggestions for dealing with the problem were seriously appreciated. But ultimate success, I concede, eluded me, though certainly not for want of trying or good faith.

Among other aspects of communal life, kashrut supervision was of considerable importance, as there was a large export trade in kosher food products. In my early years in Dublin, the Irish Government had promised a handsome gift of kosher meat to the Jews of Israel, and as we did not have sufficient local personnel (nor, I suppose, the necessary reputation in Israeli Orthodox circles), a number of Lubavitch Chasidim came from Paris to carry out the work.

This was my initial encounter with the Lubavitch movement, and for the first – though certainly not the last – time, I discovered the problems involved in dealing with people who, if nominally under my jurisdiction, in practice accepted the rulings of only the Rebbe in Brooklyn on any major point. But at least the kashrut labels carried my name, and that of my dayan, far afield. I seem to recall that the local shochetim were also prone to experiencing, or creating, problems. In pre-freezer days, communities were highly vulnerable to strike action, or the threat of it.

Of great variety and interest in my work was the constant stream of callers stepping daily across the threshold of my home. Over 400 *meshulachim* pleaded their causes before me, every one of them at least two or three times. Scores of American visitors and hundreds of tourists from Britain and elsewhere came to pay their respects or to inquire about Jewish 'sights' in Dublin.

Among the distinguished callers were many eminent Jewish leaders from all parts of the world, and I was honoured to welcome in my home, privately or as host at formal receptions, the Papal Nuncio and four Ambassadors, five Lord Mayors, several ministers of State and church dignitaries, two generals, prominent writers and scientists, including the director of the American Geo-Physical Year, together with his Jewish fellow-astronomers, attending an international conference in Dublin.

But my home witnessed experiences of a different type, too. Often, the walls of my study felt like shedding tears as they listened to the harrowing tales of broken marriages or intended intermarriages (which, if they materialised notwithstanding my pleas, usually also ended up in tragedy).

Many called to unburden their cares, their business worries or their anxiety over growing communal deficits. Some came to ask old-fashioned *shaalas*, others to suggest new panaceas for solving the problems of the community.

Sometimes, the temperature of my room would rise in the heat of discussions with shochetim, or with butchers, or among excited *din Torah* parties; then it would drop again in the cool, happy air of academic arguments on the moral concepts of Judaism in the faithful circle of my Tuesday-night youth study group.

Forever cherished, too, will be the memory of the festive *sheva berachot* for half a dozen religious young couples celebrated in my home, and the gay Simchat Torah and Purim parties of earlier years.

No less interesting were my experiences outside my home. Meeting the great of this country at a presidential garden party in honour of some visiting cardinal, or attending an academic event at Trinity College, or lecturing to some church group on a Jewish topic, or pleading some Jewish cause with Irish political and religious leaders – my contacts with our non-Jewish fellow-citizens were always cordial and stimulating, in stark contrast, as I have mentioned, to my pre-war days in Germany.

Memorable, too, were some of the special religious services I was privileged to conduct on great State or Israel occasions, especially the first civic service ever held in a synagogue in the Republic on the momentous election of Robert Briscoe as Dublin's first Jewish Lord Mayor.

Particularly thrilling were the occasions I had to represent my community at international Jewish gatherings, or to participate in conferences with my leading colleagues abroad to discuss some of the fundamental Jewish religious problems of our age. Whether at such conferences in London, Amsterdam and Zurich, or at the rousing welcome extended to me by 40 Jewish communities in the United States and Canada, I could never fail to sense the honour attached to my high office.

But all these activities and experiences were, after all, only ancillary to my principal work and concern. My success or failure as spiritual guide could not be measured in the applause or criticism which greeted my speeches, nor in the 101 little services I was able to render to individuals or institutions. The real criterion lay, of course, in the extent to which I guarded and enhanced the religious life of the community, promoted Jewish observance and learning, and consolidated a spiritual outlook among the community's members.

The attainment of these objectives could not be easily ascertained. Souls can no more be compounded in test-tubes than their content can be measured in them. Even piety and religious understanding defy means of accurate evaluation. Nor can one apply any quantitative gauge to such values of the infinite and the eternal.

The reclamation of one human soul from the abyss of despair or irreligion may be worth more, in terms of lasting achievement, than rousing a whole congregation to a crescendo of momentary inspiration by the most stirring sermon. A little seed of profound faith and religious vision planted in a single human heart may ultimately bear more precious fruit than the work of great institutions.

And no one will ever know whose life may have been vitally affected and enriched by some stray word of mine here or some solution of a perplexity there. These matters are of 'the secret things which belong unto the Lord'. The true results of rabbinical efforts simply cannot be assessed.

Somewhat more tangible, however, are the means to estimate tendencies in the overall religious character of a community. The proportion of strictly observant Jews in Ireland probably did not fall during my ten years there. In fact, judged by such criteria as the number of private succot, or of the devotees of the family purity laws, or of the participants in some regular Torah study, it rose considerably.

If this was due partly to very Orthodox immigrants, it had to be offset against the fine religious young people lost by the score through emigration to Israel or England. Had we been able to retain this wonderful element and integrate it into the leadership corps of the religious institutions, Dublin might well have become a model community.

In spiritual terms, the slogan 'Export *or* die!' became 'Export *and* die!' Emigration, more than balanced as it then was by a steady trickle of new settlers from Britain and elsewhere, may not have affected the quantitative stability of the community to any appreciable degree, but it drained our human resources of their most valuable assets.

This drainage, combined with the effects of modern entertainment's ever more powerful distractions and of the worldwide flagging of the Zionist ideal following its realisation with the establishment of Israel, inevitably led to increased apathy and a growing dearth of dedicated communal workers.

In the face of these embarrassments, it was not always easy to cope effectively with the most urgent communal problems. The thinning and ageing ranks of the old guard of solid *baalei battim* were not generally replenished by equally energetic recruits from the younger generation.

And it was on that generation, and its educational interests, that my pre-occupations were largely centred. To some achievements I look back with considerable satisfaction.

The total number of children receiving regular instruction increased fairly well. But I regard as my principal successes in Ireland the introduction of

Hebrew tuition into the morning sessions at Zion Schools and, above all, the foundation and successful expansion of Stratford College.

After those ten years, Dublin had at least the makings of two truly Jewish day-schools, with an aggregate roll of 220 pupils – nearly 40 per cent of all Jewish schoolchildren in the city – of all grades from kindergarten to the leaving certificate, where before it had only a secular national school for Jewish children, with Hebrew classes under separate auspices in the afternoons. It was also gratifying that the roll at Zion Schools more or less held its own.

Stratford College, in particular, promised to revolutionise Jewish education in Dublin. With Jewish studies compulsory up to the age of 16 years and over, with Hebrew recognised as an official teaching and examination subject by the Department of Education, and with conversational Hebrew taught from the earliest grades, Jewish education enjoyed an altogether new status and intensity.

Thanks to an agreement reached with the Torah department of the Jewish Agency, the college was also fortunate to obtain the services of an Israeli director of Jewish studies, whose enthusiasm and efficiency were soon reflected in the intense Jewish spirit and educational progress at the school. The new methods adopted may not have produced the outstanding results of former years – the two or three boys and girls who used to proceed annually to higher Jewish studies abroad – but they resulted in considerably increasing and broadening the Jewish knowledge of the average pupil.

There was one problem which, throughout my ten years, caused me the most acute anxiety, and to solve which I fought consistently, but with little avail: the stabilisation of educational finances.

Whatever expansion had been achieved was gained at the expense of an aggregate debt of £16,000 owed by the Talmud Torah and Stratford College, a debt rising by over £1,000 annually – at that time an enormous sum. This crushing burden rendered the most essential improvements impossible. Above all, it vitiated our efforts to raise the status and efficiency of the teachers – the most vital servants of any Jewish community.

Even after my success in piloting a resolution for considerably increased levies through the general meetings of all the major synagogues, their contribution to Jewish education remained inadequate and altogether out of tune with the situation in other communities. I cannot claim that I accomplished my aim – spelled out many times elsewhere in the ensuing years – of making the community conscious that Jewish education costs money, and that good education costs more money.

These were the main practical problems that agitated my mind continuously through those ten years. But all of them were more than balanced by the personal affection, loyalty and friendship I enjoyed in such rich measure. I was sustained in my work by the willing assistance of so many lay leaders and the devotion of my colleagues, particularly Dayan Zalman Alony, who never spared himself in the service of the community.

With all the pettiness and peculiarities inevitably to be found here and there in a relatively small and, for long, isolated community, people showed themselves warm-hearted, kindly and co-operative. And with all the undercurrent of drift from religious observance, Dublin remained basically a strongly traditional community, probably more so than any other set into a similar cultural pattern. To work with and for it was both a pleasure and a rare privilege, one I was to cherish long after I had left Ireland's shores.

Away from communal concerns, family responsibilities were happily developing apace. Five of our six children – Yoel (Julian), Shmuel (Samuel), Esther, Shoshana and Aviva – were born in Dublin (Elisheva came later in New York), and our prime consideration was to achieve a proper balance between our concerns for the community and those for the family.

This is not always an easy matter in rabbinical circles, and many problems have been caused where the family has seen too little of the father, or the community too little of the rebbetzin. Very skilful management of time is required – and here, of course, husband and wife must co-operate in complete harmony. Judging by the results, Amélie and I were fortunate to get the mixture right, and we never had a generation gap alienating our children and their basic way of life from us.

Despite the pressures and responsibilities, I was resolved to obtain the university doctorate which I had always regarded as my next scholastic aim after securing my rabbinical diploma.

I registered with the University of London and, on 18 May 1950, the board of studies in Oriental and African languages and literature recorded my qualifications to undertake research for a PhD. The topic was 'The concept of the biblical commandments in talmudic and midrashic literature, dealing with that literature's treatment of the Bible's legislative material, its interpretations and classification'.

This subject may surprise many who know of my final thesis. My Hirschian background had, however, given me a great interest in the rationale of halachic rulings (*taamei hamitzvot*, in rabbinical parlance), for I hoped that, by assembling and elucidating the underlying concepts, one would be in a better position to apply the lessons to the solution of contemporary problems, or to the interpretation of Jewish law and thought in modern terms.

Many years earlier, I had written one or two essays on aspects of the criminal law and the sacrificial system, and had also published work on rabbinic legislation. Nevertheless, when asked by the board of studies for further clarification of the field of research, my interest must have waned – or been superseded by new attractions – and I realised instead that the considerable store of material I had already gathered on religio-medical matters provided a substantial foundation for further research.

By this time, I had also acquired some acquaintance with the comprehensive Roman Catholic system of pastoral theology – or Catholic medical ethics, as they called this well-developed discipline – with its detailed expositions of the laws and ideology relating to every aspect of physical and moral life, including the practice of medicine. I realised how little, in comparison, had been done to present Jewish teachings in any systematic fashion and therefore, in reply to the board, I changed my application to an alternative field of research – Jewish medical ethics. (Not since my one day at Queen Mary College in London can there have been such a speedy academic U-turn!)

The proposal was accepted and, on 3 August, I was informed that Charles Singer, the renowned professor of the history of medicine, was willing to act as my adviser. The professor's father was none other than Simeon Singer, the celebrated translator of the *Authorised Daily Prayer Book* (universally known as the *Singer's Siddur*), but the son had long been identified with the Liberal Synagogue.

This did not stop us having a very amicable relationship, although it turned out to be far too brief. The professor normally lived in Cornwall, not easily accessible from Dublin, and he proved rather elusive. He was to have attended the oddly named Prehistoric Congress in Dublin in September 1951, but he failed to appear (I learned later) because of ill-health.

I heard nothing from him until April 1952, when he told me that, owing to the pressure of work involved in editing a history of technology, he was giving up all PhD supervision. This was a great disappointment, as I badly needed his guidance in marshalling my material, which by then had grown significantly.

The agreed subject was finally defined as 'Jewish medical ethics: a comparative and historical study of the Jewish religious attitude to medicine and its practice, with special reference to the sixteenth century'. This was the first time the term 'Jewish medical ethics' had been used, and when, in later years, I lectured on the subject, I would occasionally remark that my interest in it had been awakened, or at least strengthened, by 'my Roman Catholic background in Ireland'.

In the spring of 1955, the work was completed and the obligatory 12 copies prepared. The thesis ran to 476 pages, all typed by myself. In addition to Professor Singer, Rabbi Dr Isidore Epstein, the principal of Jews' College – who had frequently been of great help to me in the course of my researches – and Professor Siegfried Stern were my examiners. They found the work too long for publication and thought it contained enough for five theses; for production in book form, they urged me to shorten it to two-thirds of its length. By the end of the year, the modified version had received approval, and I was at last known as Dr Jakobovits.

Subsequent events were to show that, while furthering my own career, I had simultaneously initiated a new discipline in rabbinic studies. Had I written a thesis in line with my original suggestion, I doubt whether it would ever have been published, for it would have aroused little interest in Jewish circles, and even less outside. Work on medical ethics, however, forced me into the study of sources, and introduced me to scholars and institutions far removed from the normal limits of the rabbinical world.

The publication of my thesis, none too easy to arrange, finally took place in New York (Bloch Publishing Company, 1959); it gained increasing interest and gave me a very real footing with scholars.

I was fortunate in my timing, for developing Right-wing attitudes in Orthodox Judaism were soon to put secular studies under a cloud. A university degree for a rabbi ceased to be any sort of desideratum; a doctorate much less so. Any young rabbi now contemplating the sort of research I had undertaken would probably be warned that his pursuits were unconventional and not without some risk of evoking charges of hetero-orthodoxy – particularly in the 'comparative' part of the study.

In my earlier London days, I had often been critical of the way in which the Chief Rabbi was forced to spend so much of his time in activities which, to my mind, were unproductive, and little related to authentic Jewish religious leadership. Experience, however, was to prove to me that these outside contacts were an inescapable syndrome of Chief Rabbinical life.

I had not been very long in Dublin before I had to call on a newly appointed Papal Nuncio to convey the congratulations of the Jewish community. Over the years, I had frequent occasion to meet members of both the Roman Catholic and Church of Ireland hierarchies. One meeting had a disconcertingly medieval flavour when the Catholic Bishop of Cork warned me that he would not be answerable were there to be an outbreak of popular violence if the local Jewry interfered with the apostasy of one of its members.

Considering the very small number of Irish Jews, it is remarkable that, in my time, two rose to such eminent positions in the wider community. As already noted, Robert Briscoe became Lord Mayor of Dublin, while Arthur Goldberg was elected Lord Mayor of Cork. Numerically, at least, one can only compare this to a Catholic becoming mayor of Jerusalem or Tel Aviv.

It was, in fact, Briscoe's great success as a lecturer in the United States that prompted me to undertake a similar tour. The title of Chief Rabbi of Ireland proved fascinating to the Irish Americans – they did not come to my lectures, but they did boost the publicity – and most of my talks had an Irish title or slant. A newspaper in Savannah, Georgia, named me in its report of my lecture as 'Jack O'Bovits'.

One major international involvement during my Dublin days was related to the question of calendar reform. The aim of regulating the calendar was to fix permanently the days of the week to correspond to the calendar date through the insertion of an annual 'blank day' (two in a leap year), thus causing – in Chief Rabbi Hertz's phrase – a 'nomadic Sabbath'. This would have been calamitous to the age-old Jewish observance of a day of rest every seven days. The attempt had been defeated in Geneva in the late 1920s, and Dr Hertz had led 'the Battle of the Sabbath', as he later called his account of the episode, with all his wonted determination.

Thirty years later, the agitation resurfaced, with what threatened to be a serious additional complication. The Roman Catholic Church, previously averse to the idea, was now seemingly neutral. This appeared to be the only interpretation to be placed on an article in the *Osservatore Romano* of 28 June 1954, by the director of the Vatican Observatory, the Rev Daniel O'Connell, an Irish Jesuit.

Shortly afterwards, the official line was modified: Father O'Connell had been 'misunderstood'. Meanwhile, the Indian government had announced its intention of raising the issue at the United Nations. A meeting of Chief Rabbis was convened in London in November at Rabbi Brodie's residence to discuss what action to take to ward off the threat to Jewish life of such a 'wandering Sabbath'.

All present undertook to raise the matter with the religious and political leaders of their respective countries. I had a special responsibility in the affair, because of my contacts with the Irish hierarchy. Fortunately, I had valuable support from the director of the Dunsint observatory in Co. Dublin, Dr H. A. Bruck, who – unlike the Astronomer Royal in England – had little enthusiasm for calendar reform, which he attributed to a shallow desire for uniformity, and had shown himself very sympathetic to the Jewish cause. He was also credited with considerable influence in Vatican circles.

It was not long before the steam went out of the agitation. In February 1955, Chief Rabbi Brodie called on Pandit Jawaharlal Nehru, the Indian Prime Minister, while he was on a visit to London and obtained a statement denying that the Government of India had lent its support to the proposal to introduce the World Calendar. In the following month, the Papal Nuncio in Montevideo announced that the Vatican had always been totally opposed to 'blank days'.

There was a brief reawakening of concern in 1962, before the Second Vatican Council was convened: the Church Fathers were thought to be re-examining the matter. I was asked to undertake a mission to Castel Gandolfo, the Pope's summer residence near Rome, where the papal observatory was located.

I duly met with Father O'Connell in August 1962 and found him extremely friendly and understanding. He assured me that the 'blank day' proposal was not on the agenda for the Vatican Council meeting. With this assurance, the calendar reform proposal was dropped from the international agenda – and I may have found a tiny niche in universal history's record!

Both the Vatican and the rabbinate – and it is fair to point out that Progressive Jews gave their full support – would be willing to consider any system of calendar reform which did not tamper with the seven-day progression of the Sabbath. There are a number of such schemes, but none of them was further pursued.

By the time of my meeting at Castel Gandolfo, I had ceased to be Chief Rabbi of Ireland. My change of status had resulted from an important interview during my American lecture tour. I had never intended to remain in Dublin for more than ten years and had promised Amélie to this effect. My position could only shrink in stature and potential, for Dublin – in common with all the smaller centres of Jewry – had no possibility of reversing the drop in numbers caused by emigration or the attraction, for the younger element, of larger and more active communities.

Lecture tours meant that I enjoyed the challenge of a wider audience, but they were no compensation for a shrinking home base. On one of my American tours, I profited from the advice of Hymie Ross – formerly of Belfast, and then living in New York – to meet the four leaders of a new congregation in the process of establishment. The aim was to create an Orthodox presence on Fifth Avenue; hitherto, Orthodoxy was virtually *verboten* in that elegant area, dominated as it was by the vast and prestigious Temple Emanuel of the radical Reform movement – reputed to be the largest synagogue complex in the world.

The four were Hermann Merkin, Henry Hirsch, Max Kettner, and the celebrated author Herman Wouk. It was clear that the congregation would lack neither public interest nor financial backing. The synagogue was being built, but they were still seeking a rabbi.

The change would mean adjusting to a very different and probably very demanding congregation – and I would become a small fish in a very large pond. But the big fish included some of the greatest figures in the rabbinate, and New York offered scope for religious initiative untrammelled by the existence of an Establishment.

Both Amélie and I already had family in New York, so the travails of re-settlement would be lessened. After ten very happy years, we prepared to leave Dublin, amid mutual regrets – but I had no qualms over whether I had taken the right step.

Fragments from an unpublished autobiography

CHAPTER THREE

Pastures Green

Rabbi Jakobovits arrived in Dublin from London on the last day of January 1949. When asked at the airport by an *Irish Times* reporter what he thought of Eire's failure to recognise the State of Israel, he replied that Eire, as a country which strongly opposed partition, was probably reluctant to recognise a State based on partition.

Two weeks later, Chief Rabbi Israel Brodie visited Dublin, principally to induct Rabbi Jakobovits into office. On the Sabbath morning, Rabbi Brodie preached at the synagogue, Dolphin's Barn, and expressed deep satisfaction that Ireland had, that same weekend, joined other nations in recognising Israel.

The installation of the new Chief Rabbi was held the next day at the Adelaide Road Synagogue. Referring to the responsibilities of the exalted office Rabbi Jakobovits was about to assume, his duties to the various congregations under his leadership, and the duties of the congregations to their spiritual chief, Rabbi Brodie wished the new Chief Rabbi success in his ministrations.

In his sermon, Chief Rabbi Jakobovits said that there had been few periods in human history when the demands on spiritual leadership had been more exacting than they were now. Values and ideals that had stood the test of time for thousands of years had been swept aside by the gigantic and ever-growing machines of State and science. The moral foundations on which the world rested had been largely shed, and their place was being taken by ideological slogans and formulae.

Religious observances had become a subject of arrogant derision among those who opposed them and ridiculed them as matters of empty convention among those who held them dear. As a result, many young people, in particular, had ceased to regard religion as a vital factor in their lives or in the affairs of society. The world cried out for leadership, and that demand would be the general background to his activities among them.

A dinner to mark the installation was held at Greenville Hall. Among the guests of honour was the Taoiseach, John Costello.

Following his induction, and for many years thereafter, Rabbi Jakobovits conducted a busy round of communal meetings, lectures, sermons and pastoral visits to congregations and congregants alike. One of his first engagements was a visit to Cork to consecrate the grounds, halls and memorial tablets at the new Jewish cemetery.

Rabbi Jakobovits and the Rev B. Kersh, the local minister, were received in private audiences at the palaces of the Catholic and Protestant Bishops of Cork, and at University College, Cork, by the president, who introduced the Jewish students to the Irish Chief Rabbi. In a sermon at the synagogue, Rabbi Jakobovits complimented the Jewish community on its standard of kashrut (100 per cent purchased kosher meat) and Hebrew education (100 per cent of local children attended Hebrew classes). He addressed a reception in the communal rooms, and inspected the Hebrew classes, where he expressed satisfaction with the syllabus and the progress of the children.

Other meetings followed in quick succession. The annual meeting of the Zion Schools was told that a scheme for the reorganisation of Hebrew education in Dublin, started the previous year by Rabbi Jakobovits, was working satisfactorily. Religious and Hebrew education was now integrated into the regular school programme of the Jewish Day School at Zion Schools, while the Hebrew and religion classes at Grosvenor Road, for those who did not attend the Jewish Day School, had greatly improved.

An important extension of Hebrew and religious education in Dublin was the establishment of a *yeshivah ketanah* (preparatory talmudical college), associated with the Dublin Talmud Torah, at Zion Schools. Classes for advanced Jewish study were open to senior pupils attending the non-talmudic classes of the Talmud Torah.

In August 1953, the new synagogue at Rathfarnham Road, Terenure, Dublin – the largest to be built in Ireland for 35 years – was formally opened and consecrated. The service was conducted by Chief Rabbi Jakobovits, assisted by Dayan Z. Alony and Rabbi J. Shachter, of Northern Ireland.

Speaking at the ceremony, Chief Rabbi Israel Brodie expressed the hope that the synagogue would play an important role in the spiritual lives of the Irish Jewish community and that, together with the other synagogues which had served as centres of their spiritual lives for many years, it would 'make a notable contribution in maintaining the Jewish traditional life in all its fullness'.

Addressing a parents' meeting in early 1954, Chief Rabbi Jakobovits declared that the establishment of Stratford College, the only Jewish secondary school in Ireland, had been 'the most promising communal event' since he had taken up duties in the country. He stressed the great benefits which Jewish children would derive from secondary education in a true Jewish environment.

T. M. Shiel, the headmaster, announced that Hebrew had now been recognised by the Republic's Department of Education as a secondary-school subject that could be taken for the intermediate, as well as the preliminary, examinations of the local universities.

At the college's first prize distribution, a year later, Chief Rabbi Jakobovits said that the school had been born of a twin motive: necessity and the vision of an ideal. In secondary education, Jewish religious instruction had formerly to be superimposed on an exhaustive programme at the most disadvantageous hours of the day; in that school, Hebrew instruction was integrated into the general school syllabus.

Jewish pupils at non-Jewish schools were deprived of the most vital factor of true education – the fashioning of character and personality through religious guidance as part of their ordinary school work. The Chief Rabbi characterised as hollow and humiliating the attitude of many parents who felt that, in sending Jewish children to Jewish schools, they were 'segregating' them from the bulk of the population.

Another event of communal importance was the opening of a new poultry-house for the Dublin Board of Shechitah. The building was of the most modern design and incorporated a revolving pen designed by S. Sevitt, vice-president of the Board and chairman of the building committee, with the assistance of D. Lev, a civil engineer.

At a dinner marking the occasion, Chief Rabbi Jakobovits said that he deplored 'the increasing laxity in matters of Jewish observance'. In their parents' day, the rabbis' rulings had been sought by the lay leaders; nowadays, however, the rabbis and lay leaders did not always see eye to eye, and on occasion the rabbis were given a hint to 'look the other way'. As a result, they had to become militant and to fight for the strict observance of the law. The Dublin Board of Shechitah, on the other hand, had 'always carried on the old tradition and upheld the rulings of the rabbinate'.

At the opening of the reconstructed mikvah at Adelaide Road, later that year, the Chief Rabbi expressed the hope that the ritual baths would be utilised by an increasing number of people. It was, he said, the first major improvement since the baths had been erected some 50 years ago. The cost, approximately £800, had been met by contributions from the local synagogues and other religious organisations, as well as from private donors.

Early in 1957, Chief Rabbi Jakobovits left for a lecture tour of the United States and Canada under the auspices of the National Jewish Welfare Board's Jewish Centre Lecture Bureau. He had been invited to address the American-Irish Historical Society and the Rabbinical Council of America, and his programme was to include a series of lectures on Jewish and Irish topics, and medico-religious subjects, in New York, Boston, Baltimore, Chicago, Toronto, Montreal, and other North American cities.

In an address to the Rabbinical Council of America – which embraced 700 Orthodox spiritual leaders serving more than a million Jews in the United States and Canada – the Chief Rabbi urged leaders of Orthodox Judaism in North America to help revitalise Jewish life in Western Europe. He asserted that American Jewish communities 'must fill the spiritual void in Europe left by the destruction of East European Jewry in the Second World War'.

Flourishing centres of Jewish learning and culture in Eastern Europe had at one time provided West European Jewry with a continuous stream of educators and rabbis to meet the needs of those communities. The disappearance of such East European Jewish institutions, Rabbi Jakobovits said, 'has caused a serious shortage of trained personnel and religious thinkers in Western Europe and thereby stifled the urgent task of rebuilding these war-shattered areas'.

Dr Jakobovits appealed to American Jews, and the Rabbinical Council in particular, 'to come to the rescue of West European Jewry by supplying them with a large reservoir of Jewish community leaders such as social workers and religious counsellors. American Jewry would then be in a position to bring about the rejuvenation of a spiritually vital Jewish way of life in a free democratic Europe.'

The Chief Rabbi's tour extended over some 10,000 miles. Of the United States, which he was visiting for the first time, he said that it was 'a new world in every sense and an inspiration to behold. It is also a democracy at work. The people's feelings are animated and vocal and are the final influence on all decisions.' Less than a year later, he left for a second American lecture tour, at the invitation of the National Jewish Welfare Board. Over a period of five weeks, he visited 21 cities in Florida, Texas, California, British Columbia, and many other parts of the United States and Canada. Civic welcomes were extended to him wherever he went.

On his return to Ireland, he described his tour as 'an exhilarating experience', during which he had been warmly received. Everywhere, he said, there were indications of a groping for more solid religious bearings and a growing awareness that the spiritual emptiness of the past had to be replaced by a fresh emphasis on traditional values.

The ramifications of the visit soon became apparent. In a letter – dated 30 June 1958 – to Professor Leonard Abrahamson, chairman of the Jewish Representative Council of Ireland, the Chief Rabbi wrote:

'This is about the most difficult letter it has ever been my lot to write. I have to inform your Council – and, through it, its affiliated organisations – that, after much thought, I have decided to relinquish my present office in order to assume the spiritual leadership of the new Fifth Avenue Synagogue in the heart of New York.

By the time I propose to leave you, it will be for almost exactly ten years – the most momentous ten years in the second half of Jewish history – that I have had the great privilege to preside over the spiritual destinies of Irish Jewry. During this period, the bonds of affection linking me with all sections of my community have grown into something far more intimate and precious than is common in the relations between a rabbi and his congregation. I have enjoyed a measure of respect, loyalty and, above all, friendship which, to my knowledge, is altogether rare in rabbinical experience. My years here have been filled to capacity with joy, contentment and harmony, and I could not wish to find a more pleasurable assignment anywhere in the discharge of my sacred vocation as a servant of the Almighty and His eternal Law.

If I have nevertheless decided to vacate this high office, it is mainly, as you are aware, for overriding personal and family reasons, combined with the prospect of meeting an even greater challenge for the advancement of the ideals to which I have consecrated my life. My new congregation, with its magnificent facilities under the dedicated leadership of some of the finest strictly Orthodox businessmen and intellectuals in America, holds out the promise of developing into a pioneering model to show how the loftiest traditions of Judaism can be harmonised with modern thought in the midst of the largest Jewish community in the world.

This is not the occasion to articulate the profound feelings which overwhelm me as I contemplate my separation from those I have loved and served for so long. Nor can I here express adequately my abiding gratitude for all I owe to the leaders and members of the many institutions, congregations, societies and committees with whom it has been my pleasure to work. All I feel I must now record is my humble awareness that, with my endeavours to raise the Irish Chief Rabbinate into one of the most distinguished rabbinical offices anywhere, my own stature, too, has risen, thanks to the charge with which you have honoured me. For this alone, I will forever be indebted to Irish Jewry. I only hope I have, in turn, justified the faith reposed in me ten years ago, by upholding the dignity of the office, preserving the good name of the community among our neighbours, and conscientiously promoting the religious interests of young and old alike. At the same time, I wish to assure you that, during the ensuing months, I will certainly bend every effort on assisting you to secure the services of an acceptable successor, as well as to solve the host of problems, particularly in our synagogal and educational set-up, requiring urgent attention.'

The newly built Fifth Avenue Synagogue, which was to be inaugurated for the High Holy-days three months later, was situated in one of the most important residential sections of New York, its congregation consisting of some of the leading Orthodox businessmen and intellectuals in America. *The Irish Times* spoke for many Dubliners –

Gentiles and Jews alike – when it voiced sadness at the Chief Rabbi's forthcoming departure:

DYNAMIC AND COSMOPOLITAN

The news that Dr Immanuel Jakobovits, Chief Rabbi of the Jewish Communities of Ireland, has accepted a 'call' to officiate at the newly constructed Fifth Avenue Synagogue in New York has been received with considerable regret, mingled with genuine good wishes, not only by his coreligionists of this country but also by the many non-Jewish clergy and laymen who have come in contact with this dynamic personality.

Dynamic is, indeed, an apt description of this 37-year-old Jewish prelate-in-chief of Ireland's 1,000 Jewish families, who have acknowledged him as their spiritual leader for the past ten years. He assumed office on 1 February 1949, after a meteoric career in the service of British Jewry.

At the precocious age of 20, he was appointed minister of the Brondesbury Synagogue, one of the largest and reputedly one of the most critical of Orthodox Jewish communities in London. His reputation there attracted the attention of the Chief Rabbi of the British Empire, who, in 1947, sanctioned his appointment as minister of London's Great Synagogue, popularly known as 'Anglo-Jewry's Cathedral Synagogue' – a post which had been, until then, vacant for 105 years. Rabbi Jakobovits jocularly says that this august appointment automatically made him 'the Archbishop'.

There is not, however, anything particularly 'Anglo' in either the physical appearance or the psychological make-up of this black-bearded six-footer. If it were not for the irresistible pull which drew him to study for his rabbinical diploma at Jews' College, London, when a 16-year-old German-Jewish refugee, he would probably have been today eminent in whatever field he chose. His thesis for his doctorate of philosophy at the University of London, 'Jewish Medical Ethics', is in itself a pointer to a possible reputation in either of two other intellectual occupations – medicine or philosophy.

Outside his parochial field, his interests can be described as cosmopolitan rather than international. What else can really be expected from a German-born Chief Rabbi of Ireland, educated in England, whose charming wife is French, and whose five children (two boys and three girls) are all Dublin born, speak some Irish as well as Hebrew and English, and will enter the United States next year as Irish citizens?

Dr Jakobovits is no religious stick-in-the-mud. He has travelled extensively in Europe and America. In November 1957, he was a delegate at a rabbinical conference in Holland. The Dutch Queen expressed a desire to meet the delegates. It says as much for the dignity of Ireland as it does for that of the Chief Rabbi himself that, in honour of his adopted nationality, the royal carpet on which both royalty and rabbi met was coloured an emerald green.

This was not the only occasion, Dr Jakobovits relates, that he was precipitated into the role of unofficial ambassador of the Republic. Some two or three years ago, while undertaking a lecture tour of America, he was invited by the Jewish owner of a factory in St Paul, Minnesota, to 'look over the works'. By coincidence, a large proportion of the workpeople of this particular factory were Irish-born or of Irish descent, all of them Catholics. To his embarrassment, a special delegation met him, conspicuously dressed in green, 'in honour', they explained, 'of the rare experience of meeting an Irish Chief Rabbi'.

In Ireland, his flock comprises some 5,000 Jewish souls, consisting of eight separate congregations in Dublin (about 95 per cent of the total), plus one other organised community in Cork. The former small Jewish communities in Limerick and Waterford had already been dissolved long before he took office.

These congregations are entirely independent groups, each with its own rabbi or minister representing varying shades of Orthodox Judaism; and it says much for the ability of the Chief Rabbi that his authority is unquestioningly recognised by all of them. However, as he himself points out, the Jewish historical and religious tradition is deeply ingrained in the Irish community.

Although it is the smallest organised Jewish community in Western Europe, and makes up a tiny fraction of the population (only one-sixth of 1 per cent), assimilation through intermarriage – the Achilles heel of most Western Jewish communities – is virtually nil. The fact is, of course, attributable as much to Christian as to Jewish loyalty to the faith.

Firmly believing that the future of Judaism lies in the maturing youth, the Chief Rabbi has revitalised the Jewish schools, with the sympathetic support of the Government, and today some 40 per cent of the total Jewish children of school age are receiving secular as well as Jewish education there.

Ireland has been particularly fortunate in her Jewish rabbinical leaders. Dr Jakobovits' predecessor was Dr Herzog, whose well-merited promotion to the position of Chief Rabbi of Palestine in 1936 created a spiritual vacuum which remained unfilled, for want of an incumbent of equivalent status, for 13 years. It was, therefore, an indication of the stature and reputation already acquired by Dr Jakobovits that he was chosen to succeed Dr Herzog as the Chief Rabbi of the small Irish community of Chosen People.

Once again, Ireland's loss is New York's gain.

Chief Rabbi Jakobovits, with Mrs Jakobovits, left for New York early in September to participate in the opening of the Fifth Avenue Synagogue and to conduct its Rosh Hashanah services. He returned to Dublin for Yom Kippur, with plans to take up his new post at the end of the year.

His departure was marked by a reception at Greenville Hall, Dublin, where all sections of Dublin Jewry, together with representatives of the Cork community and the Jewish communities of Northern Ireland, gathered to bid him farewell. Professor Abrahamson made a communal presentation to the outgoing Chief Rabbi and said that, when the history of Irish Jewry came to be written, there would no doubt be a reference not only to the 'Herzog era' but also to the 'Jakobovits era'. He paid tribute to Dr Jakobovits' 'sterling work' as spiritual leader, his personal qualities that had endeared him to all, and, above all, the impact he had made on the non-Jewish communities of Ireland.

Reviewing his years in Eire, Rabbi Jakobovits said that he had given them the ten best years of his life, and they had given him his ten happiest years. He had tried, he said, to work in the interests of all sections of the community, and was glad to see at the reception 'members of a section over which I had no jurisdiction'.

Four days later, a large crowd gathered at Dublin airport to wish Rabbi Jakobovits and his family *au revoir*. Before his departure, he was received by the President of Ireland, Prime Minister De Valera, the Minister of Education, and other prominent Government officials.

CHAPTER FOUR

Jewish Medical Ethics

In June 1955, the University of London announced the award of the degree of Doctor of Philosophy to Rabbi Jakobovits, then Chief Rabbi of Ireland. He had presented a thesis on 'Jewish Medical Ethics', which surveyed 'the development of the halachic approach to medico-religious and medico-moral problems in classic and especially medieval, as well as modern, times'. In the preface to the first edition of its subsequent publication, in 1959, he wrote:

'Moral autonomy or moral automation – between these alternatives lies the most fateful choice confronting mankind today. As long as the moral law reigns supreme, the spectacular advances in science and technology will be effectively controlled by the overriding claims of human life and dignity. Man will be safe from the menace of his own productions. But when the quest for knowledge and power is unhemmed by moral considerations, and the fundamental rights of man, as conferred and defined by his Creator, are swept aside in the blind march to mechanical perfection, the ramparts protecting mankind from self-destruction are bound to crumble. Today, the contest between science and religion is no longer a competitive search for the truth as in former times. It is a struggle between excesses and controls, between the supremacy of man's creations and the supremacy of man himself.

In the past, the human inventive genius served mainly to aid nature in the amelioration of life. Now it bids fair to supplant nature, replacing it by an artificial, synthetic existence in which the deepest mysteries of creation are not only laid bare but subjected to the arbitrary whims of mechanised man. The push of one button can now exterminate life by the million; psychologically waged advertising campaigns can determine the eating habits of whole nations; chemical drugs can curb or release human emotions at will, and break down the most determined willpower to extract confessions. The control over man's conscience, over procreation and extinction, over human existence itself, is being wrested from God and nature and surrendered to scientists and technicians.

In this new dispensation, the physician, too, is playing an ever-more vital role. Human life, which he can artificially generate out of test-tubes and terminate out of syringe-needles, is now at his bidding. Psychiatry can help him to bring even human behaviour under his sway, almost like a robot plane guided by a remote radio operator. But who will control the physician and the growing army of other scientists?

There can be little doubt that, of all practical sciences, it is pre-eminently medicine with which Judaism, historically and intellectually, enjoys a natural kinship, and to which Jewish law is best qualified to address its reasoned, pragmatic rules of morality. For many centuries, rabbis and physicians, often merging their professions into one, were intimate partners in a common effort for the betterment of life. The perplexities of our age challenge them to renew their association in the service of human life, health and dignity. Indeed, they challenge Judaism itself to reassert its place as a potent force in the moral advancement of humanity.

This work is a modest attempt at helping to meet that challenge.'

A revised edition of *Jewish Medical Ethics*, published in 1975, contained an extensive additional chapter on 'Recent Developments in Jewish Medical Ethics', mainly as reflected in the voluminous rabbinical writings of the previous 15 years. Rabbi Jakobovits wrote in the preface:

'During this period, some striking medical advances have raised altogether new moral problems. Heart-transplants and the widespread recourse to oral contraceptives are but two examples of new procedures which have aroused fierce debates among professionals and laymen alike. Popular attitudes, too, have undergone radical changes. For instance, many countries have liberalised their abortion laws in response to these changes, while euthanasia, though not yet legalised, is more widely practised than before. On some subjects, such as autopsies, Jewish controversies continue to be unresolved.

On these and many other modern medico-moral issues, the additional chapter traces the evolution of Jewish law, as revealed in rabbinical judgements and discussions, through the ongoing process of applying timeless principles and precedents to the changing social and scientific conditions of the times.'

From the early 1980s, the Chief Rabbi found himself increasingly called upon to comment on the general, moral and social considerations applicable to the issues of human fertilisation and embryology then being discussed by a government committee of inquiry, the Warnock Committee. The *Jewish Chronicle* reported on one such instance in May 1983:

> The erosion of the family founded on marriage as the basic unit of society was a greater social and moral evil threatening the stability of society and its fundamental values than the suffering of individuals caused by disease or childlessness, the Chief Rabbi has stated. Hence, relief from such suffering must never be purchased at the cost of impairing the sanctity of marriage and its function as the sole legitimate agency for the procreation of children.
>
> He said that more important than to 'manufacture' children was to secure conditions under which they would be raised by parents in homes providing love and compassionate care. It was every child's inalienable birthright to have identifiable natural parents.
>
> Society was under an obligation to promote the moral and physical health of its members. To this end, medical science should harness human ingenuity and all available resources in the battle against disease and physical disabilities.

These included infertility, so long as this was done without infringing overriding moral imperatives, such as upholding the sanctity of life, the dignity of every individual, the inviolability of marriage, and the distinctiveness of all natural species.

Dealing with specific issues, the Chief Rabbi said that, where medically indicated, AIH (artificial insemination by the husband) could be applied, provided that there were absolute safeguards to ensure that only the husband's semen was used to inseminate the wife. AID (artificial insemination by donor), however, was not morally acceptable, even if, technically, it constituted no adultery, nor imposed the disabilities of illegitimacy or bastardy on a child so conceived.

The objections, he stated, lay in the profanation of marriage; the deception of the public whereby the paternity of the child was fraudulently registered in the barren husband's name; the clandestine manner in which the operation was performed; and the concealment of the donor's identity. Additionally, there was the possibility of incestuous unions between the parties closely related through or to the donor.

Equally repulsive to the moral conscience, the Chief Rabbi declared, was the use of 'host mothers', quite apart from the cruelty of eventually wresting a child on its birth from the woman who had carried it for nine months. Such a perversion of motherhood might also prematurely impair the bonds between mother and child. There was no moral objection in principle to genetic engineering or manipulation, provided that such deliberate interference with the building blocks of life served exclusively well-tested therapeutic purposes to eliminate physical or mental defects caused by hereditary or genetic disorders.

The critical difference was between 'improving' nature and correcting it. Thus, the cloning of human beings or the predetermination of their sex before birth might lead to a preponderance of, for instance, intellectuals or males which could destroy the delicately balanced fabric of society. 'Man has neither the right nor the competence to compete with nature, or Providence, in its preserves,' said the Chief Rabbi.

The deliberate wastage or destruction of germinating human life, inevitable in all these procedures, was also totally unacceptable. The freezing of human semen or embryos was likewise objectionable, if used to facilitate, as contemplated, the impregnation of women long after their husbands were dead, thus deliberately raising orphans. It might, however, be considered in exceptional circumstances, where a husband was about to undergo treatment for cancer or Hodgkin's disease, which could damage the chromosome content of his semen.

The Chief Rabbi said that the trans-species fertilisation between humans and animals, or between different species of animals, might offend against the laws of morality and nature. If such fertilisation could not develop beyond the two-cell state, it could be used for test purposes. There were also serious objections to the generation of human embryos purely for experimental use or for organ transplantation.

In late 1984, the Chief Rabbi urged the Government and the medical profession not to adopt the Warnock Committee's report on human fertilisation and embryology as it stood. In his response to the report, under the heading 'Major Omissions and Flaws', he warned that 'tampering with nature could have results even more devastating than a nuclear explosion. The long-term effects may be quite unpredictable and imponderable at present, but one misses some warning of the potentially awesome implications of the issues discussed in the report.'

He continued: 'The report turns marriage into an accepted casualty of technological progress. It appears no longer a matter of urgent public policy to safeguard the most essential unit [the family] of the social fabric.'

Referring to the interests of the child, the Chief Rabbi warned against the 'deliberate creation of orphans (by freezing semen, eggs or embryos for possible use after the owner's death); the permanent deception of children on their paternity (by AID and the fraudulent entry of the mother's barren husband as the father); or conceiving children by one mother to be borne by another as a "surrogate", with the prospect that both may one day lay conflicting claims to the child. Altogether, to raise children who will never be able to identify their immediate ancestry nor their closest blood relations for certain is an affront to human dignity as well as to the moral order.'

The Warnock Report was also flawed by its recourse to arbitrary lines of demarcation 'between what is to be morally acceptable and criminally culpable ... Experimentation on embryos is either morally totally inadmissible, or else it is acceptable for reasons other than being within the 14-day time limit (allowed for embryos).'

The Chief Rabbi welcomed the proposal to set up a statutory body to regulate research and infertility services, and expressed high praise for the 'moral norms postulated in the report'. He also endorsed calls for a moratorium on experiments on *in vitro* embryos, pending further study and legislation, and cautioned against undue haste 'in the blind pursuit of scientific and technological progress. Whether certain revolutionary break-throughs in medical progress occur a few years earlier or later will, in the long run, matter far less than whether our ethical advances keep abreast of our physical progress.

'Catastrophes stretching from the thalidomide tragedy to the recent horrendous chemical gas disaster in India could be but a foretaste of massive suffering inflicted by negligence or misjudgement in ensuring proper controls and safeguards which place the sanctity of every human life above any new scientific conquests.'

Prior to the publication of the Warnock Report, a group of medical scientists, theologians and philosophers had collaborated, under the aegis of the King's Fund, in a debate on the practice of *in vitro* fertilisation as a remedy for human infertility, and the attendant research on human embryos. Their views, later published in *The Status of the Human Embryo: Perspectives From Moral Tradition* (King Edward's Hospital Fund for London, 1988), included the following essay by the Chief Rabbi:

THE STATUS OF THE EMBRYO IN THE JEWISH TRADITION

'The criteria determining the status of the embryo in Jewish law and thought are varied, and the relevant opinions of authentic teachers are by no means monolithic. But on one fundamental principle there is complete agreement: full human status is not acquired until birth, and until then the destruction of a product of conception does not constitute homicide culpable as murder.

In fact, the determination of the embryo's status, or perhaps rather non-status, derives primarily from the laws of murder, at least in their biblical formulation. Bloodshed is a capital offence for the express reason that man was made in the Divine image (Genesis 9:6). However, in the law revealed at Sinai, such guilt is limited to the killing of 'a man' (Exodus 21:12; Leviticus 24:17).

Jewish exegesis interprets this as 'a man – but not an unborn child'. Accordingly, the destruction of a foetus, resulting from an attack on a pregnant mother, carries a monetary liability for the payment of damages (Exodus 21:22), and such monetary obligation is always excluded in cases of capital acts. All these passages clearly exempt foeticide from the laws of murder, and they therefore firmly refuse to establish full human status before birth.

Parenthetically, it might be mentioned here that the parting of the ways between the Jewish and the Christian traditions has its origin in the differing versions or translations of the Exodus passage on assaulting a pregnant mother. While the Hebrew text, as authentically interpreted in the earliest rabbinic commentaries, applies the crucial words 'if there be no accident' to the mother surviving the assault, the Septuagint (evidently based on a variant Samaritan reading, or simply on a mistranslation) renders these words 'if it be without form' – that is, if the foetus has not yet assumed human shape, thus exempting the attacker from capital liability only up to that stage of foetal development, but making him liable to the death penalty for the destruction of the foetus thereafter. This position was maintained by the early Church Fathers and later upheld for many centuries until the distinction between formed and unformed foetuses was eventually eliminated to treat as murder the destruction of any germinating human life from the moment of conception, an attitude maintained by the Catholic Church in principle to the present day.

Returning to Jewish sources, once the embryo is denied full human status, the definition of its remaining 'rights' is complex, and authentic rabbinic opinions are often considerably at variance with each other.

Again, agreement unites virtually all authorities only in conferring some degree of protection on the embryo from the moment of conception until birth in various stages of increasing human identity. In part, this identity is without any intrinsic autonomy. For instance, some schools in the Talmud speak of the foetus in certain legal contexts merely as 'a limb of the mother', not treated as a separate entity, corresponding to *pars viscerum matris* in Roman law. Indeed, several later authorities object to a non-therapeutic abortion only as an extension of the prohibition against 'spilling the seed in vain'. This severe interdict (of what is loosely called onanism) is itself merely the obverse of the biblical precept to 'be fruitful and multiply' (Genesis 1:28; 9:1) – that is, as implying a prohibition on frustrating the procreative act.

Again, some authorities in the Talmud deem the embryo during the first 40 days following conception as 'mere water', but the context in which this particular formulation occurs deals only with the levitical laws of impurity normally following a birth or a miscarriage (Leviticus 12:1–5). Nevertheless, as we shall see, some later decisors use this source for adopting the most lenient attitude to abortions carried out during the first 40 days – in other words, for attributing the least 'rights' or status to this initial period in the life of an embryo.

Two indirect references, though of no legal consequence whatever, may appear to have some bearing on the place of the embryo in Jewish thought. The Talmud ascribes certain spiritual attributes to children before birth. For instance, babes in their mothers' womb are said to have joined in the Song of Moses and the Children of Israel after their safe deliverance from the Egyptians at the Red Sea. Similarly, they were a party to the Covenant sworn between God and Israel at Sinai and on entering the Land of Israel. Into the same category of practically inconsequential, yet theologically not insignificant, statements belongs the argument reported in the Talmud between the Roman Emperor Antoninus and Rabbi Judah, the compiler of the Mishnah, on the entry of the soul, with the rabbi eventually conceding that this must occur at the time of conception rather than (as he had originally held) on the embryo's assumption of human form, or on its physical completion at birth, and this revised opinion was supported by the verse 'and Your visitation has preserved my spirit' (Job 10:12). Interesting as these passages may be in theory, they have never been used in practice to determine the status of the embryo in Jewish law.

Far more relevant, and yet not entirely conclusive, as an indicator of embryonic 'rights' or status is the rule on the suspension of the Sabbath laws if their observance would cause the slightest risk to life. Whether this suspension rule also applies to the saving of a foetal life *in utero* if otherwise deemed to be at risk is not expressly treated in the Talmud itself, except in the case of a mother who died in childbirth, when permission was given for the Sabbath to be violated in an effort to rescue her child by a Caesarean operation. However, it is only among medieval and later rabbis that consideration was given to the violation of the Sabbath rules expressly for the sake of a foetus otherwise in danger during an earlier stage of gestation. Some permitted this specifically out of regard for the life of the unborn child, but others contemplated setting aside the Sabbath law for a foetus only because any risk to its life might also endanger the mother for whose safety the Sabbath would certainly have to give way.

But there are reservations in conclusions on the status of the embryo to be drawn from the readiness of the rabbis to rule leniently on the Sabbath laws when these might conflict with the safety of foetal life, inasmuch as the normal Sabbath regulations demand their suspension in the face of not only a definite and grave threat to life but even a remote risk.

As against these last-mentioned sources, which clearly attach some significant status to the foetus demanding protection, there are others which tend in the opposite direction. For instance, in discussing the fate of a pregnant woman sentenced to death (however hypothetical this is, in view of the virtual abolition of capital punishment in Jewish law some 2,000 years ago), the Talmud weighs two conflicting interests: the child's in being delivered before the execution, and the mother's in not having the agony of suspense between the sentence and its execution drawn out. The decision is in favour of the mother at the expense of the unborn child, unless the process of birth had already begun. In that case, the child is regarded as 'a separate body', and the sentence is not carried out until after the birth is complete. By the same token of disregarding the foetus as an entity separate from the mother until birth, the conversion to Judaism of a pregnant mother (completed by her immersion in a ritual bath) automatically includes the child on being born, and its Jewish status is established without any further ceremony. Based on the same reasoning of legal non-status, a foetus cannot acquire things, and the assignment of any gift or property to an unborn child is invalid, except when made by its own father (because – to interpret the relevant source rather broadly – in the father's subjective mind, his child constitutes a real person with consequent legal rights even before birth).

None of these opinions or rulings provides absolutely conclusive evidence for the status of prenatal life in Jewish law; indeed, some are quite marginal or altogether irrelevant. Moreover, these judgements, while they usually represent a consensus of rabbinic opinion, are by no means universally endorsed. In most cases, they are subject to considerable arguments, and often to reservations and variations in matters of detail which could not be listed here. What does emerge quite distinctly is, on the one hand, a refusal to grant full human inviolability to the unborn child from conception, and, on the other hand, clear recognition that the potentiality for life must not be compromised except for the most substantial medical reasons.

It is only in the more recent writings of the rabbinical responsa (that is, written and usually published collections of verdicts on Jewish law by leading rabbinical scholars) that we find the status of the embryo defined in terms directly applicable to the current debate. These are notably in the form of answers to inquiries on abortions at different stages of gestation and in varying circumstances in the grey area between a life-hazard to the mother and some lesser concern for the welfare of the mother or the normality of the child to be born. These practical conclusions are quite often unrelated to the assertion or negation of foetal entitlements mentioned earlier.

What we have, then, are several somewhat vaguely distinct stages in the evolving status of the embryo. During the first 40 days following conception, the embryo is generally regarded as 'mere water' and lacking any specifically human 'rights', at least in the view of most authorities. At this stage, its inviolability derives purely from its potential growth into a human being, not from its actual endowment of human qualities, however rudimentary or as yet infinitesimal. The destruction of such a germinating conceptus is therefore not essentially different from the deliberate wastage of male semen. Both are condemned as grave offences, and perhaps even as appurtenances of murder, but only in a figurative sense. But there is certainly no distinction made between the first two weeks and the remainder of the 40-day period.

The next stage, according to the consensus of rabbinic opinion, takes the embryo up to the end of the third month, when human form is established and becomes visible on the expulsion or extraction of the embryo. During this stage, the embryo's life is more strictly protected in the sense that the indications for its destruction would have to be graver than in the earlier stage; for instance, the risk to the mother or of the child being born with abnormalities would need to be rated correspondingly higher for the pregnancy to be interrupted.

However, some authorities extend this stage even up to and including the seventh month, provided the considerations for an abortion are urgent enough. For example, if an amniocentesis cannot be carried out during the earlier stage, and there are reasons to suspect genetic or congenital abnormalities in the child,

14. Fifth Avenue Synagogue's founding rabbi on his appointment to the congregation in 1958.

15 and 16. The designer's drawings of the main prayer hall and the beth hamidrash at Fifth Avenue Synagogue, described by its founders as 'truly unique in the inspiring beauty of its architecture'.

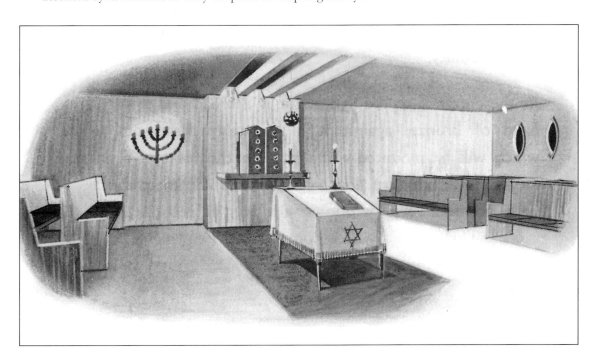

17. Fifth Avenue's Judge Sol Rosenberg (left) and Hermann Merkin present Rabbi Jakobovits with a mantle to accompany the Sefer Torah he received before taking up the post of British Chief Rabbi.

18. 'This resplendent occasion, usually witnessed but once in a generation': the newly installed Chief Rabbi at his induction service in London's St John's Wood Synagogue in April 1967.

19. A call to action as thousands gather for an Israel solidarity rally at the Royal Albert Hall, London, on 5 June 1967, the first day of the Six-Day War.

20. Conversing with excited Israelis paying their first visit to the Western Wall in Jerusalem, days after the liberation of the Old City during the Six-Day War.

21. Israeli statesman Abba Eban (centre) joins the Chief Rabbi and other communal leaders at a Board of Deputies meeting in London in March 1979 to mark the signing of the Israel–Egypt peace treaty.

22. Chief Rabbi Jakobovits looks on as Board of Deputies president Greville Janner, QC, MP, signs a declaration in 1980 opposing PLO policies.

these authorities would favour a lenient view right into the seventh month, even though viability of a premature birth could be established before then.

The final prenatal stage, when the foetus assumes a quasi-human status, is during parturition – that is, when the birth process has actually started and the foetus has 'dislodged itself from its uterine moorings'. It is then regarded not yet as a separate life, but as 'a separate body', to the extent that its destruction at this stage could be sanctioned only by applying the 'aggressor' argument – that is, if the foetus posed a direct threat to the life of the mother, for instance, by a breach birth which cannot be delivered without a grave hazard to the mother. Following in particular the Code of Maimonides, the inferior status of the unborn child would then no longer be sufficient by itself to warrant its destruction for the sake of the mother without recourse to the special law of 'pursuit', which demands the elimination of anyone threatening an innocent human life.

Biblical sources and major principles

To facilitate the reader in linking the principal relevant considerations in Jewish law with their biblical origins, it may be helpful at this point to list these sources and then to define the considerations derived from them:

Man's creation 'in the image of God' (Genesis 1:27) confers infinite value on every innocent human life and renders its destruction into a capital offence. While this absolute inviolability – whereby no life may ever be deliberately sacrificed even to save another or any number of others – sets in only at birth (Exodus 21:12, 22–23, and Jewish commentaries), the unborn child, too, enjoys a very sacred title to life, in different stages from the moment of conception, to be set aside only in exceptional circumstances, such as a serious hazard to the mother.

Judaism lists the duty of procreation ('Be fruitful and multiply' – Genesis 1:28; 9:1) as the first of its 613 commandments. Conversely, it deems the destruction of the human seed as a grave violation of this law. While Judaism therefore sets the highest value and importance on the fulfilment of marriage through children (see Genesis 30:31), it sanctions the generation of life exclusively through the bonds sanctified by marriage.

Judaism's strict code of sexual morality, especially the laws on incest (Leviticus 18:1–30; 20:8–27), presupposes that the (biological) father and mother of a child are known and can be identified with absolute certainty. No legal contract or artificial act can suspend, override or replace natural relationships based on consanguinity.

The duty to preserve human life and health is a religious precept (Deuteronomy 4:9, 15), which includes the Divine sanction to intervene in the course of nature or Providence by the practice of medicine (Exodus 21:19). But this sanction conferred on doctors is limited to acts of healing, or procedures intended to serve therapeutic ends.

Man, created to 'hold dominion over the fish of the sea and the birds of the heavens and every living thing crawling on the earth' (Genesis 1:28), is entitled to exploit animals in his service and for his health, provided they are protected from all avoidable suffering.

Moral and social considerations derived from these sources

From these basic postulates derive the following general guidelines germane to the issues related to the status of the embryo, notably in the treatment of infertility and experiments on embryos:

Society is under an obligation to promote the moral and physical health of its members. To this end, medical science should harness human ingenuity and all available resources in the battle against disease and physical disabilities, including infertility, so long as this is done without infringing overriding moral imperatives, such as to uphold the sanctity of life, the dignity of every individual, the inviolability of marriage, and the distinctiveness of all natural species.

The erosion of the family founded on marriage, as the basic unit of society, is a greater social and moral evil threatening the stability of society and its fundamental values than the suffering of individuals caused by disease or childlessness. Hence, relief from such suffering must never be purchased at the cost of impairing the sanctity of marriage and its function as the sole legitimate agency for the procreation of children.

More important than to produce children is to secure conditions under which they will be raised by parents in homes providing love and compassionate care. To deprive children of this security even before they are born is a betrayal of our human trust and responsibility. Moreover, it is every child's inalienable birthright to have identifiable natural parents, even if sometimes their identity is not publicly divulged or given to the child himself, as in cases of adoption. In these exceptional circumstances, the parentage must still be carefully recorded, with such privileged information being made available to specialised agencies for the prevention of incestuous unions or on other legitimate grounds in the interests of the child.

When the sperm and the ovum are taken exclusively from a husband and his wife, there is no essential difference in principle between *in vitro* fertilisation (IVF) and artificial insemination from the husband (AIH), but the controls to guard against the possible admixture or confusion of the vital cells from other donors, whether deliberately or by mistake, require special surveillance, possibly by two independent supervisors. The sanction of IVF must pass every reasonable test to avoid any undue risk to the mother and possible damage to the embryo before applying the procedure to an otherwise infertile marriage.

The destruction of an unborn child, let alone of an embryo in the earlier stages of gestation, does not constitute murder, since the unqualified entitlement to life – equal to the claim to inviolability of any other human being – sets in only at birth. Nevertheless, the germinating product of conception enjoys a very sacred title to life which may be set aside by deliberate destruction or abortion only in the most exceptional cases of medical urgency, notably to save the life of the mother if this would otherwise be at risk.

There is no moral objection in principle to genetic engineering or manipulation, provided such deliberate interference with the building blocks of life serves exclusively well-tested therapeutic purposes to eliminate physical or mental defects caused by hereditary or genetic disorders. On animals, the sanction for such manipulation also includes experiments or procedures designed to advance human health and nutrition.

In all these operations on human genes, the critical difference is between 'improving' nature and correcting it (or between positive and negative eugenics). The elimination of any abnormality or defect to ensure the health of children to be born is morally no different from any other medical or surgical intervention to overcome nature's disabilities. Such acts of healing, whether performed on organs, limbs or genes, are included in the biblical sanction or dispensation granted to doctors. But this licence does not cover acts of intervention in nature lacking therapeutic justification. The ecological arguments against undue interference with man's environment are infinitely increased against such interference with man himself. So are the dangers that may result from such intervention by possibly adding to each successive generation the cumulative effect of impairing nature's checks and balances.

Thus the cloning of human beings or the predetermination of their sex before birth might well lead eventually to a preponderance of, for instance, intellectuals or males, which could destroy the delicately balanced fabric of society. Man has neither the right nor the competence to compete with nature, or Providence, in its preserves.

The only circumstance under which the freezing of gametes could be morally justified is the imminent likelihood of a parent becoming unable to consummate a conception, such as a husband about to undergo radiological treatment or a wife anticipating an operation on her ovaries. But freezing procedures for longer periods, especially for posthumous use, should be strongly opposed, and the notion of a 'storage authority' is altogether repugnant.

Experimenting on human embryos

Some of the arguments advanced against experimenting on human embryos seem irrelevant or unconvincing. For instance, the embryo's inability to give informed consent is as immaterial an impediment as 'the balance of … pleasure over pain' or being 'incapable of feeling pain' can determine the ethics of experiments on embryos. Human rights or their absence cannot be related to any of these criteria, which are completely extrinsic to inviolability. What is crucial in allowing the use of embryos for experiments is that they must have been brought into being not for research purposes but solely for the possible prospect of ensuring a successful pregnancy. The moment they are no longer potentially required, or in a fit condition, for possible re-implantation, no further experiments should be done; until then, such observation or tests as do not necessarily lead to their destruction (by irreversible damage to them) may be carried out. What matters, therefore, is not any arbitrary time span, but the motive for their generation and their potential for re-implantation.

The difficulty of defining the circumstances, if any, in which experiments and research may be carried out on *in vitro* embryos is fully recognised. None but 'spares' could be so used in exceptional cases, and then only if certain conditions (such as are set out in the Warnock Report) are met. But the arbitrary 14-day limit should be replaced by the proviso that such 'spares' should be used or preserved only if and when it is feasible to re-implant them in the mother with the prospect of normal development to a live birth.

The family and the child

The two other considerations overriding the more limited question of the embryo's rights and status concern the stability of the family and the essential interests of the child to be born. Both these considerations may be of more far-reaching consequence for promoting the essential foundations of the moral order than defining the precise point at which human life, with its absolute value, commences. This priority in the Jewish scale of concerns will be reflected in the presentation of attitudes and judgements on the wide diversity of issues raised by the progress of medical science and techniques.

A direct result of man's capacity to supplant the natural generation of life is the threat to the family. The concern for its stability, let alone its inviolability as the exclusive agency for the creation of children, seems to be almost abandoned by some proposals on artificial insemination and fertilisation. It appears no longer a matter of urgent public policy to safeguard the most essential unit of the social fabric. By expressly dissociating the definition of a 'couple' from a legal husband–wife relationship, and by legalising the false entry of AID and IVF children as born to parents who are in fact infertile, these proposals would turn marriage into an acceptable casualty of technological progress. Such indifference to mankind's oldest and most vital institution can only compound the havoc already created by the debris of broken homes on a colossal scale.

Another cardinal imperative in regulating the generation of human life is the overriding insistence on the interests of the child. It is an indefensible violation of rights which should be deemed inalienable to engage in such practices as, for example, the deliberate creation of orphans (by freezing semen, eggs or embryos for possible use after the donor's death); the permanent deception of children on their paternity (by AID and the fraudulent entry of the mother's barren husband as the father); or conceiving children by one mother to be borne by another (as a 'surrogate'), with the prospect that both may one day lay conflicting claims to the child. (Indeed, some rabbinic authorities would deem the host-mother to be the child's legal parent if transplantation occurred before the foetus was viable, since they regard maternal identity to be established at parturition rather than at conception [Reference: J. David Bleich. Medical genetics: commentary. *New York State Journal of Medicine*, August 1982: page 1374].) Altogether, to raise children who will never be able to identify for certain their immediate ancestry nor their closest blood relations is an affront to human dignity, as well as to the moral order. Children facing the trauma of such shocking conflicts and uncertainties on seeking their origins are at a grave disadvantage in building socially and morally stable lives.'

Laying the groundwork for ongoing study in the field, the Sir Immanuel Jakobovits Centre for Jewish Medical Ethics was dedicated on 11 March 1986, during the First International Congress on Ethics in Medicine, at Ben-Gurion University of the Negev. The Congress, co-sponsored with New York's Beth Israel Medical Centre, was held on 10–13 March on the Beersheba campus of Ben-Gurion University.

The international gathering, which included more than 100 doctors, nurses, religious leaders, lawyers and philosophers from outside Israel, focused on the ethical implications of medical breakthroughs creating and sustaining life.

Speaking at the dedication of the centre named in his honour, endowed by the Kaplan-Kushlick Foundation of South Africa, Sir Immanuel said: 'Medical ethics, this orphaned subject so exceedingly rich in Jewish sources but somehow overlooked throughout the years, has finally received the academic recognition it so justly deserves.'

Another facility, the Centre for Medical Ethics, was opened at Jews' College, London, in 1993 in honour of Lord Jakobovits' work in the field. In his foreword to the centre's first yearbook, the Emeritus Chief Rabbi wrote:

'Jewish medical ethics has come of age. The very phrase was unknown until the late 1950s. There existed no literature whatever in the vernacular, no textbooks, manuals or even articles to guide doctors, nurses, medical students, hospital staff or laymen generally seeking guidance on Jewish insights and laws governing the ethics of their profession. Those in search of Jewish teaching on the subject had to be among the few conversant with the intricacies of rabbinic thinking and writing.

All this has changed dramatically over the past four decades. By now, a sizeable collection of comprehensive books, popular and specialised articles, entries in encyclopaedias and even regular periodicals can be assembled in this field. Jewish medical ethics is now considered an acknowledged discipline of Judaism, alongside such long-established subjects as Jewish jurisprudence, Jewish philosophy, and Jewish art.

Spectacular advances in medicine have presented numerous moral problems unthinkable in the past, and have provoked fierce public and professional debate. Judaism has much to say about these problems, and its insights should not only help to guide Jewish religious practice, but also contribute to the public and professional debate on these issues.

There are also ever more deeply committed Jews entering the medical profession. They rely on an authentic presentation of their own tradition for solutions to the many ethical problems they are bound to encounter.

I am greatly honoured to be named patron of the Centre for Medical Ethics at Jews' College. It is the appropriate place for such a centre, and it is the right subject for such a college. It is hoped that future years will see burgeoning programmes and a vision coming true. For it is the vision of its founders and leaders that this centre shall make a very large and important contribution to Jewish medical ethics in Britain and worldwide.

Of all the sciences, it is pre-eminently medicine which enjoys a natural kinship with Judaism, historically and intellectually. For many centuries, rabbis and physicians, often merging their professions into one, were intimate partners in a common effort for the betterment of life. This partnership is growing and blossoming through the Medical Ethics Centre at Jews' College.'

THE FATHER OF JEWISH MEDICAL ETHICS

An appreciation of HaRav Lord Jakobovits by his son, gastro-enterologist
Dr Yoel Jakobovits, of Baltimore, Maryland, USA

Although my father delved into medical ethics as early as the late 1940s, it was not until he arrived in Ireland that the idea of dedicating his academic career to medical ethics began to take shape. In the early 1950s, he published several seminal articles: an edited transcript and a series of articles in Hebrew, on halachic problems at life's beginning and an early review of the history of medical practice in Jewish law and literature.

Contributions to the literature continued to appear throughout the mid-1950s. Articles were published regarding autopsies, vivisection and, in Hebrew, regarding *duchaning* by a *kohen* (the priestly benediction) who inadvertently killed someone, abortion, and euthanasia. These were written in the classic *she'elah v'tshuvah* (question and answer) style. Besides addressing these concrete halachic questions, several essays were also devoted to more general abstract issues like irrational medicine and, in French, the history of biblical medicine.

A landmark article appeared in 1958 in the first issue of *Tradition* – itself a landmark rabbinic journal. This article not only presented the halachic attitudes to autopsies but it did so in the context of a comparative and historical analysis, thus presaging the sub-title of my father's *magnum opus* published the next year [*A Comparative and Historical Study of the Jewish Religious Attitude to Medicine and its Practice*]. The volume was submitted as a doctoral thesis to the University of London in 1955 and was published in 1959. In 1966, a Hebrew edition appeared, entitled *HaRefuah v'Hayahadus*, and in 1975 a 40-page chapter on recent developments was added.

The first edition is graced by a Foreword by my late sainted maternal grandfather, Rabbi Dr Elie Munk, of Paris. Alas, my paternal grandfather died in 1947 and, although he had, and continued to have, a profound influence on my father, he was not spared to see my father's literary or other rabbinic achievements. On the other hand, my maternal grandfather lived until 1983 and provided guidance and encouragement over many years. In his Foreword, my grandfather underscored several critical points that retain their truth concerning this book specifically and my father's overall outlook generally:

The present work of our author, whose purpose is a detailed treatment of 'Jewish Medical Ethics', is … a timely one. Keeping theoretical speculation to a minimum, he records the great problems of medical practice by analysing the position of the Jewish doctrine with regard to them. Each subject is introduced by an historical and comparative study in order to permit the solutions inspired by Jewish ethics to appear in their true light. Thus, the vast subjects of medico-moral conflict … which have not ceased, over the generations, to beset the moral conscience of humanity, are treated in the light of the eternal truths whose authentic source is the biblical revelation. The positions taken are clear; they are not the result of personal or sentimental considerations, always subject to caution, nor of systematic philosophy, a product of the human spirit and, consequently, always relative in value; they are based, in the final analysis, on the solid foundations of universal morality whose charter is contained in the Decalogue. In practical life, man, faced with a crisis of conscience, can give it his confidence. It is the wisdom of Israel, derived from the most venerable sources of the history of our civilisation, which raises its voice in the midst of the mental confusion of our epoch, an epoch of which Paul Valery said: 'We no longer know how to collect all our gains in the lottery of experience. All the results speak at once. And the mental confusion confounds itself with the confusion of reality.'

And this was already true nearly half a century ago!

My father's main attention was directed at moral problems raised by medicine, as opposed to those raised by Judaism. That is to say, many widely recognised inherent ethical dilemmas exist in medical practice today, beyond the exclusive interest or concern of Jewishly observant practitioners or patients. Problems of abortion, experimental surgery, life support and euthanasia, just to name a few, fall within this category. On the other hand, difficulties in medical practice sometimes arise because of Judaism: Sabbath, Yom Kippur, kashrut (dietary regulations) and autopsies fall under this heading.

Except for autopsies, and except for *Jewish Medical Ethics*, which has several chapters on ritual problems in medical practice, my father's involvement was almost exclusively in the arena of problems prompted by medical practices. Several other exceptions include articles on circumcision and on priests *(kohanim)* in medicine, *anninut* (laws pertaining to the pre-burial period), mourning, and *pikuach nefesh* (danger to life) on Shabbat.

My father's penchant for focusing authentic Jewish teachings on the complexities of modern life was evident throughout his career, beyond the confines of medical halachah as well. In articles on abortion and contraception, as well as more general reviews, he repeatedly underscored the relevance of Jewish teachings to modern Jewish, and indeed general, society.

My father honed the ability to analyse difficult questions through the prism of halachic ethics and express his thoughts in language which projects the sublime beauty of our heritage and its transcendent applicability across time and cultures. This was a constant theme in all the many varied facets of his literary and pastoral career.

Furthermore, although his 'pulpit' changed enormously over the years, his message and approach remained remarkably even and consistent. Numerous speeches, and the essays which have preserved them, resonate with this purpose. Even in personal and familial settings, he frequently gauged his reactions and conclusions against the measuring rod of halachically derived moral sensitivity and insight.

My father's chief focus, then, was to proclaim Torah values in contemporary language and current frames of reference in ways that were convincing and attractive to modern men and women, whether committed to Jewish practice or not. In this respect, he did not distinguish between Orthodox and non-Orthodox. All Jews have the obligation to accept, and become familiar with, our heritage. Furthermore, a recurrent theme in his *Weltanschauung* stressed the overarching obligation to project Jewish teachings in a way that attracted the attention and respect of society at large.

The ultimate goal of the Jewish experience and its teachings is to heighten the moral standards of *all* men. The application of many medical halachic principles should be seen in their universal context as well as in their more confined Jewish sphere. As one of his critics wrote: 'One can say without a doubt that Immanuel Jakobovits was the first really to begin systematically to address the varied and challenging elements of Jewish medical ethics in a way intended for both scholar and lay-person, for both Jew and Gentile. Every Jewish scholar of medical ethics will be eternally in his debt for his pioneering work.'

Jewish Medical Ethics is unique and pioneering in three fundamental respects. It was the first book to review and organise the diverse sources and opinions regarding Jewish views of medical practice. Secondly, it was written in English. And finally, it repeatedly stresses the ethical dimensions embedded in these rulings. These latter two features are combined to project a general ethical view which often speaks beyond the Jewish community in universal tones as well.

In 1958, my father accepted a call to become the first rabbi of the newly founded Fifth Avenue Synagogue of New York. In sharp contrast with Ireland, this brought him to the very heart of one of the world's largest Jewish communities. In addition, New York was home to many Orthodox Jewish physicians and scientists, and Jewish hospitals. This stimulating environment provided my father with many opportunities to further develop the still-fledgling field of Jewish medical ethics.

During this period, he continued to lecture widely, locally and throughout the country. Among my warmest childhood memories are those special evenings when I would accompany him to a lecture within driving distance from home. I still recall how invigorating he found these interchanges, especially the question-and-answer periods which followed the main presentation. I remember being struck by the broad similarity in the questions among the varied audiences. Notably, there was always at least one questioner whose agenda focused primarily on attacking the supremacy of the Torah, the authority of the rabbis – particularly the Orthodox ones – and the relevance of religion altogether to modern medical practice.

It amazed me to hear how many people seemed to know of Hillel's *pruzbul* device, and how many used it as the paradigm of rabbinical flexibility. These challenges offered my father ready opportunities to expand his discussion by emphasising the broad moral and ennobling doctrines of Judaism as applied to the contemporary scene.

I also recall that many medical ethics lectures in those days began with a plea that ethical decision-making in medicine be seen as a discrete and necessary sub-speciality. Just as a non-specialist physician would turn to a specialist cardiologist or neurologist for help with a difficult cardiac or neurological problem, physicians ought to seek help from ethics specialists when faced with moral dilemmas. Frequently, these arguments prompted vigorous resistance by doctors who regarded their professional training and experience as a licence to pronounce on the ethical as well as technical nature of their ministrations. These attitudes reflected the generally unchallenged paternalistic posture of doctors in those days.

A measure of the enormous change that has occurred in this regard is indicated by the currently widespread acceptance of ethics programmes, and even ethics departments, in medical schools and university medical centres as compared with the entire absence of – indeed, resistance to – 'outside' expertise in those early days.

The Fifth Avenue Synagogue provided a venue for my father to develop important medical relationships over many years. During these years, he conducted biweekly shiurim (classes) attended by dozens of physicians, nurses, and allied medical personnel. These shiurim had a reincarnation in later years in London, where my father met every month or two with about 20 doctors and allied professionals. The purpose of these encounters was to support the bidirectional flow of information. My father acquired updated information about current medical advances and problems while the audience gained by hearing authentically Jewish insights and evaluations directly related to their practices.

The cross-fertilisation of ideas and concepts bore numerous fruits. One was the development, for the first time, of a practical guide for Jewish doctors and the institutions in which they work. The guide was designed to help doctors deal with the ritual and the medical ethical problems arising in the care of observant Jewish patients. To date, over 100,000 copies of the *Hospital Compendium*, now in its sixth edition, have been distributed. It continues to serve as a model of the application of traditional sources to modern medical perplexities. Similarly, the committee in which my father brought together rabbis, attorneys, physicians and philosophers remains a paragon of interdisciplinary approaches to vexing societal difficulties.

In spite of his increased rabbinical and communal responsibilities, the early 1960s continued to see literary activity. Articles on the history of halachah in medicine, pain control, medical aspects of circumcision, and *kohanim* (priests) in medicine, appeared in various formats.

One of the major points of divergence between halachic and general medical ethics pertains to attitudes to autopsies. In Jewish circles, the debate was greatly exacerbated by the battle which raged in Israel over the past several decades. The autopsy issue became one of the flashpoints which characterised the strained and often bitter relationships between the observant and non-observant camps in Israel, and between the rabbinical and medical professions. Thus, the issue became more than only of technical halachic interest. In Israel, government coalitions were threatened and political pacts secured in relation to attitudes on this divisive issue.

Over the years, my father discussed and documented the traditional attitudes to autopsies in several comprehensive articles, in addition to the chapter in *Jewish Medical Ethics*. Taken together, these analyse the history and development of the traditional opposition to routine autopsies. However, my father went beyond the halachic details by also stressing an overall appreciation of Jewish sensitivity and thinking as reflected in this apparently narrow ritualistic area of concern. He argued that the opposition to autopsies should be seen as something more than merely an ancient restrictive regulation. Rather, it demonstrated in a powerful way the high standards of humane care which Judaism demands of its practitioners.

The Law's ultimate goal should not be obscured by attention to detail, no matter how important such scrupulous attention is. Judaism's overriding interest is to promote dignified care and respect for people even in death and thereby underscore the even higher standards of dignified and considerate care due to the living.

The frequently encountered medical attitude which sees patients as cases and relates to them merely as scientific challenges and curiosities would be largely dispelled were the profession to insist on dignified and thoughtful approaches even to the most defenceless – the deceased – in its care.

The Torah expresses its concern for the respect of the deceased in two contexts. First, the High Priest, normally prohibited from defiling himself even for his own parents, must do so by personally attending to the burial of an unclaimed body. Secondly, the corpses of criminals, executed by the state, must be buried by nightfall. The Torah chooses to teach the high regard which obtains to the human body even in death by insisting on the respect owed to the most defenceless members of society, the vagabond and the criminal. Note how sharply this approach contrasts with that of many Christian European centres where the most likely cadavers for medical school instruction were unclaimed bodies and the corpses of executed criminals.

Characteristically, my father often developed these points as examples of how the Orthodox camp in Israel, in particular, could transmit its values in such a way as to have a reinforcing influence, as opposed to merely a restraining one, on the wider society. He encouraged Orthodox groups to vocalise the broader overarching socio-ethical consequences of adhering to the authentic values of our faith with as much vigour as they defended their civil rights in protecting their traditions.

My father devoted many articles to clarifying the halachic attitude to contraception, population control, and the problems of abortion. As in the case of autopsies, he frequently stressed the wider social implications of halachic guidelines in addition to the more narrowly focused legal aspects. He often argued that the ready availability of contraceptive and abortion services gave rise to the age of 'credit-card morality', enabling people to 'enjoy now and pay later'.

Regarding abortion, especially in Israel's current liberal social environment, he emphasised the enormous aggregate losses to the population because of widespread birth control. These numbers, which now account for many tens of thousands, if not millions, would have matured into home-grown *sabras* (native-born Israelis), obviating the need for the vast financial and human resources expended over the years in promoting immigration and facilitating absorption. The demographic and geopolitical implications of these losses can only be guessed at.

These arguments, which he also made in many personal representations to Israel's leadership, demonstrate in a concrete way how the application of authentic Jewish values has broad positive significance to contemporary society at large. Reasoning cast in this language is more likely to persuade those who do not share the commitment to, and understanding of, our Torah-based beliefs.

Limitations on Jewish procreation have great implications beyond the borders of Israel, too. My father often said that nothing is more indispensable to the strengthening of our people and the assurance of its continuity than having children.

A particularly original and enduring literary enterprise during the New York years was my father's founding editorship of the column entitled 'Review of Recent Halachic Periodical Literature'. This ongoing commentary, which he began in the autumn 1961 issue of *Tradition*, was a digest of rabbinical responsa and other articles on a wide range of issues.

Topics were varied and included items from all areas of rabbinical interest. Among the medical entries were sections on birth-control, corneal transplants, medical experimentation on animals, *kohanim* (priests) studying medicine, deformed and thalidomide babies, prayers for the sick, abortion, circumcision of proselytes, autopsies, oral contraception, circumcision by non-observant *mohalim* (ritual circumcisers), accompanying women in labour on Shabbat, the blind in Jewish law, artificial insemination, mourning for deceased babies, and experiments on humans.

Somewhat more general, but equally important, reviews discussed rabbinical decision-making and objectivity in halachah. Ultimately, the competing pressures of the British Chief Rabbinate, which he assumed in

1967, forced my father to relinquish the column, which he bequeathed to the notably adept and versatile pen of Rabbi J. David Bleich.

Euthanasia and, in its currently fashionable nomenclature, 'physician-assisted suicide', artificial prolongation of life, distribution of scarce resources, defining death, and transplant technology are among the high-profile medical issues which have captured the attention of the wider public, driving the burgeoning developments in medical ethics.

One of the more contentious areas which the new medicine forced into consideration was the definition of death. Whereas in bygone days this was mainly of academic interest, the pressing demand for viable donor organs engendered by the advent of successful transplant therapy created an urgent need for a precise, but ever-earlier, definition of death.

All cultures and legal systems recognise that the donor must be dead before vital organs can be removed, even for a needy recipient. Nevertheless, as an influential medical committee reasoned, death could be redefined in the light of new pressures.

The concept of 'brain death', in contradistinction to systemic death, was introduced. Artificial ventilatory support allows a brain-dead person, even a brain-stem dead person, to carry on vital metabolic functions, thus assuring the vitality of his organs, while still being classified as dead in a legal and moral sense for the purposes of removing vital organs.

My father's attitude to the sharp debate which ensued regarding the halachic attitude to brain-death definitions was characteristic of his personal – and rabbinic – demeanour in general.

First, he often stressed the principle that, even regarding his own views, though usually firmly argued and not infrequently at odds with the prevailing wisdom, he would never insist that others – *kablu da'ati* – should uncritically accept his view. He therefore renounced the oft-stated rigid views which characterised many opinions in the brain-death controversy.

Opinions expressed with aggressiveness are not likely to sound authentic simply because they are declared stridently. A favoured dictum cautions: *divrei chachamim b'nachas nishmaim* – 'the words of the wise are heard [as being said] softly'. Note that it does not say a wise man speaks softly: that degree of propriety is taken for granted. Rather, the dictum stresses that a wise person's pronouncements are *'heard* softly' – crafted in such a way as to be perceived as emanating from a deliberate and thoughtful mind. Declarations issued in a reflective and considered tone are 'heard'; views expressed shrilly, or as if they are 'shot from the hip', are not. In passing, one might add that this attitude often governed my father's political views, too.

Secondly, he held the view that it is necessary to establish beyond any shadow of doubt that the halachah accepts a person as dead before cancelling his hitherto unchallenged presumption of life, *chezkas chai*. Given that we are dealing here with a *safek issur retzicha,* with a possibility of murder, one should have to establish the donor's death with absolute certainty.

Since the debate regarding brain death continues unabated, one must err on the side of caution. Although of immense concern, the welfare of the recipient cannot enter the equation; depriving the donor of even a few moments of life would never be sanctioned even in order to offer the possibility of many years of life to the recipient.

Incidentally, my father once suggested a compelling mathematical rationale for the absolute halachic prohibition to shorten life, even for the sake of another *(ein dochin nefesh mipnei nefesh).* The underlying halachic principle is that all life is infinite in value. Hence, since infinity is indivisible, every fraction of life remains equally infinite in value. Conversely, infinity cannot be enlarged by multiplication. Hence the ruling by Maimonides that hostages must all submit to death rather than surrender one of their number to the enemy as a martyr. In characteristic fashion, and in contrast with secular legal systems, the halachah expresses itself in concrete cases, not in general principles. The principles of halachic thought evolve from specific cases, not the reverse.

My filial relationships and emotional ties restrict any truly impartial appraisal of my father's contributions. The fact is that little scholarly criticism has been published. One notable exception is a well-documented chapter by Marc A. Gellman, of the faculty of the Hebrew Union College, in a recent book surveying the influence of several theologians on medical ethics. Dr Gellman is the current chairman of the medical ethics committee of the Federation of Jewish Philanthropies of Greater New York and, as such, has acquired, by way of Rabbi Dr Moses Tendler as the intervening chairman, my father's mantle.

Under the sub-title 'Bringing the Ancient Word to the Modern World', Gellman first presents a biographical sketch 'in tribute to the unique scope and vigour of [Rabbi Jakobovits'] life and work' and of his 'prescience' in launching the field of Jewish medical ethics a decade before the subject attracted the attention of other philosophers, lawyers, physicians, and theologians.

Perhaps Gellman discloses his own bias by suggesting that Jewish medical ethics tests the 'flexibility and vitality of Jewish law' and the 'intellectual credibility of Jewish moral reasoning in the realm of modern normative ethical thinking'. At the same time, he recognises my father's fidelity to 2,000 years of rabbinic moral reasoning and that, although my father 'is ready to move the focus of Jewish law into the new realm of medical ethics … he is not willing to alter the Jewish legal process, which has confronted novelty before without surrendering the ancient way'.

Actually, Gellman's is the correct analysis. Indeed, this is the fundamental approach of every authentic Jewish thinker: *hafok bo, vahafoch bo, d'chulah bo –* the Torah encompasses all the guidelines, provided its depths are plumbed with commitment and consistency.

What Gellman takes to be a point of criticism was, in fact, central to my father's aim in his whole approach to Jewish medical ethics, and indeed in his rabbinic leadership and halachic writings in general.

An oft-heard complaint by non-Orthodox thinkers is that their Orthodox counterparts are not willing to be 'creative' and are bound to the standards of yesteryear. Gellman feels that this has 'reduced creative thinkers like Jakobovits … to the status of quoting responsa …'

Gellman argues that 'the layering of interpretation of Jewish sources has thrown [many] off the track and [has] reduced [many] to the Jakobovitsian move of simply citing responsa while withholding personal judgement'.

Orthodox rabbis, of course, by definition always anchor themselves to the classic sources of our faith and eschew personal opinion. As they exercise their mandate, they examine the authentic Jewish viewpoints and teachings whose basic elements are enshrined in our literature stretching over thousands of years. By conscientious and sincere investigation, rabbis in each generation have unearthed teachings founded on well-defined halachic rules and guidelines. Halachic directives derived from these techniques are applicable and relevant to the whole gamut of questions raised by the human condition.

The rabbi's role, then, is decidedly not inventive. It is, above all, interpretative. In this capacity, my father was eminently successful and renowned. His ability to marshal the sources, as evidenced in *Jewish Medical Ethics* and in his numerous subsequent publications, was matched by the conviction and consistency, eloquence and dignity of his arguments.

He used every occasion and pronouncement to imbue the halachah with the spirituality which has ensured that its message endures above the shifting standards and mercurial mores of society and locality. It is this quality that was cited by Viscount Tonypandy, a former Speaker of the House of Commons, when he nominated my father for the 1991 Templeton Prize for Progress in Religion:

'He conveys Judaism to regulate human life whatever challenges, discoveries and changes confront society. He has continuously sought to provide authoritative Jewish answers to major questions of the day. The Chief Rabbi's contribution to medical ethics is unique and remains pre-eminent. Among his extensive writings are classic expositions of Jewish law of unsurpassed knowledge and enlightened humanity. He has been the pathfinder for a great and growing literature dealing with the most controversial social and ethical problems of our age... Jakobovits' natural authority is based on his knowledge, wisdom and humanity but reflected in his genuine humility, warmth and approachability, and has made him the ultimate leader of his people. His unswerving devotion to his principles has at times led him to castigate the self-imposed isolation of spiritual leaders indifferent to faiths, cultures and social needs outside their own, while he at all times seeks to influence the society around him.'

[An expanded and annotated version of this essay, originally published in Pioneers in Jewish Medical Ethics *(edited by Fred Rosner), was updated, in booklet form, to mark Lord Jakobovits' first yahrzeit, on 21 Marcheshvan 5761.]*

FLASHBACK THREE

New York

In the early days of its evolution, New York's Fifth Avenue Synagogue was launched with the publication of an expensively produced brochure for publicity purposes. It commenced its 'story of a dream' by referring to 'a new synagogue being built within walking distance of our homes, in the midst of the city … We who first conceived the promise of this building, we who nourished the dream so long within ourselves, we feel impelled to speak. There is a restrained pride in our speech, for this synagogue is truly unique – in the inspiring beauty of its architecture and the unusual scope of its activities … but most of all in the strength and purity of the ideals which gave it birth.'

Sensitive readers in Britain may perhaps wince at its style, somewhat reminiscent of the launch of a luxury car, but it shows clearly enough that the founders were not inhibited by any lack of ambition, modesty, or resources.

Five East Sixty-Second Street was a self-contained six-storey building. There was a banqueting suite below ground level, a lobby and reception area on the ground floor, and a chapel (bet midrash) on the first. The main synagogue was on the second floor, with the ladies' section on the third. The two top floors held club rooms, later used as a kindergarten and a gymnasium.

As so much interest was generated by our 'Sabbath elevator', it might have been thought that the synagogue was at the top of a skyscraper, but New Yorkers regard walking up stairs as almost un-American. Even a second floor required a lift (they call this the third floor, which makes it seem higher; for the ladies – all-important in any American synagogue construction plan – it was one floor higher still).

The original plans were for a lift operated by a non-Jew on Sabbaths and festivals, a regular feature of some other New York Orthodox synagogues. I was not happy with this practice, which, to my mind, came uncomfortably close to the prohibition of *amirah lenochri* (instructing a Gentile to perform an act forbidden to a Jew). I would have preferred an elevator where, for Sabbaths and festivals, the controls could be pre-set, so that the lift would ascend and descend, the doors open and close, without any active participation of those using it.

The engineers were at first nonplussed by this unprecedented requirement, but soon produced a satisfactory blueprint to meet my specifications. I was aware that the lift still left some relatively minor problems halachically, and I never used it myself, but I regarded it as far less objectionable than the employment of a lift operator.

The many visitors to the synagogue found the lift of extraordinary interest, and before long I began receiving inquiries from Israeli hoteliers. I was pleased to explain our system and to refer their technical questions to our engineers.

A number of hotels had installed such lifts, but these were subsequently subjected to the rather more intensive scrutiny of the Institute of Science and Halachah in Jerusalem. One problem was that increased weight in the lift added to the amount of current consumed, so that each additional passenger, so to speak, caused an additional flow of electricity and therefore directly affected the operation. Happily, this proved to be capable of solution. (This matter provided ammunition for opponents of mine some eight years later, when it was alleged that anyone who worried so much about trivialities could have no concept of the broader perspectives of Judaism.)

Fifth Avenue Synagogue probably had a larger percentage of really observant members than a mainstream synagogue in Britain, where there is only a small Conservative movement for the less committed. Its Orthodoxy was firm, but its services were such that visitors from Britain felt themselves in a congenial atmosphere. Bernard Bloomstein, the chazan, originated from London and had been a chorister at Duke's Place. The president, Hermann Merkin, had also lived in London for some years.

In American synagogues, the prayer for the nation's President is not read with anything like the frequency or solemnity accorded to the prayer for the Royal Family in Britain. We at Fifth Avenue, however, always recited the full prayer as in the *Authorised Daily Prayer Book*, merely substituting the President of the United States for the Queen.

When Kennedy replaced Eisenhower, Hermann Merkin asked me to specify the name of the President; after all, he said, in Britain they used the name of the monarch. It mattered little to me, so I accordingly inserted the name of John F. Kennedy on the first Sabbath following his inauguration.

Our congregation's vice-president was a fervent Republican and he protested vigorously at the name of one whom he regarded as unsuitable to be mentioned in the context of a synagogue service. I replied that if that was how he thought of the President, there was all the more reason to pray for him. (Later, in London, I applied the same reasoning to some rabbis under my jurisdiction – usually Lubavitch – who refused to recite the prayer for the State of Israel.)

I recited the Presidential prayer in full on my one official visit to the White House, when I was part of an Orthodox delegation that called on President Lyndon Baines Johnson.

In one other respect, we conformed more closely to Anglo-Jewish than to contemporary American practice. One of the reasons for the breakaway of Fifth Avenue's founders from the Park East Synagogue had been a dispute over women's seating and the positioning of a *mechitzah*, the partition between the men's and women's sections, since there are no mixed pews in an Orthodox synagogue.

Not for 40 years had any Manhattan synagogue been built with a ladies' gallery; the women sat around the men's section, with some – usually not very adequate – separation device. At Fifth Avenue, they decisively turned back to the traditional style of synagogue architecture, and a regular gallery was designed from the outset. If visitors expressed astonishment at this feature, I would often explain its existence on the grounds that we always looked up to our women.

I objected from the start to the idea of draping American and Israeli flags on either side of the Ark, a practice prevalent in most American synagogues since the establishment of the State of Israel. I felt that in a house of God, only one loyalty should be demonstrated.

For similar reasons, I have always endeavoured to prevail on young couples, after I solemnised their marriage, to leave the show of their affections until they met privately following the ceremony. Only one expression of love belongs in the synagogue!

Equally, I never made political use of my pulpit. American congregations always expect their rabbis to air their political views publicly, particularly at election time. This might be thought likely to upset and disappoint congregants supporting the other party, but, in practice, I do not suppose that worshippers take any more notice of their rabbi's politics than they do of his religious exhortations.

I made a fixed resolve to avoid mentioning names from the pulpit, feeling that this was undignified. The pulpit belonged to the word of God and its interpretation, especially under current conditions. Even more untypically, I never made the slightest effort to get my sermons reported in the general press, even if this was often regarded by some leading colleagues as almost the ultimate accolade.

My routine duties at the Fifth Avenue Synagogue were not too demanding and I had reasonable opportunities for lectures and literary work, or to play some part in the general religious life of New York Jewry. I did not, however, participate in the work of the New York Board of Rabbis, whose combination of cross-section composition and political interests was not much to my liking.

But I found a congenial niche with the equally all-inclusive Federation of Jewish Philanthropies of New York, which included a Commission on Synagogue Relations. Here I was able to turn my knowledge of religio-medical matters to practical use.

I became co-chairman of the Hospital Compendium Committee, which produced a manual for doctors, nurses and hospital staff, especially in Jewish hospitals. It was largely my work, 'in response to a demand for some authoritative guidance on Jewish teachings related to medical and especially hospital practice', to quote its introduction.

Seeing that most Jewish hospitals in the United States had been in existence since the turn of the century, it may appear strange that such a publication had never been prepared before. The hospitals, however, had been founded for social, rather than religious, reasons. The immigrants, nearly all Yiddish-speaking, could not receive adequate attention in strange surroundings, while would-be Jewish medical students and doctors had much difficulty in finding places in the medical schools and hospitals.

The Jewish hospitals solved both problems. Nevertheless, they were only secular hospitals for ethnic Jews – hospitals for Jews rather than Jewish hospitals – and even the dietary laws were ignored in most of the institutions. With the rapid Americanisation of the immigrants, and the disappearance of educational and professional barriers, the need for specifically Jewish hospitals seemed much reduced, and a high proportion of non-Jews figured among both patients and staff.

The hospitals, although recipients of vast sums from community chests and Federation funds, were in danger of losing their *raison d'être*. Against this background, and the general heightening of Jewish consciousness associated with the establishment of Israel, there emerged a very real desire to study specifically Jewish attitudes to medical ethics and developments, if only to vindicate the allocation of enormous Jewish resources. This, at least, was the reasoning given to me when I was invited to lecture on Jewish medical ethics to the medical, nursing and administration staff of Philadelphia's Albert Einstein Medical Centre – Pennsylvania's largest hospital – which is supported by Jewish funds.

The *Compendium* was favourably received and was distributed to hospitals of all religious outlooks, and of none. It has been reprinted many times, with additional material, as fresh problems arose with the continually increasing range of medical and surgical treatments available. With this, as with some publications of the Jewish Marriage Council in London, I am happy to discover traces of my original work, despite all the subsequent rewriting, and to feel that I was associated with some really constructive efforts.

One specific problem facing Jewish hospitals was that of autopsies. Medical schools need a supply of cadavers for the study of anatomy. In New York, a 30 per cent rate of autopsies on all who have died in a hospital is required to obtain academic accreditation. Jews are very reluctant to allow post-mortems, even where rabbinical sanction is forthcoming in particular cases – for instance, where another life at risk might thereby be saved.

Some atavistic or sentimental repugnance was found to be present equally in all sections of Jewry, as I discovered when I chaired a committee to examine the question, and we conducted a detailed inquiry into autopsy attitudes which I later published. More remarkably, our investigation revealed that the very doctors who were themselves most vociferous in urging family consent for the maximum number of post-mortem operations were as unwilling as everyone else to permit any interference with the bodies of their own loved ones.

In one matter during my American period, I found myself opposed to one of the most deeply embedded attitudes in American Jewry, one that was accepted by nearly every grouping, from the avowedly secularist to the most undeviatingly Orthodox.

The principle of the separation of religion and State is enshrined in the First Amendment to the Constitution, the Bill of Rights: 'Congress shall make no law respecting an establishment of religion, or prohibiting the free exercise thereof.'

The ramifications of this clause are far-reaching: 'Neither a state nor the Federal Government can set up a church. Neither can pass laws which aid one religion, aid all religions, or prefer one religion over another ... In the words of Jefferson, the clause against establishment of religion by law was intended to erect "a wall of separation between Church and State" ' (Supreme Court Justice Black, in *Everson v Board of Education*).

Among American Jews, this separation became an act of faith. They believed that any breach of that wall would endanger their freedom and security, notably by strengthening the Christian church, and that in protesting against any invasion of the total secularism of public schools (I need hardly stress that the word is used in the completely opposite sense from its usage in England) by religious influences, they are thereby showing themselves truly American, loyally maintaining the Constitution against those who would subvert it to gain a religious advantage. Whether the effort was as seemingly minor as a nativity play, or obviously major like a proposal to grant State aid to parochial (religious) schools, it had to be opposed, firmly and completely.

The Regents of the New York Board of Education wanted to institute the daily recital of the following prayer (referred to thereafter as the 'Regents' Prayer'): 'Almighty God, we acknowledge our dependence upon Thee and we beg Thy blessings upon us, our parents, our teachers and our country.'

The Jewish community protested vigorously and, on its instigation and financial support, the matter was argued all the way to the Supreme Court, where the prayer was declared unconstitutional by a six-to-one majority. This was warmly hailed by Jewish leaders, who had been the only religious denomination to be so fully involved, although they had enjoyed the co-operation of groups totally opposed to all expressions of religious belief.

The New York Board of Rabbis issued an enthusiastic statement, but I felt devastated by what I regarded as a betrayal of basic Jewish values. I wrote the following letter to the *New York Times*, and it was duly published on 4 July 1962:

Lest it be thought that all rabbis concur with the recent statement by the New York Board of Rabbis praising the Supreme Court decision on prayer at public schools, I wish to express my dissent from, and utter dismay at, this strange alliance between teachers of Judaism and the spokesmen of atheism or secularism who secured and applauded the verdict.

As spiritual leaders of the people that gave birth to the immortal vision of the days when 'the earth shall be full of the knowledge of the Lord as the waters cover the sea', we can scarcely, I submit, be jubilant about outlawing the acknowledgement and worship of God from any area of life, least of all from schools, which pre-eminently fashion the outlook of our future citizens, without making a travesty of Jewish thought and history.

For many centuries, devout Jewish parents have taught their children, long before they could read or even speak properly, to include in their simple morning prayers the verse from the Hebrew Bible: 'The beginning of wisdom is the fear of the Lord', so as to instil in them the conviction that knowledge or education without a religious foundation is worthless.

The United States is now probably the only country in the world outside the Iron Curtain to brand as an offence the public acknowledgement of God in schools. How can rabbis, heirs to the prophets of Israel, rejoice over this?

Freedom cannot be maintained without religion, just as the brotherhood of man requires the Fatherhood of God. A generation of heathen hedonists, worshipping the idols of happiness and material success, will be unable to evoke the herculean strength necessary to contain the mighty tide of godlessness in the defence of liberty. Furthermore, even statistics show that only children reared in a wholesome religious atmosphere are likely to develop the maximum immunity to the scourges of juvenile delinquency corroding our society and undermining its security.

'The wall of separation' between State and Church must be constructed with ample gateways to prevent the divorce of education from religion if that wall is not to lay siege to our civilisation and starve it to death.

These are purely my personal views, but I have no doubt that they are shared by many of my colleagues, whether they are members of the Board of Rabbis or not.

I realised that I would be strongly opposed, and I was not disappointed. The fears of the majority were not to be easily dismissed; if a beginning was made with the 'Regents' Prayer', denominational prayers might follow and, sooner or later, the public schools would become liable to denominational domination.

The fear of Christian extremism, particularly of Roman Catholicism, associated in many minds, or memories, with rabid anti-Semitism in Eastern Europe, was never far below the surface of Jewish consciousness and was a good deal more potent than any idealistic theology.

It always appeared to me that there were deeper roots for this obsessive concern of American Jewry with the divorce of State and religion. The phenomenon was not found among Jews elsewhere, for instance in Britain, where they readily accept that England is a Christian country, with the Queen as the head of the Church as well as of the State.

For Jews throughout the Diaspora, emancipation meant equality as citizens. Their aspirations were fulfilled when they enjoyed full civil rights and religious freedom.

Not so American Jews. They sought equality not just as individuals but as a denomination. They insisted that churches and synagogues, or ministers, priests and rabbis, should always be mentioned in one breath. And since Judaism, professed by only some 2 per cent of all citizens, could never really be equal to Christianity – to which the vast majority owed allegiance – Jews wanted religion to be neither officially recognised nor publicly aided.

Related to this peculiar attitude, no doubt, was the extreme secularisation of most Jews. If they did not practise their Judaism, they did not want to see the promotion of religious knowledge and observance among Christians either.

All the same, after my letter appeared, a number of rabbis and Jewish lay leaders privately expressed their support. I was particularly heartened when the Lubavitcher Rebbe published an uncompromising attack on the general view and, in a lengthy statement, dated 20 November 1962, claimed that the recital of the 'Regents' Prayer' would in fact fulfil the basic requirements for daily prayer for thousands of Jewish children, since it included the three essential ingredients of the biblical precept of prayer: praise, thanksgiving, and petition.

The Rebbe wound up with a challenge: 'Can anyone raise his hand to silence this vast body of American youth, saying "Stop praising God, stop praying to Him! It is forbidden to do so in the American public school." '

In view of the adverse criticism that the Supreme Court decision – and, by inference, the considerable Jewish involvement – encountered in responsible circles, the American Jewish community tended to back-pedal on these issues in subsequent years. I had never before felt myself so closely linked with the ideology of Lubavitch, though, in later years, some of my attitudes on Israeli matters aroused their passionate condemnation.

Fragments from an unpublished autobiography

CHAPTER FIVE

Fifth Avenue

Synagogues over the city were crowded yesterday as Rosh Hashanah worshippers marked in solemn prayer and meditation the Jewish New Year 5719. Scores of rabbis emphasised in their sermons the spiritual significance of Rosh Hashanah and urged their congregants to revitalise the basic concepts of Judaism in their daily existence. A highlight of the New Year occurred yesterday morning when the Rev Dr Immanuel Jakobovits, Chief Rabbi of the Jewish community in Ireland, preached his first sermon as spiritual leader of the new Fifth Avenue Synagogue at Sixty-Second Street. The 37-year-old black-bearded rabbi made an imposing pulpit appearance in his flowing white *kittel*, or gown. Here on a two-week visit, Dr Jakobovits will formally assume his new post in December.

The New York Times, *16 September 1958*

Rabbi Jakobovits took up his duties as rabbi of Fifth Avenue Synagogue towards the end of January 1959. In his first Shabbat sermon, he declared that regard for the materialistic sides of life should be subordinate to a constant search for the spiritual and religious aspects.

Comparing today's Jews to those of the biblical era, when Moses searched the banks of the Nile for the coffin of Joseph, he asserted that while the majority of Jews were then preoccupied with the gathering of their belongings prior to leaving Egypt, the primary concern of Moses was to find the relics of his ancestors. Today's Jews were preoccupied with daily affairs that stressed pecuniary and other temporary values, and neglected to enrich their souls and minds with their great heritage.

On Sunday, 22 March, Dr Jakobovits was inducted as Rabbi of Fifth Avenue at the dedication ceremony for the new synagogue.

The following year, in an address to the sixty-second biennial convention of the Union of Orthodox Jewish Congregations (UOJC) that, in time, was to assume far-reaching significance, Rabbi Jakobovits described the post-war shift of the Jewish centre of gravity from Eastern Europe and Germany to Britain as 'the most momentous development in European Jewish life since the Holocaust'.

He told the convention that, in common with recent developments in America, 'West European communities have experienced a veritable revolution through a phenomenal rise in the number of yeshivot and day-schools.' These schools had widespread popular and State support in nearly all the European countries, 'even a country like France, where assimilation has been rampant'. With 'four major yeshivot and a fine network of day-schools, France today is the home of probably the most intense Jewish learning since Rashi', he said.

The second major event was the 'distinct movement' towards greater Orthodoxy of the European rabbinate. Dr Jakobovits cited as examples Chief Rabbi Israel Brodie, of Britain, and Chief Rabbi Jacob Kaplan, of France. The former incumbents of these posts, he said, might have been described 'in American terms as basically Conservative', but now they were 'men of unimpeachable, even militant, Orthodoxy'.

At the same time, however, there had been no parallel development of religious standards among the European Jewries, with some congregations shifting to non-Orthodox standards. Rabbi Jakobovits ascribed this 'strange phenomenon' to 'religious indifference'. He pointed to the lack of rabbinical students, declaring that 'in Europe there are simply no young men outside the yeshivot with sufficient idealism to take up the rabbinical profession when so many more lucrative openings attract bright young people'.

But it would be an 'unforgivable error' to write off the 'large, uncommitted bulk of European Jewry as lost to Orthodoxy', he stated. The drift from Orthodoxy could be arrested if 'some secure, permanent anchorage' to Orthodox units elsewhere could be found. He said that this was a challenge to the UOJC.

At the convention, the Orthodox Union's World Jewry Award – presented for exceptional achievement at international level on behalf of traditional Judaism – was given to British businessman and philanthropist Isaac Wolfson, who, in 1962, was elected president of the United Synagogue and, subsequently, chairman of the Chief Rabbinate Council and Chief Rabbinate Conference.

As his Congregation entered its fifth year, Rabbi Jakobovits took as the theme of his Rosh Hashanah sermon the significance of the number five in relation to its members:

'In establishing a citadel of traditional Judaism in the very heart of the world's largest Jewish community, in a coveted position probably more exposed to the scrutiny of critical onlookers than any other Orthodox synagogue, we must aspire to the dignity of the high priesthood, to the heights of supreme sanctity and spiritual leadership. Like the high priest of old, we can discharge our special responsibilities only if we excel in five respects:

In beauty. The widely acclaimed beauty of our cherished synagogue must be matched by the beauty of our services and the attractiveness of all our activities, that it in truth be said of us, '*Ma tovu oholecha ya'akov*' – 'How goodly are thy tents, O Jacob!'

Only by turning our prayers and religious exercises into a model of charm, sincerity and dignity can we recapture an enthusiastic appreciation of our faith in those who have strayed from the ways of the Torah which are 'the paths of pleasantness'.

In strength. In our organisational world, power means influence, and strength means security. We must aspire to that power and strength in order to secure the survival of our ideals and their increasing acceptance among American Jewry.

We must seek to raise from within our midst powerful leaders who will assume responsible positions in Jewish national organisations and thus give Jewish life in all its manifestations a traditional orientation. In a focal congregation like ours, there is no room for petty parochialism and narrow isolationism; our shoulders must be broad and strong to carry the supreme responsibilities devolving on us as front-ranking bearers of the torch of Judaism.

In wealth. 'He who pays the piper calls the tune', and he who supports institutions controls their policies.

If we want to bring our influence to bear on the spiritual enrichment of the Jewish scene, we must be among the foremost contributors to leading Jewish causes, as well as place our own house on sound material foundations. Broad-minded generosity must be the hallmark of anyone wishing to wear the distinguished mantle of the high priesthood.

In wisdom. The assertion of spiritual leadership, however, requires more than political skill combined with power and money; it needs wisdom and creative thought.

Today, Judaism and, indeed, the moral order generally are being challenged by the impersonal, soulless and materialistic overtones of modern science and technology. To meet this grave challenge, we must have profound religious thinkers and devout scientists who can reinterpret Judaism in contemporary terms.

Our Congregation should aim at producing and attracting such leaders of thought if it is to vindicate the hopes of its many well-wishers and to realise the ideals to which we are committed.

In years. In terms of his wisdom, a man is as old as the experience on which he leans. Similarly, the true age of a community corresponds to the length of the traditions to which it is heir.

Chronologically, our Congregation may be the youngest in Jewry. But by founding our ideals on the accumulated spiritual wealth of all past generations of Jewish creativity, we can belong to the oldest and most experienced. Our unflinching loyalty to the timeless treasures of our faith will make us rich 'in years' and qualify us for exercising mature and sagacious leadership.'

LOOKING BACK – AND LOOKING FORWARD

During the summer of 1966, it became increasingly evident that Rabbi Jakobovits' days at the helm of the Fifth Avenue Synagogue were numbered, as rumours reached New York of his impending appointment as British Chief Rabbi (see Chapter Six). In his Rosh Hashanah message to his Congregation, he seemed to confirm their worst fears:

'Better is the end of a thing than its beginning', says the biblical preacher. How much hope, not unmixed with some anxiety, filled us as we conducted our first service together in our beautiful new synagogue on Rosh Hashanah exactly eight years ago! How well I remember the feelings of anticipation and concern that animated me on that festival inaugural occasion, when we launched our partnership as well as our great congregational enterprise.

At that time, I looked forward to the uncertainties of the future; now I have to look back to the record of the past. How have the high hopes then entertained fared in the light of today's realities?

Many of my dreams have been fulfilled beyond expectation. Our Congregation has grown from a handful to a synagogueful of members. It rapidly conquered an enviable place for itself among the world's foremost and best-known Orthodox synagogues.

It has welcomed innumerable visitors from the ranks of the great and the humble everywhere, from Israel's President and Chief Rabbi to hundreds of school-children, who included our sanctuary among the special sights to be seen on visits to New York. More importantly, it has reclaimed the Jewish loyalties of many a straying soul, and given numerous worshippers added meaning to Jewish thinking and living.

It has provided a prominent platform to scores of distinguished speakers, and attracted hundreds of participants to Jewish studies and discussions. It has cemented innumerable friendships and welded the congregation into an intimate family sharing joys and sorrows together.

To me personally, it has brought infinite gratification, and a measure of love and affection beyond my deserts.

Perhaps inevitably, some achievements have fallen short of my hopes. Somehow, I did not succeed in harnessing our unique potential in the service of the wider community as I have continuously urged.

Our synagogue did not feature as a leading catalyst in communal endeavours. Remaining aloof from the great undertakings in Jewish education and welfare, it allowed many outstanding enterprises to go by default or unsupported. Intellectual and communal efforts it could have pioneered still await realisation, and several major community projects initiated with great enthusiasm never quite came off the ground for lack of determination to sustain them.

However, our Congregation is still young. Rosh Hashanah reminds us annually that the end of one era is but the beginning of another. May the New Year witness not only the conclusion of an epoch but the opening of one excelling in distinguished service to our people and its timeless faith. May it bring to all our members the blessings of life, health and achievement in a trail-blazing partnership to enrich Jewish life in America and the world over.

However far destiny may take me, I will always share and seek in some way to contribute to the Congregation's pride in every advance to our common goals of the Torah way of life.'

Days later, the synagogue newsletter carried the following announcement:

> As foreshadowed in our last issue, our Rabbi will be the next Chief Rabbi of the United Hebrew Congregations of the British Commonwealth of Nations. He was unanimously elected to this exalted post at a meeting of the Chief Rabbinate Conference held in London on 11 September. He is to assume his new duties in the spring of 1967.
>
> At a special membership meeting convened at his request on 20 September, the Rabbi read the text of his letter of resignation addressed to the president of the Congregation on the day of his election. In his letter, the Rabbi stated, *inter alia*:
>
> It is with the deepest emotion, and only after the most agonising deliberations in my life, that I wish to tender my resignation as Rabbi of the Congregation,

to take effect in six months' time … My decision was prompted, above all, by the unique challenge of this assignment. The British Chief Rabbinate today represents the most important rabbinical post outside Israel, with ramifications far beyond the confines of its far-flung area of jurisdiction. However hard it is to wrench myself and my family from the unlimited opportunities, happiness and affection we enjoyed in the New World, I felt morally unable to refuse the pleas of Anglo-Jewry, and of numerous friends and communal leaders the world over, to take charge of this historic and commanding office.

I will always look back to the years I was privileged to serve the Congregation as the happiest and most exhilarating in my life. From you personally, and from all leaders, officials and members, I received a measure of respect, love and extraordinary friendship which may well be the envy of any rabbi in the world.

I also realise that my efforts to build up the religious idealism, the intimate relationships and the worldwide reputation of the Congregation have been amply compensated by its immense contribution to my stature and experience, so indispensable in the awesome responsibilities confronting me.

My wife and I, together with our children raised in your midst, contemplate our departure during the ensuing year with very heavy hearts, but confident that the friendships we have forged will prove more solid than the waters of the intervening Atlantic. A part of our lives, hearts and concerns will remain with you.

In a personal statement following his reading of this letter, Dr Jakobovits explained the background and motives for his decision and appealed to members for their solidarity with the Congregation during the transition period ahead, supporting the synagogue and its activities more enthusiastically than ever before, 'so that what has been built up during the past eight years will be zealously preserved and eventually expanded'.

Later that month, in his musaf address on Yom Kippur – one of a series of farewell sermons – Rabbi Jakobovits harked back to his early days at Fifth Avenue, when he had answered his 'call of destiny' from the Congregation's leaders and set about fulfilling his mission:

'Pious, observant Jews have been living in this area [of New York] as individuals for many years. But the history of Orthodoxy, of bearing witness to the vitality of traditional Judaism in this select district, began only with the foundation of our synagogue. Our first and foremost task then, as I saw it, was to be an *edah*, a corporate witness testifying that traditional Judaism is very much alive, and confounding the prophets of doom who forecast long ago that Orthodoxy could not survive in America, certainly not amid the affluence, elegance and modernity of an area as fashionable as ours.

I am proud and happy that in this objective we have largely succeeded, in part beyond our wildest dreams. We have demonstrated a *kiddush hashem* in the most public manner for the world to see. No one, anywhere, will ever again be able to say that strict Orthodoxy is incompatible with modern life, that our unadulterated traditions are only for foreigners and old-fashioned people, that you cannot reach the top of the economic ladder and still remain faithful to all our ancient convictions and practices.

We are the *edim*, 'witnesses', to prove that it can be done, that Judaism can flourish in Fifth Avenue as in Williamsburg or Jerusalem, in the twentieth century as 100 or 1,000 years ago. It is in association with *edah* that spiritual leaders are called *zekeinim*, 'elders' or 'scholars'. My task in helping this Congregation to become an *edah* was to present to you, and through you to the community at large, the magnificent vistas of Jewish learning, some insights into Jewish scholarship, to enhance the appreciation for the Jewish faith and observances.

I regarded my principal assignment here as being your teacher, so that through knowledge you would be truthful witnesses. For on what you do not know for sure you cannot give evidence. These tasks, yours as an *edah* and mine as a *zaken*, we tried to fulfil together at our *mo'adim*, the 'appointed times' when we came together for worship and study, at our services and classes.

Our success or failure as an *edah*, and mine as its *zaken*, cannot be measured by how many people attended our services or paid us compliments, but ultimately by how many worshippers we inspired to discover God in their souls, faith in their hearts, the thrill of Torah learning in their minds, and the beauty of mitzvah performance in their deeds. The true test to prove whether we are an *edah* is whether we served as an example to other congregations, whether we have helped to intensify Jewish education, to support charitable causes, to contribute to the well-being and religious vitality of the wider community.

What congregation anywhere has a greater opportunity, more fame and resources to achieve these goals than ours? A congregation thinking only of itself and its own welfare defaults in its obligations no less than a selfish individual who is unconcerned with the needs of others. To bear testimony, to be a witness, you must convince others, you must carry a jury – or Jewry, in our case – with you. You must serve the public and impersonal cause of justice and truth, of spreading the rule of God and morality.'

The Congregation's farewell dinner to Rabbi and Mrs Jakobovits took place at the Pierre Hotel, New York, on 15 January 1967. The president, Hermann Merkin, presented the Rav with a Sefer Torah and symbolically handed over the Torah mantle, a gift from the membership of the Fifth Avenue Synagogue. In his address, Rabbi Jakobovits preceded his remarks with a quotation from Yoreh De'ah (242:16): 'A disciple taking leave from his teacher should not turn his back to him, but he should reverently walk backwards, with his face turned towards the face of his teacher.' He continued:

'My sainted father, in the name of his illustrious teacher, Rabbi Dr David Hoffmann, of the Berlin Rabbiner Seminar, often reminded me of a profound explanation of the above quotation from the Shulchan Aruch. The law provides for the manner in which a disciple has to depart from his master. Literally and figuratively, he must never turn his back on his teacher. Even as he steps away, his face should be turned to his guide and mentor. However distant he may be, the image of his master should always face and inspire him; his steps in life should always be in his teacher's direction and follow his example.

But there is no law on how a teacher should take leave from his pupil. A Jewish teacher never departs from his disciple. He leaves one he has helped to educate no more than a father leaves his child, for 'whoever teaches another person's child Torah is as if he had begotten him' (Sanhedrin 19b) or 'made him' (99b) – that is, as if he were his own child. A religious guide forever remains attached to those he has instructed and shaped. No law is needed on how *he* should bid farewell.

The Hebrew word used for 'teacher' is *rabbi*, for a rabbi is, above all, essentially a teacher. The law, then, determines how a congregation is to take leave of their rabbi. They are to keep their face turned to their rabbi, and never turn their back on him. That is my most fervent prayer at this moment of parting. Over the memorable years of our partnership, we have co-ordinated our steps in a common direction. We have walked together in the same paths and towards the same goals.

My image in the community became your image, and your reputation became my reputation. What I stood for and strove for was identified with the Fifth Avenue Synagogue in the public mind. This Congregation assumed my likeness and represented my ideals to the outside world – an outlook, a policy, a stature and stance bearing the imprint of my thinking.

My plea to you now is to retain this direction, to remain loyal to the ideals which have distinguished us. Whatever distance may separate us, I hope we will continue to walk in step with one another, facing the same way towards identical goals. May you never deviate from the course we have charted together since the birth of the Congregation, and may none of you ever turn your back on the teachings I have tried to impart to you. Your obligation, according to the Shulchan Aruch, is to keep on facing me, even as you physically depart from me.

But the law says nothing on how a rabbi is to depart from his congregation. A rabbi never leaves his congregation. You will always remain part of myself, my personality, my pride, and my concern. Your successes and your failures, your fame and your faults, will forever reflect on me and bring me personal joy or sorrow, for my heart and soul will continue to be bound up with yours.

Yours is, appropriately, the fifth synagogue or community whose leadership I relinquish since I started my career 25 years ago last month. With each of my former congregations, my wife and I retain affectionate bonds and intimate friendships to this day. We have never really left any of them, and we are still at home in all of them. These bonds with you we pledge to cherish in the future as in the past. When we hear of your *simchot*, we shall rejoice, and in your sorrows – God forbid – we shall grieve with you. To you will always belong a part of our life and our love. In this sense of never leaving you, we think of your welfare rather than of farewell.'

CHAPTER SIX

Election Fever

The Americans have a hallowed formula for Presidential candidates, who must throw their cap into the ring by announcing that they have no ambitions whatever for the Presidency, but if pressed hard enough they might consider it. Rabbi Immanuel Jakobovits seems to have absorbed the tradition during his six years as rabbi of the Fifth Avenue Synagogue, New York, judging by his statements to reporters this week. He has also confirmed that he has been 'unofficially approached' to accept the post [of British Chief Rabbi].

First inklings that a faction was grooming him as a 'favourite son' came in 1962, when he was invited for a lecture tour in Britain by the Jewish Agency's Mizrachi-controlled Department for Torah Education and Culture.

The son of a former dayan of the London Beth Din, Dr Jakobovits has written on Jewish medical ethics and will be most strongly supported by the 'Right wing'.

Dr Jakobovits is now 43. Rabbi Dr Louis Rabinowitz, born in Edinburgh and also a graduate of Jews' College and Etz Chaim, is 15 years his senior, but still full of fire and a serious candidate.

Jewish Chronicle, *12 June 1964*

Other 'likely candidates' named in this report were South African Chief Rabbi Bernard Casper, 48, described as having had 'a varied and distinguished career'; Irish Chief Rabbi Dr Isaac Cohen, 50; and Rabbi Dr Solomon Goldman, minister of London's St John's Wood Synagogue, 'perhaps best known for his quiet scholarship and concern for the broad mass of Orthodox but middle-of-the road Jews, whose position has become increasingly difficult following the polarisation of opinion in the community'.

The *JC* added: 'The community's eventual choice need not necessarily fall on one of these five – some members of the [London] Beth Din are said to have aspirations – but present indications are that they are the most likely.'

In due course, other names began to appear, including that of Israeli diplomat Dr Yaacov Herzog – who commented that he had not been approached by the Chief Rabbinate Committee and that he was unaware his name had been mentioned as a candidate – and Rabbi Dr J. B. Soloveitchik, of Boston, an halachic authority and professor of Talmud and Jewish philosophy at Yeshiva University, New York.

Rabbi Jakobovits, meanwhile, indicated that he 'might be open to a call' to succeed Dr Brodie. He told the *JC* that while he owed a 'great debt' to his Congregation, which had granted him a life contract, he would not let that stand in the way; his attitude to the London position would be 'concerned with the scope of the work rather than a life contract'. He added that he expected to see Sir Isaac Wolfson in New York that week. The president of the United Synagogue was said to be 'scouting several possibilities' in connection with the British Chief Rabbinate.

In March 1965, the *Daily Express* described Dr Jakobovits as 'the man most likely to be Britain's next Chief Rabbi', while the Sunday *Observer* named Dr Herzog as the favourite. In an interview in New York with a *Daily Express* reporter, Rabbi Jakobovits stated: 'I am not a campaigning candidate for this position. But one thing I can tell you is this: whoever gets the job will be a traditionalist.'

Two weeks later, Fifth Avenue's rabbi announced to his Congregation what seemed at the time a momentous decision:

MY DECISION AND OUR CHALLENGE

'The occasional mention of my name in connection with the British Chief Rabbinate goes back to the time when I was still in Ireland. At that time, Rabbi Brodie was due to retire at the age of 65. If I had had any ambition to assume his office, I obviously would not have crossed the Atlantic only to return a few years later. Neither then nor since did I ever feel that my destiny was to be in London.

Over two years ago, as you may recall, I visited England on a lecture tour. It was a thrilling experience; after all, I have some family and many deep roots there. England is not only the land where I studied and held my first positions; it also saved my life when I came there as a refugee from Nazi oppression. In that memorable visit, I also managed to include a brief stay in Ireland – my happy home for ten years. But in making that visit, nothing was further from my mind than to throw my hat into the ring as a candidate for Britain's Chief Rabbinate.

Nevertheless, the visit sparked widespread speculation on the possibility of my choice as Rabbi Brodie's successor, and my denials could never catch up with the distortions of my intentions in certain newspapers. Then it turned quiet again for a while, as it became known that the Chief Rabbi would not retire before 1965.

Last summer, the wheels of the elaborate election machinery were finally set in motion. The Chief Rabbinate Committee of representatives from communities all over Britain and the Commonwealth was convened to discuss the terms of the office, methods of election, and eventually the selection of candidates. To this moment, no names have been officially put forward at all.

With these developments, rumours and speculation emanating from London increased. Many most likely and unlikely names have been widely discussed, ranging from Rabbi [Joseph] Soloveitchik and myself here to several rabbinical and non-rabbinical personalities in Israel, South Africa and England itself. While to this day no official approach has been made to me – or, as far as I know, to anyone else – many people in England, and even here, have urged me to declare my willingness to accept the position if it were offered to me.

At times, I was bombarded with inquiries on my intentions from press reporters on both sides of the Atlantic, Jewish and general. However, I did not deem it necessary to cross my bridges before I got there. Hence, I answered invariably that I was very happy in my present post and that I would prefer to stay here. But if I were ever officially called to London, I would feel morally bound to give the offer my most serious consideration.

This answer I also gave to Sir Isaac Wolfson – whose friendship with me goes back much longer than his presidency of the United Synagogue in London and his *ex officio* chairmanship of the Chief Rabbinate Committee – when, in the course of his last two visits here, he asked me quite informally, and without any commitments on either side, where I might stand if a call came to me. I made it very clear that I would be happy if he found some other adequate candidate and left me out of consideration.

I would conclude this summary by mentioning that, throughout this time, I kept our president constantly informed on all developments. His counsel and understanding have been of immense help to me at all times. We both felt that, without any formal approach, it was entirely premature and unrealistic to discuss the matter officially with our board and Congregation.

But lately we felt it might be wiser to reach a definite decision now than to wait for more pressures to build up. It would be easier for me to say a firm 'No' now than to refuse the position if and when offered to me.

In other words, this is to be the moment of truth. Hence our meeting here. If I confirm my decision in our discussion this evening, it is my definite resolve to communicate it to London tomorrow or the day after tomorrow. I realise, of course, the decision must be mine, and mine alone. No one can make it for me. But you can help me make the right decision. You can give me the certainty in five, ten or 20 years from now that I was right in deciding as I did.

For me, as a rabbi, this is primarily a moral decision. If I am to justify my decision to stay here before my conscience now and in future years, I must be certain that I can achieve at least as much here in terms of religious reconstruction and spiritual leadership as I could in London. This is the crux of the problem confronting me.

Here is my plan: I propose to establish an institute through which, I believe, you and I can best combine our resources to make a significant contribution to enriching Jewish religious life and thought in America. The idea grew out of a highly successful pilot project – our medico-moral seminar which I have conducted regularly every two weeks for over six years under the joint auspices of our synagogue and the Association of Orthodox Jewish Scientists.

I want to harness the intellectual resources of the religious community in a continuous effort to co-ordinate Jewish and secular thinking; to re-examine Judaism through intensive research in the light of contemporary conditions; to open up lines of communication between religious intellectuals and the wider public; to resolve conflicts between Jewish teachings and modern thought: in sum, to create a movement which will blaze new trails of the compatibility and relevance of Judaism to the problems of our morally and religiously bewildered age.

This dream, to be realised, will exact great efforts from all of us. I am prepared to dedicate my energies to the academic and organising part of its fulfilment, but I am not willing or able to assume the responsibility for providing and administering the material requirements. This is an obligation to which I would like you to commit yourselves. Our Congregation is now nearly seven years old. We have spent this first sabbatical cycle on consolidating our own existence. It is now time for us to expand our horizons and to make our creative mark on the community to which we belong.'

Following his Congregation's immediate and enthusiastic commitment to the project (which, in the event, never got off the ground), Dr Jakobovits conveyed his decision to Sir Isaac Wolfson the following day:

'After much soul-searching, I have decided to request you kindly not to consider my name for election as the successor to Chief Rabbi Dr Israel Brodie. You will recall that I have repeatedly and consistently stated, privately and in public, as well as in my informal conversations with you, that my personal preference would be to remain in my present office in New York. I added, however, that I would feel morally bound to give the most serious consideration to any official call your Committee might extend to me. From this attitude I have not wavered ever since my name was first mentioned in connection with the forthcoming election.

While it had been my intention to wait and determine my final decision only if and when the position were formally offered to me, certain more recent developments have prompted me to reach a decision at this time.

You will surely realise that the uncertainties of the situation have continued long beyond the time anticipated by you. In these circumstances, rumours and speculation – not to mention the persistent harassment by reporters and editors – have assumed forms which are increasingly embarrassing to me, to my Congregation and, in my opinion, to the dignity of the Chief Rabbinate itself. Moreover, I felt that the elimination of my name from your consideration at this stage (albeit I was never officially asked to declare my candidacy) would cause also you and your Committee less embarrassment than a negative response in the event of my selection.

These factors merely explain why I have made my decision at this time; they have no bearing on the decision itself. This is based strictly on personal and communal considerations. Above all, I have come to the conclusion that my disposition is better fitted to meeting the challenge of spiritual leadership and academic activities posed to me in my present position at the very heart of the world's largest Jewish community.

The opportunities here offered to me are practically unlimited to pursue my communal and literary interests. For example, my Congregation only quite recently agreed to sponsor an institute of contemporary Jewish thought which I plan to establish with the aim of harnessing the intellectual resources of the religious community for studying and disseminating the relevance of Jewish teachings to present-day thought and living.

Finally, my decision is not meant, of course, in any way to reflect on the high distinction of the British Chief Rabbinate. It ranks, I believe now as before, as by far the best-organised and exalted rabbinical office in the Diaspora today. I will forever be deeply sensible to the great honour done to me by those who thought me worthy to be even considered for so high an office.

I trust that you will understand my position, and I conclude this letter with fervently wishing you every success in your historic deliberations that will determine the religious destiny of Jewry in the British Commonwealth and beyond.

PS: In view of my anxiety to end all speculation involving my name, I propose to release this letter to the press as soon as I have your confirmation of its receipt.'

A month after these events, Dr Yaacov Herzog was named as Rabbi Brodie's successor. Replying to an invitation conveyed to him at his home in Jerusalem by a seven-member delegation from the Chief Rabbinate Conference, he said: 'I am deeply moved by the honour of this unanimous call. After deep contemplation and heart-searching, I have decided to respond. Providence has directed me from the course in life which I have pursued for many years and has guided me back to the world of religious thought, a world with which my innermost essence has always been linked.'

It was later announced that Dr Herzog would arrive in London in the first week of November and be formally inducted a few days later. The installation service would take place at the St John's Wood Synagogue, the traditional place of worship of the Chief Rabbi. Within days, however, the process was thrown into disarray with a statement from the United Synagogue that there would not, after all, be a new Chief Rabbi that year. Dr Herzog had withdrawn due to a 'serious deterioration in his health'. His renunciation of office was made public after a hurried flight by Sir Isaac Wolfson to Switzerland, where the Chief Rabbi-elect had gone from Israel for medical advice. (Dr Herzog subsequently served as director-general of the Prime Minister's Office in Jerusalem until his death in March 1972, aged 50.)

Following Dr Herzog's withdrawal, the names of three candidates quickly re-emerged – Rabbi Goldman, Rabbi Jakobovits, and Rabbi Rabinowitz. A new name was soon added, that of 59-year-old Rabbi Dr Alexander Altmann, the Hungarian-born former Communal Rabbi of Manchester, who had left for the United States in 1959 to become Professor of Jewish Philosophy at Brandeis University, where he was also director of the Institute for Advanced Jewish Studies.

The Israeli religious weekly, *Panim el Panim*, reported on 27 May 1966 that Sir Isaac Wolfson had left for the United States, ostensibly on a business visit, 'but it was impossible to conceal from oneself that the principal "business" for which he was going to America was to persuade Rabbi Jakobovits to withdraw his previous refusal and accept the position of Chief Rabbi.'

According to the paper, Sir Isaac had declared that 'when I return from America, we shall be able to proceed with the election of a Chief Rabbi'.

A year after the retirement of Dr Brodie, and nine months after Dr Herzog's withdrawal, the 36-strong committee of the Chief Rabbinate Conference convened for a meeting on 26 June. Before that date, however, the name of a third serious contender was being mentioned in influential circles, that of 38-year-old Dr Norman Lamm, associate rabbi of the Jewish Centre of New York City and a teacher of philosophy at Yeshiva University. But this speculation was short-lived, for the 26 June meeting issued a unanimous 'call' to Rabbi Jakobovits to become Chief Rabbi.

He responded by saying that he was 'undecided' and doubted whether he could reach an early decision. 'The whole thing has burst upon me with the force of an avalanche', he stated, 'and I need some breathing space.' He added that he would like to consult with 'some friends' before reaching a final decision.

A month later, he and Mrs Jakobovits arrived in London for a week's visit, during which he met a cross-section of communal representatives. On his departure, he stated: 'I was exceedingly pleased with my London visit. I was received with great friendliness by all groups and individuals I have met here. I was ready to meet people from various spheres of the community in order to be able to measure up the local situation. I am now getting the feel of the temperaments.'

Among those he met were members of the Beth Din, the Haham, and other leading rabbis, as well as the honorary officers of the United Synagogue. He also held 'friendly talks' with the chairman of the Union of Liberal and Progressive Synagogues, Mr M. Slowe, and with Mr S. G. Schwab, chairman of the Reform Synagogues of Great Britain, at their request.

Rabbi Jakobovits' response to the Chief Rabbinate committee's invitation was made public within days, in a memorandum to Sir Isaac and his colleagues:

YOUR CALL AND MY RESPONSE
A Personal Preamble

'Your unanimous recommendation to call me to assume the spiritual leadership of British Jewry has honoured me with the most exalted rabbinical distinction as well as challenged me with the world's most exacting and commanding rabbinical responsibility. It has also placed me before the most agonising decision of my life.

I owe it to you, who have selected me for this supreme office, to give you some explanations for my hesitation in confirming my acceptance:

1. To exchange the peace, security, happiness and freedom of my present position for the imponderables of an unknown future will involve a very heavy personal sacrifice which could not be compensated by any added wealth or fame of themselves. I presently enjoy all the comforts and honours any rabbi could wish for. I have no factions or dissension to contend with. I am a free man, accountable to no one except my conscience. I can say what I want, write what I wish, dress as I please, and lecture where I like. Whether inside or outside my congregation, my time is devoted exclusively to constructive and literary efforts.

It will also not be easy to wrench myself and my family from our present congenial environment, particularly to transplant my children to a new soil probably offering them less educational and other facilities than they have here. Indeed, the two eldest of my six children would in all likelihood have to stay behind to complete their studies.

2. While I am fully aware of the unique and historic challenge the Chief Rabbinate would offer me, I am also all too conscious of my own limitations. This is no false modesty, but simply a questioning self-assessment in the light of the awesome responsibilities that would devolve on me in such a key position at this critical time in Jewish and human history.

It should, therefore, not be unreasonable if, before I commit myself to such a gigantic task, I reassure myself that the challenge is not entirely beyond my capacities, by personal discussions with those on whose support the success of my work will largely depend. I want my London visit to convince me that conditions exist for doing justice to my assignment.

3. Above all, I regard my ability to resolve the existing religious crisis in Anglo-Jewry as a crucial test of the community's confidence in my leadership and my own confidence in measuring up to the skills needed in the discharge of my duties.

I cannot work in a climate of continuous tension, nor under the pressure of abuse, subversion and misrepresentation. Communal peace, goodwill and unity are indispensable prerequisites to my success in the office, and therefore to my acceptance. The dignity of the Chief Rabbinate, too, cannot be upheld in a community rent by ill-will and destructive conflicts. I am not prepared, or able, to preside over a constant succession of quarrels and hostilities in which the community will be reduced to a shambles, my office to a partisan battle headquarters, and my health to a wreck.

To sum up my conclusions, I deem it my ineluctable moral duty to heed your call and to dedicate all my energies to your challenge, provided the essential conditions for a successful incumbency, as listed below, can be secured.

A. Resolving the religious crisis

I believe I can assume that all parties to the recent conflict are by now thoroughly tired of the costly strife, disenchanted with the sterile results achieved, saddened by the bitterness and disunity which have disrupted the once-solid structure of the community, and anxious to find an honourable solution.

For my part, I am prepared to go a very long way in my quest for a lasting reconciliation, based on friendliness and mutual trust as well as on respect for our sacred traditions. Of course, I realise there will have to be some give-and-take on a few matters of substance, but primarily I think the situation calls for a new outlook and attitude on all sides, the creation of an atmosphere of goodwill, and an amicable 'agreement to disagree' within some well-defined limits.

It would be premature at this stage to spell out in detail the proposals for a formula I have in mind. Meanwhile, the following basic terms of an understanding should not be beyond reach or reason:

1. The 'Left wing' must agree
   (a) to respect the Chief Rabbinate as an institution which is and will remain Orthodox, reflecting the religious loyalties, if not necessarily the views, of the overwhelming majority of religious Jews;
   (b) to leave the determination and interpretation of Jewish law to duly qualified experts, and to oppose any incitement against their rulings by pressure groups, newspapers or especially individuals who themselves neither acknowledge nor practise the dictates of the halachah;
   (c) to refrain from subversion, abuse and denigration directed at any established communal institution or its leaders; and

(d) to make the maximum positive contribution to the enrichment and unity of Jewish life.

2. The 'Right wing' must agree
   (a) to look upon the Chief Rabbinate as serving to unite all segments of the community;
   (b) to accept that dissent from tradition and authority is an inescapable fact of modern life, to be most effectively met by friendly persuasion and intelligent argument, not by denunciation and ostracism;
   (c) to concentrate its energies on enhancing its own position and public respect, not on attacking others; and
   (d) to work together with others in all areas that have no bearing on halachic considerations.

3. The Chief Rabbi must agree
   (a) to revise the functions of the Chief Rabbinate (see Section B below) so that it will meet present-day needs and command the respect of the entire community;
   (b) to promote goodwill and moderation without sacrifice of any principles he is appointed to defend;
   (c) to seek common ground for joint enterprises among all factions, and not to limit his services to those who agree with him; and
   (d) to endeavour to establish a *modus vivendi* with those who, while not submitting completely to the rabbinic jurisdiction of his office, are prepared morally, if not financially, to support it.

B. Functions of the Chief Rabbinate

The Chief Rabbinate, as a nineteenth-century institution with even far older roots, clearly requires some far-reaching modifications to meet the conditions and challenges of the present time. In its existing form, it was conceived nearly 100 years ago to provide the more or less homogeneous communities of an entire country with a single spiritual leader wielding rabbinic authority, while all other occupants of pulpits were invested merely with the status of ministers and preachers.

Since then, the Anglo-Jewish community has vastly grown in numbers and diversity, and this growth must be reflected in updating the functions both of the Chief Rabbinate and of the ministry. The manifold needs and trends of today can no longer be served by only one fully recognised rabbi.

While I must again defer detailed proposals on this reorganisation until I have thoroughly familiarised myself with local conditions, I may here present a general outline of the required changes as I see them.

1. The Chief Rabbi's foremost charge, claiming priority over ceremonial, administrative and juridical duties, must be the exercise of spiritual leadership. He must mobilise the community's religious and intellectual resources to make Judaism vibrant and relevant to the issues of our times. He must direct the interpretation of Jewish thought in contemporary terms, and he must stimulate an interest in Jewish living and thinking, especially among the youth and

intellectuals. He must frequently consult with his colleagues to evolve the most meaningful form of synagogue services, wedding ceremonies and other ministrations. At the same time, he is primarily responsible for strengthening the religious loyalties of the masses and for broadening their understanding of Judaism. He must also project a creative image of Jewish moral and religious teachings in the world at large.

Accordingly, a major part of his time should be devoted to regular meetings with rabbis and ministers, visits to Jewish student bodies at the universities, discussions with various professional groups, popular lectures, and literary activities.

He should also establish high-level contacts with the supreme rabbinical leaders in Israel, America and other countries to consult and pronounce on Jewish religious policies and moral attitudes of universal Jewish significance – an acute need so far entirely unmet.

These pursuits require much contemplation, a free mind, and a prior claim on his time.

I therefore propose reducing all other functions to a minimum. If congregations or organisations want the Chief Rabbi for lectures, conference addresses, consultations on religious direction, or even debates, they should be free to call on his services. But if they seek his presence for the opening of synagogues, the induction of ministers, the presiding at meetings or the arbitration of communal disputes, they may not find him so accessible. These duties must, in the main, be delegated to others.

2. This should be accomplished by a drastic diffusion of responsibilities. The function of the Beth Din, as the authoritative interpreters of halachah, including the administration of shechitah and kashrut, should be augmented by a Council of Rabbis and Ministers to assist the Chief Rabbi in the formulation of religious policies, directives and activities, and in the discharge of his responsibilities in other areas. Such a Council should be composed of ten to 20 members, serving in rotation for two to four years. I also envisage setting up a 'Chief Rabbi's Cabinet' consisting of six rabbis and ministers appointed to take charge, respectively, of Jewish education, liaison with students, ceremonial functions, inter-faith contacts, inter-Jewish co-operation, and Israel affairs. To be effective and to contribute to raising the ministry's status and prospects of promotion, these services must be adequately compensated.

3. To command the respect and loyalty of all groups, and to be equally accessible to them, I believe the Chief Rabbi should have no political affiliations. He would, of course, lend his special support to religious organisations, whether political or not, but only as Chief Rabbi, not as a member or an honorary officer.

Likewise, the Chief Rabbi should make all reasonable efforts to keep his office outside and above communal controversies and organisational disputes. In part, this will inevitably be achieved by shifting the main burden of his functions from representational and administrative duties to the spiritual direction and instruction of the community.'

The memorandum had its desired effect, clearing the way for Dr Jakobovits' formal appointment some six weeks later:

APPROVED WITHOUT DISSENT

Dr Immanuel Jakobovits is the new Chief Rabbi of the United Hebrew Congregations. His appointment was approved, without dissent or discussion, by the Chief Rabbinate Conference which met at Woburn House, London, on Sunday. But he will not take up his duties until next spring, a few months after his forty-sixth birthday. Until then, he will remain in New York, where he has been minister of the Fifth Avenue Synagogue since 1958.

Moving the adoption of the report and recommendations of the selection committee, the chairman, Sir Isaac Wolfson, stressed that when it met in June, he had refrained from giving his personal conclusions until he had heard the opinions of everybody present. 'It was my intention on that occasion to ensure that it was your committee who made the choice and that it could never again be said that the choice was mine and that the committee had merely "rubber-stamped" my decision.'

Sir Isaac stated that he had been immensely heartened by the fact that the choice of the committee had been unanimous and that it had coincided with the views expressed to him earlier both by the members of the London Beth Din – now acting as the Chief Rabbinate-in-Commission – and by the representatives of the ministry. He also praised the decision by Dr Jakobovits not to give an affirmative answer to the 'call' extended to him in June until he was able to come to London and 'to see for himself what prospects there were of his being successful in unifying the community under his leadership'.

Sir Isaac added: 'I think it would be fair to sum up the visit by saying, "He came, he saw and he conquered". He made a very great impression on all sides, and I am now quite certain that his decision to postpone giving an answer was extremely wise and will ultimately prove of enormous benefit to the community.' In accepting the British Chief Rabbinate, Dr Jakobovits was making 'a great personal sacrifice' and was not at all dismayed 'by the awesome responsibilities of the office'.

The chairman added that what the new Chief Rabbi longed to achieve here was 'a climate of friendship, of harmony and of people striving together to maintain our Orthodox standards and traditions and to avoid all attempts at dissension which could be so harmful in the cause which we all want to serve'. They must be prepared, Sir Isaac urged, to ensure that the Chief Rabbi was given every opportunity to evince his leadership and full support in everything he undertook. 'So great is my confidence in the rabbi whom we have chosen today that I am certain that, when he takes up his office next spring, we shall see some real awakening of the spirit of unity which is so much to be desired.

'But you and I – and indeed every man of goodwill – must take care to ensure that when we appoint a leader, we follow the lead that he gives us. We must give him the atmosphere of communal peace, of confidence and of strength. We must be prepared to be tolerant when he is tolerant, and firm when he is firm. We must ensure that he is not involved in conflicts and, when questions arise, we must learn to seek his counsels and follow his guidance.'

Jewish Chronicle, *16 September 1966*

That same week, the Chief Rabbi-elect issued the first of a number of 'messages' to the British Jewish community (and, subsequently, to various factions within it, including the general Zionists, the religious Zionists, the Agudists and the Progressives):

MY MESSAGE TO ANGLO-JEWRY

'In humbly accepting your call to the Diaspora's most important rabbinate, I am profoundly sensitive to the supreme honour conferred upon me, a distinction matched only by the equally great burdens and responsibilities imposed by the office.

My hesitation was due partly to doubts of my adequacy in the face of so awesome a challenge, and partly to the agonising difficulty of deciding to wrench myself and my family from the immense opportunities and happiness offered us in the New World, where I enjoyed all the honour and comfort any rabbi could wish for.

I also wanted first to assure myself that conditions for a constructive incumbency existed, or could be created. To this end, I recently visited London, where I met religious and lay leaders of all sections of Jewry. Their invariably friendly welcome and the encouraging reaction to my ideas and projects have convinced me that – with dynamic and sincere leadership on my part, combining firmness in principle with tolerance in approach – I can reasonably count on the loyal support of the overwhelming majority of Orthodox Jewry and on a substantial measure of respect and understanding from all others.

Chief rabbinates are today established in virtually all countries of our dispersion, in Israel no less than in the Diaspora, on both sides of the Iron Curtain (with the notable exception of America, for special historical reasons). What makes the British Chief Rabbinate unique are its unbroken continuity over the three centuries of the Anglo-Jewish settlement, the extraordinary influence it has exerted on moulding the character and religious life of Anglo-Jewry, and the exceptionally widespread loyalty and recognition it commands.

The office has prevailed through recent national and communal upheavals with remarkable strength. The transformation of the British Empire into the Commonwealth has scarcely affected the Chief Rabbinate's area of jurisdiction. On the contrary, thanks to the all-too-little appreciated labours of my revered predecessor, the office and its Beth Din now constitute the principal rabbinate of Western Europe, as the focal point for the direction and co-ordination of religious policies in communities counting over one million Jews.

From the more recent internal tribulations, too, the Chief Rabbinate has emerged more widely known and acknowledged than ever before, among both Jews and non-Jews the world over, as I can testify from the unprecedented interest in the office lately manifested in America and elsewhere.

It will be my sacred charge to preserve these traditions and to consolidate these newer gains. There never was a more urgent need than now for a strong Chief Rabbinate as the main unifying and direction-giving element in a community suffering increasing fragmentation and polarisation.

But I also recognise that some far-reaching changes will be required to meet the conditions and challenges of our turbulent times. In its present form, the Chief Rabbinate is a creation of the nineteenth century, when Anglo-Jewry was a more or less homogeneous community. Since then, it has grown vastly in numbers and diversity.

It is futile to hanker after the days of Adler, or even Hertz, for we live in an altogether different world, beset by new social, intellectual and religious problems. The functions of my office must be remodelled to reflect these changes and to grapple with the realities of the 1960s.

For instance, I contemplate shifting the major emphasis from ceremonial and administrative work to spiritual leadership in the narrower and truer sense. Delegating and sharing with my colleagues many responsibilities, I hope to devote my time and energies primarily to the presentation and interpretation of Judaism in the contemporary world, using every possible means and opportunity to enhance the appreciation of Jewish thinking and living by educational and literary efforts.

I will be more interested in the provision of more and better Jewish schools and adult-education facilities than in consecrating new synagogues; and more concerned with the Jewish spirit pervading the homes of newly-weds than with who 'authorises' their marriages, as long as they are performed strictly 'according to the law of Moses and Israel'.

To discuss Jewish views on modern social and moral perplexities with Jewish students or professional groups will attract me more than to arbitrate communal disputes or to involve myself personally in kosher meat price-fixing. To win over those who dissent or stray from the Jewish tradition will be closer to my heart than to denounce or ostracise them; and rather than aspire to be the community's principal fund-raiser or after-dinner speaker, I will be anxious to restore the supremacy of religion in the Jewish national purpose, in the life of every Jew, and in the bonds between Israel and the Diaspora.

I also envisage periodic consultations with the leading rabbis of Israel and America to discuss and pronounce on universal Jewish issues – a pressing need so far entirely unmet.

In communal relations, I intend to found my policies on the conviction that the Torah was not given to Orthodox Jews only but that it is the common heritage and charge of all whose ancestors once stood at Mount Sinai; that every Jew is his brother's keeper and partner, sharing in the credit for all achievements and in the blame for any lapses found among our people; and that every member of the community can and must make some contribution to enrich Jewish life and to promote the peace of Israel.

My goal is a vibrant, creative and hallowed community to which every British Jew will be proud to belong, and in which I will be privileged to occupy, not the most unenviable post in the world (as a few pessimists fear), but the most enviable rabbinical position sustained by friendship and goodwill.

As I will gradually formulate my plans and decisions on becoming familiarised with the local scene, it is my intention always to take the community into my confidence. I know that in this democratic age, rabbis, like all opinion-makers, must seek to carry public opinion with them to make their leadership effective. While Gallup polls cannot determine Jewish law – any more than scientific laws are validated by popular votes – an attitude of trust and understanding can determine public loyalties.

Symbolic of the revised role of the Chief Rabbinate in the community will be several material innovations. A Chief Rabbinate Centre, complete with dignified office, conference and library facilities, will shortly be erected as a munificent gift to the community by Sir Isaac Wolfson and Mr Charles Wolfson. Also thanks to Sir Isaac's generosity, the Chief Rabbinate will enjoy professional services and other amenities to facilitate intimate and effective communications between the Chief Rabbi and his far-flung 'constituents'.

In dedicating myself, then, to taking charge of the religious government of British Jewry and its sister-communities in the Commonwealth, I call on you, as Moses did before me, to support my hands, both on the Right and on the Left, to assure our joint victory over the Amalek of ignorance, apathy, strife and despair. At this time, I ask, first of all, for your confidence, your trust that all our problems, grave as they may be, can and will be resolved through high idealism, hard work and mutual understanding.

To generate this confidence, and to banish all counsels of doom and doubt, is my immediate task, to be accomplished even before I assume my new duties. On these Days of Judgement, I will fervently invoke the blessings of my Creator that He may grant me the courage and vision worthily to be His chief servant in your midst and to merit the confidence you have reposed in me.

Together with my wife and children, I look forward to sharing life and its challenges with you in the ensuing year. May it be the first of an era to shed lustre on the history of Anglo-Jewry and to open a creditable chapter in the chronicles of our holy people and its timeless faith. My heartfelt wishes for a happy and prosperous New Year to you, the entire House of Israel, and all mankind.'

FLASHBACK FOUR

London

There was a wide ocean between Anglo-Jewry and me and, inevitably, my feelings of involvement with the British scene there were becoming weaker. Our children were being educated in New York and felt very much at home with their friends at the intensive Jewish day-schools they attended.

Of the immediate family, only my brother Joseph remained in London, while all of Amélie's brothers and sisters, as well as uncles, aunts and cousins, had now settled in New York. On my side, Lotti's, George's and Solomon's families helped to fill our lives, so our interests centred on the New World, where it seemed that we were permanently settled. As with all other immigrants, we felt we had finally arrived. If we were one day to leave America, it could only be to Israel – always my preferred ultimate destination.

I was still a regular reader of the *Jewish Chronicle* and noted with pain its strident hostility to the Orthodox rabbinate, coupled with its relentless advocacy of the theology of Rabbi Dr Louis Jacobs. I had every sympathy with Chief Rabbi Brodie, but it was only the sentiments of a far-distant friend.

Some glimpses at his election, late in 1947, are relevant here. Sir Robert Waley Cohen, president of the United Synagogue for ten years from 1942, had for long been at loggerheads with Chief Rabbi Joseph Hertz. Both were dynamic, and headstrong personalities. On Dr Hertz's death in 1946, Sir Robert resolved never again to face similar strife and insubordination. He decided that future Chief Rabbis would no longer serve for life (Hertz had told him on one occasion that 'Chief Rabbis never retire, and they only rarely die!') and would retire on reaching 70.

On the death of Hertz, three candidates emerged, or at least were publicly canvassed. Dr Alexander Altmann, then Manchester's Communal Rabbi, was the most scholarly and enjoyed a worldwide reputation. But for many he was too Germanic. Rabbi Dr Kopul Rosen was a popular orator and, although still young, was widely admired for his forthright leadership. But Sir Robert's preferred man was Israel Brodie, whose mellow disposition promised to give the community a period of tranquillity.

The irony of this was to become evident some 15 years later, when the Chief Rabbinate became locked in the fiercest controversy of its centuries-old history.

Rabbi Brodie, as I have mentioned, had been my teacher for a short period while serving as tutor at Jews' College, following his ministry in Australia and then as senior chaplain to HM Forces. At his induction at the New Synagogue in 1948, I led the ministerial procession as rabbi of the oldest United Synagogue congregation. Later, as Chief Rabbi of Ireland, I worked closely with him at the Conference of European Rabbis, over which he presided since its foundation in 1957, and which I attended that year in Amsterdam. On his death, I was to succeed him as the Conference's president.

Louis Jacobs himself, by his increasing detachment from the Orthodox rabbinical world and his subsequent association with the Conservative (Masorti) movement, showed that, whatever his scholarship and sincerity, he represented a trend that could not be accommodated within contemporary Orthodoxy.

His prime misfortunes were his two leading supporters – Ewen Montagu and the *Jewish Chronicle*. Montagu had succeeded to the presidency of the United Synagogue in 1954, having been vice-president under Waley Cohen, and was thus a major personality when it came to the selection of the next Chief Rabbi. He was a member of one of the old Anglo-Jewish families who had long dominated the communal scene. At one time, this had been of no great moment, since most United Synagogue members – little better than them in standards of knowledge and observance – were quite happy with the state of affairs, the grandees combining strong feelings of communal obligation with their hereditary claims.

But times were changing. A new generation, combining higher Jewish standards and Zionist enthusiasm with little respect for the cousinhood of yesteryear, was gradually assuming control. Montagu hoped that, by appointing a Chief Rabbi with a less rigorous outlook, he would restore the community to the decorous indifference that had prevailed in the more fashionable synagogues during the Adlerian era.

The *Jewish Chronicle*, too, looked back to an earlier era, but for a different reason – because those times seemed to have conformed more closely to the usages of American Conservatism. The union of two such irresistible forces seemed to ensure easy victory.

But Montagu was defeated by history. His resignation from the presidency in 1962, over policy differences, was a clear indication of a decisive swing in public opinion. The *Jewish Chronicle*, for its part, failed in its campaign because it ignored the old axiom that you cannot fool all the people all the time. Its obsession with Rabbi Jacobs had distorted the whole balance of the journal, which persisted in seeing a cataclysmic theological struggle in what was basically a social and organisational clash blown up out of all proportion.

What I, from the distance, found most nauseating in the paper's campaign was its constant reference to 'all thinking Jews' supporting Dr Jacobs' views. This turned not only Rabbi Brodie, but Rabbi Isidore Epstein in England, Rabbi Joseph Soloveitchik in America, and such top-ranking pre-war scholars as David Hoffmann, Adolf Berliner and Ezriel Hildesheimer, not to mention Samson Raphael Hirsch, into 'unthinking Jews' because they were, like numerous others, strictly traditional in thought and practice. I exposed this arrogance in my one intervention from America in the affair.

Chief Rabbi Brodie had no idea of the importance of public relations, or perhaps despaired of competing with the ceaseless barrage of his adversaries. The London Beth Din varied the 'no comment' of its clerk with the provocative outbursts of Dayan Morris Swift.

In fact, however, Dr Brodie did a remarkable job without necessarily planning it. He was seen everywhere that his multifarious duties demanded. He was invariably courteous, gentlemanly and impressive; his diction was cultured and mellifluous, even if the content of his remarks tended to be somewhat thin.

It was difficult to associate this perfect father-figure with the obscurantist ogre vilified almost weekly in the *Jewish Chronicle*. And when, as often happened, the Chief Rabbi was accompanied by his wife Fanny, the very personification of ladylike dignity and charm, the favourable impression was complete. She, at any rate, made no secret of the near-terror with which she anticipated every Friday morning the newest issue of the *Jewish Chronicle* and the unending torrent of criticism in its news, editorial and correspondence columns.

At the end of 1961, the Brodies were on a cruise, necessitated by the Chief Rabbi's ill-health. Communal gossip had it that he no longer felt able to resist the pro-Jacobs clamour, would announce from abroad that he had withdrawn his opposition to the appointment of Rabbi Jacobs as principal of Jews' College, and would follow this up with notification of his own resignation from office. Dr Jacobs' progression to the Chief Rabbinate would thus be assured, since no other candidate of similar stature existed – as the community was being led to believe – or, in any event, would wish to become involved in such a poisoned atmosphere.

The impasse was broken by a most unlikely person. Rabbi Samuel Sperber, a quiet, retiring scholar, never accomplished much in the material sphere but was greatly admired by the few who appreciated his depth of learning and power of teaching. He was the London representative of the Jewish Agency's Torah department, which worked from the office of the Mizrachi movement and seemed, though was not, part of it.

Rabbi Sperber's budget covered the expense of bringing over each year a visiting scholar, who would address academics, groups or societies, usually under Mizrachi auspices. He had the idea of inviting me for late 1962 and, with very definite intent, making this a more public and ambitious project than usual.

For this he needed co-operation, and he turned, quite certain of success, first to communal activist Norman Cohen and then to Cyril Domb, a leading Orthodox scientist and professor of theoretical physics at King's College, London. Domb had an entrée to the B'nai B'rith Hillel Foundation, which, after a disastrous lecture from Robert Graves the previous year, was anxious to restore the balance by inviting a traditionalist for its next annual lecture.

The three were joined by Betty Boxer, chairman of the Jewish Marriage Council, an organisation that turned out to be the most enduring achievement of my Great Synagogue days. A meeting was held at Rabbi Sperber's home and a schedule of lectures drawn up.

Then Professor Domb pointed out that I had to be made aware that more was at stake than a mere lecture tour. If I came, saw and conquered, and then returned happily to the United States showing no interest in the Anglo-Jewish scene, the result would be worse for the Orthodox than if I had not come in the first place. No one, he added, could possibly write such a letter. Norman Cohen said that he could – and did, the very next morning.

Some of our subsequent correspondence has survived and has helped me to recall my attitudes at that time. I accepted Rabbi Sperber's invitation, and the visit was successful; yet I could not really be certain that I wished to exchange the settled satisfaction of my life in New York for the hazards of the British Chief Rabbinate.

My feelings about the office derived from two opposing camps, and neither was reassuring. During my Jews' College days, and in my early years in the ministry, I had enjoyed limited contact with Dr Hertz and had moved in circles where some, at least, positively venerated the office. But by the time I knew him, he was an elderly widower, in indifferent health, and far from placid in character.

As I have said, he was on exceedingly bad terms with Sir Robert Waley Cohen, and on poorish terms with large numbers of other individuals and organisations. He still wielded considerable influence, yet one felt that he was isolated and unhappy and had derived more satisfaction from his literary achievements than from his Chief Rabbinate. It struck me as a dreary, almost pathetic, end to a lifetime of courageous endeavour.

At my yeshivah, the whole concept of the Chief Rabbinate had run counter to all my teachers' principles. For them, the leading rabbi of an area had to be the one whose rabbinic skills were the most prodigious. The idea that a lay-appointed rabbi could be empowered to lay down the law to dayanim and every type of rabbi and minister under his jurisdiction had no traditional basis in halachah.

The idea of a rabbinical head over an entire country, or even beyond, had ample precedents from the patriarchs and exilarchs in talmudic and gaonic times to Chief Rabbinates in most major Jewish communities (excluding America) in modern times. Nevertheless, it seemed demeaning of rabbinical office that the holder should be obliged to spend so much time on social and representational activities, involving contacts far beyond the normal confines of Orthodoxy, or even incompatible with them.

Both these strands had led me to the conclusion that the British Chief Rabbinate was something to which I had no wish to aspire. Indeed, the feeling had been deepened by my knowledge of the ceaseless attacks launched on Rabbi Brodie over the preceding few years.

Yet the office, if at times almost suffocating with protocol and responsibilities, also possessed an enormous and unrivalled prestige, and a vast potential to lead and to influence. Duke's Place, Ireland and Fifth Avenue had all been offered to me, and I had no reason to repine at the outcome. I would not fight or intrigue to become Chief Rabbi, but I was not sure that, under the right conditions, I would refuse an invitation.

As Rabbi Brodie was not scheduled to retire until June 1965, there was ample time for rumour-mongering, press conjectures and interviews of interested parties to be provided for public delectation. Following the veto of Dr Jacobs' appointment as principal of Jews' College, there had been an abortive attempt by his supporters to reappoint him to his old synagogue, the New West End, despite the fact that no certificate to act as minister was forthcoming from the Chief Rabbi.

Sir Isaac Wolfson was now president of the United Synagogue, and in April 1964 the organisation's council voted down an effort to overturn this second veto. The result was the withdrawal of the Jacobs supporters from the New West End and the subsequent founding of the New London Synagogue. It also meant that Jacobs was no longer in the running, if ever he was, for the Chief Rabbinate.

Some of his support shifted to Rabbi Dr Louis Rabinowitz, who was perceived as being more moderate in his views than other possible candidates (his militant Zionist stance seems to have been tacitly ignored). Among his various endowments, he was an effective fund-raiser, which no doubt increased his standing in many Zionist circles. In that respect, he clearly outclassed me.

The local Mizrachi leaders had been most affable during my London visit, but their more politicised Israeli leadership felt that my Zionist loyalties were somewhat vague. I had never identified with the Mizrachi movement, or, indeed, with any other party, and independence of thought was not regarded as any sort of virtue in the religio-political set-up. But it was only later that I was to become – and publicly to declare myself – an outright opponent of the alliance between religion and party politics, and, therefore, of all religious parties in Israel.

Israel, in fact, now produced a quite remarkable candidate – Dr Yaacov Herzog, the second son of Dr Isaac Herzog, former Chief Rabbi of Israel and, before that, of Ireland. The younger Herzog was an admirable rabbinical scholar but, although holding semichah, had never had any practical experience in the rabbinate. He had been an adviser to several Israeli Prime Ministers and was tipped to be the next Ambassador to the United States.

Rumour credited his mother with a burning desire to see him carry on the rabbinical tradition, inherited from both his father and his maternal grandfather, Dayan Samuel Hillman. His appointment might have been an outstanding success; it would certainly have been unprecedented.

Yaacov Herzog's nomination was of special interest to me, for several reasons. We had been friends ever since we studied together at the Etz Chaim Yeshivah, just before the Second World War. I had always rated him as one of our leading intellects, and the only statesman in or near Israel's seats of power to see contemporary Jewish events through specifically Jewish eyes.

I thought that his London appointment, surprising as it was, might restore the respect for the office after the denigration it had suffered for many years. Even in retrospect, I felt that his acceptance helped to break the back of the pro-Jacobs campaign. I was later to be the beneficiary of this, but meanwhile was relieved that his appointment had taken the pressure and the focus of attention off me.

Potential Chief Rabbis do not present formal applications or submit to formal vetting; it is all supposed to be done with subtlety and diplomacy. I do not think, however, that these skills were much in evidence, although the early approaches to me remained discreet. But that did not stop communal dithering and press speculation involving my name, causing me some embarrassment.

In due course, I wrote to Sir Isaac Wolfson, withdrawing my name from consideration. On 31 May 1965, Dr Herzog was formally appointed. Unfortunately, he developed serious health problems and was never able to take up the post, resigning the appointment on 7 September, just two months before he was due to assume office. He never fully recovered, and he died in 1972.

Sir Isaac was understood to be bitterly dismayed by the disappointing outcome of his efforts, but had reluctantly to steel himself to resume the search. The field, though, had narrowed. Rabbi Rabinowitz, for one, was nearly 60, and the support he had enjoyed from certain circles was regarded as a doubtful boon.

Sir Isaac was a fairly frequent worshipper at the Fifth Avenue Synagogue, and his overtures to me became more insistent, while my reluctance to commit myself remained equally determined. However, on 26 June 1966, I was unanimously chosen by the Chief Rabbinate selection committee.

The endorsement of the full Chief Rabbinate Council, composed of delegates from all the 200-odd congregations under the jurisdiction of the office, remained only a formality. Most of the delegates represented United Synagogue congregations in London, a number of provincial communities in Britain and Northern Ireland, and several congregations in Australia and New Zealand.

Just three weeks before this, an event occurred which subsequently no one seemed able, or anxious, to recall, but which was one of the most decisive events in the history of the Chief Rabbinate. As it happened in Scotland, however, it made less impact than a London crisis would have done.

The Garnethill Synagogue in Glasgow had for long been in a state of virtual insurrection. Its minister, the Rev Dr I. K. Cosgrove, its lay leadership and, it was alleged, most of the members, were totally alienated from the Glasgow rabbinical authorities and had been assiduously canvassed to link up with Rabbi Louis Jacobs.

In an atmosphere of excited acrimony, a meeting was held on 6 June 1966, to effect the required constitutional changes. A motion to withdraw from 'the ecclesiastical authorities as recognised by the London United Synagogue' was carried by 181 votes to 133, less than the two-thirds majority required.

However, a second motion, 'to make contact with other like-minded congregations, including the New London Synagogue', was defeated by an even greater majority, 186 to 128. At the end of a campaign of unparalleled ferocity, directed at the most disaffected of congregations, the pro-Jacobs camp proved to be less popular than the Chief Rabbinate.

The threat of a major secession disappeared. None happened, nor was even threatened, throughout my period of office.

(To anticipate a little, all that Garnethill had really wanted was independence, and a fretful opposition continued until peace broke out as a result of my first pastoral visit to Glasgow, soon after my appointment. Following my presentation to a packed membership meeting, I was put through a gruelling cross-examination. But I could sense the tide of support moving strongly in my favour, and before the meeting was over, Dr Cosgrove made a moving declaration of loyalty. He became a valued personal friend and maintained his full support of my office until his death.)

Even at this late stage, I was still haunted by anxieties over the overwhelming responsibilities I was assuming. Amélie was even more fearful, especially when she recalled what had happened to the families of former incumbents. I consulted widely, turning to trusted leaders and friends in several countries, including the dayanim and leading rabbis in London, Rabbi Soloveitchik and others in New York, and Chief Rabbi Issar Yehudah Unterman in Israel.

They all urged me to accept – mostly because they genuinely believed I would succeed, but in some cases, I suspect, because they wanted to avoid the selection of a less acceptable candidate.

In the end, the decisive judgement came from my father-in-law, Rabbi Elie Munk, in Paris. He asserted – perhaps ruled is the better word – that morally I was duty-bound to accept the challenge and had no right to refuse it, lest the office fall into the wrong hands.

I was swayed, moreover, by the feeling that I could never justify refusing to serve the community in a country that had saved my life. Gradually, there seemed to be an inevitability about it all, and it made my final acceptance inescapable.

There followed some hectic communications on a visit to London, constant press interviews, and the drafting of 'messages' to the four principal Jewish (including Reform) journals, promising and seeking co-operation on matters uniting us. And I was still rabbi of a busy New York congregation, with my diary further loaded by what seemed an endless succession of farewell parties, lectures and dinners organised by friends inside and outside the congregation.

On looking through my files, I am struck by the enormous amount of time I spent at this period trying to ensure harmonious relationships with other Orthodox rabbinates and synagogal organisations in London.

Rabbi Dr Eliezer Kirzner had been appointed Principal Rabbi (Rav Rashi in Hebrew, though for a short while they called him Chief Rabbi) of the Federation of Synagogues. This was, and remains, a self-important body which typifies the enduring power of organisations to continue operating well after their original purpose has been fulfilled and outlived.

When the Federation was founded in 1887, and for perhaps half a century thereafter, it served a vital function by catering for the waves of newcomers who neither could nor wanted to be absorbed by the 'English' United Synagogue, established 17 years earlier. But in the 1930s and 40s, and certainly by the 1960s, all distinctions had disappeared, and most Federation members – including its president – worshipped in United Synagogue congregations.

In practice, the Federation retained its dwindling membership mainly through its burial society, and the Orthodox community could have been enormously strengthened through a merger with the United Synagogue. But personal ambition and communal inertia worked in the opposite direction, to the present day.

The continuous urge to be a parallel body to the United Synagogue, despite a marked disparity in size and activity, was always leading to communal friction. As Rabbi Kirzner was resident in New York, I thought it a good opportunity to reach a *modus vivendi*.

In fact, while still in New York, I held a series of meetings with him and Sir Isaac Wolfson, and we reached a comprehensive agreement to eliminate the utterly unnecessary duplication – at such heavy cost in wasted budgets and communal strife – of separate batei din and kashrut and shechitah authorities. Sadly, the arrangement was repudiated or sabotaged by the Federation's lay leaders before it could be operated.

Subsequent attempts to secure any form of rationalisation, or even co-operation, came to grief, on a collision course with the same rocks of petty self-aggrandisement. But it is only fair to add that the rigidity of the United Synagogue's leadership did not help to advance an accommodation.

For instance, the last stumbling block to an understanding might easily have been removed by inviting the president of the Federation to become a vice-president of the London Board for Shechitah, but this was deemed to defy the Board's constitution. It did not allow a former employee (the Federation president had been a shochet) to be an honorary officer, as if changing the constitution would not have been wiser – and easier – than threatening the institution by interminable wrangling and communal strife.

Similarly, I worked to effect an arrangement with Rabbi Dr Solomon Gaon, the Haham of the Spanish and Portuguese Jews' Congregation in London. We had been fellow-students, and remained good friends. In the end, some nebulous formulae of good intentions were produced, but they were hardly worth the time and trouble involved.

Co-operation always signifies a loss of prestige to interested parties. The London Beth Din would not contemplate sharing authority with dayanim from other congregations. The Federation did not want to accept anything that seemed to jeopardise its independence or its 'parity' with the United Synagogue, although the latter comprised the overwhelming majority of the Orthodox Establishment. The Sephardim would do nothing that implied the Hahamate was not an office of equal standing with the Chief Rabbinate.

The negotiations were tortuous, the rabbis contended with each other and with their lay leaders, and the lay leaders followed suit. Vested interests were of much greater importance than religious unity and unimpeachable standards. When kosher establishments eventually went 'shopping' for licences, some proved cheaper than others, and all the parties were hurt, but most of all the community itself.

Much of the labour at the London end devolved on Rabbi Maurice (Moshe) Rose, then secretary of the Chief Rabbi's Office. He wrote to me on 24 February 1967, *inter alia*: 'If you were to have experienced the acrimony (let alone the time-wasting) which has been aroused in the past two weeks over whether the designation "Rabbinate" or "Beth Din" of the Federation should be used for matzot, you would be surprised that you have achieved as much as you have. There is still as much suspicion and animosity between the lay leaders of the three groups as ever there was, and you will have to reckon with this in future negotiations.'

For a while it looked as if the problem with the Federation would be resolved by Dr Kirzner's decision, after only a year or so in office – into which I had inducted him, as a gesture of mutual goodwill – to return to New York.

The previous rabbinic head, Dayan Michael Fisher, was appointed as successor, initially with the title 'Acting Rav Rashi'. Although less headstrong, he for long procrastinated in the endless negotiations for an agreement with the United Synagogue and its – strictly, the Chief Rabbi's – Beth Din. The intervals between open clashes grew longer, but the destructive problems of fragmentation and dissension were never resolved.

Rabbi Gaon became decreasingly involved with his community, spending more and more of his time in New York, where he held a professorship at Yeshiva University. Ultimately, the Hahamate became (and remains) vacant – a recurrent and prolonged feature of its history. On his retirement, authority was shared between a Communal Rabbi and an Av Beth Din.

On the Right wing, there had been no spokesman for its brand of Orthodoxy since Dr Solomon Schonfeld stood down as Presiding Rabbi of the Union of Orthodox Hebrew Congregations.

The Union was a loose association of congregations, each fully occupied with its own concerns. Within this framework, outstanding achievements were recorded, but its leaders were all too willing to dissociate themselves from the general community, with whose standards and outlook they had little sympathy, or even understanding.

So, although I was not to lack critics over the years, I never had any experience of rivals for the positions I held.

Fragments from an unpublished autobiography

CHAPTER SEVEN

Rabbi and Chief

RICH IN TRADITION AND TROUBLES

The Chief Rabbi of the British Commonwealth is one of the most prestigious posts in world Jewry. As leader of more than 820,000 Jews – 450,000 of them in Britain – he is recognised by British protocol as one of the country's premier spiritual lords: at State occasions, he sits with his peers, the Primate of All England and the Roman Catholic Archbishop of Westminster. Vacant since the retirement of Dr Israel Brodie in May 1965, the post will now be filled by an Orthodox rabbi from the US: Immanuel Jakobovits, 45, of Manhattan's Fifth Avenue Synagogue.

Jakobovits, who accepted the $19,600-a-year post last week, will become titular chief of a Jewish community rich in both tradition and troubles. Jews emigrated to Britain from France as early as the eleventh century. Driven into exile 200 years later, the Jews returned during the Protectorate of Oliver Cromwell, have since blossomed into one of the world's wealthiest and least persecuted Judaic communities. By the nineteenth century, the Rothschilds, Montagus and Samuelses made Jews a force to reckon with in British finance. Today, 40 Members of Parliament are Jews, as well as 61 knights and 20 peers of the realm. Although Jews are expected to congregate at their own country clubs, there is comparatively little overt anti-Semitism in Britain – one of the few nations where Jews were never forced to cluster together in ghettos.

About 70 per cent of British Jewry is Orthodox – a fact that is no guarantee of cohesiveness. On the far Left of the community – scorned as near-apostates by Jews who observe halachah (religious law) – are the minority of Reform Jews, similar in their modernising views to American Conservative Judaism, and the Liberals, who theologically conform roughly to the Reform movement in the US. Representing the mainstream of Orthodoxy – and most of the wealthy Anglo-Jewish families – is the United Synagogue, which governs 80 congregations in Greater London. Although it defends the full authority of halachah, the United Synagogue is nonetheless suspected of liberal tendencies by the militant Federation of Synagogues, which was founded by recent emigrants from Eastern Europe, although its supporters now include many Anglo-Jewish families that have been in Britain for generations. Fearful of being absorbed by *goyim* culture, these Jews think of themselves as 'God's Cossacks', and recognise the authority of the Chief Rabbi only when he is strict enough for their taste.

Within the past two years, tensions have been rising within British Judaism. One source of conflict was Dr Louis Jacobs, sometime rabbi of London's New West End Synagogue, who outraged his fellow Orthodox rabbis by insisting that the Bible was not infallible (*Time*, 22 May 1964). Still other feuds have been created by attempts of Reform Jewish temples to join local, Orthodox-dominated synagogue conferences. Contributing to the lack of calm has been the lengthy, rumour-ridden search for a new Chief Rabbi, who was expected to be stern enough to placate the Cossacks, progressive enough to negotiate with Reform and Liberal Jews, less than 51 years old – and blessed with no trace of a foreign accent.

Jakobovits qualifies on most counts. The son of a rabbi, he was born in the former East Prussian capital of Königsberg, educated in Britain, and served for a decade as Ireland's Chief Rabbi before coming to the US in 1958. In Ireland, some British Jews recall, his advice on moral issues amounted to 'the rabbi says you mustn't'; in the US, however, he is counted among the modern Orthodox leaders who seek to accommodate halachah to contemporary issues. An expert on medical ethics, he frowns on contraception, points to the low birth rate among Jews, and fears that Judaism may some day vanish entirely. He and his wife have six children.

As Britain's Chief Rabbi, Jakobovits hopes to avoid much of the tiring round of weddings, barmitzvahs and routine social engagements that go with the job, spend most of his time writing and preaching on contemporary Jewish problems. 'Books to us are what armies are to others', he says. Orthodox though he is, Jakobovits thinks he can at least carry on a fruitful dialogue with Reform and Liberal Judaism, and says that 'the Jews of Britain are tired of conflict and yearning for a new, constructive outlook'.

Time, 26 August 1966

During the first week of 1967, Rabbi Jakobovits, accompanied by his wife, made an unannounced flying visit to London, in response to an urgent request from the lay leaders of the United Synagogue. The honorary officers felt unable to endorse the terms of an agreement the Chief Rabbi-elect had negotiated in New York with Rabbi Dr Eliezer Kirzner, the newly appointed Rav Rashi of the Federation of Synagogues, with which Rabbi Jakobovits was seeking a closer relationship.

The United Synagogue believed that Dr Jakobovits had conceded to the Federation more power and influence in communal affairs than was justified. There was, above all, an unwillingness to grant its religious head a status of equality with that of the Chief Rabbi in joint communal institutions such as the proposed unified kashrut authority.

By the end of the month, revised terms of the agreement, providing for 'the closest and most effective co-operation' between the respective synagogal groups, were approved by the lay leaders of the United Synagogue. Details were made public by the Chief Rabbinate office in London:

'Understanding' with the Rav Rashi-elect of the Federation of Synagogues

Having recently been elected to assume the spiritual and rabbinic leadership of the two largest groups of Ashkenazi congregations in Anglo-Jewry, we have had several meetings together to ensure the closest and most effective co-operation between us upon our assumption of office in London.

Determined to promote the strength of, and respect for, traditional Judaism as our supreme goal, and resolved to eliminate all past frictions, we have agreed to commit ourselves personally to, and to obtain the fullest support for, the following understanding in principle:

a) In matters affecting the representation of the Ashkenazi community at large, the Chief Rabbi of the United Hebrew Congregations of the British Commonwealth shall be recognised as its spokesman and authority, and he agrees to consult with the Rav Rashi of the Federation of Synagogues on policy decisions and public statements affecting also the Federation of Synagogues.

b) Each will give full and unqualified recognition to the other's rabbinic rulings.

c) Every endeavour will be made to combine the activities of our independent Batei Din (Ecclesiastical Courts), together with the Haham of the Spanish and Portuguese Congregation, by setting up a unified and departmentalised Beth Din.

d) We are resolved to ensure and maintain the joint administration of shechitah and kashrut (including matzot).

We will make every endeavour to extend our harmonious co-operation to all other areas of common concern, such as Jewish education. We also look forward to the eventual representation of the Federation of Synagogues on the Chief Rabbinate Council.

We realise that the success of each of us lies in a strong Orthodoxy, and each of us is profoundly interested in strengthening the other, fulfilling the prophetic vision: 'Each shall help his neighbour, and everyone say to his brother: "Be of good courage." '

We are confident this understanding will help to restore the solidarity of Orthodox Judaism as a constructive force to inspire and uplift the Anglo-Jewish community.

Statement by the Chief Rabbi-elect, the Rav Rashi-elect and the Haham of the Spanish and Portuguese Jews' Congregation

In order to promote the unity of Anglo-Jewry and give added strength to the rule of Torah in our communal life, we agree in principle to make every endeavour to co-ordinate the functions of our Batei Din.

Solomon Gaon, Immanuel Jakobovits, Eliezer W. Kirzner

Asked by the New York correspondent of the *Jewish Chronicle* to comment on the significance of the agreement he had reached with Dr Kirzner, Rabbi Jakobovits replied: 'This agreement brings the Chief Rabbinate and the Federation closer together than they have ever been in the past. Previously, there had never been any official recognition by either side of the other. This is now assured for the first time in Anglo-Jewish history. It is also, and perhaps more significantly, the first breakthrough in resolving the Anglo-Jewish crisis, reversing the process of disintegration which has embittered communal relations in the past few years.'

Endorsing this view, Dr Kirzner commented: 'This understanding is unprecedented in Anglo-Jewry and it may be a stepping stone to enable other rabbinical leaders to realise that there is very little hope and very little future, if any, in isolationism. But in co-existence leading to co-operation, there is every hope for a successful future for Anglo-Jewry. And it may also help the lay leaders to see the example set for them and follow in the right direction.'

[In November 1968, Dr Kirzner's appointment was terminated, by mutual consent, and Dayan Michael Fisher became Acting (and later full) Rav Rashi. Within a short space of time, the 'understanding' between the Chief Rabbinate and the Federation of Synagogues, shaky at best, fell apart altogether.]

Three weeks before his official induction on 11 April 1967, Rabbi Jakobovits arrived at Southampton on board the *Queen Mary*, accompanied by his wife and their four daughters, the youngest of whom was less than a year old. One of their sons stayed on in New York to complete his studies; the other was preparing to go to Israel.

Rabbi Jakobovits' arrival prompted an unprecedented leading article in *The Times* and another in the *Jewish Chronicle*.

A DIFFICULT INHERITANCE

The new Chief Rabbi arrived in Britain yesterday to take up a difficult inheritance. The divisions within the British Jewish community have been evident, and widely proclaimed, over the past few years. What makes them particularly significant is that they are now to be found within the Orthodox section itself. There was the breakaway of Rabbi Jacobs and his adherents three years ago when the former Chief Rabbi refused to approve his appointment either as principal of Jews' College or as Rabbi of the New West End Synagogue. This symbolised the conflict over the more radical approach to religious teaching. There were the difficulties in appointing a new Chief Rabbi, and the uncertainties over the extent of his jurisdiction. These indicated the weakening of respect for rabbinical authority. There was the recent affair at the *Jewish Observer*, which reflected diverging attitudes towards Israel. Is support for the Jewish State consistent with objective, and if necessary unfavourable, comment on its internal developments?

In all these cases, it is the underlying trend rather than the events themselves which are worth further notice. They all point to a reduction of traditional authority: in the realm of theology, of organisation, and of the unquestioning acceptance of collective goals. It is easy for the outsider to forget the extent to which the establishment of the State of Israel has represented to Jews in Britain as elsewhere the supreme achievement of the Jewish people – to question which in any way is to border upon the heretical. In that sense, the readiness to cast an objective eye can be interpreted as a move away from tradition.

One reason for this general trend is obviously the increasingly secular mood in Western society. All religions, and all denominations within the Christian religion, have been feeling the effects. One result has been a growing desire to adjust minds to contemporary thinking so far as conscience permits, and this has naturally strengthened the forces of liberalism. When it has blown to such effect through the Roman Catholic Church, there can be no surprise that its breezes should have been felt in the Jewish community as well. But it would be wrong to look only to general causes for an explanation of developments within British Jewry. What has happened is that the old pattern of an extremely tightly knit community is beginning to break up.

No longer is there the widespread concentration upon specifically Jewish education in depth within the family. No longer is there the same strict attention to the rituals of Jewish observance. Perhaps this is the natural consequence of the greater acceptance of Jews within all walks of British life. The less discrimination there is against a minority, the more difficult it must always be for it to maintain the full rigour of exclusive traditions. But while such a period of change and adjustment can be exciting and constructive, it poses considerable problems for those who have to lead a people through it. Fortunately for British Jewry, Dr Jakobovits has indicated that he will lead with a sensitive touch – by seeking unity on the basis of divisions, not by trying to suppress them.

The Times, *21 March 1967*

A WARM WELCOME

Rabbi and Mrs Jakobovits, together with some members of their family, who have arrived in London this week, can be assured of a warm welcome. Since the announcement of his appointment as Chief Rabbi of the United Hebrew Congregations, Rabbi Jakobovits has been at pains to make known his intention to seek reconciliation within the community. He comes from the largest Jewish community in the world, whose vigorous development owes much to the recognition by all groups of the legitimacy of different trends in Judaism. Like the United States, Anglo-Jewry has many and diverse strands, and Rabbi Jakobovits has wisely recognised this fact. As Chief Rabbi of Anglo-Jewry's largest synagogal body, he can do much to improve the stifling climate of opinion engendered by Orthodox leadership in recent years. Fences need to be repaired and bridges built within Jewry as between Jew and Gentile. Public statements and public relations, valuable though they be, are no substitute for action, and Dr Jakobovits' deeds during the coming months in the directions he has so encouragingly enunciated will be eagerly awaited. His task will be no light one, but if he courageously follows the line of principle and integrity, he will be on the highway to success. It is with this sincere hope that troubled Anglo-Jewry welcomes him and wishes him well.

Jewish Chronicle, *24 March 1967*

Watched by almost 5,000 people in London and the provinces, Rabbi Jakobovits was inducted into office at the St John's Wood Synagogue, London, by his predecessor, Chief Rabbi Brodie. In the synagogue itself were 1,800 representatives of all sections of Anglo-Jewry, as well as distinguished guests from abroad. Also present were closed-circuit television cameras which screened the service to the adjoining hall and to synagogue halls in Hendon, Ilford, Manchester, Glasgow and Cardiff.

The induction service – conducted by the ministers of the St John's Wood Synagogue and by Dayan I. J. Weiss, of Manchester, representing the provincial clergy – began with a procession of religious and lay leaders into the synagogue. Among the congregation were 50 uniformed youngsters from the various youth movements and a group of Dr Jakobovits' former congregants from New York.

Guests included the Israeli Ambassador, Aharon Remez; S. Z. Shragai, of the executive of the Jewish Agency; the Mayor of Westminster, Councillor A. Burton; and leading representatives of all synagogal bodies. Among the latter were Lord Cohen of Walmer, president of the Union of Liberal and Progressive Synagogues; its executive director, Rabbi Sidney Brichto; and Rabbi Dr Louis Jacobs, minister of the New London Synagogue.

Foreign visitors in the procession included the Chief Rabbi of France, Dr Jacob Kaplan; the Chief Rabbi of Eire, Dr I. Cohen; Rabbi H. Grunwald, of Germany; and Rabbi E. Munk, Dr Jakobovits' father-in-law. Also there were the Haham and the Rav Rashi-elect.

The President of Israel, Zalman Shazar, and the Archbishop of Canterbury were among distinguished personalities who sent goodwill messages to the Chief Rabbi. The Archbishop coupled his 'warmest congratulations' with his 'best wishes for the peace and well-being of all the Jewish congregations in the British Commonwealth'.

In his induction address, Rabbi Brodie expressed his pleasure that 'the appointment of my successor has been greeted by our community and the general public with so large a measure of interest and goodwill and friendliness.' He continued:

'I pray that our community, its leaders and members will sustain and implement their present manifestation of support and encouragement in all his endeavours in their service and in the highest purposes of our Faith. I am content in the knowledge that a successor has been chosen who, like his predecessors, will uphold with steadfastness and constancy the authority, the validity, the relevance of the Torah, Written and Oral.

Fortified by his trust in Heaven and the stimulating meritorious example of his learned, pious, lovable, saintly father, I am confident he will bring to the discharge of the manifold and various duties of his office the gifts of personality, scholarship, vision, and moral courage, wide human sympathies with which he is conspicuously endowed. The years in the rabbinate in this country, in Eire and the United States of America have witnessed his abilities as preacher, lecturer and author. He has brought an enriched, dynamic, practical experience to his newly enlarged area of activity which will give him ready access to the hearts and understanding of men and women, of young and old.

Certain and firm in conviction, mature in the gift of exposition, he is equipped to teach, to guide, to redirect and fortify those of our time who walk about as if in darkness, the doubting and the frustrated, the strayers and the discontented with the teachings and demands of our spiritual heritage. They will listen: many will respond when heart talks to heart.'

In his installation address, the new Chief Rabbi outlined his mission in stark, uncompromising yet conciliatory terms:

PROPHECY, PRIESTHOOD AND KINGSHIP: THE ROLE OF THE CHIEF RABBI

'On this resplendent occasion, usually witnessed but once in a generation, and before this august and uniquely representative assembly – covering the entire spectrum of the community like a colourful rainbow of peace after a storm – permit me to share with you some of the hopes and prayers stirring my heart, as well as a few thoughts agitating my mind on the future of Judaism and British Jewry as we consecrate our partnership.

The first day of Nisan, by an extraordinary coincidence of anniversaries, marks the beginnings of the three classic forms of Jewish leadership: prophecy, priesthood and kingship. On this day, in the first dated event in the history of prophecy, God told Moses and Aaron: 'This month shall be unto you the first of months', proclaiming to the Children of Israel the dawn of freedom when time, the count of months, would belong to them and not to their Egyptian masters, as before. On this day, a year later, the Tabernacle was completed and the Jewish priesthood began to function. And on this day, 'the New Year of the Kings', the kings of Israel started to count the years of their reign.

In some respects, the rabbi today is heir to all three roles of leadership. Let me, then, outline my aims and responsibilities in this triple capacity as I see them.

'Who are the kings? These are the rabbis', says the Talmud. Ever since the lapse of temporal sovereignty, Judaism has invested rabbis with certain royal prerogatives in guiding the destinies of our people. They directed its thoughts, inspired its actions, initiated its great historical movements, and gave Jewish life its sense of destiny and moral purpose.

In this capacity, it will be my charge to help in directing the community's internal and external affairs, and to suffuse them with religious content.

I will seek to bring the influence of my office to bear on promoting world peace and the moral regeneration of society – our most urgent universal task; on alleviating the religious attrition and communal isolation of our Russian brethren – the most painful Jewish problem of our day; on cementing the bonds of our common heritage between Israel and the Diaspora – our most acute national problem; and on moving with prudence and caution in the uncharted territory of inter-faith understanding and co-operation – the most serious post-war challenge to religious statesmanship. Within our community, I will encourage friendliness in our relations, imagination and originality in our planning, and a constant search for dedicated talent and high idealism in our communal work. I will use every available means of communication with the public in pursuit of my determination always to take the community into my confidence.

In particular, it will be among my major objectives to enhance the status of the Anglo-Jewish ministry. I realise that the intense concentration of rabbinical power and authority in the Chief Rabbinate is bound to stunt the growth of a dynamic ministry. In fashioning my office to meet the needs of our time, I will try to strike a judicious balance between excessive decentralisation, leading to religious chaos, and over-centralisation, stifling ambition and responsibility among ministers, reducing them to mere functionaries. Having myself risen from their ranks and once joined the brain-drain for bigger opportunities abroad, I know their frustrations. I would like our spiritual leaders to assume unquestioned spiritual command in their congregations, and increasingly to participate at the highest level in the direction of the community and its religious policies. Only thus will we attract our finest sons to a rabbinical vocation.

I am also charged to assume some principal functions of the ancient priesthood. Perhaps this gives a little sense to the curious reference to Britain's earlier Chief Rabbis as 'High Priests of the Jews'. Moses defined the tasks of the priests as: 'They shall teach Thy laws unto Jacob, and Thy Torah unto Israel; they shall put incense before Thee, and whole burnt-offerings upon Thine altar.' Let me here, then, come to the heart of my responsibilities as teacher and guardian of Jewish law, coupled with the duty to make Judaism sweet as incense and also to exact sacrifices for it.

Far above all else will be my obligation to promote the study of the Torah. I want to assure the inalienable birthright of every Jew to an adequate Jewish education. On this I stake the success of my ministry, for on this will depend Jewish survival. During the post-war period, Jewish education has made vast strides in many lands. There are today tens of thousands of Jewish children, even outside Israel, who master Hebrew fluently, to whom immortals like Isaiah and Rashi and Maimonides speak in familiar accents, who have completed several tractates of the Talmud before they leave school, and who freely consult the genius of Judaism for authentic answers to the social, moral and intellectual perplexities of our age. If Jewish education ends, instead of starts in earnest, at barmitzvah age, is it any wonder that the products are juvenile Jews, quite incompetent to assert their faith in an adult world, their love of Judaism too flimsy to resist the temptation of intermarriage and the allurements of pagan philosophies? Just imagine were we to stop our children's natural growth and their secular instruction at 13 years of age; would they not become physical and intellectual cripples?

Wherein lies the glory of beautiful synagogues if tomorrow they will be empty monuments to our neglect; what is the profit of the finest kashrut supervision if kosher homes will continue to decline, and of all our Zionist work without committed Jews in the next generation?

In this emergency of appalling defections among our youth, our expenditure in money and energy on Jewish education represents our defence budget in the communal economy, and it must be given the highest priority over every other Jewish effort.

What Judaism is it I will teach and defend? It is the vibrant faith found in synagogues filled every week, and equally evident 'when you sit in your home and when you go about' your business, sanctifying life at work and at leisure, as a guide to professional ethics in public and to sexual morality in private.

It is the Judaism which was never in step with the times; which was as much out of date when it preached the brotherhood of man in pagan antiquity as when our martyrs defied the enticing attractions of Hellenistic culture and the savage bigotry of the Middle Ages; the Judaism which will never be in accord with the times until the times are in accord with Judaism. But it is also the Judaism which is ever dynamic and creative, addressing its eternal message to each generation in terms of its needs and accents; the Judaism which produced the prophets in response to the challenge of immoral paganism; which evolved the Talmud as a reaction to our encounter with Greece and Rome and to our dispersion among the nations; and which created Jewish philosophy to articulate Jewish teachings in an age of scholasticism and theological speculation; the Judaism which will now have to project its teachings in terms of the scientific thinking and intellectual stirrings of our times.

It will be my priestly duty to offer you, as best I can, this Judaism, fragrant and refreshing like incense, to make it meaningful and attractive.

But in my priestly charge, I must also insist on sacrifices. Do not ask me to make Judaism easier or cheaper, to devaluate its worth to the soft currency of convenience. I can no more offer you a programme without toil and sacrifice than you can offer me a life of ease and leisure. There is no instant Torah, prepared in one or three hours a week of study and practice, no Judaism without tears, just as there is no creation without travail and no triumph without hardship. Remember always, a religion which demands nothing is worth nothing, and a community which sacrifices nothing merits nothing.

Let me here make this quite clear: I am resolved to preserve the Orthodox traditions of my office and the predominantly traditional character of our community. To borrow from the memorable words uttered, in Britain's finest hour, by the man to whom we all owe our lives and our freedom: I have not become Anglo-Jewry's First Minister in order to preside over the liquidation of British Judaism.

I will do my best to serve and unite all sections of the community, but I am not prepared to replace the Torah by an umbrella, either open or closed, as the symbol of my office. In any event, I anticipate fair weather rather than rain or hail, and we should not require any umbrellas.

For, in my priestly capacity, I also want to be among the disciples of Aaron in 'loving peace and pursuing peace'. In my attitude to all my fellow-Jews, I will look to the example of the saintly Rabbi Kook's boundless 'love of Israel', and of my revered father's broad tolerance. In our free society, I cannot ensure that everyone will submit to my decisions, but I can aspire to earn respect for my convictions and for my right to make decisions as my conscience dictates. I cannot bend or compromise Jewish law which is not mine to make or unmake, but I can administer it with compassion and despatch.

To those whose faith in the Divine origin of the whole Torah is weak and who do not accept the discipline of Judaism as entrusted to me, may I say this in all solemnity: Never forget the immense tragedy of our religious differences. Should your and our hearts not bleed with grief when we, your brothers and heirs to a common tradition, cannot worship in your synagogues, cannot eat in your homes, and sometimes cannot even marry your sons and daughters, because laws which we recognise as Divine and sacred have become meaningless to you, because what has united us for thousands of years now estranges you? I will never cease pleading with you to rediscover the thrills of traditional Jewish living and the awesome magnificence of our faith: the Divinity of the Torah, the truth of the prophets, the authority of the halachah, and the messianic vision of the future, born of hope and toil. Nor will I ever surrender my firm belief in the promise of our prophets that eventually the entire House of Israel will be reunited in the service of our Creator.

Meanwhile, it will be my privilege and my duty to do all within my power and authority to close the gaps within our people, and I appeal to all segments of the community for help in this vital effort. To this end, I pledge all the skills and resources I command, for God will hold me to account for the failings of any Jew I can influence, as well as for my own many short-comings.

Nevertheless, I recognise dissent as an inescapable fact of Jewish life today. I will seek to befriend those who dissent, and to work with them in Jewish and general causes unaffected by our religious differences. After the devastating losses we have suffered by slaughter, repression and assimilation, every Jew's contribution to the enrichment of Jewish life is now more precious than ever, and I will encourage all British Jews to give of their best to the common good.

Finally, I am summoned to provide the vision and inspiration of the prophet, whose mantle, according to the Talmud, was bequeathed to the rabbis from the day the Temple was destroyed. Unlike the priests, who expected the people to come to them in the sanctuary, the prophets went out to the people to proclaim their message. I shall likewise seek out my brethren wherever they are. Those who do not visit me in the synagogue I will try to meet in their surroundings, speaking and debating with them wherever they allow me to appear, and writing to vindicate the Torah wherever it is challenged.

As successor to the prophets, the rabbi today must demonstrate the relevance of Judaism to the contemporary experience. He must also spiritualise the mechanics of Jewish observance, showing the moral grandeur of religious discipline, the stirring uplift of true prayer, and the holiness of lives daily consecrated to God's service.

He must interpret the interplay between faith and reality, between ritual and ethics, between Israel and the nations. He must make manifest the gap between the laws of nature and the moral law, between impersonal science complacently dealing with things as they are and personal religion impatiently dealing with things as they ought to be. He must demand commitment, denounce indifference, and ennoble the aim of life as a quest for living in the image of God instead of the selfish pursuit of happiness and personal success.

Living in the aftermath of the most turbulent age in the annals of man and of Israel, our generation faces a special challenge in matching our gigantic material strides with a commensurate spiritual advance. The past generation experienced unparalleled bloodshed, first in a world war of unprecedented proportions, then in the heinous Holocaust which claimed more Jewish lives than all the medieval massacres combined, and finally in the restoration of Jewish rule to Zion. Such an afflicted generation, however heroic, could not evince the capacities, the vision and peace of mind, to concentrate on spiritual endeavours, any more than King David, conqueror of Jerusalem, because he had spilt blood, could build the Temple.

It is our assignment, blessed as we are with peace and prosperity, to complete the rebirth of Israel. As they restored the soil of Israel, we must restore the soul of Israel.

A generation ago, the Jewish problem was the survival of Jews. Today, it is the survival of Judaism. A generation ago, one-third of our people was annihilated. Today, one-quarter of our people is forcibly denied the right to live as Jews, and at least another quarter wilfully abdicates the right to live as Jews, being just as ignorant about Judaism, just as estranged from the synagogue, from Jewish traditions and literature by choice as the Jews of Russia are by compulsion. Even in the most catastrophic periods of the Middle Ages, when the total number of Jews in the world exceeded scarcely one million, and when they were exposed to slaughter, oppression and destitution, no Jew ever worried about Jewish survival as we do now in this age of unequalled freedom, affluence and opportunity. How passionately would our prophets indict our generation if we now failed to bestir ourselves to rebuilding our destroyed sanctuary, to invest Jewish existence with meaning, and to turn the martyrdom of the past into the consecration of the future.

In the broader arena of mankind's tortuous evolution, we have also just passed an age of unrivalled conquest and material advance.

In the process, life has become mechanised, and man the victim of his own inventive genius. Man today lives longer, he has more time through labour-saving gadgets and faster communications, and yet he pants, too short of breath for contemplation and spiritual pursuits, his moral sense blunted by the hunt for pleasure, his vision obscured by the glitter around him, and the temple within him crushed under the weight of his technocracy.

As history's religious pioneers and moral pathfinders, we are summoned to reassert our national purpose in ministering to our fellow-men as 'a kingdom of priests and a holy people'.

If we expect the world to take up our cause when we are in trouble, we must also be prepared to involve ourselves and our teachings in the travails of mankind.

I pray that in the office I now assume, I may be granted a humble share in re-orienting the aspirations of our people and our fellow-men towards these prophetic goals. I pray especially that Anglo-Jewry may occupy an honoured place within the world Jewish community in the fulfilment of these ideals.

In the past, British Jewry has enjoyed an enviable reputation for stability and service. From these isles radiated an example of communal solidarity and religious loyalty. From these isles went forth the great translations of our Jewish classics, casting our sacred Bible, Talmud, Midrash and Zohar into new vessels of understanding from which all may drink. From these isles came aid and intervention for suffering Jews everywhere. And from these isles, through their genius and ours, issued the Balfour Declaration 50 years ago, title-deed to Israel's rebirth. As the principal survivor of the European catastrophe, Anglo-Jewry must now assume an even more eminent position of leadership and responsibility.

In our shrinking and inter-dependent world, Anglo-Jewry can no more afford to be insular and self-contained than Britain can afford to withdraw from the rest of the world. We must share with, and contribute to, the Jewish experience of other communities. And we must consolidate our part in the upbuilding of the Land of Israel, by encouraging aliyah and by freely aiding the spiritual and material growth of Israel as a land flowing with the milk of Torah and the honey of prosperity.

I pray that I may always be worthy of your support, trust and friendship. I plead with our eminent dayanim, our learned rabbis and all my distinguished colleagues: uphold my hands on the right and on the left. Thus will my arms be firm, the one as 'a mighty hand', to defend 'the Law of Moses and Israel', and the other as 'an outstretched arm', to grasp with love those who stray or falter. I call upon our dedicated lay leaders, perhaps with a touch of homiletical licence: You take charge of our administrative wants, supply our material needs, and give me the freedom to devote myself to things of the spirit, as we share in equal parts, like Issachar and Zevulun, the efforts and rewards in building a flourishing Torah society.

I turn with special fondness to our youth, bright hope of our future, whom I am so delighted to see represented here for the first time in such numbers: Make me at home in your midst, stimulate me by your questions, rejoice me by your response, and humble me by your restless search for depth and meaning beneath the shifting sands of passing fads as you prepare yourselves to become tomorrow's guardians of yesterday's heritage.

To all my brothers and sisters in the far-flung dispersion of the Commonwealth I say: Let us seize each other's hands across our distances to form the most wonderful family of communities cheerfully responding to Jewish history's greatest challenge in these exciting times.

Let us so acquit ourselves of our diverse tasks that no Jew will ever spurn his heritage, and that, as promised in the Torah, 'all the nations of the earth shall see that the name of the Lord is called upon us'.

As for myself, what do I crave in this hour of destiny? Upon King Solomon's accession to his high office, he had a dream in which God said: 'Ask what I shall give you'. His response is my response: 'O grant to Thy humble servant an understanding heart to judge Thy people, to know between right and wrong'.

I seek neither power nor authority, for no rabbi today can impose himself upon unwilling people, or enjoy their respect without earning it. Rather do I seek the wisdom to judge and make the right decisions, the inspiration to guide and persuade, the mind to instruct, and the heart to comfort. I crave the ability to elicit understanding, not submission; to win partners, not subordinates.

We have now reached the end of the beginning. In responding to your call, I am sustained by a vision. In its fulfilment I have abiding faith. And I desire you to come and share with me this vision, as I now impart it to you in the sight of Him Who is the Sovereign of us all:

My vision is that 'out of the cruel shall come the sweet'.

My vision is that out of the age of monstrous depravity there arises the great vindication of the age-old Jewish faith in the brotherhood of man, now a more universal hope than ever before.

My vision is that out of the religious hatreds of the past, polluted by rivers of Jewish blood, there is born the great confrontation between Judaism and the world, an encounter not of theological parleys, but of the world religions – secure from bigotry within and missionary subversion without – attacking the common enemy of evil and godlessness, and acknowledging their debt to

Judaism as the enduring fountainhead of all that has inspired moral progress in the human story.

My vision is that out of the age of soulless materialism and the blasphemy of 'God's death' there stirs the search for a higher morality transcending reason, a quest for the living God to replace the sham gods made to order by today's pseudo-theologians.

My vision is that out of our people's agony there is reborn Zion restored to its glory, radiating the Word of the Lord everywhere, and there prosper Jewish communities living in tranquillity and harmony with our fellow-citizens.

My vision is that out of Anglo-Jewry's past tribulations there emerges a happy, forward-looking community, confounding the defeatists and routing the strife-mongers, as a mighty fortress of our spiritual treasures.

And my vision is that out of the clash of opinions, and sparked by the eternal fire of the Torah, there are released the massive energies to raise us to the peak of achievement, towering majestically in a universal panorama of peace and basking in the everlasting sunshine of God's choicest blessings.'

CHAPTER EIGHT

Peace and Morality

'Promoting world peace and the moral regeneration of society'

HUMAN RIGHTS AND HUMAN DUTIES

'I must admit that, when just over a year ago I somewhat reluctantly agreed to leave the fleshpots of America for the headaches of the British Chief Rabbinate, in response to one of the more unusual bids by Sir Isaac Wolfson, the chairman of the Chief Rabbinate Conference which elected me, I certainly did not realise that the honour of addressing this august Conference of Directors would be part of the bargain.

My presence here at this conference before Britain's captains of industry is not so incongruous as might appear. I am the director of a fairly large and tricky business – the business of selling traditional Judaism to critical and sometimes hesitant buyers in a highly competitive world in which the market is being flooded by many cheaper substitutes which imitate the article I have to offer. And since, moreover, all the customers I seek – some half a million of them – are Jewish, my powers of salesmanship are severely put to the test.

Today, restlessness is universal. The oppressive feeling that things are far from what they should be, the critical search for purpose and meaning – all these tides of unsettlement and instability engulf the entire world. This dissatisfaction with the existing order may well be the most characteristic mark of our age. Never before in the history of man have so many people and so many nations wanted so much they do not have. Never before have the discontent with the present and the longing for change been more universal.

Human society is in a state of unprecedented turbulence, tossed about in the ocean separating hope from reality, and plunging precariously between peace and war, between industrial rest and unrest, between social security and strife, between racial equality and riots, between political universalism and chauvinism, between scientific mastery and human mechanisation, between religious ecumenism and moral impotence. Much of the current restlessness and discontent irritating human relations in all these areas must no doubt be attributed to the sudden shrinkage of the world. The speed of modern communications may have reduced distances, but it has also widened the gap between the haves and the have-nots.

23. With Israeli Prime Minister Yitzhak Rabin at a meeting of world Jewish leaders in Jerusalem in 1976.

24. Congratulating Israeli Prime Minister Menachem Begin on the completion of the peace talks with Egypt.

25. With Israeli Foreign Minister and Deputy Premier Shimon Peres at a London meeting in 1987.

26. Welcoming Israeli Prime Minister Yitzhak Shamir at a communal gathering in London in 1990.

27. Left to right: Chief Rabbi Jakobovits and Israeli Chief Rabbi Shlomo Goren with the Archbishop of Canterbury, Dr Michael Ramsey; the Archbishop of Westminster, Cardinal John Heenan; and the Rev A. S. Cooper, Moderator of the Free Church Federal Council.

28. Queen Elizabeth the Queen Mother conversing with the Chief Rabbi and violinist Yehudi Menuhin at a Westminster Abbey concert in aid of the Council of Christians and Jews and the Royal Silver Jubilee Fund, 1977.

29. The Duchess of Kent with (left to right) Sir Sigmund Sternberg, Lord Coggan and Chief Rabbi Jakobovits at a reception in London.

30. With the Archbishop of Canterbury, Dr Robert Runcie, after receiving a Lambeth degree in 1987.

Underlying the malaise of our age is that we want more than we can get, and that today's philosophy of life encourages us to want more than we can get. This gnawing sense of unfulfilment and deprivation frustrates us and bedevils all our human relations, whether personal or collective, whether between individuals or between groups and nations.

What can I, as a spokesman for Judaism, offer as a contribution towards mitigating this malaise? Perhaps the most significant feature of our contemporary social and moral philosophy is that we define our basic human imperatives mainly in terms of rights. We speak and think of human rights, constitutional rights, international rights, political rights, labour rights, student rights, racial rights, and what have you. The whole motivation of our social behaviour is galvanised by our clamour for rights which we are pressed to assert as our due. The demand of rights we consider inalienable fuels the machine of our ambitions and kindles the fires of our discontents and frictions.

Now, in Judaism we know of no intrinsic rights. Indeed, there is no word for rights in the very language of the Hebrew Bible and of the classic sources of Jewish law. In the moral vocabulary of the Jewish discipline of life, we speak of human duties, not of human rights, of obligations, not of entitlements. The Decalogue is a list of Ten Commandments, not a Bill of Human Rights.

In the charity legislation of the Bible, for instance, it is the rich man who is commanded to support the poor, not the poor man who has the right to demand support from the rich. Or, to use its phraseology, it states: 'Thou shalt surely open thy hand unto thy poor and needy brother.' It does not state that the poor man shall open his hand to demand his share. Economic and social justice is to be achieved by impressing upon the privileged the duty to give, and not upon the underprivileged the right to demand.

Likewise, in labour relations, as in all other laws affecting the social order, the accent is invariably on the debt of him who has, not on the claim of him who has not. Even in Jewish medical ethics, which happens to be my specialised interest, the same principle applies. In Jewish law, a doctor is obliged to come to the rescue of his stricken fellow-man and to perform any operation he considers essential for the life of the patient, even if the patient refuses his consent or prefers to die. Once again, the emphasis is on the physician's responsibility to heal, to offer service, more than on the patient's right to be treated.

In a profoundly meaningful passage nearly 2,000 years old, dealing with the sanctity and equality of human life, the Talmud requires witnesses in capital trials to be cautioned, with the following argument: 'Why was but a single man created as the progenitor of the entire human race? So that no one should say to his fellow: "My father is greater than your father."'

Mark this, it does not say: 'So that every man may claim, "My father is as great as yours"', but rather that people shall not claim, 'My father is greater than yours'. In other words, it is not the one who feels inferior who shall claim equality, but the one who is in a superior position who shall grant equality. We want to teach people to think not in terms of what they may demand from others but of what they owe to others.

Herein, surely, lies the curse of our age – and its cure. The accent today is on demands, not on obligations. Everyone thinks of what society owes to him, not of what he owes to society. Already our youth are conditioned to ponder on what they can get out of life, and not on what they must put into life. And just as a family in which the relationships between parents and children are predicated on the rights children may demand from their parents rather than on the duties parents owe to their children must flounder, so a society whose catchwords are 'success' instead of 'service', 'leisure' instead of 'work', 'rights' instead of 'duties', must come to grief and disillusionment.

What is needed, then, if we are to reverse the tide of restlessness and frustration is to change radically our focus in human relations. We must expunge the word 'rights' and replace it by 'duties'.

If, for instance, management felt that the onus of improving the workers' lot rested more on management granting better conditions than on labour unions demanding them, we would have no strikes, and if the workers sensed the urgency of deliberating on how better to serve the country by increased productivity and a greater pride in work, we would have no economic crises.

If people were trained to regard their obligations to serve others, and not their addiction to personal success and selfishness, as the *leitmotif* in their preparation of a career, we would not have the growing problems of delinquency and narcotics, not to mention immorality, on our hands, for they all stem from a perverse insistence on rights without duties. If our newspapers and other mass media provided the people with what they need rather than with what they want, public enlightenment and entertainment would encourage service through publicising virtue, and not crime through publicising scandals, vice and agitation. And if the incentives to international trade and agreements were the obligation to help other nations rather than sheer national self-interest, we would have neither war through conflicting interests nor the suppression of war through a balance of terror; we would have peace throughout the brotherhood of man.

Instead of asserting rights at the expense of others, let us assert duties at our expense. Instead of drifting aimlessly in quest of new purpose and meaning, let our purpose be the service of others and our meaning to secure equality by granting it. In setting our sights on these soaring peaks in the wonderful panorama of human evolution, we may yet confound the prophets of doom who see nothing but strife and disenchantment in store for us.

The fatalistic prognosis of so many of our political and social doctors may well be overruled by a superior second opinion, granting a new lease of creative life to ourselves and to all our fellow-men, every one of them a director of our human destiny, created to live in the image of the Divine Director of us all.'

The Institute of Directors, London, 9 November 1967

This excursion into national and international affairs, delivered barely six months after he assumed office, was the first of many the Chief Rabbi was to make over the ensuing years. The following are extracts from a number of major addresses and articles on moral and ethical issues that received widespread attention both in Jewish circles and beyond.

RELIGION IN PUBLIC LIFE

'Mankind is now almost equally divided into three camps: the religiously developed, the underdeveloped and the maldeveloped. Perhaps just over a billion people, at least nominally, profess one of the three monotheistic faiths of Judaism, Christianity and Islam. Another billion, spread over vast lands in Asia and Africa, are religious neutrals – uncommitted – neither acknowledging nor rejecting God. And about another billion, alas, are in militant rebellion against God.

For the first time in history, we have not only individuals but powerful States dedicated – indeed, constitutionally committed as a matter of national policy – to the overthrow of all religion and to the eradication of belief in any deity from the hearts and minds of men. To my mind, this is fundamentally the crux of the ideological struggle between East and West, even more than differences in social doctrines or economic systems. For, after all, Communism as such teaches a lofty doctrine of human equality and brotherhood, a doctrine not entirely unrelated to our prophets' passion for social justice. How can we explain, then, that it has nevertheless been perverted into such a mighty instrument of oppression, that it has led to prisons engulfing almost whole continents, to the brutal suppression of freedom of speech and literary creativity, to the degradation of man into a soulless machine?

The answer is quite simple, apparently too obvious to be noticed. There can be no brotherhood of man without the Fatherhood of God. It is only as children of a common God that we humans are brothers. Take away the link, and the chain of human fraternity and understanding disintegrates. Dethrone God, and the dignity of man created in His image is bound to collapse.

In staking this claim, I am all too painfully aware of the terrible wars, persecution, intolerance, torture and slaughter so often inflicted in the name of religion – from the medieval Crusades to the intractable agony of Northern Ireland in the present day. But these manifestations of inhumanity are an abuse and perversion of true religion, entitling us to blame and banish religion itself with as much logic as we ought to ban and condemn science because it created an atom bomb, or to proscribe music and literature because some of history's most evil tyrants resorted to these arts and prostituted them in the pursuit of their fiendish frenzy.

Let me now turn to the role of religion nearer home, and the vindication of my belief that our contemporary dilemma represents basically a profound moral crisis.

Take our tottering economy as one example. Even worse and more devastating than the inflation of prices and the devaluation of money as a cause for our tribulations are the inflation of selfishness and the devaluation of moral values and ideals. Our age is conditioned to think only in terms of rights, never of duties and obligations, only of what people can get out of life, not what they must put into it. Contending parties and politicians have only recently told us that we face a crisis which was never so bad – when, incidentally, they told us not so long ago that we never had it so good. They then proceeded to display an assortment of programmes which would raise Britain out of its economic doldrums, but none dealt with the root of the crisis, which is simply that we do not work hard enough.

We can no longer match the growing demand for rising living standards with the declining will to work, with the waning pride and pleasure in producing the means of personal and national wealth. In today's competitive world, a nation without extraordinary resources cannot prosper on a 30-odd hour working week (interspersed by two-hourly tea-breaks or afternoons off for golf), periodically disrupted by strikes, and compromised during work by indifference to the job.

The real crisis betrays a perverse sense of values, a warped philosophy of life, in which pleasure is the *summum bonum,* in which comfort and the avoidance of work are a greater virtue than diligence, and in which the pursuit of selfish interests is the legitimate road to success and power.

Naturally, an effective challenge to work harder, to place the serving of others above, or at least on a par with, promoting one's own interests, such an unpopular demand can hardly come from those vying for massive votes in popularity contests. Who, if not religious leaders, can advocate the application of the Golden Rule of loving one's neighbour as oneself to the wider sphere of social relations, of caring for the welfare of others as for one's own – now that this may well be a key to economic survival no less than to personal salvation?

Selfishness is also at the root of the increasingly bitter and potentially explosive polarisation of society – or confrontation, in the contemporary parlance. This threatens to lead not merely to economic bankruptcy but to civil strife and political instability of unpredictable consequence. In this day and age of instant communications, when the wealth and comforts of the rich are constantly portrayed on the screens of the underprivileged and disadvantaged in their very homes, the inequalities between the haves and have-nots, or have-less, are bound to arouse greater envy than ever before and to erupt into desperate, sometimes even violent, action to redress the balance.

In the face of these realities, we surely ought not to wait for pickets and demonstrators to denounce and eliminate the social injustices which still maintain an indefensible differential between the wages of some labourers and the incomparably higher earnings of those in management, or entertainment, or other recipients of rewards unrelated to output, training, skill and effort. The equitable redistribution of wealth should be a powerful moral challenge to unite the nation, not a political slogan to divide it. Its fiercest advocates ought to be the appointed custodians of the nation's moral conscience rather than the partisans of class and party.

At the same time, religious leadership might be expected, by a concerted effort, to help in devising a more civilised and less damaging method for resolving industrial conflicts than by crippling strikes, which cause millions of innocent citizens who are not a party to the dispute – not to mention the national economy – to suffer grievous harm, untold misery and hardship, appalling losses and sometimes even death as a result.

Religious leaders would have to take the lead in both pressing more rigorously for social justice with civic responsibility and helping to find a system of adjudication or mediation which would render arguments between sections of industry amenable to the same orderly and fair process of resolution as we take for granted when individuals have conflicting claims.

Perhaps an even more disturbing phenomenon calling for the greater involvement of religious leaders in public affairs is the problem of the rising tide of violence and its corollary, the cheapening of human life.

Significantly, with the end of the long Vietnam War, and the mercifully short armed conflicts in the Middle East and Cyprus, the world is now without an international war for the first time in decades. But, instead of conflicts fought over international frontiers or for military targets, war has now moved into the streets and homes of our cities, into shops and offices, banks and public houses, railway stations on the ground and civilian planes in the skies. Hijacks, kidnaps, car-bombs, letter-bombs, incendiary devices, muggings, vandalism – these words are now among the most common terms in our contemporary vocabulary, bringing the threat of violence in any innocent mailbag to unsuspecting citizens everywhere, and exposing even children as deliberate targets of political blackmail and extortion.

The wave of indiscriminate violence is only one aspect of the current assault on the supreme value of life. There is the threat to life from atom-bomb tests prompted by a false national vanity. There is the ecological peril to our environment which, through our reckless abuse of the bounty of nature in the name of economic progress, threatens to poison our food, pollute our rivers and choke us in the very air we breathe. There is the legalised cheapening of human life; at its inception through wholesale abortions for reasons of personal convenience, at its conclusion through the despatch of the incurably sick and aged urged by the agitators for euthanasia, and – in the period between swaddling clothes and the shroud – through experimentation on humans in the interests of medical science.

If, in an ostensibly civilised society like ours, the absolute sanctity of life can be legally set aside for selfish reasons of national pride, political dogma, material advantage, personal comfort and social convenience, or even for what has been medically justified as 'important research procedures', can we be surprised that fanatical or misguided groups or individuals apply the same reasoning, with equal logic, to justify murder and violence for political ends? In a climate of disdain for life, can we wonder there are those who seek political domination or social revolution through terror and anarchy, or engage in extortion by violence to support these or lesser causes?

Worse still, we are now told, often by representatives of the very agencies responsible for the enforcement of law and order, that we will have to learn to live with violence as an accepted fact of modern life. This is the counsel of despair and the surest prescription for failure. It is like telling a person with a nagging toothache that he should learn to live with it, instead of repairing to a dentist to have it cured. Or like telling a school committee concerned with the indiscipline of unruly children in a classroom that they must accept the situation, instead of devising ways to improve the training of teachers and children – and perhaps also of parents – in order to eliminate the problem.

The moment society or groups of individuals are prepared to come to terms with injustice, to say 'it's too bad; we will have to learn to live with it', then they will indeed have to live – and suffer – with it, for they surrender the will to ameliorate their lot and lose the hope of improving their condition. The great glory of this country in 1940, 'its finest hour', was precisely that its people were not prepared to come to terms with evil.

Unless religious teachings help to restore the infinite regard for the sanctity of life, we will face catastrophe; as our cities turn into jungles, and terrorist gangsters, holding up to ransom governments, citizens and including even children, will rule the world at will in an orgy of human self-destruction. I stress religious teachings, for only religion postulates that no life is expendable, that life being infinite in value is indivisible, making one human being worth as much as a million others and conferring on each equally infinite value.'

University of Leeds, 15 October 1974

PARENTAL CONSENT

Sir, Having signed, together with other national religious leaders, a statement in support of Mrs [Victoria] Gillick's case against the DHSS guidelines permitting doctors to prescribe contraception to girls under 16, even without their parents' knowledge or consent, I naturally applaud the judgement of the Court of Appeal.

I welcome this important decision for two quite distinct reasons. The 'professional guidance' by the General Medical Council, endorsed by the BMA, had stated: 'If the patient (under the age of 16) refuses to allow a parent to be told, the doctor must observe the rule of professional secrecy in his management of the case.' In other words, any conflict between parents and doctors in claiming the confidence of children is to be resolved in favour of the doctors.

The Appeal Court ruling has restored the supremacy of the Ten Commandments' 'Honour your father and your mother' over the medical profession's self-proclaimed guidelines. This is bound to be greeted with immense relief by all who seek to reassert the rights and duties of parents and who see a major cause for the rampant rise of crime and vice in the widespread breakdown of family life, aggravated by officially encouraged challenges to parental control.

The BMA has argued that the new judgement will 'force doctors into actions that will betray confidences and damage a fundamental principle of medical practice'. That may well be so. But surely even doctors will not argue that this principle is more fundamental than the respect owed to parents. Indeed, no other profession – teachers, clergymen or lawyers – ever made any such claim, demanding stronger bonds of trust with themselves than children have with parents.

The second reason for acclaiming the court ruling is that it represents a notable reversal of the trend towards an ever-more permissive society.

The BMA document quite rightly affirms the strong belief 'that if people under 16 know that their parents will be informed against their wishes, many more will just not seek contraceptive help, and more girls will become pregnant. It is likely that abortion rates would rise in consequence'.

These consequences are unfortunate and may indeed be inevitable, at least for a while. But what the document does not consider is that an even greater number of girls (and their boyfriends) will now think twice before they irresponsibly embark on sexual adventures, and hold back from the brink of temptation by the very fear that a moment's pleasure may no longer be concealed from parents, or its effects neutralised by the simple expedient of a doctor's prescription.

Doctors themselves ought to feel relieved that they will no longer be unwillingly exploited for the promotion of promiscuity.

Immanuel Jakobovits, Chief Rabbi
The Times, 31 December 1984

ONLY A MORAL REVOLUTION CAN CONTAIN THIS SCOURGE

I have delayed publicly expressing a view on the awesome menace of Aids now hanging like a monstrous medieval plague over mankind, despite pressures from within my community and beyond to make some authentic Jewish pronouncement. This is due not merely to the fact that most authoritative Jewish statements on the moral issues were made thousands of years ago.

The earliest sources of Jewish law and morality are quite unambiguous. The Bible brands homosexual relationships as a capital offence (Leviticus 20:13), and execrates any sexual licentiousness as an abomination, whether in the form of premarital 'harlotry' (Deuteronomy 23:18) or of extra-marital adultery (Leviticus 20:10). Equally stern are the warnings of national doom consequent on any defiance of these principles: the land itself will 'vomit out' peoples violating these injunctions (Leviticus 18:28–29).

My hesitation in adding a Jewish voice to the many religious and moral statements already widely publicised, and worthy of endorsement, has been accentuated by the uncompromising nature of these biblical strictures. The difficulties go beyond the dilemma of choosing between soothing platitudes and unpalatable truths. I am still racked by doubts on how to react to such a horrendous threat, how to address an age not exactly attuned to the puritan language of the Bible, how to transcend the perplexities which baffle medical and government experts, and how to present deeply held convictions without causing offence, panic, or disdain for the very teachings I espouse.

There are questions to which I simply know of no categorical answers. Some are practical: is it right to advocate 'safe sex'? Or, should all citizens be subjected to screening tests to identify carriers, and if so, how is this information to be used? Some questions are theological: can a disease like this, patently discriminating against certain sections of society, be attributed to divine wrath, or altogether be adjudged in moral terms? And some are purely human: how can one reassure without spreading complacency, warn without condescension or self-righteousness, and highlight the horrific without inducing immunity to shock by horror? Altogether, are habits and behaviour susceptible to change by moral exhortation, by publicity campaigns, or even by medical information?

Inscrutable as the answers may as yet be, and rudimentary as may be our understanding of the long-term effects of Aids and its spread, not to mention the prospects of halting its ravages, certain facts seem incontrovertible as a basis for some conclusions in the light of Jewish insights and moral principles.

Both at the individual and the public level, we are certainly never entitled to declare a particular form of suffering as a punishment for a particular manifestation of wrongdoing. We can no more divine why some people endure terrible ills without any apparent cause than we can comprehend why others prosper though they clearly do not deserve their good fortune. Even less are we ever justified in being selective, subjecting some scourges to this moral analysis while exempting others (Aids, yes; but earthquakes or floods or droughts, no). There is no such simplistic relationship between evil and misfortune, if only because there are too many exceptions. According to Jewish exegesis, the prophet Isaiah had his lips scorched because he sinned in saying, 'I dwell in the midst of a people of unclean lips' (Isaiah 6:5–6).

There is all the difference – even if the distinction is a fine one – between ascribing massive suffering to personal or social depravity as a divine visitation, and warning that such depravity may *lead* to terrible consequences. If I warn a child not to play with fire, and it ignores the warning and gets burned, the hurt is not a punishment but simply a consequence. If people recklessly indulge in infidelity and end up in the agony of a broken marriage, they suffer no vengeance; they simply pay the inevitable price for moral negligence or turpitude.

Public information campaigns should therefore be explicit and unequivocal: Aids is the price we pay for the 'benefits' of the permissive society which, helped by the pill, liberal legislation and more 'enlightened' attitudes, has demolished the last defences of sexual restraint and self-discipline, leading to a collapse of nature's self-defence against degeneracy.

An even greater price in human misery than deaths from Aids is being paid for violating the imperatives of sexual morality: the devastation of the family, with millions of casualties, especially among young people driven to vice and crime by the absence of a loving home. The provision of condoms, condoning and facilitating sexual irresponsibility, is therefore hardly the answer, even if they temporarily reduce the transmission of Aids. They would only increase the ravages of personal degradation and social disintegration. In any case, what has to be carefully weighed is individual safety against the erosion of public standards. The principle is illuminated in a striking precedent – Jewish law and thought must invariably search for guidance in earlier sources.

A leading fifteenth-century Spanish-Jewish scholar objected to the establishment of facilities for communally controlled prostitution to keep licentiousness from running wild – even if this objection meant failing to prevent married partners from committing the capital offence of adultery (as implied in the Ten Commandments, Judaism makes no difference between killing a person and killing a marriage). He argued that, however culpable individual indiscipline is, its mitigation cannot be sanctioned at the expense of the slightest public compromise with the Divine Law (Rabbi Isaac Arama, *Akedat Yitzhak*, Gate 20).

True, in Jewish law the saving of life overrides all religious precepts. But even this pro-life stance has three cardinal exceptions: forbidden liaisons, murder and idolatry are proscribed even at the cost of life. This, too, would seem to rule out recourse to any measures, such as condoms for unmarrieds, which would encourage indecent conduct, though the rule might be invoked to treat more leniently the distribution of clean needles for drug-abusers. No less important than clean needles are clean speech, clean thoughts and clean conduct. What will be crucial is the cultivation of new attitudes calculated to restore reverence for the generation of life and the enjoyment of sexual pleasures exclusively within marriage. Nothing short of a moral revolution will in time contain the scourge.

The role of governments in achieving these objectives is admittedly limited. Morality cannot be legislated, nor can politicians and civil servants become preachers. But the administrators of our national affairs cannot remain morally neutral either, when the eventual cost may be counted in millions of lives.

Governments can help to refine human behaviour – for instance, by opposing any legislation liable to weaken the bonds between husband and wife or parents and children. Equally, governments can, by the careful use of language in official speech and documents, eliminate from the common vocabulary the kind of euphemisms or misnomers that make perversions acceptable. I think of words like 'gay' for homosexual, 'heterosexual' for normal, 'safe sex' for inadmissible indulgence, and 'stable relationships' for unmarried couples.

The Jewish experience demonstrates that, in the final analysis, only spiritual power is invincible as a shield against lust. This is perhaps reflected in observant Jews, however addicted to smoking, finding the Sabbath prohibition against lighting a cigarette far more effective than the most alarming health warnings in securing complete abstention from smoking for one day in seven. They have also discovered that a conscience so trained prevails even in the most intimate relations between husband and wife: the religious ban on any physical contact for some 12 days in every normal month, regularly rejuvenating the marriage through an iron self-discipline, achieves more than the most skilled marriage counsellor could in regulating the rhythm of love and longing. Natural urges can be bridled in submission to a higher law.

What is needed, then, is a massive campaign mobilising government resources and citizens of all faiths and of none to strive for moral excellence, to avoid the arousal of passions in literature and entertainment, to extol the virtues of fidelity, and to promote the utmost compassion for those struck by a hideous killer as a result of failings which may not be theirs but the society's into which they were born, and which to ennoble is the charge of us all. Every action to promote these ideals has now become a life-saving operation – including saving marriages as the sole legitimate origin of all human life.

The Times, *27 December 1986*

HOPE IN A BETTER FUTURE

I want to draw attention to a striking paradox. In this age of constant moaning over declining morals and mounting perils, we should also hail some very solid advances towards social justice and human brotherhood achieved in our life-time at a speed and on a scale unprecedented in all the thousands of years of man's tortuous evolution.

The dismantling of colonialism, leading to the emergence of scores of newly freed nations; the rise of the Welfare State, providing care for the sick, the aged, the workless and the poor formerly often abandoned to destitution; the ability of the mass media to arouse millions to protest against suffering, oppression and hunger among people thousands of miles away; the upgrading of 'human rights' to the top of the international agenda at summit meetings and global conferences: all these represent momentous progress.

And here comes the paradox. All these ideals of compassion, equality, freedom and brotherhood are basically the essence of religious teachings. We may therefore have expected these forward thrusts to be generated primarily by religious forces. Yet nothing of the sort happened. The role of religion and religious leadership was at best only marginal in the advances I have mentioned.

The initiative for all these remarkable developments in the refinement of the moral and social conscience came invariably from secular or purely humanist sources. Perhaps it is precisely because these gains lacked a spiritual dimension that they are now in danger of being swept aside by new scourges of drugs, terrorism, shameless promiscuity and a novel form of economic conquest and exploitation. Perhaps the relative impotence and irrelevance of religious leadership explains why a more caring society, which we undoubtedly witness today, can yet be more careless about the wreckage of marriages or the desolation of unemployment.

Even the activists campaigning for a better world need spiritual directives to sustain their efforts and keep their goals in sight. The noblest campaigns for human rights become worthless if the campaigners themselves become demoralised through idleness, or insensitive to suffering through the surfeit of violence in entertainment and the media, and aimless in life by despair in human progress.

The strangest inconsistencies now abound in human affairs. Yes, the world is more egalitarian and classless today than ever before. Yet, the gap between the haves and the have-nots is constantly growing, and hardly a shoulder is shrugged when we are told that 900 million people are threatened with starvation, or that the industrial nations spend 20 times more on armaments than on aid to the Third World.

Labour-saving technology enables us to reduce the time spent on work and on travel to but a small fraction of what was needed only a couple of generations ago. What are we doing with all the time we save? One would imagine that people would be more relaxed, more cultured, better read and more free to devote themselves to spiritual pursuits. In fact, the contrary is true. Those who are busy are more harassed than ever, and those who have time on their hands kill it with mischief and frustration, making everyone more prone to irritation and aimlessness.

There are major defects in our moral judgements. Well-meaning libertarians protect the interests of criminals sometimes at the cost of their victims; these campaigners defend the peddlers of pornography, and they agitate for the freedom of the press to be open for character assassins and hate-mongers, while the freedom and security of the law-abiding majority are under ever-mounting pressure.

More odious still is the selective morality which singles out some countries for international boycotts and ostracism while passing in silence over the far worse violations of human and democratic rights in other countries. Such discrimination is morally indefensible and ought to be challenged by religious leadership.

By concerted action, religious leadership – transcending the often quite legitimate self-interest of politicians and industrialists alike – could contribute to improving the human condition, for instance – as I have suggested before – by urging an international ban on all arms sales, perhaps the most immoral blot afflicting us. Since 1945, the world has witnessed some 150 wars, with more than 20 million fatal casualties, all fought with conventional arms freely sold and shipped for political or commercial gain.

We raise a few million pounds to relieve hunger in war-ravaged countries such as Ethiopia, Sudan or Mozambique. How many more lives would we save, quite apart from the victims of violence, if by denying arms to all these countries they would be forced to divert their national economy from arms purchases to building a healthy infrastructure, a flourishing agriculture and an effective network of educational enterprises?

Above all, religion is summoned to sustain hope, especially in an age afflicted by much resignation and despair. I once heard a police commissioner in Britain, commenting on rising crime rates, say that we would have to learn to live with crime. This is the counsel of despair. The opposite is true: we have to learn not to live with crime, to abhor it as unacceptable and intolerable. The moment we get used to evil, it will never be conquered. Only by confidence in a better future can and will the impediments to it be eliminated.

I know from my pastoral experience in visiting hospitals that a patient who does not believe in his own recovery can often not be helped by the best doctors and nurses. Hope is the key to getting better. Hope is the first condition to the betterment of life, to overcoming the evils, the fears and the scourges besetting so much of our stricken world. Without confidence in a better future, there will be no better future, and it is up to religion to generate this hope.

The Times, *13 February 1989*

[*This article was based on an address to the World Economic Forum in Davos, Switzerland.*]

Pronouncements such as these led in time to international recognition of the Chief Rabbi's courage and fearlessness, often in the face of widespread criticism. In March 1991, he received the ultimate accolade:

WORLD'S MOST VALUABLE PRIZE

Chief Rabbi Lord Jakobovits has won the world's most valuable prize, worth £410,000. This week he became the first Jew to be awarded the prestigious Templeton Prize for Progress in Religion. He will receive it formally from Prince Philip at Buckingham Palace in May.

Lord Jakobovits, who was in New York this week for the announcement of the award, said that he would use the prize money to establish a Jakobovits Foundation, which would fund 'innovative and ground-breaking research intended to promote the impact of religion in every area of Jewish life'. He hopes to attract leading experts to conduct research into areas such as family stability, including the cause of marriage break-ups; marriage and sex education for schoolchildren; business ethics; race relations; and relations between governments.

The Templeton Prize is the brainchild of a Presbyterian millionaire, Sir John Marks Templeton, who lives in the Bahamas. It is awarded annually to 'a person who has advanced humankind's understanding of God'. Lord Tonypandy, former Speaker of the House of Commons, who was among those who nominated Lord Jakobovits for the prize, said that the Chief Rabbi had shown 'exemplary originality and courage in interpreting the traditional values of Judaism and in their application to the spiritual and political problems which today beset Jews'.

The first recipient, in 1973, was Mother Teresa. Other previous winners include Billy Graham and Alexander Solzhenitsyn.

Speaking at a press conference after returning from New York, Lord Jakobovits said that he planned to launch a campaign against the worldwide trade in conventional arms. 'More wars have been fought with imported weapons since the Second World War than at any other time in history', he said. 'These weapons of destruction are recklessly available. This is a moral issue, and we need to bring religious teaching to issues such as this that bedevil our world.'

He said that campaigns against nuclear weapons were already led by church leaders, but conventional weapons needed to be added to the campaign because they had killed so many people.

Lord Jakobovits expressed the hope that the Jakobovits Foundation would apply religious teaching to present-day concerns through research and publicity and through the promotion of the work of fellow scholars. These concerns included the problems and responsibilities of marriage, business ethics, race relations, international relations, and the weapons trade. 'I would like to strive to achieve ideals set in the past, such as stable marriage', he said. 'I would like honesty and decency to become trendy.'

Discussing a theme that had endeared him to former Prime Minister Margaret Thatcher, he asserted that the Jewish religion was precise on business ethics. 'We don't look askance but applaud people whose objective it is to gain, as long as that gain is acquired legitimately and is shared. There is a moral dimension to gaining wealth, and Judaism has whole volumes dealing with the laws of charity.'

Lord Jakobovits said efforts must be made on both sides to solve the problem in the Middle East, 'because there can be no peace in the world if there is no peace in the Holy Land'. Peace could be obtained if Israel were no longer regarded as a miscreant by her neighbours, and if Israel responded by recognising legitimate Arab aspirations. 'The indignity inflicted on Arabs in the refugee camps is unacceptable, especially to Jews who know what it is to be outcasts. Jews should be the first to awaken the conscience of the world to collective suffering.'

As a religious leader, as opposed to a political leader, the Chief Rabbi wished to generate hope that the problems could be solved. 'Despair is the problem, and far too many people have given up hope that the problem can be solved. We must generate the conviction that the problem is able to be solved.'

Jewish Chronicle, *March 1991*

ON RECEIVING THE TEMPLETON PRIZE

'On a global scale, the fortunes and misfortunes of religion since the Second World War have been without precedent. Pressed from opposite sides, religion was caught in a vice which nearly strangled it – in the East by militant atheism, and in the West by equally godless materialism. It is surprising that religion survived this twin assault altogether.

Within religion, seeds of doubt were also sown, and a whole school of a 'God-is-dead' theology sprang up. The trauma of the Second World War, culminating in the Holocaust, threw up questions never asked before, leading to the challenge: Where was God at Auschwitz?

For myself, the question is unanswerable – but no more so than when God's justice is challenged by a cot death striking an innocent infant and devastating the lives of bereaved young parents. Infinity cannot be multiplied, and the inscrutable death of one child or a million, or the six million butchered simply because they were Jews, all cry out equally: Where was God?

The Nazi barbarities may have manifested a dehumanisation of man rather than a dethronement of God. That is true. Nevertheless, they shook the religious faith of many who could not embrace the simple logic of a famous Jewish savant earlier this century who said: 'For those with faith, there are no questions; and for those without faith, there are no answers.'

Has religion progressed? There were, to be sure, some astounding moral as well as political and social advances in the wake of the war. The clamour for human rights and national freedom gained powerful momentum. The grossest inequalities of centuries came to an abrupt end.

Colonialism was dismantled, empires dissolved, and the dominance of the white man was abrogated. Scores of new nations were born, asserting their right to be free and their claim to an equal voice among the newly emergent United Nations. These are strides without parallel.

Yet, on the whole, these forces of liberalisation were motivated not by religion but by plainly secular nationalism. I believe the only really significant exception is Zionism as the Jewish national liberation movement. It was, and remains, activated above all by religious aspirations rooted of course in the Bible. But otherwise, even the vision of the United Nations itself was hardly conceived by religious promptings.

Of course, the great religions themselves made enormous progress in their inter-relations in the post-war world. For the first time in history, they entered into dialogues with each other. Religion vested the very term 'dialogue' with a new meaning.

But these advances were probably influenced by the secular trend towards greater tolerance rather than by purely religious dynamics. After all, only a few years earlier, the great religions looked the other way, and even came to terms with history's most monstrous tyranny.

Since then, the pages of contemporary history have been further soiled by what I can only call the unacceptable face of religion. Religious extremism and fundamentalism have lately led to brutal oppression and violence gripping millions.

Then there are the world's most intractable conflicts, such as in Northern Ireland and in the Middle East, to show how hard it is to extinguish fires lit by the combustion of religious zealotry. As further examples, I am bound to include the hawkishness of religious parties in Israel, and, on a different level, the offensive campaigns of aggressive evangelism.

Still on the debit side must be listed the pronounced pacifism, amounting to craven appeasement, among many religious leaders and groupings. By a strange irony, such pacifism is the obverse of religious militancy, but the result is the same. The knowledge that violence will not be resisted inevitably encourages men of violence.

No one has yet invented a method of overpowering violence in self-defence without force; and where even the threat of force is withdrawn, criminals and oppressors are bound to prevail. Religion all too often prevaricated in this struggle against tyranny and terror.

Again, why has not religion spoken out more forcefully against the worst international evil: the vast and indiscriminate international arms trade? By arousing the world's conscience against this evil, religious energies would do more to preserve human life than umpteen appeals for food or money to relieve starvation.

This leads me to the credit side of religion. Its momentous contributions are often belittled or ignored. Religion remains our principal defence against the erosion of moral values. The Bible is still by far the world's leading best seller.

Perhaps the most urgent contribution religion can yet make in our age is to counter the individual's sense of impotence and irrelevance, that we are but insignificant bystanders in the drama of events in which the really fateful historic decisions are made by a handful of political leaders and some outstanding scientists, industrialists, and a few others who leave their fingerprints on the tapestry of history.

Religion wants to endow each human being with a sense of uniqueness. We all must aspire to contribute something which no one else could give. Our ambition must be to ensure that the world would not be the same without us.

I recall that in 1957, when I was still Chief Rabbi of Ireland, I went on my first lecture tour of the United States and Canada. Here I made a proposal which, though widely reported, was never acted upon. I now repeat it some 30 years later, in the hope that my Templeton distinction may give it greater resonance than a fluttering shamrock leaf driven across the Atlantic in 1957.

The United Nations had proclaimed a 'Geo-Physical Year', calling on the world community to undertake special projects to promote the exploration and understanding of the physical universe in which we lived. That global effort helped considerably to advance our scientific knowledge.

I then said, and I propose it again today: why not similarly proclaim a 'Geo-Spiritual Year' in which countries the world over would be urged to participate in an unprecedented global effort.

Let the world's finest brains and resources explore man's spiritual condition, and how best to enhance it. Could not underwater or outer space research and other scientific exploits be matched in excitement, and in usefulness to human progress, by worldwide projects

- to study the causes of marriage breakdowns;
- to experiment on new approaches in the fight against crime and vice;
- to find out scientifically how we can make our youth less selfish and more committed to the service of others;
- to study the impact of the ethical issues raised by the quest for justice and peace;
- to cultivate ambition and to nurture a taste for art, literature and culture generally.

Perhaps during such a Geo-Spiritual Year, schools the world over might be encouraged to participate in substantial prize essay competitions on some outstanding feats of virtue, on singular examples of nobility of heart and mind, on charity at its finest, or on some spectacular success in turning a dropout into a noble citizen, such essays to be published in the world's press to create widespread public interest and involvement. Let our finest academic minds be harnessed

- to study the role of religion in human refinement;
- to analyse the religious factor in business honesty and human decency;
- and to probe into the relationship of religious faith to political creativity and social stability.

In an age when we can peer into the mysteries of the genetic code inside us, of the sea beneath us, and the heavens above us, let us try to discover the one formula which still eludes us: how to build two homes next to each other that happiness reigns inside them and peace between them.

Thus could my fellow-humans share in my debt for the Templeton Prize as an encouragement not only of progress *in* religion but of progress *through* religion.'

From Lord Jakobovits' Acceptance Speech, Nineteenth Presentation of the Templeton
Prize for Progress in Religion, Vancouver, Canada, 29 May 1991

(The printed record of the presentation ceremony, published by the Lismore Press, Nassau, Bahamas, noted, *inter alia*: 'Lord Jakobovits, Chief Rabbi of Great Britain and the Commonwealth, is a man whose steadfast principles and unwavering integrity have extended his moral authority far beyond the Jewish community. In 50 years of rabbinical leadership, Lord Jakobovits has developed a reputation as a rock of un-yielding ethics. His efforts to advance Judaism have set him on an often-lonely path, sometimes putting himself at odds with many of his own faith. Even those who do not agree with him, however, admit that they are charmed by this man who exudes warmth, humour and extraordinary scholarship ...' In his address, Sir John Templeton stated: 'The Templeton Prize does not encourage syncretism but rather an understanding of the benefits of diversity. It seeks to focus attention on the wide variety of highlights in present-day religious thought and work. It does not seek a unity of denominations or a unity of world religions; but rather it seeks to encourage understanding of the benefits of each of the great religions ... Each of the 20 winners has been very different from the others. We rejoice in the increasingly rich diversity of religion. Millions of people in all nations are uplifted and inspired by studying the life and work of each recipient ...')

CHAPTER NINE

Soviet Jewry

'Alleviating the religious attrition and communal isolation of our Russian brethren'

Sir, The right of free worship enjoyed by all in this country will shortly be very fully exercised by our Jewish community during our forthcoming High Holy-days. We are profoundly aware that, by sad contrast, our fellow-Jews in the USSR sorely yearn for similar freedom to practise their faith, to instruct their children without harassment, and to be reunited with their people in the land of their forefathers. To our deep sorrow, our Russian brethren are deprived of the most basic spiritual comforts and the elementary means of religious expression.

Moving testimony is given in the following letter, a photographic copy of which has just reached me. It is addressed to Rabbi Levin of Moscow:

'I apply to you because, unfortunately, there is no rabbi now in our city. And you in effect represent the religious Jews before the Soviet State, and you often speak in their name. I hope that you will examine my request and will answer me. My brother, Yosef Mendelevich, has been sentenced by the Supreme Court of the RSFSR to 12 years of imprisonment for an attempt to go to Israel illegally. At present, my brother is in the investigation isolation ward of the Leningrad Department of State Security … I tried to transmit to my brother a prayer-book issued by the Moscow Jewish religious community in 1968, and a Bible issued in Berlin in 1903. However, the head of the investigation isolation ward refused to accept these books for transmission, for the sole reason that they are religious literature.

'My brother is deeply and sincerely religious, and the lack of religious literature causes him additional moral suffering.

'I ask you to petition the Soviet authorities that my brother should receive these books.'

A second case poignantly typifies the plight of Soviet Jews. In a desperate plea, Rabbi Shalom Yosef Schapira wrote to me as follows:

'My wife and I were born and lived in Chernowitz, Bukovina. In 1940, when the Russians conquered my home town, I was arrested and spent five years in a camp, and 21 years in Siberia. In 1967, God helped us and we were allowed to leave Russia for Israel. But our only son and his family were refused per-mission, though it is four years since he has been requesting a permit to leave the country.

'For us, as bereaved parents, life is very difficult without our child. I am 70 years old, my heart is weak, and my only ambition in life is to save my son and to bring him to his parents in Israel, to live a proper Jewish life, as he lives in a place that has not even one Jew. His name is Benjamin Yosifowitz Schapira, and he lives with his wife and daughter in Belgorod.'

It is our heartfelt prayer that these anguished cries from the depths will be answered with humanitarian compassion.

Immanuel Jakobovits, Chief Rabbi
The Times, 10 September 1971

In February 1972, the Chief Rabbi and his personal assistant, Rabbi Maurice Rose, spent three days at a reception centre for Soviet Jewish emigrants in Vienna, followed by a short visit to Israel. In an address to ministers and synagogue presidents soon after their return, Dr Jakobovits warned that 'if the revolutionary fervour of Soviet Jews arriving in Israel is allowed to run wild, the problems caused by the Black Panthers would be nothing compared with the trouble the latter could create. The dangers are so great that this could become a major irritant in Israeli society. But, if we harness their spiritual resources and their longing for spiritual inspiration, and if we give them this rooting in tradition and daily life, then we may stand at the gates of the golden age of religion, arts and science in Israel.'

The Chief Rabbi commented: 'This new element is going to bring to the scene in Israel an entirely different sort of immigrant. I believe that we are standing here before one of the most crucial crossroads of alternatives that are opening up to us. Every Russian Jew we met confirmed that our demonstrations are of the utmost importance. The Russians don't want to become embarrassed. It's not just that … They say the Jews are encouraged. It is most important that we maintain public pressure.'

A month after the visit, the Chief Rabbi's Office launched a £100,000 scheme, administered by the Federation of Jewish Relief Organisations, to provide religious inspiration to Russian Jewry inside the Soviet Union, on transit to Israel, and during the integration of new immigrants in Israel itself. The scheme, under the auspices of the Conference of European Rabbis, was financed by contributions from Jewish communities in Europe, Australia and the United States.

The Chief Rabbi called on all ministers and synagogue officials to ensure that every congregation established a local aid committee for Soviet Jewry and collected the funds for the various projects being undertaken. In Israel, a full-time director, Rabbi David Refson, formerly of Britain, was appointed to co-ordinate the efforts of voluntary bodies with those of official agencies.

A memorandum prepared by Chief Rabbi Jakobovits and Rabbi Rose, following their visits to Vienna and Israel, discussed the religious requirements of the newcomers from Russia. Among the practical steps taken was the provision of 'extra amenities' to newcomers in Israel and transit migrants in Vienna. Two thousand parcels would be provided, each containing a tallit, tefillin, Siddur, yarmulka, tzitzit and chalah-cloth. Half the total cost would be met by the Israeli Ministry of Religious Affairs.

In December 1975, the Chief Rabbi – together with Moshe Davis, the executive director of his office – paid an historic visit to the Soviet Union, at the official invitation of the Moscow Great Synagogue. The initiative came from Rabbi Yaacov Fishman, Rav of the Moscow Synagogue, and the lay leaders of the city's Jewish community.

Hearing of the invitation, some 50 Jewish academics who regularly met in Moscow, as the scientific and cultural seminar under the leadership of Professor Mark Azbel, issued their own invitation to the Chief Rabbi. They described themselves as 'a group of Jewish scientists resident in Moscow and fighting for our right of emigration to Israel'. Most had lost their academic positions – and thereby their means of livelihood – after applying for exit visas.

'Feeling a great regard for you personally and for you as a representative of Jewry of Great Britain,' they wrote, 'we invite you to visit our group, which includes more than 50 scientists and intellectuals denied emigration to Israel. Your visit would be extremely valuable and exciting to us. Some of us are religious in the Orthodox sense of the word, but the majority are interested in the philosophical, historical and practical aspects of Judaism as the basis of our national existence and our spiritual life.'

On his arrival in Moscow, the Chief Rabbi declared in a prepared statement: 'I have come to visit my Soviet brethren, to learn something about their life and concerns, and to strengthen the bonds between us – forged by a common history, a common faith and a common destiny. We want Soviet Jews to know how close they are to the hearts of all of us in the rest of the world. To this day, our religious and cultural life is inspired by what was created here, and our communities are often still led by rabbis, teachers and communal workers who were born and sometimes even trained here. So we obviously feel a special kinship with Soviet Jews and an exceptional affection for them.'

At the outset, a number of 'very positive suggestions' for Anglo-Jewish assistance in the religious sphere were put forward by Dr Jakobovits to government officials in Moscow. He discussed his proposals during a two-hour meeting with Viktor Titov, deputy chairman of the Council for Religious Affairs, a special department of the Council of Ministers. No details were disclosed, but Mr Davis, who was present at the talks, described them as 'helpful and very useful'.

Returning to Moscow from a two-day visit to Leningrad, the Chief Rabbi held a second meeting with senior Soviet officials, this time from the Ministry of the Interior, responsible for Jewish emigration. He thus fulfilled a pledge given before his departure that the two themes he would pursue during his Soviet mission would be 'Let my people live as Jews' and 'Let my people go'.

On the Shabbat, hundreds of Moscow Jews crowded into the Central Synagogue to hear Rabbi Jakobovits address them in Yiddish. So intense was their interest, and so emotional the event, that every member of the congregation insisted on standing. The Chief Rabbi, introduced by Rabbi Fishman, spoke of his joy at seeing Soviet Jewry and of the sadness at the suffering they had undergone. The great question was: Is the spirit of Russian Jews still alive? This was the central problem, Dr Jakobovits declared.

The following day, he attended the weekly scientific seminar organised by Professor Azbel. More than 60 scientists overflowed on to the stairs outside a small first-floor flat in the outskirts of Moscow. Expressing his admiration for the refuseniks, the Chief Rabbi said: 'Many of our students in our own community would not identify with Jewish life if it were not for you. You have awakened their Jewish consciousness.'

On his return to London from his nine-day visit, Rabbi Jakobovits spoke to the *Jewish Chronicle* of hopes held out by the Soviet authorities for the alleviation of the plight of the Jews. He said that new avenues would have to be carefully explored as a result of the visit.

'In our talks with high-ranking Soviet officials, first in the Department for Religious Affairs and then in the emigration and visa office of the Ministry of the Interior, we were able to raise the entire gamut of our concerns – ranging from emigration, the imprisonment and harassment of Jews who wish to leave for Israel, to the cultural, religious and communal needs of the majority who will be remaining in the Soviet Union.

'On the question of religious, cultural and communal facilities, we put forward to the Department of Religious Affairs a number of practical suggestions, including assistance by our own community in the field of exchange programmes, the training of rabbinical and religious officials, and the provision of literature. We also pressed for the only official Jewish journal, *Sovietish Heimland*, to be published in Russian as well as Yiddish, since few of the younger people (especially in the Baltic republics and Bessarabia, incorporated into the USSR during the war) know Yiddish. We also argued that Hebrew be accepted as an appropriate language for study.

'We were told that there was nothing in the law which barred the existing officially recognised Jewish religious communities from forming themselves into a federated and centralised body, as is the case in Romania, if they so wished. They had by tradition remained separate, with the rabbi of the Central Synagogue in Moscow acting as head.'

On a second visit to Moscow, in March 1976, Moshe Davis raised the question of allowing the printing of Jewish religious publications in the Soviet Union and the distribution of Hebrew books for religious Jews. During a three-hour meeting with Viktor Titov, he made a number of representations concerning the religious and cultural life of Soviet Jews.

Later that month, in an interview with *The Guardian*, the Chief Rabbi described progress on the Soviet Jewry issue as 'hopes deferred'. Little tangible or concrete had been achieved since he had visited the Soviet Union and made firm proposals. But, he added, the Russians seemed keen to maintain the contact and 'still want us to be confident and hopeful that certain positive developments are likely to ensue on all fronts – on exit permits, releases, and on cultural and religious rights'.

Contacts were indeed maintained, on the initiative of the Soviet authorities, both directly with Moscow and through the Russian Embassy in London. These included Soviet requests for further official visits and, particularly, participation in a Religious Peace Congress to be held in Moscow in June 1977. The Chief Rabbi's Office replied, however, that 'such responses cannot be contemplated until some substantial progress is made on the submissions presented to the authorities during and after his visit'.

A memorandum detailing these submissions, and the responses to them, was subsequently sent by the Chief Rabbi's Office to Viktor Titov. Among them were the following requests (responses in italics):

1. Training and exchange programmes
a) It is suggested that the British Jewish community assume responsibility for the training of three to six rabbinical students at Jews' College, London (the leading Jewish theological seminary in the British Commonwealth, with courses leading to university degrees combined with the rabbinical diploma), in special intensive and shortened courses, enabling qualified rabbis to return after three or four years' study for service in Soviet Jewish communities.

During our discussions in Moscow, this idea was fully explored. It was indicated that names of prospective students would be submitted. No such list was ever received and there has been no response to this request.

b) Pending the completion of this programme, we are prepared to make available competent rabbis for short-term services (ranging, perhaps, from three months to one year) at congregations in the Soviet Union, naturally subject to the approval of the respective synagogue leaders and the Soviet authorities.

c) We would wish to give every encouragement to communal and cultural exchange programmes, including periodic visits to and from Soviet Jewry by communal leaders, student and academic groups, participation in joint conferences and seminars, etc.

So far, the response has been negative, despite the obvious importance of such a programme as part of the Helsinki emphasis on cultural exchanges and religious contacts.

2. Organisation and representation

a) Jewish communities should be accorded the right, if they so desire, to organise themselves on a national basis by establishing a central council composed of delegates from existing congregations and other approved organisations and institutions which may be set up, plus such other Jewish notable individuals as may be invited to join the council in order to give it the widest possible representational character.

b) This Council of Soviet Jewry should be entitled to convene periodic meetings to discuss matters of common interest, including the provision of religious requisites, literature, training programmes, etc.

c) This Council, as the representative body of Soviet Jewry, should be free to participate with similar bodies representing Jewish communities in other countries in inter-Jewish religious conferences which may be convened both inside and outside the Soviet Union, as well as in official exchange visits, on the lines pioneered by my recent visit.

While such facilities are available to approved churches, they are completely absent on the Jewish scene. As a result, there is no formal contact whatever between Jewish communities in the USSR on the religious or lay levels, nor is there a representative council. This is not the case with the other religious denominations. This deficiency forces each of the few remaining synagogues to remain completely isolated, thus stifling any form of organised Jewish life.

3. Religious observance

a) The acute shortage of statutory books required for synagogue worship (particularly editions featuring the original Hebrew, together with a modern Russian translation) should be met either by fairly large-scale printing within the Soviet Union or by permission to import the required quantities. Suitable texts for reproduction or export are now freely available in various countries. There is also a considerable demand for phylactaries (tefillin), doorpost scrolls (mezuzot), prayer-shawls (tallitot) and other religious requisites, which it should be lawful to import without hindrance, as required and requested.

Permission for this was never granted. The only exception was permission to import a limited number of reprinted pre-World War I archaic Russian translations (specifically designated by the Soviet authorities as the Vilna 1914 edition) which obviously do not meet the requirements.

b) It should be officially reaffirmed that Jews who so desire may perform, or submit to, Jewish traditional observances at home or in the synagogue without let or hindrance.

Unfortunately, the opposite is the case. Further restrictions on the freedom to meet have been introduced. Almost on the eve of the signing of the Helsinki Accords, on 23 June 1975, a new Soviet 'Law on Religious Associations' was introduced, amending the 'Law on Religious Associations' of 8 April 1929. This was the first major legislative Act on religion for 46 years. Although this new law contained improvements in the status of religious associations, it introduced new restrictions, some of which affect Jewish religious practice with particular severity.

c) Where requested, sanction should be given to the establishment of Jewish cemeteries or special Jewish burial grounds, together with facilities to perform the Jewish traditional rites prior to interment, for those anxious to be buried in accordance with tradition.

In many major communities, no such facilities are available, despite repeated requests by the local religious Jews.

4. Culture and literature
a) While it is recognised that the teaching of religion to minors up to the age of 18 years (outside private instruction in the home) contravenes Soviet law, this clearly does not include the teaching of Hebrew as a language. There are today probably several thousand Soviet Jews (and possibly some non-Jews, too) intensely desirous to learn Hebrew, as a key to an understanding of the synagogue service and of the Jewish heritage generally. Jews inside and outside the Soviet Union would therefore greatly welcome an official statement acknowledging Hebrew as a legitimate subject for school instruction and the right publicly to conduct and announce classes in the Hebrew language. The same facilities, should, of course, exist for the teaching of Yiddish, although the demand for this is likely to be substantially smaller.

Despite the statement made in Izvestia *on 24 December 1976, that no language teaching is prohibited (including Hebrew and Yiddish), Hebrew teachers and schools are being refused registration, accompanied by a demand to stop teaching, with the argument that 'Hebrew is not part of Soviet curricula'. Hebrew-language books are being confiscated, homes are being searched, and books sent through the mail are being stopped. The teaching of Hebrew, even merely as a language, is therefore being virtually suppressed.*

b) The prohibition on religious instruction does not extend to cultural and literary pursuits, as was made clear to us. Hence, synagogues should be officially granted the right to arrange lecture programmes on the history and literature of the Jewish people, for applicants of all ages.

This has been completely resisted. The key to Jewish religious survival in the Soviet Union lies in this request.

c) Similarly, it would be appreciated if official confirmation were given that there is no objection to meeting individual or communal requests for modern books (in Russian) of Jewish cultural or literary interest. Such books are now becoming increasingly available for reprinting within the Soviet Union or for importation as required.

No permission was granted.

d) To meet the patent hunger for contemporary literary material, and for an organ to give Soviet Jews a sense of cohesion as a recognised nationality, it is further suggested that sanction be officially granted for the issuance of a religious periodical magazine (on the lines of the *Journal of the Moscow Patriarchate*), to be published by the Moscow Jewish community, with the help of an editorial board of experts to be appointed. The editor of the *Sovietish Heimland* declared to me his willingness to undertake the production of such a magazine. Its distribution would, of course, be handled by the synagogue throughout the country, and the magazine should also be freely available by subscription.

This suggestion continues to be resisted and clearly illustrates the discrimination against the Jewish faith.

e) Facilities should be accorded for the setting up of clubs, institutes, seminars and other desired amenities, both inside and outside the synagogue, to provide such Jews as are interested in opportunities for social, recreational, artistic, literary or scholarly self-expression.

Seminars such as suggested above were planned with full legality and were severely clamped down upon. Raids were conducted in the homes of the organisers, and they and their families were subjected to grave harassment.

The lack of progress was reinforced by the Chief Rabbi in a statement from his office on 6 December 1976:

A DETERIORATING SITUATION

'A year ago, I visited the USSR. It was for me a momentous and moving experience, which I described on my return in several articles, lectures and addresses, and during interviews on radio and television. Following my visit, and at the suggestion of the Soviet authorities with whom I had held personal discussions, I submitted written memoranda dealing with both religious and cultural matters. I also appealed for clemency on behalf of a number of prisoners, and made submissions for exit visas to be granted to a limited number of individuals who, for over five years, had failed to obtain permission to leave the country. It was indicated to me that a positive response would be made, and, indeed, about one-third of these visa requests have been granted. But the bulk of my proposals still remain to be implemented. Ongoing contacts with the Soviet authorities are being maintained.

Regrettably, overall, this last year has seen a deterioration in the situation of the Jewish community in the USSR. While some concessions were made – High Holy-day services this year were undisturbed, and a memorial service was permitted to be held at Babi Yar – prisoners of conscience still continue to languish in confinement. Cultural activities, completely within Soviet law, meet with rebuff. Attempts to hold seminars have resulted in searches of private houses and confiscation of material. Tens of thousands of parcels of matzo despatched from abroad were confiscated by the Russian authorities, although I have now been assured that no obstacles will be placed on the future delivery of such gifts.

Religious freedom for all faiths is seriously restricted. In any review of human rights in the Soviet Union, this must feature as a principal concern. It remains my firm belief that we must continue to press with all means at our disposal for the alleviation of the Jewish situation, both religious and cultural, within the USSR; and, indeed, to assert the rights of all individuals wishing to leave the country to be able to do so freely and without harassment.'

In December 1980, Chief Rabbi Jakobovits, as president of the Conference of European Rabbis, was asked at short notice to lead a rabbinical delegation to plead the cause of Soviet Jewry at the European Security Conference in Madrid. The delegation also comprised the Chief Rabbis of France, Italy, Holland, Ireland, Switzerland, Denmark, Norway, and Spain. They represented all the Chief Rabbinates in Western Europe, apart from that of Belgium, which was vacant. In a report written after the visit, Rabbi Jakobovits summarised his conclusions:

'It was clear that the British were deeply and genuinely committed to the cause of Soviet Jewry, which featured centrally in their presentation on human rights. When I asked whether any movement at all was discernible on the Soviet side, I was told that while no major breakthrough or meaningful concessions were to be expected at this conference, other than possibly a few individual accommodations, such as the unification of some families, nevertheless it was considered significant that the Soviets had not repudiated their accountability, or indeed their commitments, under the human rights section of the Helsinki Accord. In fact, the Russians had listened and responded to the torrent of accusations and challenges from the West with relative patience and lack of outspoken exasperation.

The Russian manoeuvre was to tell the West that progress on human rights (Basket 3) could not be expected until their demands for disarmament (Basket 1) were met or at least dealt with. The British and other Western delegations were strongly opposed to any such linkage, arguing that each 'Basket' was an entirely separate and independent commitment which could not be traded off for progress on others.

I then asked whether the West should not turn the tables on the Russians by arguing linkage in the opposite direction: if there was no substantial advance on human rights, should the Russians not be told that the West would question what was by far the greatest gain of the Russians at Helsinki, i.e., the international validation of the post-war East–West frontiers, which confirmed the territorial annexation of the vast areas by Russia and her allies?

Mr Harry Spence [the British delegate in charge of human rights] replied that no government delegation could press this view, since it would undermine the Western argument against any linkage. But he saw no reason why non-governmental agencies, such as Chief Rabbis, should not remind the Russians of the enormous advantages they got out of Helsinki.

Generally, the British view was that the intense pressure of world opinion was not altogether ignored by the Russians, and that 'with patience' some gradual relaxations might be anticipated. But this would also very much depend on extraneous developments, such as in Afghanistan and Poland.

All in all, I think we have every reason to be profoundly gratified by the British stand (and by their personal courtesy and helpfulness).

I told Mr S. A. Kondrachev [of the Soviet delegation], who had agreed to meet me after we discovered that no arrangements had been requested for the Chief Rabbis to meet his delegation, that – as he apparently knew – I had myself been on an official visit to Soviet Russia five years ago and maintained ongoing contact with the authorities there, as well as through the Soviet Embassy in London. Many of the hopes held out to me at the time had not been fulfilled; on the contrary, the repression was now more acute than ever. I had with me a detailed document listing the various submissions made to the Soviet authorities following my visit, and our assessment of the practical responses on each item, in most cases absolutely negative. When I suggested I leave the document with him – it was not a submission or a petition but merely a report – he firmly declined to receive it, arguing that he was flooded with documents and would in any case find no time to read it. If I so desired, I could forward it through the Soviet Embassy in London.

Turning to specifics, I mentioned our anguish, shared throughout the world, over the continued incarceration of Jewish prisoners of conscience, several of whom I named. He answered that in a few individual cases there were 'complications' which were being dealt with, but he could not understand why these few cases should cause such a worldwide furore. To this I replied: was it worthwhile, for the sake of these relatively few individuals, to arouse such bitterness and agitation throughout the world, and would it not be wiser simply to release them and thus put an end to campaigns which evidently caused so much irritation to the Soviets? [He responded that] the cases were complicated and would continue to receive attention.

On the repression of religious and cultural rights for Jews in the Soviet Union, I mentioned specifically the ban on Jewish literature and the teaching of Hebrew, although 150 languages were officially recognised. He replied that there were only 80 classical languages so recognised. I commented that Hebrew was surely the oldest and most classical of them, a point he conceded.

At the end, he tried to reassure me that the situation was constantly under review, but he was not authorised to give me any definite commitments.

It is evident that the Soviet Jewry campaign has aroused the intense concern of Western governments as the principal item on the human-rights agenda. It is also clear to me that Jewish campaigners throughout the world have been far more successful in highlighting the plight of Soviet Jewry than Christian or other ethnic communities have been in mobilising world opinion on behalf of other oppressed minorities. I also have a distinct impression that the mounting world pressure on human rights is not a matter of indifference to the Soviet Union, which is acutely embarrassed and irritated by the agitation.

What I am not sure is whether – however successful the campaign in the West, and however much supported by Western governments, and however anxious the Russians may be to avoid irritations – the Russians are likely to be forced into any realistic concessions on the human-rights front. Past experience is hardly encouraging. The intensified campaign for Soviet Jews has not succeeded in easing their plight, which is, if anything, more grim today than at any time since Stalin. Nor have far more powerful Western pressures, including trade and other boycotts threatening détente itself, made the slightest impact on Soviet policies in Africa and Asia, especially lately in Afghanistan.

It seems unlikely, therefore, that Russian attitudes to Soviet Jewry will be materially affected by outside agitation. The Soviets are exceedingly sensitive to not being seen to 'capitulate' to Western pressures, as already shown by the drastic emigration decline following the Jackson Amendment at the time. It is far more likely that the fate of Soviet Jews will be determined primarily by global calculations, such as Russia's strategic and economic interests, East–West relations generally, and Soviet attitudes towards Israel and the Middle East.

In the end, efforts to secure any significant advance on human rights, including relief for Soviet Jewry, may have to contemplate some form of linkage with other Soviet concerns, much as the present Western opposition to such a notion is appreciated. On the other hand, Jewish Soviet Jewry campaign policies, which have hardly changed over the years, may also not be entirely blameless for the present pitiful situation, particularly regarding the appalling dropout rate, which deals such a devastating blow to the whole campaign.

We are now paying a heavy price for neglecting the demand to 'Let My People Live' almost exclusively in favour of the slogan 'Let My People Go'. They go, or went, but of late mostly not to Israel. The only motivation for aliyah, what-ever the hardships and uncertainties, in preference to settlement elsewhere, is the overriding desire to live a fully Jewish life, inculcated by an appreciation of Jewish values. Had efforts over the years at spiritual rehabilitation been intensified inside the Soviet Union as well as during the often-prolonged transit of migrants in Rome, far more Soviet Jews might have opted for Israel because they want to live as Jews, rather than for other countries because they want to escape as Jews.

Moreover, the Soviet authorities are more likely to make some internal concessions to relieve repression of religious and cultural activities than visibly to relax policies on imprisonment and emigration. Regarding the former, we should not forget, Jews are far worse off than other religious or national groups, while in respect of the latter, Jews are treated no differently from other discontented minorities who also seek to emigrate and whose leaders also suffer cruel incarceration and exile.

The conclusion seems inescapable that the 'Pros' of the establishment guiding world Jewish policies on Soviet Jewry are still often governed by assumptions and slogans which are now long dated. What is needed is bold fresh thinking in a constant reassessment of the ever-changing conditions determining Soviet attitudes.'

Enlarging on the 'appalling dropout rate', the Chief Rabbi spelled out his concerns in an article written soon after his Madrid visit:

SOVIET JEWISH DROPOUTS: WHOSE FAILURE?

The 'dropout' rate among Soviet Jews has for some time now given cause for alarm. Lately, the proportion of such Jews, choosing settlement in America or elsewhere in preference to Israel, on leaving the Soviet Union with Israeli visas, has reached nearly 90 per cent. This entirely unexpected phenomenon puts a heavy black border around what might have been one of the brightest episodes in modern Jewish history.

It is an immense spiritual tragedy for the dropouts themselves. Instead of being reclaimed to Judaism and the Jewish people, most of them are likely to be lost as Jews, unable or unwilling to be integrated into the Jewish life of the communities receiving them. Many may also suffer cruel disillusionment as they discover that the struggle of adjustment can be harder than they anticipated.

It is a national calamity for Israel, as the principal reservoir of new immigration is drying up. No other major sources of mass immigration are now in sight, and the already precarious population figures are threatened with further erosion by the current excess of *yeridah* over aliyah – a trend as ominous for physical survival as it is psychologically dimming the Zionist vision.

It is a catastrophe for Soviet Jewry, whose hopes for eventual deliverance have been gravely compromised by the refusal of so many emigrants to abide by the terms under which the Soviet authorities were prevailed upon to allow them to leave, thus providing an excuse for further restrictions on the granting of exit visas.

It is a colossal burden for Jewish communities in America and elsewhere. They face enormous financial and social demands without the prospect of seeing their Jewish life enriched by the newcomers in return.

Above all, it is a devastating blow to the most intensive campaign ever mounted by the Jewish people throughout the world in modern times, next to Zionism itself. No Jewish cause outside Israel has agitated so many, so much and for so long as the Soviet Jewry campaign.

In the face of this campaign's virtual collapse, it is not surprising that the Jewish Agency has for some time considered and urged draconian measures to redirect the flood-turned-trickle of Soviet emigrants to Israel, by denying all Jewish aid to emigrants who refuse to go on aliyah. But can such methods be morally justified? The implications and consequences are grave indeed. Such a policy calls into question the integrity of the claim, vociferously made over the years, that human rights demand the freedom of people to move from one country to another of their choice. Any Jewish opposition to this fundamental right is all the more disturbing in the light of its emphatic endorsement quite recently made by the American State Department.

Moreover, the denial of aid to fellow-Jews in need, however deficient their Jewish loyalties may be, is without precedent in our history. Abandoning them the moment they reach freedom would drive them either to mischief or into the outstretched arms of the missionaries. In either case, we would provide highly inflammable material for the fires of anti-Semitism, an inevitable price exacted from the betrayal of what, after all, is the most deeply ingrained Jewish tradition of caring for fellow-Jews.

Even the efficacy of such a policy, were it to succeed, is highly questionable. Involuntary immigrants to Israel are likely to be the first to leave when they have a chance. *Yeridah* is even worse than *neshirah* in terms both of damage to the morale and of costly wastage of resources. But overriding all these considerations is what caused the problem in the first place. The very organisations which now shout and act with such alarm may themselves have contributed much to the failure of the policies they directed.

Ample warnings of what might happen have been given for years. I was lonely, but by no means alone, in urging not to make 'Let My People Go' the exclusive dynamic of the Soviet Jewry campaign, lest lack of Jewish commitment, on which we had to work at least equally hard, would make them go – but not to Israel. The officialdom remained unconvinced, arguing all that mattered was to get the Jews out of Russia and brushing aside any suggestion to divert part of the campaign and its resources to their rehabilitation as Jews, whether inside Russia or in the transit camps, where those who had left often spent months of idle waiting for visas to their destinations.

Lately, with the dramatic rise in the dropout rate, the policies were changed, and some cultural work inside Russia was encouraged. But it was too late and too little to turn the tide of defections. Yet perhaps it is not too late to learn from this tragic experience, now aggravated by the rising flood of *yeridah*, that only Jews with a passionate commitment to Judaism, nurtured by intensive learning and practice, are likely to be sufficiently attracted to Israel to prefer its hardships and risks to the comforts enjoyed elsewhere, as demonstrated by the disproportionately high ratio of religious aliyah and correspondingly low rate of religious *yeridah*. The more attractions Israel has to offer to this element, the more will come and help Israel to be strong and secure.

Without Judaism, there will be no Jews; and without Jews, there will be no aliyah – and eventually no Israel.

OUR GRAVEST CHALLENGE

'Soviet Jewry numbers two million – two-thirds of European Jewry. If we could rescue them, or even a fraction of them, as Jews, what a difference this would make to Jewish fortunes for centuries to come.

The present challenge cannot be compared to the two million who left Russia between 1881 and 1914: they were still soaked in Jewish culture and learning. Today's Jews are drained, most of them completely alienated. And even the memories have faded.

So the task is gigantic. Yet the world Jewish response so far has been pitiful. True, Israel has absorbed some 150,000 – perhaps 'received' would be a better term – and this, we should never forget, is well above the percentage of Jews from the West who have gone on aliyah (as the Soviets reminded me when I was in Russia nearly 14 years ago). Yet the campaign itself has proved disastrous.

It is dramatically clear that the Gorbachev era has inaugurated many farreaching changes, including – for Jews – the freedom of emigration, of communication, and of religious and cultural pursuits undreamed-of but a few years ago. To all intents and purposes, there are no more 'refuseniks' in terms associated with the heroic struggle by and for Soviet Jews. As a result, numerous Jewish groups and individuals hitherto dedicated to this struggle are now out of business.

A new role must be found for them, and I am afraid it will be rather harder and more demanding than just protesting and demonstrating. So, what can and should be done, now that we no longer have an excuse for inaction?

Aliyah is, of course, the ideal, both to save Russia's Jews from Jewish oblivion – inside and outside Russia – and to gain them for *binyan ha'aretz*. But it would be dangerous to force them: worse than *noshrim* are *yordim* who spread a sense of failure and resentment.

We have to re-create a *chalutzic* spirit of idealism, which will require years of intensive educational work inside Russia. Equally important is reviving the spirit of excitement among Israelis at the newcomers' arrival, instead of the miserable treatment which is often accorded them.

The price of providing these essential services will be enormous. But we are either in earnest about retrieving Soviet Jewry, or our entire past campaign will turn out to have been a mockery.

Remember, too, that the vast majority will remain in Russia. Their restoration to the Jewish people calls for massive help on two levels: micro-schemes and macro-schemes. Under the former, I classify everything directed at individuals, whether a cultural centre, a yeshivah, a musical group, or any other expression of Jewish identity – all of them requiring enormous investments of human resources.

Under the latter, I include the reconstruction of national organisations – above all, communities – providing not only religious and educational facilities, but the normal range of communal services: kosher restaurants, old-age homes, defence organisations.

The challenge is not only how we can help Russian Jews, but equally: how will our own Jewish lives be affected?'

From an address by the Chief Rabbi to the Jewish Agency Executive, 25 June 1989

In 1990, after an interval of 15 years, the Chief Rabbi visited Moscow for a second time, accompanied by the executive director of his office, Shimon Cohen. Lord Jakobovits was invited by the New York-based Global Forum on Environment and Development for Survival to its international conference in the Soviet capital.

In addition to participating in the conference, he addressed students of Mekor Chaim, the talmudical academy established by Rabbi Adin Steinsaltz, as well as Iggud Hamorim, the Soviet Hebrew Teachers' Association. On the Shabbat, at the invitation of Rabbi Abraham Shayevich, he delivered the sermon at the Moscow Central Synagogue.

On his return to Britain, he called on world Jewry to establish twinning arrangements with Soviet Jewish communities in order to assist the estimated million Soviet Jews who, he believed, would elect to remain in their country to rediscover their Jewish consciousness.

Interviewed by the Glasgow *Jewish Echo*, he warned that the opportunity presently available should not be missed, as it occurred 'perhaps once in a century'. While Israel and the Jewish Agency would need help in looking after those Soviet Jews who wished to leave for Israel, he wanted to emphasise the requirement for assistance for the vast majority of Jews who were 'drained of any semblance of Jewish life'. The Chief Rabbi said that a 'massive and unprecedented effort' was required to begin to do justice to both the challenge and the enormous opportunity that now existed.

He believed that about 200,000 Soviet Jews would want to emigrate to Israel. Their passage, he said, would have to be eased, their absorption facilitated, and housing and work assisted under the direction of the Jewish Agency. But he added a warning that even with the physical absorption problems resolved, they had become so alienated from any Jewish background that he believed the 'intensification of their Jewish consciousness and the realisation of the spiritual values that link Jews as a people' was today the most urgent task. 'Unless some priority is also given to that, one will not succeed in integrating them into Israeli society.'

As for the 'vast majority' who, for the foreseeable future, would stay in Russia, he pointed out that their children did not even know the names of the biblical patriarchs Abraham, Isaac and Jacob. Lord Jakobovits called for a massive effort from world Jewry to make religious facilities available to them. As a prime need, he called for the provision of rabbis and teachers, suggesting that those who had emigrated to Israel from the Soviet Union and had been trained there might now be prepared to return.

Lord Jakobovits suggested that groups of students should visit Russia, and Soviet students invited to the West, coupled with the dispatch of Jewish literature, to overcome the problems faced by Soviet Jews, 'divorced as they are from any anchorage in the Jewish people, let alone Jewish history, Jewish consciousness and Jewish religious observance'.

He wanted in particular to start formulating detailed programmes for individual communities. 'We need to ensure that one person, at least, will go to each community to help reorganise some form of Jewish communal life, which will include not only religious and educational facilities but social facilities as well. There is a need for old-age homes – enabling Jews to end their days in a Jewish environment – and for cultural activities for youth, such as art and music, to enable them to identify as Jews.

'Above all, however, we need to reconstruct some form of community life, whereby Soviet Jews can gradually give corporate expression to matters of deep concern.'

In September 1990, the Chief Rabbi published the essence of an exchange of correspondence he had had with Mendel Kaplan, chairman of the board of governors of the Jewish Agency. In his initial approach, he wrote:

'... As you know, I attach the utmost importance to the spiritual aspect of absorption. Unless the new generation of immigrants, particularly from Soviet Russia, is to be successfully integrated into Israeli society as a stable and creative factor, there are others besides Natan Sharansky who fear that these new elements may be among the first to join the queues for emigration from Israel. If they are not allowed to strike root and find fulfilment in the traditions, loyalties and disciplines of our people and our heritage, there may be little to bind them to Israel in preference to other options which may become available.

Such a backlash of new Soviet arrivals turning their backs on the land that has claimed them so insistently over the past decades could be a calamity without parallel in the history of modern Israel. The demoralising effect itself would be catastrophic.

The urgency of such a programme of spiritual integration is underscored by the experience that the aliyah rate from Soviet Russia, as indeed from other countries, is by far the highest among groups who have undergone some intensive spiritual training and religious education. The rest, whatever their love of Israel, suffered a 90 per cent dropout rate on leaving Russia, and an even much larger proportion of Western Jews for whom aliyah has never even been a serious option.

By the same token, I place the highest possible priority on the reclamation of Soviet Jews to Judaism inside Russia. The bulk of the rest are likely to be lost to Israel and to Judaism alike. As I have argued from the beginning of the present campaign, when I attended the Jewish Agency conference in Jerusalem last summer, the 'Jewish Agency *for Israel*' can hardly be expected to work for the consolidation of Jewish life and communal organisation in the Diaspora, least of all in the Soviet Union, except among the minority of Jews who are likely to prepare for aliyah. We clearly cannot abandon the rest and write them off as Jews.

Hence, it could become entirely counter-productive if Soviet Jewry campaigns, such as the JIA special appeal in this country, were to block other efforts to assist in the rehabilitation of Soviet Jewry, for instance by twinning communities with a view to organising student exchange visits, by providing well-trained personnel, by setting aside, say in our case, £1 million out of the estimated campaign proceeds of £10–15 million for the type of work inside the Soviet

Union that I have described. I believe the lead must come from Israel, if we are to avoid unnecessary rivalry in the Diaspora and equally unnecessary losses among Soviet Jews inside and outside Russia.

At this season of 'Let My People Go', let us never forget – as I have argued for the past decade and a half – that they will 'go', but not to Israel unless we add 'so that they shall serve Me'. Moses could not do it otherwise, and I doubt that we can.'

Mendel Kaplan's reply included the following:

'… All fund-raising for Operation Exodus is being maintained in a separate account at the Jewish Agency, together with the expenditure needs of this aliyah. Our expenditure covers transportation, initial absorption, housing and employment. We are obligated by our board resolution to expend every dollar of income received from the special campaign only in designated budgetary areas. We are, in fact, covenanted to this decision and under no circumstances would allow expenditure of funds collected through Operation Exodus outside the Jewish Agency framework for this aliyah alone.

The Jewish Agency has a small budget for work inside the Soviet Union whose main activities are directed towards the promotion of aliyah …

… I do not share the pessimistic view of Natan Sharansky and must point out to him and yourself that of the nearly 200,000 Russians who arrived in the 1970s, less than 3 per cent have emigrated. This is the lowest percentage of any aliyah from the West. I am confident that the key to successful absorption is employment, and we look forward to overcoming this major factor in the development of Israel.'

Following a visit to Israel, the Chief Rabbi wrote again:

'… Yes, I can also confirm from my many conversations with people famous and very ordinary in Israel that the Russian aliyah so far has gone remarkably well. It is enthusiastically welcomed by most Israelis, and the quality of the new immigrants is rated high on the whole. The Agency certainly deserves, and is given, the highest praise for handling this huge operation with consummate skill and care.

Of course, I accept the Agency board resolution to expend all income from the special campaign only in designated areas, of transportation, initial absorption, housing and employment, as well as for a very limited programme of activities inside the Soviet Union, concerned mainly with preparing potential olim.

But that being so, other organisations clearly must be free to conduct their own campaigns for vital work of Jewish rehabilitation among the hundreds of thousands, if not millions, of Soviet Jews who are likely to remain behind for the time being – whether by choice or by the limitations in Israel's capacity to absorb newcomers.

One needs no special wisdom to appreciate that if these completely alienated Jews are to be abandoned by world Jewry – left without rabbis, teachers,

31. Alongside a portrait of Rabbi Menasseh ben Israel, Hindu leader Shree Pramukh Swami presents a menorah to the Chief Rabbi at an inter-faith ceremony in London in 1980.

32. With communal leaders at a commemoration in London in 1983 to mark the fortieth anniversary of the Warsaw Ghetto uprising.

33. Discussing with the Bishop of Stepney Holocaust relics at a memorial exhibition in the East London borough in 1983.

34 and 35. The Chief Rabbi with a group of refuseniks at the Moscow home of Professor Mark Azbel during his historic first visit to the Soviet Union in December 1975.

36 and 37. Alongside memorial stones and plaques to victims of the Holocaust during a 1993 visit to the remnants of Jewish communities in Belarus.

38. The Duke of Edinburgh assists with the fixing of a mezuzah to the doorpost of a new building at Nightingale House home for aged Jews in 1983.

39. Helping with flower arrangements during a craft session at Sinclair House, the Redbridge Jewish youth and community centre.

40. With Nobel Laureate Elie Wiesel (centre) and Jewish Educational Development Trust chairman Stanley Kalms at a JEDT dinner in 1983.

communal organisers, youth leaders, educational institutions, social workers, etc. – the bulk of them will be lost to our people for ever. The stakes are high and urgent …

… That you have had a less than 3 per cent emigration rate of Russian Jews from Israel can hardly be regarded as proving anything. Many are or remain in Israel because they have nowhere else to go. In the long run, a disaffected population in Israel 'under duress', as it were, is likely to escape at the first possible moment and thus eventually swell the *yeridah* figures …

… I would therefore deem it both unjust and shortsighted to exclude 'spiritual absorption' from the specified budget items. In five years' time, the price exacted may be heavy indeed, just as it was for the past 20 years when the neglect of Jewish religious and educational activities inside the Soviet Union led to a 90 per cent dropout rate so long as the American alternative still existed. We would not want this costly error to be repeated. Sharansky's perspectives may be somewhat different, but his practical conclusions appear incontrovertible …'

The rest of the dialogue was conducted in person.

SPREADING TORAH IN THE FORMER USSR

Everyone who can do so should visit Russia now, says Emeritus Chief Rabbi Lord Jakobovits, who returned on Monday from a visit to Minsk, Belarus. Now that one can travel freely and without oppression, an atmosphere of *techias hameisim* prevails in that vast territory, he said, and the responsibility on us to replant *chiyus* there is consequently very great. Our yeshivah-educated youth would be especially welcome to teach and spread Torah. The conditions are primitive, but one can live there, he added.

Lord Jakobovits was accompanied by his wife, Amélie, and by some 20 rabbonim from Eretz Yisroel, America and the former USSR itself – six were from Belarus, the Ukraine and Moscow. He was invited by the young Chief Rabbi of Belarus, Rabbi Yitzchok Wolpin, of Brooklyn, New York, the 23-year-old nephew of Rabbi Nisan Wolpin, of the American Agudah.

Lord Jakobovits spoke of visiting a winter camp in a resort outside Minsk, where he met 40 youngsters in the sparse conditions who, until recently, did not know *alef beis*. Now young people like them are trying to keep *kashrus* and walk long distances to attend *tefillos*. He also reported seeing a *mohel* from the United States and noted how people were literally queuing up for *brisos*.

The Emeritus Chief Rabbi visited Volozhin, where he witnessed the handing back of the three-storey building that once housed the famous yeshivah to the local Jewish community – which now has only 25 members. He also went to Radun and said *tefillos* at the *kever* of the Chofetz Chaim, which has a new *matzeva* listing all his *seforim*. In Radun, there is also a mass grave of 2,500 of our people.

Similarly, in Vilnius (Vilna), Lord Jakobovits recited *tefillos* at the *kevorim* of the Vilna Gaon and Rav Chaim Ozer Grondzenski, which were both moved at the end of the war but are in perfect order. The *beis olam* in Vilna is still used. There are 4,000 Jews now living in Vilna, but only three are *shomrei shabbos*. Truly a double Holocaust, mused Lord Jakobovits – physical under the Nazis and spiritual under the Communists.

Minsk, where Lord Jakobovits was based, has lost its *beis olam* altogether – it is now a football pitch. Of the several million Jews who once lived in Belarus, only 160,000 remain.

The group was received for over two hours by Belarus President Branislav Kavitz, Deputy Prime Minister Michail I. Demtchuk, and Foreign Minister Piotr K. Kravchenko. They confirmed the return of the Volozhin yeshivah to the Jewish community and the stoppage of work at the Pinsk cemetery.

The group pleaded that shuls and communal buildings in Minsk should likewise be returned to the local community, where they are now urgently required. The Ministers promised to help bring this matter to the desired conclusion.

Jewish Tribune, *14 January 1993*

CHAPTER TEN

Israel and the Diaspora

*'Cementing the bonds of our common heritage –
our most acute national problem'*

On 5 June 1967, there were 10,000 people present at a communal rally at London's Royal Albert Hall expressing solidarity with Israel. Pent-up emotions on this first day of the Six-Day War were running high, and the audience responded spontaneously to every call for support. Chief Rabbi Immanuel Jakobovits announced that, in conjunction with the Haham, he was convening a conference for rabbis and ministers from all over the country and setting up an Israel emergency office to co-ordinate and direct the efforts of Anglo-Jewry. His address was a passionate call for communal co-operation:

'SHALL YOUR BROTHERS GO TO WAR ...?'

'Nearly 30 years ago, my illustrious predecessor, Chief Rabbi Dr J. H. Hertz, addressed a massed assembly in this very hall to arouse the conscience of the world on the catastrophe that lay ahead for European Jewry. Alas, the cry was too weak and too late to avert disaster.

Today, we have reached another turning-point in Jewish history, perhaps more fateful than any in our long and chequered past. From the land of our first oppression in biblical days, a new oppressor has arisen – a tyrant so cruel that he does not flinch from using poison gas on his own Arab brothers – with the avowed and often-proclaimed aim to destroy Israel and to drive its population into the sea.

We are here this evening to make quite sure that we will not be too weak and not be too late this time. We are not going to have another Holocaust in the martyred history of our people. The hope of two millennia, and the toil and sacrifice of two decades, is not now going to be wiped out in two weeks or two months.

Israel, as we were foretold in the Bible, *hen am levadad yishkon*, 'a people that will dwell in loneliness' [Numbers 23:9], is the only nation on earth without alliances – except for the Jewish communities. We are Israel's only allies. We are assembled here this evening to make it clear that an attack on Israel is an attack on every Jewish community throughout the world, and that we are at least as united in the defence of the land that is dear and cherished by us as our adversaries are in their resolve to destroy us.

Together with you, I am proud and elated by the magnificent response of the overwhelming majority of our community in rising to this historic occasion. We have been flooded with volunteers who wish to offer their lives and their service to our people, and with those who are coming forward to give of their means towards the consolidation of Israel in this hour of trial.

This grave emergency calls first upon the Jewish people. We hear tonight an anguished cry, a cry that Moses once uttered when two of our tribes of Israel wanted to remain on the other side of the Jordan without participating in the battle that lay ahead for the rest of them, and he said to them: '*ha'achechem yavo'u lamilchamah ve'atem teishvu po*, Shall your brothers go to war and you will remain and sit idly by here?' We are not asked, thank God, to go to war or surrender lives. But we are asked to identify ourselves and make common cause with those who do, so that not merely they will live, but that we will live as a self-respecting community.

You may ask: 'What can I do in this emergency?' The industrialist who gives a million or the little Jewish child who pours out his heart in prayer to God to have mercy over our people, the volunteer who gives his service in order to prop up Israel's economy, or our communal leaders who now fight for Jewish survival against the scourge of assimilation with redoubled vigour – they all stand in the front-line of the battle against Jewish extinction. They all help to make sure that together we prevail.

Specifically, my Office – in trying to co-ordinate, and to assist in, the gigantic efforts that will be demanded of us – has taken a number of steps, together with the Haham.

First, I have convened a conference of rabbis and ministers from all over the country for tomorrow to consult together on the help we can render in directing and co-ordinating efforts to mobilise our community, and, indeed, to mobilise public opinion on a local as well as a national level.

Second, we have opened an office, an Israel Emergency Office, to receive inquiries and direct offers of help.

Third, we are asking all synagogues during the present emergency to remain open all day for those who wish, in a moment of anxiety or inspiration, to commune with their Creator and seek the strength and comfort of which we stand in need in this awesome moment of test and trial. Two-and-a-half million Jews cannot, by the ordinary laws of nature, win out against 50 million adversaries without the help of God; and side by side with our material mobilisation, we are going to mobilise our spiritual resources to storm the gates of Heaven and plead to God to be at our side in this moment of destiny and danger.

Fourth, we are appealing to all members of our community, during this crisis, to curtail personal parties and functions and to use the resources that had been set aside for these purposes as contributions to Israel, that it may prevail.

Fifth, we are asking Jewish communal organisations throughout the country during this emergency to suspend all campaigns for communal projects, with the sole exception of any venture connected with the intensification of the Jewish education of our own children. For, let us make no mistake: the battle of

Jewish survival is being fought in our own midst just as grimly as in Israel. How can we survive, and what kind of a people are we going to be, if our children will be aliens to our heritage; and if we are going to suffer more casualties than our troubled and martyred people has already sustained through massacre, through repression and through assimilation in the past 30 years?

There also goes out from us here a call to the British nation. An Israeli friend of mine, a Member of the Knesset, told me a few years ago of an interview he had had at the White House with the then President Truman. He asked the President what made him decide on the day of the establishment of Israel to give his historic recognition to the newly born State. Mr Truman answered that he felt 'Providence had summoned me to complete the Balfour Declaration'.

Tonight, in the fiftieth year of the Balfour Declaration, Britain is being summoned by Providence and destiny to complete the Balfour Declaration. I plead with the leaders of Parliament with us here and, through them, the leaders of this great and gallant nation, which also was once in the depths of danger and appealed to the world to come to its rescue. I plead with them as a Bible-loving people: you can help to make not just Jewish history but British history.

And we call upon the nations of the world. Israel is the only nation that has been created by the United Nations. We are surely, as anyone with the scantiest knowledge of Jewish history knows, a peace-loving people. Never in our history have we embarked on building empires by aggression. Never in our history have we gone out on crusades in order to convert others to Judaism by force. Throughout our history we have been at the receiving end of persecution. We have never meted out persecution to others.

Tonight, on this evening of Jewish solidarity, how we think of our three million brethren in the Soviet land who, if only they could, would join with us and whose spokesmen we are, and who are a living witness that we are victims of persecution and will never impose persecution, let alone extermination, on others. Let the world take up our cause. We have 4,000 years of history behind us to prove our case. We will get along in peace and constructive endeavour with our Arab cousins and neighbours.

Let me conclude on a note of confidence. We are told in the Book of Books: 'And it shall be, when you draw nigh to war, that the priest, the spiritual leader, shall approach and speak to the people, and shall say to them: "*Shema Yisrael,* Hear, O Israel, you draw near this day to war against your enemies; let not your heart be faint, fear not, nor be alarmed, neither be affrightened at them, for the Lord your God will go with you, to fight for you against your enemies to save you."'[Deuteronomy 20:2–4].

May I mention to you, as a token of the spirit of the land which today has been plunged into war, that I was advised through the Israeli Embassy that, on this first day of war, the children of Israel went to school and took examinations at school. Likewise, the Ambassador has told me that, since the delivery of the mail in Israel has been taken over by the youngsters, it has become more efficient and more expeditious that ever before. That is the spirit of the newly born Israel, and that is going to be our spirit.

We cry out on this evening of decision to God, the guarantor of Israel's survival. In the words that we recite every time we open the Holy Ark: *'Vayehi binso'a ha'aron vayomer mosheh, kumah hashem veyafutsu oyevechah veyanusu mesan'echah mipanechah.'* And as the Holy Ark of Jewish history is once again on the march, we call out: 'O Lord, arise and scatter Your enemies, and let those that hate You flee from before You!'

We also call out to our brothers and sisters assembled here this evening. We hear a distant cry from our brothers in Israel, and I am here to convey it to you. That cry is identical with the words which the British nation, through its greatest son, once used when it was in danger and addressed itself to others. Our Israeli brethren call to us tonight: 'Give us the tools, and we will finish the job.'

May we so acquit ourselves of one of the greatest challenges of Jewish history that we may, with God's help, on next 5 Iyar, celebrate the twentieth anniversary of Israel with greater joy, with greater comfort and, indeed, with a greater assurance of permanent peace than ever before.'

On the initiative of the Chief Rabbi, and backed by its honorary officers, the United Synagogue in 1969 set up an Israel department as its 'instrument of identification' with, and commitment to, the Jewish State. In an interview with the *Jewish Chronicle*, in which he publicly disclosed his new venture for the first time, Dr Jakobovits recalled that, soon after the Six-Day War, an Israel department headed by Rabbi Maurice Unterman was established within the Chief Rabbinate Office to give it an Israel orientation and to provide liaison with the Jewish State, as well as with the Israeli Embassy and with all communal bodies working on behalf of Israeli institutions and causes.

'As a further extension of the Israel orientation of the Chief Rabbinate, I have for some time been urging the honorary officers of the US to set up an Israel committee, on a par with its existing departments, with the object of forging an instrument of identification with, and involvement in, Israel', Dr Jakobovits said.

'Under the heading of identification with Israel, I would mention specifically the encouragement of emigration, the organisation of group visits, the provision of scholarships for study there, arranging seminars and lectures on Hebrew culture and Israel, as well as every sort of activity that would strengthen the awareness that religious organisations such as the US must regard the Jewish State as one of its major sources of inspiration. I also believe that such identification with Israel would help the US itself to become more relevant as it would reflect more than it did hitherto some of the things that stir the Jewish world and particularly our youth at the present time. In addition, the committee should serve as a spokesman and representative of our congregational body in all matters affecting Israel and its religious life.'

Dr Jakobovits added: 'The religious community in Britain so far has been silent too often and not sufficiently alert.'

Towards the end of that year, the Chief Rabbi made his first significant public statement on the plight of the Arab refugees, a topic that was later to spark the most heated controversy of his career. Addressing the national leadership conference of the Union of Orthodox Jewish Congregations of America, he declared: 'We must manifest much more clearly our sensitivity to the humanitarian aspects of the Arab refugee problem.'

He told the 800 delegates and guests: 'We must re-establish – for the State of Israel and for the entire Jewish people – the classic, authentic image of the Jew whose hallmark has always been compassionate identification with the weak, the needy, the suffering and the persecuted, wherever they may be.'

The Chief Rabbi asserted that 'the double standard of morality and justice so patently applied by the nations [of the world] to Israel is indicative of the fact that, somehow, Israel has not fulfilled their expectations. These expectations lie in the moral and religious dimension and are not satisfied by its political and economic advances.'

Dr Jakobovits expressed distress that 'the present image of Israel is not fulfilling the moral quest and yearning of many of our young people who feel a void when confronted by the present rather harsh image of self-reliance which Israel presents to the world.'

By the turn of the decade, as the Chief Rabbi later observed in *If Only My People*, the euphoria of the Six-Day War had evaporated. 'So had the short spell of spiritual re-awakening, to be replaced by a creeping growth of crass materialism, ethnic strife between the privileged and the under-privileged, and political complacency under the imaginary shelter of invincibility. This was shaken neither by the enervating War of Attrition nor by the ascendancy of the PLO in spectacular acts of terrorism and obscene receptions accorded by the United Nations. Then the Yom Kippur War burst upon us.'

Eight days into the war, on 17 October 1973, Rabbi Jakobovits sent the following message to President Ephraim Katzir of Israel:

'While our efforts are insignificant compared with the supreme sacrifices being made by the sons and daughters of Israel, in defence of our common heritage, we have elicited an unprecedented response to our call for a total mobilisation of our resources in support of your epic struggle. We are endeavouring once again to set an example to the Jewish communities throughout the Diaspora.

As partners – united by a common faith, history and destiny – we share your confidence in the vindication of Israel's cause. We join you in reverent tribute to the fallen, in extending comfort to the bereaved, and in praying for the healing of the wounded. We plead daily to our Father in Heaven for a speedy end to your ordeal.

From the depths of our hearts, we pray that the concluding days of the Feast of Tabernacles and the Day of Rejoicing of the Law will strengthen our abiding trust in God, the Rock of Israel, that he may speedily spread the Tabernacle of Peace over Israel, and enable our people to resume our historic role as a spiritual beacon of light unto the nations.'

President Katzir responded with a message expressing profound gratitude for the faith and support of British Jewry and the hope that they would soon see 'the Tabernacle of Peace' over Israel. The following week, at a unique ceremony at London's Kingsbury Synagogue, six Torah scrolls were handed over by the Chief Rabbi to a representative of the Israeli Embassy. The scrolls had been urgently requested by Israel's Chief Rabbinate and Defence Forces to serve units on the battlefront.

In his address, the Chief Rabbi said that religious Jews in Israel had made supreme sacrifices in the Yom Kippur War. Many yeshivah students had volunteered to conduct services at army outposts and a tragically high number had been killed or wounded. It was therefore particularly fitting that the religious community in Britain should make an unprecedented response to the needs of Israel, both financially and spiritually. The presentation of Sifrei Torah was 'a declaration of belief in the religious faith which has sustained the Jewish people in all its tribulations and which will, once again, guarantee the protection of Divine Providence over Israel and its gallant defence forces'.

At a crowded meeting of United Synagogue ministers, council members and other communal leaders on 30 January 1974, the Chief Rabbi discussed some of the major issues and challenges thrown up by the war:

THE LESSONS OF THE YOM KIPPUR WAR

'The Yom Kippur War revealed a spiritual crisis at least as alarming and critical as lapses in the sphere of logistics. It marked the collapse of an attitude of mind, of a whole philosophy of life, no less than the collapse of a military strategy and of a foreign policy. It slaughtered some very sacred cows and exploded quite a few hallowed myths just as ruthlessly as it brought to an untimely end thousands of precious lives and dashed many cherished hopes and assumptions.

Let it be stated at once and emphatically: we are all responsible for our predicament and we can exonerate from blame neither secular Zionism nor the religious parties, neither our national leadership nor our rabbinical establishment, neither non-observant nor observant Jews, neither in Israel nor in the Diaspora. We are united in guilt as we must be united in repentance and a common endeavour to overcome our difficulties. None of us can undo the past; but we all can and must learn our lessons to secure the future.

In the double crisis, eroding both the quantity and quality of Jews, in addition to threatening their security, Israel and the Diaspora will increasingly now have to merge their respective roles in a common drive to consolidate the Jewish spiritual commitment. Paradoxically, while the establishment of the Jewish State has greatly intensified Jewish consciousness and identification in communities everywhere, it has also weakened the main common denominator between them.

In the Diaspora, many Jews have found vicarious refuge for the expression of their Jewish identity in the existence and support of Israel. For them, living as Jews by proxy has conveniently replaced the personal discipline of Jewish living.

In Israel, again, large numbers of Jews have found in their national allegiance a substitute for traditional Jewish loyalties. For these Jews, the Diaspora became the vicarious haven of their residual Jewishness, so poignantly attested by the many Israelis who discover their Jewish feeling and identity only when they visit the Diaspora and find communication with their faith and with fellow-Jews in the synagogue. Thus, Jewish statehood helped to accelerate the secularisation, or despiritualisation, of Jewish life both at home and abroad, leading to an ever-widening gap between Jews and Judaism.

The Yom Kippur War will force us to recognise that a secularist Jewish State, itself a contradiction in terms, cannot be viable in the long run, as we will find the ultimate answer to many of our most pressing problems in a growing emphasis on our spiritual assets.

To ensure greater spirituality and improve the quality of Jewish life, there must be a shift in our national (and communal) scale of priorities and public recognition. For instance, financial resources are certainly vital to sustain the fabric of our corporate existence.

But if wealth alone becomes the main qualification for communal honour and respect, it is bound to devalue the coinage of the spirit and inflate the currency of material success. In a truly Jewish society, the teacher, the scholar, the thinker, the man of piety and moral nobility generally must command at least the same power and respect. In the hierarchy of leadership, too, men of vision, competence and culture, rather than mere party faithfuls, will have to reach the top if we are to harness our finest brains in the tough struggles ahead.

Such a return to Jewish traditional values would also, incidentally, help to regain the involvement in Jewish affairs of numerous gifted talents, especially of the younger generation, whose disenchantment with the bureaucratic and materialistic value system of our age has alienated them.

Aliyah itself, also now more urgent than ever, is likewise affected by religious considerations. It is sad to reflect that, during 25 years of Jewish independence, Jews driven to Israel by oppression far outnumber those attracted there from the free world. Most Diaspora Jews living in comfort still look upon the Jewish State – apart from being a source of great pride and self-respect – as a home for the homeless.

However small the aliyah rates, immigrants from Western countries came, and will continue to come, disproportionately from groups whose idealism was nurtured by their strong traditional background and education. Again, among immigrants from Arab and Soviet lands, those who remained or became religious eventually presented fewer problems of integration, both because they share a common way of life with their new neighbours and because their religious commitment makes them less liable to social indiscipline and moral fall-out.

The uncertainties created by the Yom Kippur War will greatly accentuate these trends, perhaps even in a shocking new form. Already one hears in Israel of Sabras who are unwilling to expose themselves and their children to the chronic risks of war and insecurity. Unfortunately, some even consider emigration. For them, Israel is principally a haven; once they believe its security is in doubt, they will seek the greater safety of foreign lands.

No truly religious Jew thinks that way. For him, Israel is primarily the only place where he can live a fully Jewish life. What attracts him there is its holiness even more than its security. The religious commitment will therefore increasingly determine the rate of aliyah from the West, the degree of successful integration from the East, and conversely the rate of emigration from Israel.

To this very limited catalogue of religious principles with a bearing on pressing current issues must be added the overriding quest for peace, the greatest and most oft-repeated Jewish religious yearning of all. As has now been so cruelly demonstrated, even distant borders and military strength do not of themselves secure or guarantee peace. Genuine peace springs not from a balance of power, and certainly not from an imbalance of fear. It slowly grows out of mutual trust, encouraged by each side showing the same understanding of the other's apprehensions and sufferings as it seeks for itself.

The traditional Jewish compassion over ancient Egypt's losses in the Red Sea, still marked in our annual Passover observances, well illustrates an approach, the challenge of which hardly lacks contemporary parallels, not least regarding the sensitivity to the plight of Arab refugees, whatever the cause of the problem. Only through an intensely religious conscience can such high moral standards be attained as will eventually reassure our adversaries that they can dwell securely and without fear.

Real peace is a state of mind, rather than an expedient accommodation. Little wonder that the Psalmist speaks not of wanting or loving peace, but of 'pursuing peace', and that in our synagogue usage, when reciting the prayer for peace at the conclusion of the Amidah and Kaddish, we draw back three steps before coming forward again.

Whether people do or do not agree with the religious interpretation of our present perplexities, what is clear is that the crisis has fundamental spiritual ramifications far beyond its purely political or military manifestations. It is equally clear that, in guiding the perplexed of our times and ensuring that we prevail over our immense difficulties, spiritual leaders and the religious community generally are called upon, as they were throughout our past, to make a decisive contribution towards bringing the ship of our destiny to safer waters.

In particular, we are summoned to apply ourselves to three distinct tasks: to provide comfort, hope, confidence and encouragement to those of our people whose faith is tottering in adversity; to explain the meaning of our current tribulations and our response to them in the light of our historical experience and religious insights; and to respond to the intense search for spiritual values evoked by the trauma of the Yom Kippur War by arousing a massive religious re-awakening to restore our people everywhere to its timeless purpose and destiny.

In addition, in the Diaspora it is primarily for the religious community and its leaders to stimulate a mass movement of aliyah, by redirecting Jewish education to this end; by transferring ever-more seminars, schools and yeshivot to Israel; by sponsoring projects to encourage all school-leavers to spend at least a year in Israel, with the prospect that out of many thousands going annually, many hundreds will stay; and above all, by cultivating in our youth the faith and idealism which will predispose them to prefer a full Jewish life in Israel, even under conditions of some risk and hardship, to the spiritual hazards of their exilic existence, even in relative prosperity.

Mindful of the historic responsibilities devolving on our spiritual leadership at a critical time like this, I have urged the Chief Rabbinate of Israel ever since the Yom Kippur War to convene an informal consultative meeting of leading rabbis to evolve a meaningful response, intellectually as well as in practical terms, to the enormous spiritual challenges now facing us.

Such a meeting was eventually held in Jerusalem two weeks ago, with the participation of some 20 principal rabbis from Israel, Europe, America and South Africa. From it emerged a common resolve, in great part along the lines of this appraisal, thoroughly to revise our priorities, with a view to promoting the spiritual foundations of Jewish life, the unity of the Jewish people, sober confidence in the future, and the implementation of specific projects to be undertaken by joint action.

Of uppermost concern to me were the potentially disastrous effects on Israel's spiritual strength and stability resulting from the absence of any religious teaching or experience for two-thirds of the country's children, on the one hand, and the bitterness and divisiveness engendered by the ongoing debates on pro- or anti-religious legislation, on the other hand. I therefore pleaded with my colleagues to consider a dramatic gesture to replace the present religious policies by a supreme effort to win at least the rising generation for an appreciation of the Jewish commitment, founded on deep faith, intensive learning and devout observance.

To this end, I suggested, at any rate during the present emergency, when religious faith and national unity are such indispensable assets to Jewish survival, that we press for some regular religious instruction and practice at all schools, and in return agree to a moratorium on all new legislation of religious significance, such as on conversions, civil marriage, public Sabbath observance or autopsies – all subjects on which fierce divisive controversies continue to rage and which, to my mind, however vital in themselves, are now irrelevant to the overriding need of fortifying our spiritual defences, by raising God-fearing and practising Jews.

I even doubt the wisdom of the 'Who is a Jew' agitation at this time, not because of the foolish argument that Jews outside Israel have no right to meddle in Israeli affairs – for 'Who is an Israeli' is the business of Israelis, while 'Who is a Jew' must obviously be of vital concern to every Jew – but simply because I believe this agitation is futile and counterproductive, so long as the majority of Jews do not share our religious convictions.

To advance the future prospects of a truly Jewish State, I would rather concentrate all religious efforts on securing the Ministry of Education and forgo all other portfolio claims, than to persist in legislative battles which cannot but further erode Torah influences by hardening anti-religious attitudes, based today primarily on the objection to what is regarded as 'religious coercion', now the principal stumbling block to regaining for our spiritual leadership the confidence of our entire people.

Omitted so far from my review of the relevance of Judaism to the security and quality of Jewish life is the attitude of halachah to the ceding of territory now under Israeli control in the quest for peace. The views of rabbis, as of laymen, vary widely on this vexing and fateful question, a subject here left to the end because of its topical importance.

No rabbinical authority disputes that our claim to a Divine mandate (and we have no other which cannot be invalidated) extends over the entire Holy Land within its historical borders and that halachically we have no right to surrender this claim. But what is questionable is whether we must, or indeed may, assert it at the risk of thousands of lives, if not the life of the State itself.

Any religious law is set aside, even fasting on Yom Kippur, if it involves a danger to life. Rabbis, in giving such rulings in respect of individuals, are required to rely on expert medical opinion to determine what constitutes such danger in particular cases.

Similarly, it would seem, we are halachically compelled to leave the judgement on what provides the optimum security for Jewish life in Israel to the verdict of military and political experts, not rabbis. Included as a major factor in this difficult judgement must also be the overriding concern to preserve the Jewish character of Israel, which may clearly depend on the proportion of Jews within the State. For, in the suspension of religious laws for life-saving purposes, the threat to Jewish spiritual life and to physical life is considered alike.

Most importantly also to be borne in mind must be some more intangible factors of supreme Jewish religious and moral concern. The present ceding of some territory, if necessary and consistent with security requirements, may conceivably be justified as a ringing act of faith to promote regional, and indeed international, peace and as a goodwill gesture of immense value to establish friendly relations with the neighbouring peoples, ideals of human fellowship to which Judaism is passionately dedicated.

In an altogether unique category is Jerusalem. It enjoys a sanctity of its own and is the common possession of all Jews, wherever they may live, the gateway of all their prayers, the symbol of all their hopes, and now happily also the spiritual heart of Jewish learning, circulating inspiration to the most distant parts of our dispersion. To save life, one can amputate a limb or even excise parts of some internal organ. But not the heart!

The Jewish right to Jerusalem should be asserted not only by Israel, but by world Jewry, and especially by the religious community, who have never forgotten, throughout the long and bitter years of exile, the Psalmist's oath to set Jerusalem above their chiefest joy, yearning for its restoration in every prayer, every grace after meals, every blessing of joy to bridal pairs, and every greeting of comfort to mourners.

We should also expect the Jewish title to Jerusalem – now completely free for the first time to the adherents of all faiths – to be recognised by the community of nations in acknowledgement of the people who originally sanctified it, who have maintained an unbroken association with it for 3,000 years, and who have constituted the majority of its inhabitants for the past 150 years. The recognition of this title will ensure continuing rights of access and freedom of worship for all, as well as the social and economic progress of the Holy City in the best interests of its entire population.'

The Chief Rabbi reverted to the future of the territories, and of Jerusalem, in an October 1975 address to the Anglo-Israel Friendship League of Manchester:

CEDING TERRITORY

'You ask me about the Jewish attitude to the internationalisation of Jerusalem. In any final peace agreement, consideration would certainly be given to the creation of autonomous or extra-territorial enclaves within which the different faiths would exercise complete control over their places. But I cannot imagine that Israel, or indeed any Jew, would ever agree to the redivision of Jerusalem and its renewed desecration by barbed-wire fences separating the Jewish and Arab communities with the barrier of no man's land – in the city which is meant to be every man's land.

To achieve peace, Israel may have to be prepared to cede territory which historically belongs to the Holy Land assigned by Divine mandate to the descendants of Abraham, Isaac and Jacob and sanctified by the Jewish people. In an operation to save life, one may have to amputate a limb or excise part of an organ. But one cannot amputate the heart. And Jerusalem is the heart of the Jewish people, restored to health through its unification – a heart large enough to encompass the affections of, and to bring inspiration to, all faiths. Thus will the 'Faithful City' vindicate its name as the 'City of Peace' and as 'the House of Prayer for all peoples' (Isaiah 56:7).'

Preoccupied with the spiritual crisis confronting Israel and the Jewish people, the Chief Rabbi again drew attention to his anxieties in a letter circulated, two months later, at a leadership conference convened in Jerusalem by Prime Minister Yitzhak Rabin:

THE KEY TO SURVIVAL

'Why [he asked] has Zionism, meant to eradicate anti-Semitism and to 'solve the Jewish problem' by making us equals among the nations, now become the principal 'Jewish problem', a main generator of anti-Semitism and Jewish loneliness among the nations?

Only the semantics have changed. Anti-Semitism has become anti-Zionism, and instead of sporadic pogroms, we have periodic wars and continual terrorism. How can one explain our subjection by the world community to the very double standards Jewish independence was intended to eliminate? The inescapable answer is that our premises were false and we have built our expectations on an illusion.

Our spiritual starvation is now nothing short of a national disaster. At a time when the assets of deep faith, idealism, self-discipline and pride in being Jewish are absolutely vital in the armoury of Jewish self-preservation, it is an invitation to national despair, if not suicide, to tolerate the spiritual alienation of two-thirds of Israel's children, and the totally inadequate Jewish education for most Jewish children elsewhere, to the point that many never even see Jews at prayer and remain complete strangers to traditional Jewish thought, values and observance.

I realise, with much pain, that our religious establishment is at least as responsible for this blight as our secularist leadership. Torn by strife and preoccupied with political battles over legislation rather than with persuasion, religious leaders all too often abdicated their prophetic role as moral mentors and spiritual guides to the perplexed, thereby estranging the masses of our people instead of attracting, enlightening and uplifting them.

Between the extremes of the introvert traditionalists and the rabid secularists, we have produced the great divide of polarisation and fragmentation which now threatens to add to our external peril the bane of internal dissension, so ominously reminiscent of the 'causeless hatred' which sealed the fate of the second Jewish Commonwealth. Only a national return to our common spiritual commitment can repair this potentially catastrophic breach in the unity of our people.

Additionally, and more specifically, I would set out several propositions which events force us to acknowledge as the key to survival through regeneration. I list these points neither as a summary or conclusions, nor in any order of importance, but simply as examples for the application of Jewish teachings and insights to our situation:

1. It is significant that three novel questions, never previously asked or debated in our long annals, have been raised simultaneously: 'Who is a Jew?', 'What is "Jewish identity"?', and 'How do we ensure Jewish survival?' The moment we are no longer certain and agreed on who and what we are, Jewish survival becomes problematical.

2. The question 'Why Jewish survival?' troubles not only some spiritually impoverished Jews; it bedevils the world at large. Why indeed, if we are widely regarded as being at the heart of so many of its gravest crises and perils; if, in the public image, we create problems rather than solve them?

3. Having long exceeded the life-span of other nations, and in a callous world insensitive to the death of millions by starvation or violence, we can hardly expect support and sympathy for our claim to national survival, possibly at the risk of the world's economic stability if not its peace, unless we make an indispensable contribution to mankind's enrichment as a model society dedicated to moral excellence, ethical integrity and a passion for social justice as its national purpose. Without such purpose, the Jewish people becomes redundant and expendable by history.

4. Were we to be the one people on earth striving as our supreme objective to eradicate crime, vice, selfishness, social inequality, the breakdown of marriages and the generation gap – through self-discipline trained by religious idealism – our image in the world, among Jews and non-Jews, would be vastly different and we would not be exercised by the problem of Jewish survival.

5. The claim – to which we now increasingly resort (in the absence of any other which cannot be invalidated) – that 'the Bible is our mandate' to legitimise our title to the Land and our Zionist aspirations, is a sham if used by Jews who do not accept the dictates of this mandate in their own lives while expecting non-Jews to subscribe to it at their cost.

6. The quest for equality, together with its corollary, the abrupt disengagement from our spiritual commitments, has already deleteriously affected the ethos of our national existence, and even our security. While the benefits of equality have eluded us, as the nations still do not treat us as equals, the liabilities of equality afflict us, as we now sadly experience many social and moral aberrations which used to be unknown in Jewish society.

7. As any objective observer knows, only Jews intensely committed to Jewish learning and living are now completely immune to the erosion of faith, as they are to the inroads of assimilation and intermarriage on the wider front in the global struggle for Jewish survival.

8. They now also constitute the bulk of Western aliyah, since what attracts them to Israel is its holiness rather than the security it may offer.

9. Moreover, this is now the only element of our people, because they live in strict accord with the precepts of Jewish ethics on birth-control and abortion, which is numerically prolific and immune to physical attrition, both inside and outside Israel. Had Israel's Jewish population at large been prepared to face similar hardships in upholding Jewish law, it would now number over five million, including at least two million more Sabras who would have been raised without the colossal costs and problems involved in the transportation and absorption of immigrants amounting to but a small fraction of this number.

10. Finally, and in a special category, the abandonment of Jewish spiritual values has political ramifications bearing on Jewish security, too. As an example, I would refer (after much anguished thought) to the vexed problem of Arab refugees. Whoever and whatever caused their plight, had we as Jews – faithful to our heritage of special sensitivity to the sufferings of the stranger and the homeless – cried out in protest against the intolerable degradation of hundreds of thousands inhumanly condemned (albeit not by us) to rot in wretched camps for over a generation; had we aroused the world's conscience over a tragedy of such magnitude (even if we could do little about it), and not left it to terrorist gangsters to draw the world's attention to this stain on humanity – who knows? – we might have prevented the growth of a monster organisation which has already destroyed so many precious lives and now threatens, with the blessings of the world community, the existence of Israel more acutely than the Arab armies ever did, not to mention their worldwide dissemination of anti-Semitic venom.

May I therefore urge, Mr Prime Minister, in the spirit of the timeless ideals which have preserved us through all our vicissitudes to this day, and for the sake of the millions of our fellow-Jews who are no longer bearers of our heritage through apathy, defection or repression, that we call for a massive mobilisation of all our spiritual resources, so as to assure the unity, faith, courage and vision of our people in the resumption of our historic assignment.

These supremely anxious times demand not only the reappraisal and sublimation of the Zionist purpose, but the revision of our national priorities. The moral and spiritual training of Israeli youth is just as vital as their military training, and Jewish schools in the Diaspora, too, are in the front line of our national defences. In the past, we often triumphed over the most fearful odds without physical might, but never without spiritual strength, born of Jewish learning and Jewish living.'

'ANOTHER WAY'

On 23 June 1978, the *Jewish Chronicle* published a leading article on the Middle East, entitled 'Another Way', in which it declared:

What Israel has to seek and espouse is a long-term peace strategy combining her maximalists' primary concern for territorial safeguards with the minimalists' overriding yearning for an accommodation. There is such a way, but it needs boldness. It must offer the Palestinian Arabs sovereignty and self-determination in exchange for peace. But, the onus is upon them to prove *in advance* that such a peace would be genuine and lasting, and this proof would have to be adduced before Israel vacated one inch of the territory presently under occupation. What is required of Israel is an undertaking to withdraw from occupied territory, with negotiated adjustments, *following and subject to* an agreed period of normal diplomatic, trade and tourist relations with all the Arab States at present in a state of war with her, starting with immediate revocation of the Arab boycott; the cessation of all and every act of terrorism by States or organisations; Palestinian renunciation of force or any designs against Israel's territorial integrity; and a firm agreement, internationally underwritten, that all territories vacated by Israel will remain completely demilitarised, except for a police force for internal security.

Chief Rabbi Jakobovits responded with the following letter:

Your bold editorial, 'Another Way', raises issues transcending even peace with the Arabs. It might also affect peace among Jews, now threatened by more perilous divisions than any other controversy in the history of the Jewish State.

Your proposals seem to offer an alternative to, and a compromise between, the two sides in the present debate for and against territorial concessions. While stipulating a period of genuine peace with *all* Arab States *before* ceding any territory, the proposals would yet break the current deadlock by a firm commitment *now* to meet Arab claims in exchange for convincing proof of peace, supported by other safeguards spelt out by you (border adjustments, demilitarisation and international guarantees).

Apart from turning the tables on the Arabs by challenging their sincerity in the quest for peace, your formula would thus also narrow the gap between our internal factions, taking account of some major demands and fears on both sides of the big divide, in seeking peace with security.

Of course, your proposals are still liable to encounter opposition, mainly from three groups (partly in combination): (1) those who reject them for reasons of security; (2) those who insist on retaining 'the historic Land of Israel' at all costs on religious grounds; and (3) those who object to Jews outside Israel expressing any views, other than in support of official Israeli policies.

1. I claim no competence on the security aspect. But one need not be a political or military expert to ask whether the existing *status quo* will prove tenable, and whether the likely alternative to an *eventual* withdrawal *on Israeli terms*, holding out some prospects of true peace, will not be a *speedier* withdrawal *without any returns*, enforced by America, as happened in 1956.

(Your correspondent last week, by dismissing your proposals both because he cannot accept 'some sovereign Palestinian entity' even *after* a period of completely normal relations with all Arabs, including the Palestinians, and because 'it is easier to believe that pigs will fly' than that the Arabs will accept your proposals, surely misses the whole point. This, as I understood your formula, was precisely that nothing would be given up until the Arabs had accepted, and prolonged evidence of peaceful relations was at hand.)

Nor is much sophistication required to appreciate the tremendous diplomatic gain which would accrue to Israel from seizing the initiative instead of merely reacting to events or to the initiatives of others (Dulles, Rogers, Kissinger, Sadat – and soon, no doubt, Carter-Vance).

Again, in the event of Arab acceptance (unlikely though that may be), would not the security risks after several years of peace be infinitely smaller than the present situation, with its constant threat of continual terror and renewed warfare?

2. Here, as a rabbi, I am on safer ground, and need not ask questions or speculate. Paradoxically, the most intransigent stance today is generated by religious elements. But vociferous as their 'rejectionist' clamour is, it should not drown out the 'small still voice' of 'moderates' like Rabbi J. B. Soloveitchik and many others.

No religious Jew disputes our claim to a Divine mandate (and we have no other which cannot be invalidated) extending over the entire Holy Land. What is arguable is whether we must, or indeed may, at this time assert it at the risk of thousands of lives, if not the life of the State itself.

To be sure, there are authentic sources and valid precedents for both views. I have analysed them in some detail in my book, *The Timely and the Timeless*, and in an article, 'The National Idea – Differing Religious Attitudes', in *L'Eylah*, Spring 1977. But the preponderant opinion in Jewish history and literature seems to favour conciliation and peace, notwithstanding the cost of territorial sacrifices. Even Joshua and Ezra did not complete the occupation of the entire Land.

Obviously, for religious Jews, settlement in Israel has a special dimension as a religious ideal – hence their quite disproportionate share in the aliyah rate. But, by the same token, their conscience must be particularly sensible to other, perhaps overriding religious imperatives, too, such as to the pursuit of peace as Judaism's highest ideal; to the preservation of life which suspends all other laws; to the inhuman condition of thousands of Palestinians in wretched refugee camps, whatever and whoever the cause; to the justice of some Arab claims even when they conflict with ours; and, above all, to the Jewish character of Israel, which would be vitiated by retaining a large Arab population within her borders, especially when, on present demographic trends, Jews would be in a minority within the next 15 years.

Even more alarming are the avowedly messianic components in the policies of some religious groups. The pages of Jewish history are littered with the lethal shrapnel flung out by the explosion of pseudo-messianic movements. As high expectations of imminent deliverance were cruelly shattered, they left behind them a trail of devastating disillusionment, stretching from the collapse of the Bar Kochba rebellion to the fearful aftermath of the Shabetai Zvi debacle.

Messianic *hopes* are the essence of faith and indispensable to our survival. But to base national policies on the certainty of such expectations can invite catastrophic consequences.

Altogether, the battle-cry 'not an inch', with its 'all-or-nothing' overtones, evokes ominous echoes of Massada – an episode without parallel in Jewish history and entirely out of tune with Jewish teachings.

Never before or after this epic has a Jewish religious sect declared its preference for collective death with dignity (totally ending all hopes for the future) over survival without immediate fulfilment of all national aspirations (but retaining faith in ultimate redemption).

If such a philosophy had been embraced by our entire people, Jewish history would have ended long ago with national euthanasia.

3. Here simply as a Jew I find myself least vulnerable. The cry to stifle participation in the great debate on Israel's future comes strangely *from* those who constantly remind us of the partnership between Israel and the Diaspora. It comes just as strangely *to* those who are committed to the centrality of Israel in their lives and who express their views only because of their supreme concern for Israel, realising that on her security now depends their own security.

The attempt to silence dissent and constructive criticism also sits particularly ill with a people which cannot forget the awesome price paid for silence in the face of suffering and injustice not so long ago.

Are we, of all people, again to become the 'Generation of Silence', responsible for aberrations or missed opportunities by default? Rather should we heed the Prophet's cry: 'For the sake of Zion I will not remain mute, and for the sake of Jerusalem I will not be silent'.

The Chief Rabbi's response elicited the largest postbag the *JC* had received in years, in addition to a flood of letters sent to him personally. They prompted the following statement:

'YOU WROTE WHAT MANY OF US THINK'

'The sharp criticism aroused by my letter was hardly unexpected. This was not the first time I had brought worldwide controversy on my head. I had fared no better when, alone among Orthodox rabbis, I opposed the 'Who is a Jew' agitation as futile and counter-productive, and when I advocated adding 'Let My People Live' to the slogan 'Let My People Go' in our campaigns for Soviet Jewry to secure their spiritual rehabilitation as well as their emigration. In both cases, subsequent events and policy revisions vindicated my stand, bitterly taken to task as I was at the time.

On this occasion, what did astound me were the widespread support I received and the irrelevance of much of the criticism directed at me. Judging by my mail and numerous other personal reactions (with the frequent refrain: 'You wrote what many of us think'), the current official line, both political and religious, is nothing like as widely endorsed as claimed. I now come to wonder if the silent majority does not share my attitudes, at least in great part.

The gravamen of my epistle lay, of course, in the religious argument. In our present predicament, I believe, it is critically important to demolish the sedulously fostered notion that all religious Jews belong to the 'intransigent' camp, or that Jewish teachings, because some interpret them as sustaining the 'not-an-inch' stand, are responsible for the present political impasse and the perilous consequences that may ensue.

I penned my letter out of the conviction that nothing would be more damaging to Judaism, to the image of the Jewish people, and to the current peace prospects than such an assumption. Without questioning the authenticity of the religious 'hawks', I was anxious to show that some 'doves' were at least equally 'kosher' …

Altogether, few critics addressed themselves to the core of the issues, or really answered the three key questions which troubled me and prompted my letter:

1. Why should not Israel seize the initiative by challenging all Arab States to establish completely normal relations in return for a commitment now to make substantial concessions after conclusive evidence of genuine peace is at hand? In what way would such an offer, whether accepted or rejected, spell greater risks for Israel's security than the present deadlock, with its continued toll of terror and threats of renewed warfare?
2. Assuming these proposals are unacceptable, what is the alternative? How do those who rely on the existing borders for Israel's security, and who despair of an eventual understanding with the Arabs, envisage the future – both short-term in view of America's capacity to impose a settlement, and long-term in view of the inevitably faster growth of Arab power, now commanding unlimited human material and soon also technological resources? How can relatively diminishing military might secure Israel's survival, let alone peace, unless, in the long run, one believes in an ultimate accommodation with the Arabs?
3. How is the Jewish State to be preserved when one-third of the present population are Arabs, increasing at double the Jewish rate?

The first two questions were completely ignored, and the last elicited the inaudible answer: 'Work for aliyah!' (as if I had not done so for years). The optimum estimate of new *olim* from the West does not exceed 30,000 annually – a figure more than twice wiped out by Israel's phenomenal abortion rate (which makes a mockery of all aliyah campaigns). And even if this figure were a net gain (i.e., with a zero *yeridah* rate), it would still fall far short of the Arab net increase, delaying their becoming the majority by just a few years. How can serious people resort to such a spurious argument and be so blind to reality? …

To retain world support, especially among friendly nations, we must persuade them not that we all think alike (which they know is not true), but that we genuinely wrestle with the problem of peace, even to the point of publicly disagreeing on the best way to attain it. We also have to show that our religious faith, far from being an impediment to a settlement, bids us to 'seek and pursue peace'.

These objectives I endeavoured to promote, although my letter was addressed to readers of the *Jewish Chronicle* and I had no desire to see it publicised in the non-Jewish press.

To those adding heat rather than light to the debate, I can only say: if we seek tolerance and understanding from others, we must first practise these virtues among ourselves. And to those who put their entire faith in borders and military hardware, the Prophet exclaims: 'Zion will be redeemed through justice, and her inhabitants through religiousness.'

THE VENICE DECLARATION

On 17 September 1980, the Foreign Secretary, Lord Carrington, addressed the Board of Deputies, mainly in defence of the European Community's Venice Declaration on the Middle East, issued earlier that summer. A week later, the Chief Rabbi wrote to him, 'setting out some reflections which have for some time exercised me and which were accentuated by your exposition':

'… If the response evoked by your address and your replies to questions was more agitated than is usual on such occasions, it reflected the uneasiness on HM Government's policies towards Israel widely felt among Jewish citizens, and I feel I ought frankly to tell you that your presentation did not give us much cause for reassurance …

As you are well aware, while Jews the world over are united in staunch support of Israel's vital interests, on opposition to any redivision of Jerusalem or to the establishment now of a Palestinian State – which at this stage would be suicidal for Israel – yet in wrestling with the quest for peace, Jewish opinion inside and outside Israel is sharply, often bitterly, divided. I have made no secret of my own leanings …

I am convinced that if Arab expressions of moderation had been comparable, in strength and influence, to Jewish conciliatory voices, especially among many Israelis themselves, the Arab–Israeli conflict could have been resolved long ago. I also believe it is self-evident that a mutually acceptable settlement will be possible only if and when a spirit of conciliation prevails on both sides.

Hence, any third-party intervention or initiative can be helpful only if it encourages and strengthens the moderates on each side.

To me, sadly, the EEC Venice Declaration, with Britain's support, did the opposite. Instead of urging participation in the peace process by countries hailed for their 'moderation', such as Saudi Arabia and Jordan, it called for the association of the PLO with the negotiations, just after the PLO had reaffirmed its commitment to the destruction of Israel and again asserted its sole reliance on continuing the 'armed struggle' (i.e., terrorism) against Zionism.

Such support for the most intransigent element in the Middle East situation was bound to harden attitudes on both sides and to dishearten the moderates. The stand of the latter, based on confidence in the balanced influence of friendly powers, has now been seriously eroded by this upgrading of an avowedly terrorist organisation. Conversely, the boost to Israel's mortal enemies by a world apparently indifferent to her fate was bound to stiffen a back-to-the-wall mentality of defiance, and I have little doubt that the EEC thus contributed directly to the Knesset passage of the Jerusalem Law.

For Israelis, the alternative to security is not defeat but extermination. Unless and until this fear is removed through the cultivation of mutual trust, there can be no lasting or just peace.

For years, I have publicly urged that as Jews – no strangers to refugeedom – we cannot be indifferent to the plight of the Palestinians in their wretched camps (though millions of refugees elsewhere have been successfully resettled during the past three decades). But it would be a supremely immoral travesty to relieve this festering problem at the cost of dismantling a sovereign State – and one itself created as a haven for the homeless!

Should not Britain, therefore, with its enviable tradition of fairness and tolerance, take the lead in pressing for a show of Arab moderation to match the very real and widespread spirit of accommodation already existing in Israel and among Jews everywhere? Your attribution of 'moderation' to Jordan and Saudi Arabia may be true in respect of the global East–West encounter, but sadly it has little basis in the reality of the Arab–Israel conflict.

We have yet to hear a single authentic voice from those quarters, let alone from Syria and Iraq, prepared to acknowledge the legitimacy and inviolability of Israel (wherever the borders) or to denounce the PLO terrorism! All Arab countries (apart from Egypt) are far more intransigent than the most uncompromising political grouping in Israel in their mutual attitudes to each other, and it is this gross imbalance which 'honest brokers' should redress to create an accelerating momentum of reconciliation.

To my mind, moreover, present European policies transcend the imperilling of Israel's security. With rampant inflation and unemployment scourges not unrelated to the 15-fold oil price rise in the past seven years already gravely destabilising Europe's economy, I recognise that oil and trade must feature prominently in any political calculations to placate the Arabs. Governments owe it to their citizens to protect them from economic collapse, threatening social chaos, political impotence and large-scale suffering. There need be nothing immoral in such pursuit of the national self-interest. But will these aims be achieved, and if so, at what cost?

The respectability conferred on terrorism, implicit in the invitation to the PLO, is only one item. And this is terrorism not in the 'accepted' sense of a liberation movement resorting to warfare or sabotage against the oppressor, but of the kind which first introduced into the history of human brutality deliberate attacks on children, air passengers, sportsmen and other innocent victims who are not a party to the dispute. Such overtures cannot but encourage terror, already wreaking havoc in Europe as elsewhere.

More significant, to my mind, is the blatant acknowledgement of Europe's mendicant status. In recent decades, its political and cultural influence has been on the wane, as the ascendancy of the Communist and Third Worlds has progressively turned democratic countries, governed by human values forged in Europe, into an ever-smaller minority among the United Nations. In the world arena, European civilisation is under siege, if not in retreat, for the first time in 2,000 years.

These values were safe in Europe itself in the post-war period, as even East–West tensions could not erode Europe's political, economic and cultural independence. But that is now being threatened, not by super-power military might, which is being resisted, but by the tyranny of petrodollars, with effects more devastating on Europe's economy than any Communist subversion.

If Mr Heath (*The Times*, 19 June) can declare explicitly (as is implicit in the EEC Declaration) that 'political incentives' to maintain high oil production rates must include '*sustained* indications by the Western countries that they are determined to make progress on the Palestinian problem', then political vassaldom is no longer concealed. And tomorrow's demands for such 'incentives' may prove even harder to deliver than Israel's security.

The global dangers appear even more ominous. The increasing transfer of the world's wealth to a few oil-rich countries to make them richer still, having already amassed the greatest wealth ever accumulated in history, cannot but lead to destitution and starvation on a scale never previously experienced in history.

Social injustice of such terrifying magnitude must in the end create a global imbalance far more dangerous than any nuclear disparity in overkill capacity between the superpowers. Such a new hegemony will inevitably also affect the freedom and cultural heritage we still enjoy, threatening to drive Europe, too, back to the Middle Ages.

I believe a halt can be called to this spiral of subjugation. The solidarity of the West, on whose protection most Middle East rulers still depend for their survival, could resist unreasonable demands. (The withdrawal of military and technical aid from them would lead to collapse more speedily than their withdrawal of oil from us – as we are now likely to see in Iran!) Such Western solidarity could equally induce the Arabs to adopt a truly moderate stance. I have little doubt that such moderation, provided it is convincing, will consolidate the strength of similar moderation in Israel, once the fear of annihilation is removed.

In our volatile and brutal world, statecraft is, to be sure, a daunting exercise in which the urge for sheer self-preservation may for a while obscure moral refinements. But, in the end, only 'righteousness exalteth a nation', and 'where there is no vision, the people perish'. In these tempestuous times, a sturdy ship of state built to the specifications of a millennial civilisation and guided by the fixed stars of eternal values may yet prove safer than the most modern super-tanker flying the flag of convenience or expediency.

On behalf of my people, which has helped to inspire this civilisation and to preserve these values at the cost of immeasurable suffering, I plead for your understanding and wish you every strength in upholding our common ideals and interests.'

Lord Carrington replied as follows:

'I agree that peace in the Middle East will ultimately depend on the creation of a genuine spirit of reconciliation and mutual acceptance. I, too, wish that the voice of Arab moderation would make itself heard with greater clarity and courage.

However, I do not agree that to acknowledge the support the PLO enjoys among the Palestinians, and to accept that the PLO must be associated with peace efforts if lasting peace is to be achieved, is to discourage the forces of moderation in the Arab world.

On the contrary, countries such as Egypt, Jordan and Saudi Arabia point to the Venice Declaration as evidence that the West is committed to a reasonable and balanced settlement. This strengthens their hand (and that of moderate elements inside the PLO) in arguing for the continuation of the search for a negotiated settlement through political means.

I do not believe I can be fairly accused of over-optimism about the PLO; I condemn their proclivity to talk in public of the destruction of Israel and their failure to signal clearly their readiness for a negotiated settlement. But it is surely wrong to assume that the PLO cannot ever be brought to a reasonable position. We have not endorsed their intransigence, but have accepted their importance. This gives us the best possible basis on which to press them to accept Israel. I can assure you that we take every opportunity to do so (as we do with all the Arabs).

I must also protest against your assumption that our policy in the Arab/Israel dispute is based on a 'mendicant' stance towards the Arab world because of their oil and consequent wealth. Leaving aside our own oil resources, our policy is not based on a desire to appease the Arabs but on our conviction that only a settlement which will ensure a secure and dignified future for both Israelis and Palestinians alike will bring lasting peace.

Of course we cannot ignore our very considerable interests in the area. Naturally, we wish to see a major irritant removed from our relations with both sides to the dispute. But I do not share your apparent conviction that this desire to encourage a lasting peace is somehow a sign of moral decay. And your suggestion that by pressure we should quickly bring about the collapse of the moderate regimes in the area seems, if I may say so, to be a recipe for disaster, in which Israel, too, would be engulfed.

I can assure you that our policy will continue to give full regard to the concerns and needs of both sides. We are committed to Israel's future. No settlement will have our support (or will ever be possible) which does not meet this basic requirement.'

With the situation in the Middle East continuing to deteriorate, Israel's 1982 incursion into Lebanon prompted the following message from the Chief Rabbi to Anglo-Jewry:

THE AGONY OF LEBANON

For British Jews, the war in Lebanon is a triple agony: the critical injury inflicted [weeks earlier] on Israel's beloved Ambassador, Shlomo Argov, as the war's first victim; the grievous loss of life on both sides as the war proceeded; and the hostility of Britain's Government, media and people as the poisonous fall-out from the war. How can – and should – we react as Jews, as lovers of Zion, as British citizens?

There is no single answer acceptable to all. We must recognise that this is the first war in Israel's history to divide rather than unite Jewish opinion – most acutely so in Israel itself. The moral, political and local defence problems raised by this war are too complex for a monolithic response. The first prerequisite for any reaction must therefore be to cultivate greater tolerance for diversity of views, preserving our solidarity with Israel and the cohesion of the community by uniting on basic essentials, while still respecting inevitable differences on attitudes.

Not everyone who blindly supports every action of Israel serves her best interests, and not everyone who criticises her policies is a traitor. Israel prides herself on her democratic way of life, the complete freedom of speech and opinion she permits and encourages, even in wartime. We would betray this ideal, which the Western world shares with Israel, if we were to restrict such democratic freedom among ourselves.

What may be arguable (as is heatedly debated between the Coalition and Opposition in Israel) is whether the campaign should have stopped short of Beirut once the PLO guns were out of range of Israeli settlements by a 25-mile *cordon sanitaire*, as was the original war aim, thus reducing the toll of civilian deaths and suffering. It may also be legitimate to question whether the action is likely to bring any nearer a lasting solution to the Arab-Israeli conflict in the long run, so long as the root problem of the Palestinians festers and is aggravated by increased bitterness and despair. It is also debatable at what point the cost in innocent lives becomes too high, especially under conditions of siege laid to a vast city.

What should be indisputable among Jews is that, in self-defence, Israel's action was morally as just as any war in history; that Israelis fought brilliantly and at heavy cost not only to protect their northern settlements from the constant threat of terror (which could have led to the eventual flight of most Jews from Upper Galilee), but to save all Israel from what might have been a mighty onslaught by the vast PLO arms stores found in Lebanon. They fought also to protect Europe's Jews (whose security now depends more than ever on Israel's security) from terrorist outrages. They flushed out the world headquarters of international terrorism training murder gangs for numerous other countries, thus making every citizen in the world safer.

So long as the PLO, by its National Covenant, remains committed to the 'armed struggle' (i.e., terrorism), it would be immoral, as well as futile, to negotiate with them. Jews ought also to appreciate that the PLO initiated an altogether new breed of terrorism, the first to introduce into the history of inhumanity the deliberate assault on civilians, especially children, and the threat to the lives of people not even a party to the dispute – such as air passengers – for political ends.

Also beyond argument must be our deep concern over the transparent anti-Israel or pro-Arab bias in Government statements, and especially in the presentation of the conflict in the media, now spilling over into very unfriendly public opinion. We cannot but be shocked by the widespread insensitivity to Israel's struggle for sheer survival, particularly as survivors of the Holocaust which, as now more fully revealed, left Western statesmen at the time virtually unresponsive to the cries for help.

The chorus of indignation against Israel, led by Europeans of all nations, contrasts with the silence and unconcern on the far larger carnage of Christians and Arabs in Lebanon's civil war, or on the 100,000-plus deaths in the Iran-Iraq war. There has been total indifference to the crucial distinction between accidental civilian casualties inevitable in any war and civilian targets being deliberately chosen to terrorise the population, not to mention the PLO rejoicing over the slaughter of Jewish children they had taken hostage.

Vastly and maliciously exaggerated as the civilian losses and damage reported in our media may have been, however, we must not fall into the trap of the 'numbers game'. In Jewish law and moral teaching, one innocent human life is as infinitely precious as a million, and our grief is not reduced by revising the figure of accidental casualties from thousands to hundreds, or of those rendered homeless from hundreds of thousands to tens of thousands. Nor is that grief diminished by arguing that the PLO inflicted far more massive cruelties on the Lebanese people, many of whom now hail the Israelis as liberators from a nightmare afflicting them for over a decade. The Jewish sensitivity to human suffering is absolute and unconditional, and it applies to the bereaved mother of a terrorist no less than to rocket victims in the Galilee.

At a time like this, when the danger of character refinements being dulled is so great, we must be particularly concerned to preserve, and to be seen to preserve, the special virtue which has always distinguished our people as *rachamim b'nei rachamim*, 'the compassionate, the sons of the compassionate'.

More open to discussion may be the reasons for the bias against Israel among British leaders and, indeed, in much of the free world at large. It is cold comfort for Anglo-Jewry to know that elsewhere in Europe attitudes are even more hostile than here, as I can testify from recent conversations with the Chief Rabbi of France and several other friends in some European countries.

I do not doubt that Israel is being judged and condemned by standards not applied to any other nation. But I think it is neither true nor wise to attribute this discrimination simply to anti-Semitism. Not true – because I know any number of prominent non-Jews who have for long been strongly slanted against Israel and yet have a genuinely friendly disposition towards Jews, highly respecting them as fellow-citizens, denouncing any manifestation of anti-Semitic discrimination, staunchly supporting the cause of Soviet Jewry, and similarly identifying with Jewish concerns. And not wise – because I fear that such attribution can only tend to be self-fulfilling.

By charging people with anti-Semitism, you help to breed anti-Semitism. You give aid and comfort to the real anti-Semites and their movements, and you alienate true friends. You also undermine Jewish confidence in the basic decency and tolerance of the society around us, and thus contribute to Jewish insecurity, whether subjective or objective. I believe that, generally, the unqualified equation of anti-Zionism with anti-Semitism holds true only in the Communist and Third Worlds.

The causes for the antagonism towards Israel are many and complex. Among other factors, there are vested interests in relations with Arab countries; there is a residue of Christian hesitation to come fully to terms with the restoration of Jewish sovereignty in Zion; there is the genuine sympathy with the sufferings of the Palestinian refugees; and there is estrangement caused by a certain abrasiveness not uncommon with some Israeli leaders and spokesmen, not to mention their policies.

For my part, I accept that we are being subjected to double standards. If this means that a higher morality is expected from us than from others, I take this as a compliment, nurtured through the biblical heritage by respect for Israel's role in moral pioneering.

Above all, what must unite us all without dissent at a trying time like this is our common commitment to Judaism as well as to Israel, and our resolve to strengthen both. Whatever our arguments on Israel's policies, they cannot and must not affect our identification with Israel's brave and long-suffering people, nor our faith in the future of the Jewish State as the principal gateway of all our hopes. Anyone who uses disagreement with Israeli actions as an excuse for withholding support is like a father punishing his son for some disagreeable behaviour by starving him.

Israel needs, and is entitled to, more than enormous financial help from us. In their loneliness, Israelis want to see us, and we should make extra efforts to plan visits there. They want to hear from us. Write or phone to your relatives or friends there. Inquire about their well-being. Tell them about the activities for Israel in your congregation. Reassure them that you share their bitterness over the distortion of the facts in our media. They yearn to know that they are not alone in their travail, and that we do all we can to plead and explain their cause. Of course, most heartening to them would be an increase in our aliyah.

No less important is the strengthening of our spiritual defences, the mainstay in all our tribulation over the ages. If you really believe the Almighty is our ultimate salvation, go to the synagogue and pray harder and more frequently.

Our children are not asked to defend the Jewish people by giving up the best years of their life for army service, and sometimes to make the supreme sacrifice. But surely we can demand of parents that they raise their children as creditable Jews, proud of their faith and familiar with their heritage, so that we do not face the appalling catastrophe of losing more by assimilation than by war, terror and persecution. Perform some extra mitzvot, sanctify your homes as happy havens of truly Jewish living, and exemplify the finest Jewish virtues through absolute integrity and caring for others.

Surely our grim predicament should unite us all in seeking to redress our distorted image not as a people of the sword, so sadly imposed on us in a cruel world, but as a people meriting Divine favour and human respect by striving to live up to the Torah injunction: 'And all the peoples of the earth shall see that the Name of the Lord is called upon you, and they shall have reverence for you.'

Jewish Chronicle, 16 July 1982

TERRITORY FOR PEACE?

As the first signs of a Middle East peace initiative between Israel and the Palestinians began to unfold in the late 1980s – assuming concrete expression with the Madrid conference of October 1991 – the question of 'territory for peace' resurfaced. Chief Rabbi Jakobovits clarified his stand in an address to the United Synagogue on 14 November 1989, during which he declared:

'However much I support the moderate line, I have never and would never endorse the 'Peace *Now*' formula. Indeed, in 1978, when I was first embroiled in a public debate on the subject, I always insisted that there can be no ceding or surrender of any territory before a period of genuine peace with all Arab States has convinced us that peaceful co-existence is possible.

Alas, we have not reached that assurance yet. I believe that, even at this time, the PLO cannot be a partner in peace negotiations until and unless they change their Covenant (which calls for an 'armed struggle' to eliminate Israel) and they officially adopt the non-violent option which, though open to them, they have just recently again rejected.

My argument is one of attitude rather than of decision or policy. I think the fact that as yet we have no responsible Palestinian leadership ready to enter into meaningful negotiations ought to be regretted by us, and we ought to show that we feel depressed by this sad fact of life.

Not everyone agrees. Many important sections of our people are happy that we cannot trust the Arabs and negotiate with them; for they oppose in principle any territorial accommodation, even for a genuine peace.'

The Chief Rabbi returned to the subject the following spring, in the columns of the United Synagogue's house journal, *Hamesilah*:

A TIME TO SPEAK AND A TIME TO BE SILENT: TO TELL OR NOT TO TELL

The substance of my inaugural lecture on 'Territory for Peace?' in the United Synagogue adult education series appears in the current issue of *L'Eylah*. Here I want to present *Hamesilah* readers with a more intimate *en famille* digest of that lecture and to share with them the meaning of the above sub-title, 'To tell or not to tell'.

When the title of the lecture 'Territory for peace' was first presented to me, I insisted that it should be treated not as a statement but as an inquiry; therefore, a question-mark must be added to emphasise that it was asking a question. The theme, I feel, is perfectly appropriate for the United Synagogue to sponsor and for me to deliver. The United Synagogue, as Anglo-Jewry's largest membership organisation and as the principal guardian of its religious loyalties, must relate to the problems of the moment and provide a platform for a new dimension of thinking on all current issues not found in newspapers or heard at purely political meetings. After all, the subject is on top of the national Jewish agenda today, in Israel, the United States and elsewhere. Opinions are sharply divided throughout the Jewish world, above all in Israel itself.

Even more important, perhaps, in my context, each side in this argument for and against the territory-for-peace proposition believes that its stand advances Israel's security, and equally that those opposing the proposition are endangering the security of Israel. Therefore, it should not occasion any surprise that this subject arouses intense fervour and passion. If opinions we hold with profound conviction will either promote or impede the quest for peace, then this is bound to stir passionate argument. What is not justified is that the debate should be conducted with rancour and intolerance, with the clamour for the denial of the right to express views that are sincerely and genuinely held out of a deep love for Israel.

In this lecture, I seek to contribute whatever I can to the promotion of mutual respect and of understanding between the two sides. My constant concern is the memory that our Temple was once destroyed not because there was a conflict of opinion – as there was – on how to face the Roman threat, but because, according to our sages, of 'causeless hatred', because of intolerance. Similarly, two generations later, Bar Kochba was defeated in the last attempt to establish (or re-establish) Jewish sovereignty after the Roman conquest not because there were arguments, as indeed there were, over how to meet that challenge. He was defeated because, among the disciples of Rabbi Akiva – who presumably were the main supporters of Bar Kochba and his rebellion – 'they did not show respect for one another'. And once they fell apart, the revolt failed, and we have been suffering the consequences of *galut* ever since, right up to the re-establishment of Jewish sovereignty some 41 years ago.

My views are well known – they are on record. Those who expect provocation will be disappointed. I speak here not as a politician and certainly not as a news analyst, but as a rabbi, as a teacher conducting a kind of 'teach-in' based on mainly religious and historical sources relevant to the present debate.

My reference to 'intense fervour and passion' concerns a vigorous campaign against the lecture being delivered at all. Friends with whom I work closely on Zionist as well as communal platforms pleaded with me to stop the lecture. They also approached the sponsors to have it cancelled, and, furthermore, they tried to prevail on individual members of the community not to attend. What were they afraid of? They feared that, by expressing my views on such a contentious subject, I might once again threaten to break up the unity of the community on Israel, and – worse still – undermine Israel's security. They need not have feared. I had no intention to do other than to give an academic lecture, providing the historical and religious background for the present arguments for and against territorial concessions.

I so informed my challengers, but they were still not altogether reassured. Nor did they recall that nothing untoward happened when I did make certain 'provocative' statements on Israel some ten years ago, their dire warnings then of the consequences notwithstanding. Israel survived unaffected, the community survived undivided in its solidarity – and I survived!

I admit the problem is a problem, and I do face a genuine dilemma. So do other communal leaders whose personal opinions may not always be identical with Jewish public opinion. But in my case, the difficulty is particularly acute. In very occasionally taking a public stand on policies affecting Israel, I invariably observe certain cardinal rules. I never resort to personal attack, whatever the provocation. Also, I never publicly criticise the Israeli Government or any of its decisions, such as the annexation of East Jerusalem and the Golan Heights, or the settlements policy in Judea and Samaria.

Altogether, I have always felt that the refusal occasionally to adopt a critical stance is tantamount to a denial of Israel's centrality in Jewish life. It amounts to a rejection of the belief that Jewish life the world over depends on Israel and its security. Jews, wherever they live, should feel that Israel determines their fate. They cannot disengage from major decisions taken in Israel.

Nor could I ever understand that divisions of opinion compromised the unity of the Jewish people in solidarity with Israel by undermining support for Israel among the nations of the world. On the contrary, to pretend that there is unity or unanimity when there is none is itself liable to promote Jewish disunity.

Of course, utmost caution is imperative, if criticism is not to provide grist to the mill of our enemies, or cause strife and contentiousness within the ranks of our own people. In practice, therefore, even the considerations in favour of intervention did not as a rule prevail as I am constantly wrestling with my conscience.

By contrast, people holding radical Right-wing views have never in my experience felt the need for any reticence, even when those views conflicted with official Israel Government policies. For instance, when Lubavitch came out with full-page advertisements denouncing Prime Minister Begin for surrendering Sinai, I cannot recall a charge of promoting disunity or giving aid and comfort to our enemies, who were only too keen to present Israel as intransigent. Or, more recently, when Israel's officially sponsored peace proposals were widely attacked by some Jewish speakers in the Diaspora, as well as in Israel, I have yet to hear the charge that this was calculated to undermine the interests of Israel by publicising disunity within our ranks. The whole argument is rather tendentious and one-sided.

Now well into the fifth decade of Israel's existence, we ought perhaps to be a little less self-conscious. We certainly should not lay ourselves open to the charge made by my sainted predecessor Chief Rabbi Dr Hertz when he spoke, albeit in another context, of the 'trembling Israelites'.

Referring, in an interview a year later with *Evening Standard* writer A. N. Wilson, to the plight of the Arab refugees, the Chief Rabbi sparked off a controversy as great as any encountered by him throughout his rabbinical career:

A MAN WHO BELIEVES IN ABSOLUTE RIGHT

Immanuel Jakobovits retires this summer as Chief Rabbi covered with honours. In 1988, Mrs Thatcher, who made no secret of the fact that she admired him more than most of her own bishops, made him a peer of the realm. This year, he has been awarded the £410,000 Templeton Prize ...

Lord Jakobovits is smaller than his patriarchal photographs would suggest. His animated face glows with intelligence. Because of his admiration for Mrs Thatcher, and his apparently simplistic views of sexual morality, he has been branded in some quarters as nothing better than an old reactionary. In fact, as I soon discovered from talking to him, it is not easy to classify him in any crudely political or religious stereotype.

'I dislike signing on dotted lines. That is why I have never belonged to a political party. It is perfectly true that I admired many aspects of the Conservatism of the last 12 years. But, in social matters, I have much sympathy with the Labour Party. I believe that society has a duty to help the underprivileged – but to help them to be self-sufficient; to get them on to the point where they can help themselves.'

He went on to quote approvingly the old proverb that 'God helps those who help themselves'.

I said that this seemed a good proverb for a Jew, since there had been precious few Gentiles in the history of the world who had been prepared to help the Jews. Was this not supremely exemplified by the establishment of the State of Israel in 1948?

Yes, it was, said Lord Jakobovits. But he is very far from being an uncritical supporter of the present Israeli Government.

'I am not in any way suggesting that the Palestinian refugee problem was caused or aggravated by Jewish complicity, but that has nothing to do with *feeling* with them.'

His voice rises three octaves. 'This is a stain on humanity – people locked up in these wretched refugee camps for 40 years. We ought to cry out to the world, we ought not to wait until terrorists draw attention to this. We could enlist the help of friendly Arabs. After all, there is no lack of wealth there. It ought to be possible to build secure lives for these people without threatening anyone.'

Is he suggesting that there should be a separate Palestinian State?

'I do not know what the ultimate solution will be. But we cannot forever dominate a million and a half Arabs, lord it over them. In less than 30 years they'll be in the majority. This blinkered attitude is self-destructive. One has to recognise that the Palestinians have legitimate aspirations which cannot be denied forever.' ...

The Chief Rabbi has provoked howls of dissent from among the ranks of his fellow Jews with some of his 'Thatcherite' politics, or his simple view that homosexual acts are in all circumstances wrong, as well as with his liberal views on Zionism. But among the British public at large, he has earned very widespread respect at a time when the Church of England is failing to supply leaders who seemed either pious or clever.

Why is Jakobovits an impressive figure? Because most of us recognise what his namesake Immanuel Kant (his father named him after the great philosopher) regarded as moral imperatives.

There are rights and wrongs in life, there is a moral law which we did not make up for ourselves. To articulate what this law is, and to say how it applies in the complex world of today, might be thought to be the prime function of a great religious leader. It requires deep faith but also a very lively intelligence. It is because Immanuel Jakobovits is so liberally endowed with both that he has made such an impact – and, on the whole, such a benign impact – on our generation.

The interview provoked fierce reaction within the British Jewish community, leading to this report in the *Jewish Chronicle*:

Lord Jakobovits, the Chief Rabbi, came under unprecedented public attack this week for his remarks on the Palestinians to the London *Evening Standard* – with two planned fund-raising events cancelled, and a trustee of the Jakobovits Foundation resigning in protest.

The wave of recrimination followed the Chief Rabbi's description of the Palestinian refugee problem as 'a stain on humanity'. Comments from the interview were used in a front-page splash story headlined 'Chief Rabbi shames Israel'.

In the wake of the interview, the Chief Rabbi spent hours in discussion this week with the head of the Horeb Schools of Jerusalem, Rabbi Mordechai Elon, who was in London for a planned fund-raising dinner on Wednesday under Lord Jakobovits' patronage. An additional dinner, also with the Chief Rabbi as guest of honour, is scheduled for Israel on 24 June.

Despite the last-minute talks, the London dinner was cancelled, although it appears that the event in Israel might still go ahead after a negotiated statement by the Chief Rabbi clarifying his remarks in the *Standard*.

On Shabbat, Rabbi Jonathan Sacks, the Chief Rabbi-elect, gave a sermon at Hampstead Garden Suburb Synagogue, in London, which many congregants took as a criticism of Lord Jakobovits. But Rabbi Sacks rebutted this interpretation, telling the *JC* that he supported 'any rabbi's right to speak on a matter of principle'.

Of Lord Jakobovits, the Chief Rabbi-elect said: 'I admire his moral courage, and there is a very deep kinship between us. My views are not significantly different from his own. Lord Jakobovits has pointed out the moral dilemmas facing Israel and the Arab world, with great courage.'

Lord Jakobovits, who will retire in September, reiterated many of his views this week.

'I'm a rabbi. I'm not a statesman or a politician. My job is to propagate Jewish teachings as I understand them, and that is to care deeply for the sufferings of anyone, even of our enemies. That does not mean that I want them to enjoy rights which would undermine the security of Israel', he said.

The 1993 peace agreement between the PLO and Israel was greeted by Lord Jakobovits – with reservations that were to prove increasingly justified as the decade drew to a close – in the following feature in the national press:

LIVING TOGETHER ON THE EDGE OF A SWORD

When the Prime Minister of Israel, Yitzhak Rabin, shook hands with the Palestinian leader Yasir Arafat on the White House lawn yesterday, it was a single, simple gesture fraught with the most awesome consequences and symbolism. For me, it was the single most significant historic event of the century: a moment of unimaginable grandeur, carrying with it the expectations, not just of Jews and Arabs, but of the whole world. It signified the end of the longest bloody feud of the post-war world, between the Palestinians and my people, the Jews. I watched it with a mixture of supreme hope and some trepidation.

That hope would have seemed barely imaginable even a few weeks ago. After all, Israel has not known a single day of peace for half a century, and I had hardly dared cherish such a sudden and unexpected prospect. But now we must nourish hope, for out of it peace is constructed.

The agreement signed in Washington is a vindication of the views I have expressed over many years that the PLO must renounce terrorism if Israel's security is to be assured. Now they have made that enormous leap of faith.

Peace is not merely a piece of paper or a handshake – it is an attitude of mind. Now, with the right kind of fruitful collaboration between Jews and Arabs working together in harmony, I wonder whether the Middle East might once again see a Golden Age from which the whole world will benefit.

Consider the effects of economic collaboration between the oil-rich Arab countries and the Jews; the marriage of intellectual capacity and the strength of economic co-operation. I say, advisedly, that the effects will be global, for the land of Israel, established as it was by Moses at the crossroads of Asia, Africa and Europe, has historically had an enormous impact on world events and the progress of civilisation.

In the Cold War, it was the Middle East battleground for the superpowers, America and Russia. And now that the threat of new war has receded, and years of enmity between Arabs and Jews have ended, I am quite sure that the reverberations will be felt around the world. Yesterday's historic agreement will,

I am convinced, encourage moves towards peace in other trouble spots world-wide. Perhaps even the Protestants and Catholics of Northern Ireland will be inspired by it to find some common ground.

Consider, too, that far more Arabs have been killed by Arabs during decades of hostilities than have been killed by Jews. This mutual accommodation must be an immense relief to Arabs as well. These factors have contributed to a growing affinity between Palestine and Israel, crowned by this spectacular pact between two hitherto sworn enemies.

So, when I saw that momentous handshake, my feelings were divided: on one hand, relief; on the other, trepidation. We cannot and must not forget that the hand proffered in friendship has also been drenched in blood: the blood of innocent athletes murdered at the Olympics, the blood of those who perished in the hijacks of aircraft and the numerous acts of terrorism. One could not help but feel a stirring of fear and revulsion, to see the man responsible for the killings of hundreds of Jews standing side by side with his old enemy on the White House lawn.

So trust and friendship will not be easily won. We would not be human if we expected decades of hostilities and bitter memories to be wiped out in a handshake. Yet we want to look forward rather than back. Mr Arafat has committed himself to a peaceful resolution of the conflict. He has recognised the right of Israel to exist in peace, and we must now hope that forthcoming negotiations will include safeguards against renewed aggression.

For, to the Jews, peace is not merely a means by which people live together in amity – it is a religious ideal. Jews use the word *shalom* (peace) more than any other. No other blessing has more meaning. So no one rejoices more at the prospect of peace than those who are living by a religion inspired by the ultimate ideal of peace. For me, it is not just a cause for physical rejoicing, but the attainment, at long last, of a religious yearning.

King Solomon, the 'King of Peace', built a Temple in Jerusalem, the capital of the Jewish people. David, conqueror of Jerusalem, could not build it, for he had shed much blood. It is now my most fervent hope that this accord will be the foundation on which we will build another edifice that will bring a moral dimension to the word 'peace'.

These are my views. I have expressed them to Mr Rabin on my frequent visits to Israel. I am full of admiration for him and Mr Peres, that they should lay aside the prejudices of generations and signal the dawn of a new era with this meeting.

I know that there is not universal approval for the agreement. Unanimity on such momentous issues is impossible, and passions are bound to be inflamed. But nothing justifies the outbreaks of violence – in Gaza, Hebron and Southern Lebanon – that preceded the signing of the protocol. My feeling, however, is that the overwhelming majority of Arabs and Jews endorse the agreement, and my hope is that those who do not should use democratic, not violent, means to express their views.

But I do cherish great hopes and dreams for the future unfolding of a collaboration of two ancient peoples, symbolically signalled in the signing of papers in Washington yesterday.

How appropriate, too, that America, the greatest democracy on earth and home to the largest Jewish community in the world, should have been the setting for an event of such colossal consequence and significance.

There is a saying in Jewish lore that a man and a wife can live together on the edge of a sword if there is happiness and accord between them. But once their love is no longer, a bed 60 cubits wide is not big enough! There is room for all in the Middle East, provided they live in amity.

I have such hopes for the Arabs and Jews. And once we have achieved a degree of co-operation, nourished by hope, then the sky is the limit: Israel, once again, will be one of the most flourishing areas of the globe. There will, of course, be disappointments, some of them grave; but we must keep our minds riveted on the ultimate aim.

Daily Mail, 14 September 1993

WHITHER RELIGIOUS ZIONISM?

The massacre of Arab worshippers in Hebron over Purim 5754/1994 – wrote the editor of *Tradition*, the journal of the Rabbinical Council of America – 'placed a spotlight on the tiny number of Jewish militants who are followers of the late Meir Kahane, many of whom are self-styled Orthodox Jews and Religious Zionists. Because of this – and the fact that some of their more militant doctrines seem, here and there, to have found a positive response within some small sections of the larger Orthodox community over the years – attention has recently been focused on Religious Zionism as a whole. *Tradition* therefore asked a number of prominent thinkers from the wide range of Israeli and Diaspora Orthodoxy to address the issue. They were asked the following questions:

- Has the leadership of Religious Zionism and that of the more general Orthodox community been clear enough in teaching the difference between the philosophy of a movement that is willing to fight militarily for the establishment and maintenance of the State of Israel, on the one hand, and that of a group whose symbol is a fist and in which violence has been an ever-present threat, on the other?
- What are the fundamental differences between Kahanists and those for whom a rejection of "land for peace" is an integral tenet of Religious Zionism?
- Has Religious Zionism failed to take seriously the criticisms posed by non-Zionist Orthodoxy? Has it been guilty of unjustly denigrating "traditional *galuti* values"? Has it erred in its theological or halachic judgements and presuppositions?
- Has Religious Zionism been guilty of cultivating a negative stance towards Gentiles? How can Israel's chosenness (*behirat Yisrael*) be so formulated as to avoid its being misinterpreted as either another form of secular nationalism or an endorsement of negative attitudes towards non-Jews?'

The following was Lord Jakobovits' response:

Religious Zionism was clearly derailed long ago, abandoning the historic tracks laid by its early pioneers and their followers.

In its original form – as the Mizrachi – it was always a movement, or a political party, committed to moderation as a cardinal principle, a bridge-builder seeking the middle ground between extremes, whether religiously by making undeviating Orthodoxy compatible with the Zionist enterprise, or politically by opposing all forms of extremism and militancy.

Today, the National Religious Party (NRP), with a few fading exceptions, finds itself firmly allied with other extremist Right-wing groups, inside and outside the Government of Israel. Oddly, the same radical shift towards the Right has occurred within the Agudah and the major Chasidic movements – all of them once political moderates, now, overwhelmingly, supporters of the most militant policies.

This applies even to those groupings which continue to deny religious recognition or legitimacy to the State of Israel – a contradiction dramatically demonstrated by Lubavitch in particular.

That these trends should have encouraged the emergence of a movement like Kach committed to violence was perhaps inevitable. Its active supporters may be few, but those who are at least ambivalent in denouncing it as utterly un-Jewish are not so insignificant.

To state these facts may be easier than to explain them, let alone to reverse them. Some conclusions seem inescapable.

Apart from the shrinking remnants of genuine ideologues who believe in Greater Israel for purely religious ('halachic') reasons, the bulk of the rest hold their Right-wing view on nothing but secular grounds: 'You can never trust the Arabs'; 'The only language they and the world understand is military power'; 'The old borders are indefensible' (as if ruling over two million Arabs were not, Jewishly if nothing else, at least as indefensible); and so forth. The political philosophy of Orthodoxy is now completely secularised as well as radicalised.

Maybe this has something to do with the shift of power and influence to America and away from other Diaspora communities. America being a more volatile society than, say, Europe, the demand for power is far more in evidence among American Jews than elsewhere. Neither Kach nor Lubavitch could ever have been indigenous to Israel; perhaps even Gush Emunim owes its strength to American support.

I see the eventual solution only in the gradual disengagement of religion from political parties, and of the rabbinate from State control. Apart from gaining far greater public acceptance as custodians of true religious thought and leadership, this might also shift the overriding concerns of the religious community from political manifestation towards mobilising Israel's spiritual forces – no doubt the ultimate determinant of Israel's destiny.

THE ASSASSINATION OF YITZHAK RABIN

Britain's Jewish community was united in shock, grief and mourning yesterday as it tried to come to terms with the assassination of Israeli Prime Minister Yitzhak Rabin [wrote Ruth Gledhill in *The Times* of 6 November 1995]. At a meeting in Switzerland today, Jewish leaders will debate the implications of the assassination.

At the Conference of European Rabbis' meeting, Lord Jakobovits, Britain's former Chief Rabbi and conference president, will discuss 'the shock, the grief, the shame' of Mr Rabin's death. He said last night: 'This presents a particular challenge to the religious community, since this was born out of religious fanaticism. It also represents a distortion of Jewish values.'

He added: 'The religious community will have to do some very profound stocktaking. We may well have to revise our education system to ensure such a thing can never happen again.'

In recent correspondence with Mr Rabin, Lord Jakobovits urged him to reassure the settlers that their concerns were understood. In his letter, Lord Jakobovits said they felt abandoned. 'They believe the Government does not sufficiently care. They need constant reassurance that their present despair is well understood.

'They are alarmed by the growing threat of complete secularisation, by the alienation from Jewish spiritual, moral and family values, and by the acute apprehension that, on the attainment of any peace between Israel and its neighbours, Israel will lose more of its Jewish distinctiveness.'

In his reply, Mr Rabin agreed that additional efforts must be made to reassure Israelis living in the territories. He appreciated their 'tremendous concerns'.

A PALESTINIAN ENCLAVE IN JERUSALEM

Emeritus British Chief Lord Jakobovits has called for part of Jerusalem to become a self-governing Palestinian enclave as part of a final peace plan for the disputed city.

The peer, who as Chief Rabbi attracted criticism for supporting the exchange of land for peace, mooted the controversial idea in an authorised biography – *The Lord Rabbi*, by Israeli journalist Michael Shashar – due to be published next week in Israel. [Entitled *Lord Jakobovits in Conversation*, an English version was later published in the UK by Vallentine Mitchell.]

Lord Jakobovits told the *Jewish Chronicle* that his plan was for Jerusalem to remain the 'united capital of the Jewish State'. However, he added, 'while the Jewish part should be under Jewish municipal control, the Arab areas should also be self-governing. If they want to fly the Palestinian flag there, then they can. And they can call it the capital of whatever entity they make.'

Lord Jakobovits, who has on several occasions been attacked by Right-wing communal figures for his views on the Middle East conflict, said he was aware his ideas would be controversial. 'I know they will raise a few eyebrows. But one has to find a workable solution for Jerusalem', he said. 'I am afraid that if you want to be true to yourself, you have to be prepared for controversy.

'My remarks on Jerusalem were actually based on an idea that originated with the former mayor, Teddy Kollek, who wanted to divide the city into

Jewish and Arab boroughs', he said. 'It is also based on the belief that it is easier to reach agreement if you avoid moving populations. If you do that, you build up grievances that can last for generations.'

Passions ran high on the future of Jerusalem, Lord Jakobovits declared. And although it was 'much more than just a capital' to the Jews, it was also important to the Palestinians. 'There has to be give and take', he said. 'In fact, it would probably have been wiser to start the peace negotiations by settling the future of Jerusalem. If agreement is not reached, Jerusalem could become a festering wound.'

Jewish Chronicle, *15 December 1995*

WHY RELIGIOUS JEWS SHOULD SUPPORT THE PEACE PROCESS

I do not relish being involved in public controversy. But I am even more averse to suppressing my views when these concern vital Jewish interests, and especially when I anticipate being vindicated ultimately – as happened before.

Rabbis – or indeed religious Jews generally – are no greater experts on Israel's military or physical security than anyone else. But they should be expected to be more proficient than others on Israel's spiritual security – and this may in the end prove to be the decisive factor. On the specifically Jewish aspects, we ought to be the more competent.

My own very occasional forays into the public arena on Israeli politics are made purely as a rabbi, charged to promote Jewish values. Several such values are now at stake. For me, the pursuit of peace is a supreme Jewish ideal, second only to the preservation of life itself.

The present opposition of the religious Establishment to the peace process is, as I see it, based on purely secular arguments. These include: ceding territory will endanger Israel's security (I would argue, perhaps, not ruling over two million disaffected Arabs will make Israel safer – it would certainly make the State more Jewish); the old borders are indefensible (with missiles from Baghdad hitting Tel Aviv, borders are almost irrelevant – and from the 'indefensible' pre-1967 borders came the biggest victory in Jewish history, while the near-disaster of the Yom Kippur War sprang from the 'ideal' borders of the Suez Canal and the expanded Golan area); and, one cannot trust the Arabs (I have often advocated that Israel should not cede any territory until the Arab State in question has conducted at least five years of normal diplomatic, trade and tourist relations with Israel).

In Jewish thought, we pray not to destroy our enemies, but to 'confound their counsels' – that is, to make them change their minds. I am not naïve enough to believe that they have suddenly turned murderous hostility into genuine friendship. This can happen only if our interests converge.

Yasir Arafat knows very well that he has more to fear from fundamentalist fellow-Arabs than from Israelis. Indeed, far more Arabs than Jews have been killed by these extremists. Arafat's security, and that of other Arab 'moderates', may well lie in making common cause with Israel. We should encourage such convergence of interests.

Still more important as a religious consideration is the realisation that unyielding attitudes are liable to lead to another war, with – Heaven forfend – catastrophic casualties dwarfing past losses.

Nothing can weigh more heavily on the Jewish religious conscience, with Judaism's attribution of infinite worth to every single life, not to mention the collectivity of the Jewish State which could also be threatened.

Which leads me, above all other considerations, to Israel's spiritual security. To this, as religious Jews, we have everything to offer.

We ought to know, and to believe, that in the long run the Jewish people cannot survive in the Land of Israel without keeping faith with the Divine Covenant which conferred our claim to the Land in the first place.

We must accept, and proclaim with conviction, the twice-daily declaration of the Shema that, without a firm moral and spiritual foundation, our people 'will be destroyed from off the good land which the Lord has sworn to give our fathers' – as the experience of repeated destruction and exile has proved in our history.

Many religious Jews, I suspect, do not genuinely believe this warning. So many are more convinced with the quantity of the land under Jewish control – where the borders are to be – than with the quality of its life.

Preoccupied with physical power and strength, we rely on material calculations (strangely nowhere more so than in religious quarters), lacking the conviction that, in the end, Israel's security will depend on factors which we alone can contribute.

If immoral imports into Israel – lechery, drugs, marital infidelity, dishonesty and much other evil – still exceed the export of Torah from Zion, religious Jews should feel deeply worried. For such a negative balance sheet spells the failure of the religious element to set the tone.

Religious Jews would have much to answer for if, instead of this primary concern, there would be a calamitous derailment of the Jewish destiny.

I am absolutely confident that the Jewish purpose will prevail, however long it may take. After all, nearly half a millennium elapsed between Joshua's first conquest of the Land and the establishment of Israel's sovereignty over Jerusalem and the building of the Temple there.

Equally, I believe the peace process is irreversible, and some concessions compatible with security will be made over the Land, including Jerusalem, yet retaining its status as Israel's undivided capital – forever if we merit it.

As a salutary by-product of such a stance, religious Jews may regain the respect which they have at present widely forfeited, and which they need in order to exercise any influence on our people and its fortunes.

Lord Jakobovits, Jewish Chronicle, *16 August 1996*

CHAPTER ELEVEN

Inter-Faith Relations

'Moving with prudence and caution in the uncharted territory of inter-faith understanding and co-operation'

In contemporary terms, we need to emphasise the tremendous innovation of Judaism and Christianity groping for the first time for an understanding, instead of regarding each other as rivals. I believe that this revolution may perhaps ultimately have a more crucial effect on the future course of human history than the scientific, economic or political revolutions that have taken place over the past few decades.

This realisation that we all have an assigned role to play in history, and that numerous social and moral issues which bedevil human relationships today can be resolved only by a broad *religious* attack, is itself one of the most hopeful signs of our era. It has brought the great faiths much closer to each other than at any time throughout their existence.

Consequently, what we have in common [with Christianity] is not only our heritage and our origins, but the joint enterprise of meeting together some of the social evils which plague human society. Among these are the rise in crime, the break-up of family life, and the 'New Morality' which so often gnaws at the roots of the moral order as we jointly understand it.

If these things are to be effectively countered, they will require, I think, a great deal of partnership between the faiths.

Chief Rabbi Immanuel Jakobovits
Sunday *ecumenical magazine, November 1967*

JUDAISM AND CHRISTIANITY: ADVANCES AND LIMITS

'Few of the revolutionary changes which have reshaped the post-war world can be greeted by us with greater satisfaction than the dramatic improvement of inter-religious relations generally, and particularly the attitude of Christianity to Judaism. Great faiths, for millennia implacable and often mortal rivals, now reason together. We witness formerly undreamed-of manifestations of tolerance, exemplified here by the Council of Christians and Jews under the patronage of the Queen and the joint presidency of the heads of denominations, and culminating in the Vatican decision to modify age-old teachings offensive to Jews, including the murderous 'deicide' charge.

It is no credit to civilisation that these revisions were not effected until well into the twentieth century. Had they come 1,000 years earlier, untold millions of human lives might have been saved from degradation and slaughter. Nevertheless, late as they are, these radical developments are obviously welcome.

These new trends challenge as well as relieve the Jewish people. The olive-branch of peace and understanding signifies more than an end to the past flood of blood and tears, and the present overtures envisage more than the unilateral rectification of historic wrongs. A new era is being ushered in, with ecumenism as its watchword, aiming at some as-yet undefined inter-denominational reconciliation, in which demands will also be made of Judaism. What are these demands, what prompts them, and how far can they be met?

The ecumenical movement, aimed at 'Christian Unity', is, of course, a purely internal affair within Christendom. The forces generating this movement are not born, and cannot be expected to be born, solely out of altruistic motives, any more than the internationalism of the United Nations is sustained without a measure of self-interest by the Great Powers.

With the end of European colonialism diminishing the hopes of converting to Christianity one-third of mankind, and with militant atheism ruling another third, not to mention the rebellion against religion in the remaining Christian world, Christianity is on the defensive for the first time in its history. This momentous turn of the tide is bound to produce pressures for consolidation from within, to compensate for the inroads from outside.

Clearly, the same pressures also call for some accommodation with Judaism, to strengthen the ramparts of the 'Judaeo-Christian patrimony' against the 'common foes' of materialism, secularism, atheism and sheer paganism sweeping the world.

From the Jewish point of view, some Jewish and Christian interests converge, while others will always remain irreconcilable. Jews certainly have an interest in Christians being good and faithful Christians, not only because – in the very phrase first coined in medieval times – '*wie es christelt sich, so juedelt's sich*'. Judaism obviously cares deeply for the advancement of the moral and religious values promoted by all monotheistic faiths.

There are also many specific areas in which inter-faith co-operation should prove of common interest. Consultations and joint efforts are surely desirable to ensure better religious educational facilities, including aid for denominational schools; to defeat morally unacceptable legislation, from abortion on demand at the start of life to euthanasia at its end; to fight racial or religious discrimination; and generally to cultivate the moral and religious conscience of society.

But traditional Judaism shrinks from inter-denominational activities and debates in areas on which our religious differences impinge. Our aversion to theological dialogues and inter-faith services, for instance, is founded both on practical considerations and on the dictates of Jewish law.

We regard our relationship with God, and the manner in which we define and collectively express it, as being so intimate and personal that we could no more convey it to outsiders than we would share with others our husband-wife relationship. We feel it is improper to expose one's innermost beliefs and mode of worship to the judgement or comparative scrutiny of those who do not share the same religious commitment.

Moreover, any parleys between Judaism and Christianity would be between two essentially unequal partners on several counts, quite apart from the gross disparity in dominance and numbers in Christian lands. Christianity may well have seen a need officially to define its doctrinal attitude towards the faith from which it emerged and eventually broke away. But neither the recognition of this need nor the resultant relationship can be entirely reciprocal.

Judaism, antedating Christianity by many centuries, had no occasion or cause to include in its official doctrines any formal views on a faith which sprang up long after these doctrines were formulated in all essentials. It lies in the nature of their history that the New Testament can refer to the Old, while the Old cannot refer to the New.

An even more important element of inequality lies in the fundamental divergence of views on evangelism, a subject of special sensitivity to a people already decimated by persecution and assimilation. While Christianity aspires to convert all human beings, uniting them within one universal religion, Judaism has no such aspirations.

It is content to remain for all time a minority faith, 'the remnant of Israel', restricted to those born into it and the few who may spontaneously seek to embrace it, without any encouragement or inducement. Even if Christians were to forswear any missionary intent in theological dialogues with Jews, their traditional division into two groups – the one seeking to absorb the other – is historically, if not theologically, so deeply rooted as inevitably to compromise their equality.

Judaism accepts religious diversity and cultural pluralism not just as an inescapable fact of life, or a temporary condition to be tolerated, but as a desirable state to enrich the human experience. Diversity, we believe – in creed, race, nationality, political views and other spheres – is as essential to create the dynamics of human progress as are the distinctions and tensions between male and female or between positive and negative poles, which are required to generate all life and energy. A human race made up of identical beings would be as dull and as uncreative as a symphony played by a single-instrument orchestra.

Judaism teaches that even in messianic times, when the Kingdom of God will be accepted universally, religious differences will still exist. At 'the end of days', in Micah's famous prophecy, 'all the peoples will walk each in the name of his God' (4:5). This is the real significance of the verse from Zechariah (14:9) with which we conclude every Jewish service: 'In that day shall the Lord be One and His Name One'.

From a sermon delivered by the Chief Rabbi
St John's Wood Synagogue, London, 12 June 1971

At a reception in London, in October 1975, to mark the tenth anniversary of the Second Vatican Council's Declaration on the Jews, Chief Rabbi Jakobovits and the Archbishop of Westminster, Cardinal John Heenan, expressed hope for closer understanding between the Roman Catholic Church in Britain and the Jewish community.

The Vatican declaration was defined by Dr Jakobovits as a 'colossal historical event' and one of the most important turning-points in the history of human relationships. He said that he was looking forward to a greater awareness of Jews among the Roman Catholics as a people with a homeland in Israel.

Cardinal Heenan said that the declaration had outlawed anti-Semitism in the Roman Catholic Church and had banished forever the belief that the Jewish people were an accursed race. He pointed to the common Jewish–Catholic attitudes to many moral problems facing present-day society.

[On Cardinal Heenan's death, only ten days after this meeting, the Chief Rabbi issued a statement paying tribute to him as 'a fearless champion of moral values in British society ... His deep humanity also found expression in his repugnance of anti-Semitism and, in particular, in his constant concern for the plight of Soviet Jewry ... Cardinal Heenan left an historic mark on Jewish–Roman Catholic relations.']

In 1982, during a visit to Britain, Pope John Paul II met the Chief Rabbi and other leading members of the Jewish community, including Dr Lionel Kopelowitz and Martin Savitt, vice-presidents of the Board of Deputies. As *The Times* reported, the meeting took place in Manchester because the Sabbath and another Jewish festival fell while the Pope was in the south of England. Nevertheless, the meeting at Heaton Park was especially pleasing and appropriate because the venue lay in the heart of one of the biggest Jewish communities in the North-West.

The Pope told the Chief Rabbi that it was a joy for him to extend his fraternal greetings: 'On this occasion of my visit to Britain, I wish to express my personal sentiments of esteem and friendship for all of you. At the same time, I wish to reiterate the full respect of the Catholic Church for the Jewish people throughout the world.'

The Chief Rabbi delivered the following address to the Pope:

'Your visit to this country, although officially of a pastoral nature, is an historical event of significance far beyond Catholic friends. British Jews join their fellow-citizens in warmly greeting you not only as the world's most widely acclaimed spiritual leader but as a charismatic personality of rare distinction, deeply respected for your vision, dynamic qualities and human virtues.

Your visit's ecumenical aspirations, while primarily of inter-Christian concern, are of course of profound interest to Jews as well, all the more so since the papacy had often been a cause of conflict and suffering in the long history of the Jewish people. Happily, past tragic relations have lately been reversed, notably by the enlightened policies of Catholic–Jewish reconciliation pioneered by Pope John XXIII, a momentous turning-point to which the late Cardinal Heenan gave such powerful momentum.

As Pope John Paul II, you have maintained and further promoted this inter-faith understanding. Yourself hailing from a country in which you witnessed and shared the supreme agony of the Nazi Holocaust, including the massacre of three million Polish Jews, your election aroused special interest among the Jewish people. Also of particular relevance to Jews are the as-yet unpredictable consequences of the religious stirring within the Communist world, sparked by the Catholic revival in Poland under your spell. These consequences may well eventually alleviate the bonds of more than three million Soviet Jews among the repressed religious communities in the USSR and her satellite countries.

As senior progenitors of the Judaeo–Christian heritage which nurtured Western civilisation, the Jewish people watched with profound gratification your immense efforts to reassert the moral and spiritual values we have in common against the disruptive inroads of violence, the blighting depression of materialism, and the despiritualised secularisation which threaten everything we have built up over the ages, and which may endanger human survival itself.

While enormous strides have been made in advancing Jewish–Christian harmony, some items on our common agenda remain to be resolved. They include the elimination of the last vestiges of religious prejudices against Jews, and some residual Christian hesitations in accepting the State of Israel as the fulfilment of millennial Jewish dreams. We seek understanding for our love of Jerusalem, a city holy to three faiths because Jews first sanctified it as their capital 3,000 years ago.

At this anxious time, when our country is sadly once again at war [in the South Atlantic], with grievous loss of life in defence of freedom and the rule of law, we pray with special fervour that your visit may contribute to the advancement of conciliation and peace. We also hope that it will prove a unique spiritual experience, bringing to all our citizens the gift of your inspiration and the blessing of rededication to the noblest ideas of human brotherhood.'

Echoes of these sentiments were heard a year later in the Chief Rabbi's address to the annual meeting of the Council of Christians and Jews in London:

ANTI-SEMITISM AND ANTI-ZIONISM

'For Jews the world over, this past year has been a traumatic experience. The fallout of the tragic war in Lebanon has gravely hit us all – in the United States, in Europe, behind the Iron Curtain, in all corners of the world. In its wake there has been a noticeable upsurge of anti-Semitism worldwide which, we thought, would have been brought to an end with the catastrophe of the Holocaust and with the creation of the State of Israel.

Let me record with immense appreciation and gratitude that the Jewish community in this country has been protected by the climate of tolerance and decency prevailing here. We ought to record our infinite gratitude to God Almighty that he has blessed us in this way largely through the existence of a body such as this Council [of Christians and Jews]. It constitutes an altogether unique concept of Jewish–Christian partnership and co-operation, functioning under such illustrious auspices as the patronage of the Queen herself. In the CCJ, we have an instrument not matched anywhere else, through which we enjoy a relative immunity from some of the worst excesses of anti-Semitism.

Some weeks ago, I participated in the International Hearing on Anti-Semitism in Oslo, convened by the Manson Committee in association with Elie

Wiesel, the head of the Holocaust Commission of the President of the United States. We heard experts, historians, journalists, religious leaders, leading statesmen and politicians give their assessment of the present state of anti-Semitism, its causes, its roots, and the methods with which to counter it.

When Elie Wiesel, that brilliant thinker and writer, said that after three days of intensive deliberations we had come to the conclusion that anti-Semitism is not a good thing, he added: it is not good for the perpetrator, it is not good for the victim, and it is not good for the bystanders, who may be neither perpetrators nor victims but allow it to happen by their silence.

The hearing agreed that there was a worldwide resurgence of one form or another of anti-Semitism. More importantly, it stressed that the factors responsible for this ominous revival of previous prejudice were substantially different from the causes of anti-Semitic excesses in the past. Accordingly, it came to the conclusion that our response to this threat must likewise be different from what it was in the past.

Foremost in this reassessment was the recognition that Israel is now central to Jewish life and Jewish aspirations. This fact must therefore be the key to attitudes towards Jews in general. You cannot divorce attitudes towards Israel (not the policies of Israel but the right of Israel to exist) from attitudes towards Jews.

In this morning's otherwise highly welcome and admirable *Times* leader on Jewish–Christian relations, this basic fact is glossed over. Israel is not even mentioned. This is like discussing road accidents without referring to cars. It may be debatable whether all anti-Zionism can be attributed to anti-Semitism, an assumption which I, for one, do not accept and will continue to challenge. But what is indisputable is that anti-Zionism fuels anti-Semitism. In other words, anti-Zionism is a cause of anti-Semitism even if anti-Semitism is not necessarily always a cause of anti-Zionism.

Enormous strides have been made in Jewish–Christian relations, pioneered largely by the enlightened policies of Pope John XXIII and the subsequent historic Guidelines on Relations with the Jews, of Vatican II. But this momentous improvement has always stopped short of coming fully to terms with the restoration of Jewish statehood. The Guidelines on Relations with the Jews therefore urgently requires some similar guidelines to revise relations with Israel and Zionism if the forward thrust of Jewish–Christian reconciliation is to be maintained. In fact, I presented this plea personally to the present Pope in Manchester when I was privileged to meet him on his momentous visit to this country.

No one asks for an unqualified endorsement of Israeli policies or actions. Even Jews, I need hardly tell you, have fiercely conflicting opinions on the wisdom, and sometimes the morality, of these policies. But by withholding formal recognition from Israel, as the Vatican still does, or by adopting a distinct bias against Zionism and Israel as such, as the World Council of Churches frequently reflects in its statements, all Jews are bound to feel adversely affected, as such unfriendliness – apart from its intrinsic injustice – cannot but provide grist to the mills of anti-Semitism.

We should not forget that anti-Semitism eventually challenges the moral health of society at large, threatening the security of Jews and non-Jews alike. History has warned us, at such frightful cost, not so long ago. Hitler began with the Jews. No one cared until he ended up plunging the world into history's most catastrophic war. That war could have been avoided if human fellowship had extended to Jews when they were still the sole victim of the tyrant's frenzy.

However, not only devastating hatred and unparalleled suffering began with Jews. The story of monotheism, of the brotherhood of man, the pursuit of social justice and the promise of universal redemption and salvation also began with Jews.

We can only look forward to the time when, through understanding of each other and working as partners in the service of God, we may speed the day when there will be the greatest of all elections – the election of man in the bond of conservative values combined with the labour of love, leading to an alliance between all humanity with our common Father.'

Jewish expectations of a rapprochement with Christianity had been exaggerated in some circles, including Jewish ones, and misunderstood in others, the Chief Rabbi declared in London some months later.

Delivering the fourth Lambeth Inter-Faith Lecture on 'Jewish understanding of inter-faith encounters', at Lambeth Palace – at which Dr Robert Runcie, the Archbishop of Canterbury, presided – Sir Immanuel told Jewish and Christian ministers and distinguished lay leaders that Jews did not seek, at least within the Orthodox community, theological dialogues in the sense of subjecting each faith to the critical scrutiny of the other. 'Jews do not aspire to joint religious services, or to inter-faith activities of a specifically religious nature, as an expression of mutual trust and respect', he added. There was 'much unfinished business on our common agenda, but modifications in our forms of worship and probes into each other's beliefs are not among the items'.

He recalled that he had spelled out traditional Judaism's reservations to inter-faith activities in a sermon in 1971 [see above]. At that time, he said: 'We regard our relationship with God, and the manner in which we define and collectively express it, as being so intimate and personal that we could no more convey it to outsiders than we would share with others our husband-wife relationship.'

The Chief Rabbi suggested that instead of items that touched on the distinctiveness and integrity of another faith, he would prefer to see a continuing examination and, if necessary, a revision of the pragmatic relationship between Judaism and Christianity; and a look at the common approaches to moral and social issues which challenged religious leadership and religious conscience in general. With regard to the first, the Chief Rabbi said that pride of place would go to the rising centrality of Israel in Jewish life, and its effects on Jewish–Christian relations.

He noted with regret that the emergence of Zionism and concern for Israel's security as the principal dynamics of Jewish life had been countered by the shift from anti-Semitism to anti-Zionism as expressions of anti-Jewish prejudice. Any changes in the Churches' attitude which failed to take account of this situation were both dated and incomplete. Opinions on Israeli Government policy were irrelevant, said the Chief Rabbi. What was needed was a reappraisal of religious attitudes divorced from all political overtones and considerations about the importance of Israel in contemporary

Jewish life, and a recognition of Israel's legitimacy as a sovereign State, and of its right to a peaceful and secure existence.

CRITICISM OF THE VATICAN

The Chief Rabbi has added his voice to other Jewish criticism of the latest Vatican document on Jewish–Christian relations. In a statement to *The Times* yesterday, Sir Immanuel Jakobovits called the document's reference to the Nazi Holocaust 'painfully casual'. He said it lacked an outright condemnation of anti-Semitism, or any expression of remorse. 'Even more disturbing is the continued denial to the Jewish State of both religious significance and of any formal recognition, an attitude now shared only by Arab, Communist and some other hostile states', he went on.

The document, issued this week in Rome, is in the form of guidance to preachers and teachers on 'the right approach to Catholic–Jewish relations'. It is in the name of the Pontifical Commission for Religious Relations with the Jews, and is largely a commentary on the Second Vatican Council's decree, *Nostra Aetate*, of 1965, in which the Catholic Church formally condemned the idea that the Jewish people may be held responsible for 'deicide' – the killing of Christ.

The International Jewish Committee on Inter-Religious Consultations had previously issued a statement from its New York office calling the document a retreat from more positive positions in earlier Vatican documents.

The Chief Rabbi said in his statement that Jews would welcome the emphasis the new document placed on the Jewish component in Christianity's origins and teachings, and said it was an undoubtedly genuine effort to advance Christian–Jewish understanding.

'The major defects in the document will cause all the more regret among British Jews in the light of the felicitous relations between Catholics and Jews in this country', he said. He praised the British newspaper, the *Catholic Herald*, for having pointed out the document's weaknesses.

The document, called *The Common Bond*, urges Catholics to deepen their knowledge of Judaism. The object was not merely to uproot the remains of anti-Semitism among Catholics but to bring them to 'appreciate and love' the Jews because of their unique bond with Christians.

The passage on which most Jewish objections have focused states: 'The existence of the State of Israel and its political options should be envisaged not in a perspective which is itself religious, but in their reference to the common principles of international law'.

The Chief Rabbi said Jews would 'find it difficult to fathom the meaning of this enigmatic statement … when in fact, throughout the ages, the vision of the Jewish return to Zion has been essentially religious.'

Clifford Longley, The Times, *29 June 1985*

Later that year, the Chief Rabbi found himself at the centre of inter-faith attention following an approach to him by the Archbishop of Canterbury. It related to the release of *Faith in the City: A Call for Action by Church and Nation*, a report prepared by the Archbishop's Commission on Urban Priority Areas (under the chairmanship of Sir Richard O'Brien) and published for the General Synod of the Church of England by Church House Publishing.

FAITH IN THE CITY

I have pleasure in enclosing a complimentary copy of *Faith in the City*. This is the Report of a Commission I appointed in 1983, with the following terms of reference:

'To examine the strengths, insights, problems and needs of the Church's life and mission in Urban Priority Areas and, as a result, to reflect on the challenge which God may be making to Church and Nation; and to make recommendations to appropriate bodies.'

I hope that this Report will be of interest to you and I shall appreciate any comment you may care to make when you have had the time to read it. I know that you share our deep concern for the quality of life in the inner-city areas.

Letter from the Archbishop to the Chief Rabbi, 27 November 1985

I was pleased to have received your letter of 27 November, together with a copy of the Report of your Commission, *Faith in the City*, which I shall read with much interest, and then write to you again with some of my impressions.

Needless to say, we are all deeply concerned with the need for the enhancement of the quality of life in the inner cities, and I commend your initiative which seeks to meet the ever-growing challenge.

The Chief Rabbi to the Archbishop, 3 December 1985

FAITH IN THE CITY: **THE COMMISSION'S CONCLUSIONS**

15.1 Chapter after chapter of our Report tells the same story: that a growing number of people are excluded by poverty or powerlessness from sharing in the common life of our nation. A substantial minority – perhaps as many as one person in every four or five across the nation, and a much higher proportion in the Urban Priority Areas – are forced to live on the margins of poverty or below the threshold of an acceptable standard of living.

15.2 The present acute situation of our nation's Urban Priority Areas demands an urgent response from the Church and from government.

15.3 The Archbishops' Commission on 'Church and State' concluded its report in 1970: 'The Church should concern itself first, and indeed second, with the poor and needy, whether in spirit or in body'.

15.4 We echo these words. The Church cannot supplant the market or the State. It can, as we recommend, mobilise its own resources in a way that accords high priority to the poor. It must by its example and its exertions proclaim the ethic of altruism against egotism, of community against self-seeking, and of charity against greed.

15.5 But we are conscious that we have only scratched the surface of some of the major concerns to have emerged from our work. To draw out the implications of some of these, such as the Church's response to the prospect of persistent long-term unemployment, will require more time and resources than have been available to us. There must also be a major national debate on the future of our cities, in which the Church must play a full part.

15.6 Perhaps the most important wider question concerns the structure of our society. One submission to us put it bluntly: 'The exclusion of the poor is pervasive and not accidental. It is organised and imposed by powerful institutions which represent the rest of us.' The critical issue to be faced is whether there is any serious political will to set in motion a process which will enable those who are at present in poverty and powerless to rejoin the life of the nation.

15.7 Here is a challenge indeed. It will call, among other things, for a clear resolve on the part of Church and government to have faith in the city.

From Faith in the City, *30 September 1985*

THE CHIEF RABBI'S RESPONSE

Black people should learn self-reliance and cultivate the work ethic to solve their problems in the inner cities, according to Britain's Chief Rabbi. Sir Immanuel Jakobovits says in a report published today that his community has much to teach Britain's blacks, as the Jews have first-hand experience of struggling from the 'ghetto' to a life of prosperity and security.

His report, *From Doom to Hope*, is a response to the controversial Church of England document on the inner cities, *Faith in the City*, which was openly critical of Mrs Thatcher's Government.

Rabbi Jakobovits criticised the document for showing, in places, 'a measure of patent political bias' and for failing to appreciate the importance of work and self-reliance. But he stresses the right of the Church to speak out on social issues and to criticise Government economic policy if necessary. He is openly critical of what he sees as a tendency in the black community to assume that the ethnic majority have a duty to support them and bend to their 'street culture' way of life. He criticises, too, the Welfare State mentality which rejects hard work for modest rewards.

At the same time, he acknowledges that blacks, because of their skin colour, can face prejudices in addition to those experienced by Jews. He calls for patience instead of the 'give it to me now' attitude; the development of strong family ties with strong moral principles; and, above all, a major effort to educate young blacks to a standard at least as high as the host community, a technique long and effectively used by Jews. He insists that blacks should, like Jews, enforce the strongest discipline in their own communities to stamp out crime, which can only alienate them from the host community.

Rabbi Jakobovits writes in his report: 'How did we break out of our ghettos and enter the mainstream of society and its privileges? Certainly not by riots and demonstrations. Above all, we worked on ourselves, not on others. We gave a better education to our children than anybody else had. We hallowed our home life. We channelled the ambition of our youngsters to academic excellence, not flashy cars. We rooted out crime and indolence from our midst, by making every Jew feel responsible for the fate of all Jews. We did not gate-crash into our Gentile environment; we made ourselves highly acceptable and indispensable by our industrial, intellectual and moral contributions to society.'

Rabbi Jakobovits concludes that the Jews could make no greater contribution to the inner-city problem than by helping to shift the emphasis 'from rights to duties' and 'from having a good time to making the times good'.

Daily Telegraph, *24 January 1986*

The Chief Rabbi's response provoked strong criticism within the Jewish community. The director of the Jewish Social Responsibility Council, Dr Edie Friedman, called it 'patronising' and 'not terribly helpful for black–Jewish relations', while the director of the Sternberg Centre for Judaism, Rabbi Tony Bayfield, feared it would prove 'offensive' to blacks. 'Nowhere does it discuss whether society discriminates against ethnic minorities. The question that should be asked is: "Do we live in a society that offers equality of opportunity to everybody who wants to help himself?" I don't think we do.'

Henry Morris, chairman of the Board of Deputies' defence committee, said: 'It is possible for those … who have criticised the Jewish community to distort this into a justification for the accusation that we are led by Right-wing, reactionary forces.'

In response to the criticism, the Chief Rabbi's Office pointed out that he had received a large postbag on his report and that all but two comments had been favourable.

Speaking after a meeting, at his request, with the Chief Rabbi, the Secretary of State for the Environment, Kenneth Baker, welcomed *From Doom to Hope* as 'a positive response to the challenges which all communities face'. He said: 'We discussed his emphasis on individual enterprise within the framework of support for the family and for law and order. There is a lot to be learned from the Jewish experience in creating in urban areas the conditions in which enterprise and ambition can flourish to the good of the community as a whole.'

A REPLY TO THE CRITICS OF *FROM DOOM TO HOPE*

The overall response to my *From Doom to Hope*, on the plight of Britain's inner cities, has been strangely inconsistent: predominantly critical in Jewish quarters, and overwhelmingly favourable in the general press and in the nation at large. I find the Jewish reaction rather baffling and quite disturbing. One wonders whether it derives from gross political bias among Jews, an undue sense of insecurity, or a wide Jewish divergence from public opinion at large.

The blacks were the only other community to voice some severe criticism, fanned partly by Jewish misinterpretations of the parallel I drew between our escape from Jewish ghettos in the past and the hope for inner-city dwellers to overcome their deprivation in the future. I can see nothing patronising or self-righteous in giving today's ethnic minorities the benefits of the Jewish experience as an assurance that they will eventually triumph over their travails. I am sure immigrant Jews suffering poverty and discrimination would have been only too grateful had there been some earlier immigrants providing advice and reassurance based on actual experience.

Looking over my transcript of an interview I gave on the BBC Radio London programme, 'Black Londoners', I find that even there the discussion ended on an amicable note. They must have sensed that my sole concern in any reference to ethnic minorities was to be of help. I wonder why my own members did not feel likewise.

I never charged blacks with being 'work-shy'. I believe the entire country needs a different work ethic to become prosperous, and thus to help solve the economic and social problems besetting the inner cities. I resorted to Jewish teaching to emphasise the difference between jobs and work. Granted we suffer from grievous mass unemployment. But that is no reason for keeping people idle, which is an even greater curse.

There may as yet be few jobs, but there is plenty of work – there certainly ought to be enough to keep every able-bodied citizen busy in welfare services, public works, perhaps even American peace-corps type of activities here and overseas, or at least in creative educational or leisure pursuits.

Many are impoverished not because the rich earn too much, but because the country as a whole produces too little, because all too many people – whether in management or in the work-force – prefer killing time to using it creatively. Here, religious teachings can crucially affect economic standards.

All this has nothing whatever to do with political partisanship. While the laudatory motion in Parliament by some 160 Conservative MPs came as a pleasant but complete surprise to me, my document was totally open to support from all parties alike. It was political only to those who made it so.

In individual attacks on my paper, I have seen few reasoned arguments, and none challenging my statements as representing authentic Jewish teachings. When speaking on moral issues, I am clearly expected to be a spokesman for Judaism, and not necessarily of the Jewish community, just as the Archbishop's Commission spoke for Christianity and not for the opinions of the parishioners. Consequently, such specific criticisms as were directed at me struck me as not only irrelevant, but often as entirely baseless. For instance, one called my intervention 'unsolicited', when in fact it was solicited and published in response to a request from the Archbishop himself. Another complained that I had 'carefully avoided' any biblical reference to 'justice'. If my critics would open their eyes wider they would discover that 'social justice' and 'righteous-ness' were my central biblical themes, supported by quotations in which the fate of cities 'was determined by righteousness in human relations'.

To sum up the object of my intervention and my charge on what Jews could contribute as Jews to ameliorate the hopelessness and squalor of the inner cities today: If I visit patients, it is not my function to tell the doctors how to diagnose symptoms of pain or what drugs to prescribe. Yet my pastoral services can be just as vital as the professional care given by doctors and nurses. First, I try to change the mood of the patient from despair to hope. This can be just as important for his health as the best medical treatment. I might achieve this by telling the patient that others in a similar condition have recovered through confidence and perseverance. Next, I can use my expertise in the moral sphere to influence attitudes – perhaps to make the doctor more caring, or the patient more receptive to accepting medical instructions, or decisions on the allocation of scarce resources more attuned to moral priorities. And I may want to advise the patient and his family on their relationship in the face of their travail.

Applying this to our inner-cities situation, the first task is to strengthen hope among those who presently feel despondent and abandoned. In this, the Jewish experience is unsurpassed and we ought to share it with those now afflicted with despair, whatever the very substantial differences between Jewish ghettos of the past and their modern urban counterparts. Revisions in attitudes to work and to the family can similarly provide a specifically Jewish dimension to the solution of our inner-cities' problems, quite apart from increased direct forms of financial and social help which I so strongly advocated.

Chief Rabbi Jakobovits, Jewish Chronicle, *14 March 1986*

LAMBETH DEGREE FOR CHIEF RABBI

There will be no risk of rabbinical ears being offended when Dr Robert Runcie, the Archbishop of Canterbury, confers a Lambeth degree on Sir Immanuel Jakobovits, the Chief Rabbi of Great Britain and the Commonwealth, sometime next month. Nor even rabbinical eyes.

The coveted degrees are normally bestowed in the chapel of Lambeth Palace, as five others will be on 17 June. But not so the doctorate of divinity going to Sir Immanuel, Chief Rabbi since 1967. The degree being awarded, says Lambeth Palace, is a tribute to his leadership of the Jewish community, and in recognition of his contribution to the development of co-operation and understanding between the Jewish and Christian communities. It will be conferred in a room other than the chapel and, it is understood, it is more than likely that all references to Christ in the accompanying ceremony will be discreetly omitted.

This is in deference both to Sir Immanuel and to Jewish law. As a spokesman at the Chief Rabbi's Office carefully put it: 'With the full understanding of the Archbishop, the Chief Rabbi is not able to attend inter-denominational services. Jewish law prevents that, so the Archbishop will hold a special service later on.'

According to a Lambeth Palace spokeswoman, 'to the best of our knowledge, this is the first time someone of another faith has received a Lambeth degree'.

Yorkshire Post, *15 May 1987*

[The degree was conferred on the Chief Rabbi at a ceremony at Lambeth Palace on 8 September 1987. The Archbishop of Canterbury, the Church of England Newspaper *reported, 'has had the authority to grant degrees ever since the passing of the Peter Pence Act in 1533, during the reign of Henry VIII. This formally gave the Archbishop many of the rights which he had previously enjoyed as the representative of the Pope. Degrees are granted in theology, law, arts, music, and medicine. Recipients wear the academic dress of the university of which the Archbishop is a member.']*

The Chief Rabbi warmly welcomed a resolution on inter-faith relations which 500 bishops from all over the world approved at the Lambeth Conference in August 1988. In a statement, he said that he hoped it would lead to 'a new era in Jewish–Christian relations, centred on what we have in common, as well as on respect for our differences'.

He expressed particular gratification at 'the acknowledgement of the Jewish roots of their faith, the appreciation that a distortion of Jewish teaching has often led to persecution in the past, acknowledgement of the centrality of Israel in contemporary Jewish life, the rejection of all forms of anti-Semitism, and the recognition that religious teaching provided the basis for traditional anti-Semitism culminating in the Holocaust'.

Lord Jakobovits described the 'qualified rejection' of evangelism directed at converting Jews as 'an advance', but said that the 'Jewish community would have welcomed an outright condemnation of all forms of missionary activity'.

The resolution, proposed by the Right Rev Richard Harries, Bishop of Oxford and adviser to the Archbishops of Canterbury and York on inter-faith relations, recommended delegates to 'initiate talks, wherever possible, on a tripartite basis with both Jews and Muslims'.

A background document to the resolution said that Christians today were being called into 'a fresh, more fruitful relationship with Judaism'. There was a common concern 'to be sensitive to Judaism, to reject all proselytising, that is, aggressive and manipulative attempts to convert, and, of course, any hint of anti-Semitism. General sharing', the document added, 'requires of Christians that they correct all distorted images of Judaism and Islam.'

Even the gospels, it conceded, 'have at times been used to malign and denigrate the Jewish people. Anti-Jewish prejudice promulgated by leaders of Church and State has led to persecution and pogrom and finally provided the soil in which the evil of Nazism was able to take root and spread its poison.'

REPRESENTING THE QUEEN AT AUSCHWITZ

In January 1995, Lord Jakobovits accepted an invitation to represent the Queen at the commemoration of the fiftieth anniversary of the liberation of Auschwitz, despite anger in some circles over Poland's failure to include the recital of Kaddish in the official ceremony. He said he was aware of the controversy but had decided to go 'because the Jewish presence should not be reduced any further'.

Visibly moved by his participation in the commemorative events at the former death camp, Lord Jakobovits later told the *Jewish Chronicle*: 'My overwhelming feeling, never having been to Auschwitz or Poland before, was that I could walk out of Auschwitz – walk out alive. Auschwitz was a gigantic black hole. It sucked in Jews from all over Europe. There was no exit.

'I was privileged to be able to walk out – I'm grateful to come out, and to carry on Jewish life. If Hitler is not to have a final victory, we must not just remember but rebuild. We must not simply grieve over past wounds. We must seek to be moral pioneers, spiritual pathfinders.'

The vast cemetery of Birkenau, the camp where most of the 1.6 million Auschwitz victims died, was the scene of two major ceremonies marking its liberation. Jewish participants held a separate ceremony outside the framework of the official events because they felt that the planned commemorations did not reflect the unique Jewish dimension of Auschwitz.

The official commemorations were attended by heads of state and other representatives of more than two dozen countries.

After the trauma of the two events, said Lord Jakobovits, Jewish spirits were buoyed by an extraordinary Shabbat of feasting, song, dancing and prayer, held at an hotel in nearby Cracow. Attended by visiting Jewish dignitaries, and by local Jews just beginning to rediscover their religious roots, the occasion – 'a commitment to carry on Jewish life' – contrasted sharply with that of the death-camp ceremonies. 'It was healthy to have Shabbat right after the commemorations', said Lord Jakobovits. 'It was a balm on our wounds and a comfort to our broken hearts.'

CHAPTER TWELVE

Communal Leadership

'Within our community, encouraging friendliness in our relations;
imagination and originality in our planning; and a constant search
for dedicated talent and high idealism in our communal work'

'The United Synagogue will have to set the pattern. It will have to be the pioneer. No one else will move unless we do. We are the strongest and have the greatest resources in men and material means.

We have to attract into our ranks, especially our leadership ranks, young new people. Hence I was so insistent on having representatives of the district synagogues at this meeting as well. The bulk of the young couples in our community, who have a personal concern in education for the sake of their own children, the great majority of men of enterprise, are to be found today in our suburbs. We have to bring into the top leadership of our community more and more of that excellent manpower to be found in our suburban communities, notably in the district synagogues.

There are also large numbers of young people, intensely committed and with a profound Jewish education, who are outside the United Synagogue altogether, and who have come to me and said: 'Create an opening for us, enable us to make an impact, and we will come forward.' You have to create these possibilities. When you have elections, give preference to men of learning and of commitment. Make sure that anyone ready to serve, who has new ideas, will have a place in the leadership of our community. Welcome such people, listen to them, and let them share our joint responsibilities.

In this connection, I wish to express my concern and make a suggestion about the smaller communities. This, of course, is a national problem. It is not just a problem around London, where you have small groups of people struggling hard to build up new congregations without the services of an experienced minister. This is a problem even of old communities scattered throughout the country that are left without leadership. I don't think that by making our existing ministers available for that kind of service, as has been suggested, you will get an effective answer. They have more than their hands full with leading their big congregations if they are to do all the work that is really expected of them.

What I am proposing instead, and have already begun discussing with several quarters involved in this, is to create teams of 'Torah Corps', as I would like to call them, young people who themselves have had a first-class Jewish education, who are very enthusiastic – they may be yeshivah products, they may be former Study Group leaders – who will be prepared as a public service to organise, on the 'Peace Corps' basis, expeditions into the smaller communities.

If they can't go for Shabbat, let them go on a rota once a week on weekdays, to get the people together, learn or debate with them, advise them, make them feel someone cares, by coming into their midst to stimulate interest in Jewish activity. I believe that we have today hundreds of young people able and ready to do this work, provided we organise them and have a modest little budget to allow for the travelling expenditure and some other expenses involved.

I would like to see the United Synagogue open a vibrant youth department, which would help in creating flourishing youth centres attached to every one of our larger congregations. If the United Synagogue would invest as much money, active interest and efficient personnel in such a youth department as it does in its burial society, then indeed we would make sure that we not only bury people according to Jewish law but cause them to live according to Jewish law.'

Chief Rabbi Jakobovits, 'Looking Ahead'
United Synagogue Council, 26 November 1967

With this call to his core constituents, the new Chief Rabbi launched his campaign for radical improvements on four fronts: leadership, youth, small communities and fund-raising. They were joined by an uninvited fifth – women's rights – some years later. Each of the four was a key element of his vision, spelled out in his installation sermon, of 'a happy, forward-looking community … a mighty fortress of our spiritual treasures'.

TOMORROW'S LEADERS

At the forefront of these efforts were attempts to combat the dearth of potential leaders, upon which the success of all other communal campaigns depended. The Chief Rabbi used the platform of his United Synagogue centenary address, on 19 July 1970, to concentrate on the issue, in characteristically outspoken terms:

'Let me here utter this warning with every emphasis before this distinguished gathering: if the United Synagogue will ever decline and fall, financial insolvency will not be the cause. We may be certain, as our sages tell us, that 'a community never goes materially bankrupt'. If we make the priceless values and services we have to offer sufficiently appealing, people will gladly pay for them, just as they generously pay for other causes they really cherish.

The United Synagogue will collapse only if we suffer bankruptcy in our religious and human resources, if we cannot generate enough excitement and commitment to fascinate and involve the rising generation as the active members of the future, and if we fail to attract our finest sons – and daughters

– to breathe fresh air and vitality into the leadership of our religious community. We have nothing to fear except stagnation.

We are caught between two grinding millstones threatening to pulverise us. The upper millstone will squeeze out of our ranks the finest of our synagogue family, the young religious intellectuals, the idealistic youth who will be drawn to the better day-schools, the yeshivot and girls' seminaries, gravitating from there either to Israel or to congregations more fervent than ours. And the bottom millstone will be littered with the chaff of the indifferent, the dropouts of our classes and congregations who, in their disenchantment with us, will sever their last bonds with traditional Judaism.

For let us be under no illusion: the United Synagogue as it is today, our organisation, our education, our services, our leadership and our whole philosophy, simply does not attract either element. It will reclaim neither the creative grain nor the wind-tossed chaff, and we will be left with the thinning ranks of the old faithfuls who are too stagnant to break with the past or rally to the future.

At the root of all these perplexities, we face an ominous crisis in leadership, a dearth of competent people to augment and succeed our present spiritual and lay leaders. How are we to meet these gigantic challenges?

What is urgently needed, in the first place, is to loosen the rigidity of our system. Our trouble is that we have today little room for people with fresh ideas, and none for rebels. On the whole, we welcome neither new questions nor new answers, in an age teeming with questions and crying out for answers.

Our leadership must be flexible enough to encourage men of high ideals, broad vision and strong will to come forward, by convincing them that they will have a chance to assert their thinking, unconventional as it may be, in the conduct of our affairs. Our congregations, too, will require more autonomy, greater rights to use the fruits of their extra exertions for their own expansion, if we are to provide incentives for local initiative, rewards for harder efforts, and opportunities for more dynamic leaders and members. The prescription for a modern vibrant community is mass participation, some decentralisation and healthy diversity, apart from an imaginative programme of constant improvement and growth.'

Addressing a conference of young British and American fund-raisers on the lack of potential communal leaders, the Chief Rabbi later described Anglo-Jewry's attachments to tradition as 'a great impediment'. The community, he said, was 'most unenterprising, backward-looking, taking pride in past achievements rather than enjoying challenges, innovations and experimentation, which are characteristic of American Jewry. With any of my new schemes, if these represent a departure from the past, my colleagues are inclined to notice their negative aspects first.'

If present trends continued, said Dr Jakobovits, Anglo-Jewry would be reduced in numbers to about 300,000, from 450,000, by the turn of the century. That smaller community, however, would be more intensively Jewish than the present one. 'It has been a feature of Jewish history that only a minority survived the challenges, but that it was always able to create the grounds for a revival.'

Frustrated by a lack of progress in the provision of leadership material, the Chief Rabbi returned to the subject at the Conference of Jewish Representative Councils, in Sheffield, in June 1974:

'There are [he said] only two possible reasons to account for the decline in leadership: either we no longer attract our finest talents to positions of leadership – they exist but we do not recruit them – or we do not train them adequately to develop their full potential to become the kind of leaders they could be. I am inclined to believe that both these causes are valid and are responsible for the present situation.

The burdens of leadership today in a difficult world and the number of problems facing us are simply too heavy, the rewards offered to those accepting positions of leadership are too few, and the penalties paid for taking on the responsibilities of leadership are too great. Even if we discount a reward in terms of material benefits, the honour and respect formerly enjoyed served as a kind of compensation. These have now often been replaced by denigration and scorn, especially in the mass media – a feature never quite so pronounced as it is today and bound to serve as a deterrent to people of talent taking up positions of leadership.

Other occupations and professions have become more competitive and therefore claim talent hitherto available for leadership purposes. There are, after all, fewer headaches and more comforts to be had in many businesses and professions than for those assuming the mantle of leadership. If, therefore, the field of public or communal service has been left wide open, then the gap has obviously to be filled somehow – not infrequently by less competent people than those who were prepared to offer their services in the past.

Deficiencies in training are, at least in part, caused by the acute shortages we are suffering, so that the problem has become a vicious circle. Candidates for high office move into ranking positions without first completing their full professional preparations or adequate apprenticeship. As a result, we get them taking up top positions long before they have really equipped themselves to assume them.

This, I believe, applies equally to our lay leadership, which today may require some formal training in situations where we increasingly have to transfer executive responsibilities to community workers. With the growing complexity in the conduct of community business and affairs, we can no longer manage with people entirely untrained in the skills of organisation, social service, administration and policy direction.

The time has come, therefore, seriously to consider – as has been done in the larger communities in the United States – setting up academic and practical programmes, in both general and Jewish studies, and in the field of social work, for those seeking to become executive directors of our community organisations. Even honorary officers should take some courses in Jewish affairs, community relations, Jewish social ethics, and the like.

Notwithstanding the significant advances in both the ministry and lay leadership, we are certainly facing a growing crisis in terms of recruitment.

We would be living in a fools' paradise if we did not recognise that prospects for the future are increasingly uncertain. Demand – as far as one can tell – will eventually far outpace supply ...

Somehow, we have failed to enlist the best available, people who are highly dedicated, who may often have had great business experience and achieved considerable success in their own fields, and who are now ready to give of their time, their wisdom, their experience and their resources for Jewish causes.

I believe there are a number of reasons for this. The whole system of our Establishment is too rigid for people with new ideas, with enterprising and imaginative minds. They feel that once you join a shul board or a communal council, all you have to do is be a 'yes man', subscribing to old-fashioned constitutions drawn up in the nineteenth century. They are powerless to give new direction and a new dimension to community enterprise.

Our young people today live in an impatient age. They are not prepared to wait until late middle age to reach the top. In our synagogue community, you move up in very slow steps. This whole process of attaining decision-making powers in community government must be cut short. We have somehow to find an opening for young people to get in and get close to the top, to exercise influence in the making of decisions, very much more quickly.

Sadly, we have alienated from community leadership what ought to be our most valuable element – our intellectuals. These are the best talents we command. Today, at virtually every level of the community – from the Board of Deputies and the United Synagogue to individual congregations – we have hardly any academics or intellectuals. This is a unique Jewish experience: it used to be the reverse.

People who were uncultured, who had no education, were left behind; those with academic training and the experience that goes with it were the first to come forward and offer their services. Today, they are the most disenchanted, the most distant from the community. Somehow they feel they cannot fit in well into the tight regime that we exercise in our communal council chambers.

We must find a way to reach out to this tremendous talent. There are many hundreds of them – wonderful personalities, potentially dedicated people, who would give splendid service to the community if only we could make them feel that there is room for them within our communal set-up.

In these tempestuous times, under the most anxious and agonising conditions of Jewish life that beset us, the need for bold, forward-looking and competent Jewish leadership is more acute than ever before. On the quality, the vision, the determination and the loyalty of our leaders will largely depend the state of Jewish life in ten years, in 50 years, from now – indeed, for generations to come.'

Despite the earnestness of this plea, nearly 15 years were to pass before any significant strides were made in the provision of leadership training. In November 1988, Anglo-Jewry's first lay-leadership programme, known as Atid (the Hebrew for 'future'), was launched in London, against the backdrop of a renewed warning from the Chief Rabbi that 'the community is not sufficiently aware of the urgent need to ensure that those in charge of guiding its destinies should have certain qualifications, even if they are lay leaders and not professionals'.

Thirty-two people, aged from 25 to 45, met for the first class in the year-long course, involving over 30 lectures, as well as group sessions, a residential seminar, and an Israel trip. The programme broke new ground in being the joint work of a local welfare organisation, the Central Council for Jewish Social Service, and an organisation raising money for Israel, the Joint Israel Appeal. Half the funding for Atid came from the Doron Foundation in Israel.

The programme featured Israel-Diaspora relations, the structure of communal organisation – including campaigning, public speaking and management training techniques – the Holocaust, Zionism, modern Jewish leaders, and the development of Anglo-Jewry. It was conducted not only by distinguished Jewish and non-Jewish academics, but also by communal personalities, among them the joint president of the JIA and the executive director of the Jewish Welfare Board.

YOUTH SERVICES

The campaign to enhance facilities for youth gained ground much more speedily, as the Chief Rabbi noted in 'Moving Ahead: A Review and a Preview', published by his office in September 1968:

'More gratifying are several results already achieved in the field of youth services. After protracted inter-communal discussions, a joint board for the appointment of full-time university chaplains has now at last been set up under my chairmanship, comprising representatives of three religiously unlabelled organisations – Hillel-B'nai B'rith, the Jewish Memorial Council, and the Inter-University Jewish Federation – together with individual nominees to ensure that specialised talents, as well as all segments of the community, are adequately represented on this board.

Efforts are currently being made to proceed with appointments at Oxford and Cambridge, out of the fair number of promising candidates who have applied for these posts. The chaplains, who need not necessarily be ministers but who must adhere to traditional Judaism in thought and practice, are to serve all Jewish students on the campus.

Another pioneering venture is the establishment of the Torah Corps, an organisation of youth volunteers in community service. This very hopeful enterprise, so far limited to a few pilot projects, is designed to fill important communal gaps by harnessing the immense resources and potential of youth leadership hitherto entirely untapped.

The Torah Corps is to train and utilise these resources for religiously servicing new and small communities, to introduce effective Jewish programmes in youth clubs, to conduct house-to-house canvassing for the enrolment of children in schools and Hebrew classes, and to promote Jewish living and identification by other activities of a similar nature. At the same time, it will foster interest and experience in public Jewish service among our religiously committed youth.

Aiming at related objectives, I am hopeful that more and more openings will be found for young people to participate in the government of our community, and that all boards and committees of the community, its congregations and organisations, will soon fulfil my request to reserve at least 20 per cent of their membership for men and women under 30 years of age. In this way, Anglo-Jewry will be rejuvenated; obsolete and hide-bound policies will give way to new thinking; and the enthusiasm and energy of our youth will be channelled to build a new community and not to rebel against it.'

SMALL COMMUNITIES

Allied to progress in the provision of youth facilities was greater co-ordination of services among Jewish communities in the outlying areas. In October 1969, the Chief Rabbi convened a conference of smaller communities, attended by some 120 delegates from 48 communities, and representatives from 23 central organisations.

In his opening address, he commended the communities on maintaining their Jewish identity under difficult circumstances, often remote from the mainstream of Jewish life. He expressed the hope that the conference would focus the attention of the wider community on the problems confronting the smaller communities and would help in servicing them more effectively from central sources. These communities should, in turn, be encouraged to use self-help and take a responsible part in carrying the burdens and making the necessary decisions regarding their activities. All communities, however small, could make historic contributions to the overall destiny of Jewry.

After the morning session – on congregational activities – the Chief Rabbi presided over a session devoted to education. He referred to the importance of parents encouraging their children to enter the rabbinical and teaching professions, in order to produce the leaders and teachers for which so many communities – great as well as small – were crying out with increasing despair.

Dr Jakobovits stressed the urgent needs of Jewish education and suggested that even if local classes were not available, remedies could be found in several other ways, such as parents instructing their children, sending them to summer camps in order to absorb a traditional Jewish atmosphere, or to Israel for at least a year after leaving school.

At its final session, the conference adopted a resolution recommending the establishment of a working party, consisting of six representatives of the smaller communities and four members nominated by the Chief Rabbi, to consider setting up a permanent Council of Smaller Communities. With its own honorary officers and an independent budget, it would work with the national agencies in London in providing religious, educational, youth and social services to the smaller communities.

Encouraged by the response to his proposals, the Chief Rabbi later drew up a programme of co-operation with the long-established Provincial Councils Conference, subsequently debated and adopted at its 1973 conference. He pointed out that 'any plans for strengthening Jewish life in the provinces, and enhancing their contribution to Anglo-Jewish vitality in general, must include efforts to consolidate Jewish life in the main centres and to extend a helping hand to the smaller and declining communities'. His four-point programme called for:

1. **Consolidation within the larger centres.** The Chief Rabbi pointed to a 'novel enterprise' in Newcastle, which, with the assistance of the United Synagogue in London, had

pioneered an association of congregations aimed at rationalising resources and effecting economies. Similar schemes, he suggested, should be attempted in Manchester, Liverpool, Glasgow, Birmingham and other centres. 'What we have, we should consolidate, and we should eliminate losses suffered by undue fragmentation and duplication.'

2. **Systems of regionalisation.** Following the establishment of a regional Beth Din of the North, based in Manchester and embracing Leeds and Liverpool, the Chief Rabbi proposed a similar Beth Din for the North-East, taking in the communities of Newcastle, Sunderland and the surrounding areas. He also suggested setting up regional rabbinates, with 'supreme rabbinical authorities' making local decisions and involving themselves in routine affairs on a day-to-day basis, without having to rely on advice and guidance from 'a remote office in London' for the solution of local and regional problems.

3. **Twinning of large congregations and small communities**. Each major congregation, said the Chief Rabbi, should adopt a small, declining community, within a 50- or 70-mile radius, and invite as its guests children for Shabbatonim and other joint activities. The larger communities should also allocate speakers, preachers and teachers at regular intervals; and the minister of each major community – once every three months, together with his family – should spend a Shabbat in 'an outlying, lost and scattered little community that faces extinction if we do not inject into it from time to time a new booster of Jewish life'.

4. **Better use of metropolitan facilities for the training of communal personnel.** The Chief Rabbi reported that his office was negotiating with the Newcastle, Leeds and Liverpool communities to ensure that they engaged in 'a common effort to expand and intensify Jewish education by joint planning, mutual aid and the judicious deployment of their limited resources'. He urged other communities and congregations to follow their example.

COMMUNAL FUND-RAISING

Hand-in-hand with the 'judicious deployment of limited resources', in the Chief Rabbi's view, was the crucial need to consolidate communal fund-raising and, based on his experience in the United States, to establish a community chest. For some time, he had been pressing communal leaders to consider a plan to combine fund-raising for Israel and local welfare institutions. He advanced this proposal in 1974 at an exploratory meeting chaired by him and attended by representatives of the Joint Israel Appeal and of the Central Council for Jewish Social Service, which included the Jewish Welfare Board, the Jewish Blind Society, the Norwood Homes for Jewish Children, and other major Jewish welfare organisations.

The plan was subsequently submitted to leaders of the Joint Israel Appeal by its chairman, Michael Sacher, but was rejected for several reasons. These included a belief that more campaigns could raise a larger amount of money, and that campaigns for particular goals should involve different people. The JIA leaders were unable to see how fund-raising for Israel and for local charities could be combined in a practical way. They were determined, however, to encourage their key-workers to participate in fund-raising efforts for local organisations outside the periods allocated to the JIA's annual campaign.

The Chief Rabbi told the meeting that his initiative was based on a deep concern for the serious financial needs of both Israeli and Anglo-Jewish institutions. Although collaboration between the JIA and the welfare organisations appeared out of the question, he was still negotiating for a JIA contribution to local educational institutions. JIA leaders confirmed that they were considering this request – which they later implemented – particularly in view of public statements by Pinhas Sapir, the Jewish Agency's chairman, emphasising the importance of Jewish education in the Diaspora as a way to ensure continued support for Israel.

In the face of sustained opposition from the Israel-based charities to the initiation of a community chest, the Chief Rabbi again pressed home his point at a 1983 meeting of Norwood. 'Money raised for charity by the Jewish community', he declared, 'should be redistributed to cover Israeli and domestic causes. We must learn to cut the communal cake and reallocate the enormous sums raised by the community to take into account the needs of Israel and our own charities. You need the capacity to adjust, the capacity to take account of changes, to be flexible. The organisations that are flexible survive; those that are rigid and ruled by the past will not.'

Ultimately, his campaign succeeded, but not before a lapse of several more years. In 1989, Anglo-Jewish leaders took the first tentative steps towards revolutionising communal funding, at a meeting convened by Jewish Care president Lord Young. His 'community chest' initiative, forcefully backed by the Chief Rabbi, was an attempt to encourage communal charities to collaborate in a united appeal, instead of competing for funds.

The immediate spur to Lord Young's campaign were changing patterns in British Jewry's population, with a growing number of elderly people and a shrinking number of people capable of providing finance. He said that money and energy were being wasted in the chase for funds. A community chest would bring Anglo-Jewry into line with other countries, such as the United States, South Africa and Australia.

Lord Young told the meeting, attended by leaders of 26 educational and welfare organisations, that the JIA and other bodies raising funds for Israel were unlikely to join the venture until the home charities had proved their ability to co-operate. A working party under his chairmanship was set up to pursue the project.

The meeting – attended by, among others, Lord Jakobovits and Board of Deputies president Dr Lionel Kopelowitz – led eventually to the establishment of the United Jewish Israel Appeal (UJIA), an amalgam of educational and Israel charities in Britain. Its declared mission was 'to secure the future of the Jewish people by mobilising the British Jewish community's support for the rescue of Jews in need throughout the world, and their absorption into Israel, and by the renewal of Jewish life in Britain, and of our partnership with Israel'.

WOMEN'S RIGHTS

The women of the United Synagogue waited until the mid-1970s before launching their battle for greater rights and for a more commanding role in communal affairs. Their champion was none other than Amélie Jakobovits, president of the Association of United Synagogue Ladies' Guilds. Addressing the association's first biennial meeting, in response to a resolution seeking the inclusion of women on synagogue boards of management, she declared: 'I feel strongly that women should have a strong liaison with men in running synagogues, particularly in anything to do with education.'

As for representation on the United Synagogue council, she said: 'I do not think we need to be there physically at the moment, but I do think we should be represented on the Kashrus Commission and the Shechitah Board.'

Some months later, the Chief Rabbi appeared to give an unqualified 'Yes' to the idea of women sitting on synagogue councils and boards of management, following a call to this effect from Lady Janner at a session of the Provincial Councils Conference in Leeds. He said he would be 'only too happy' to sponsor a working session on the subject of women's representation on such bodies.

Responding under pressure to calls for positive action on the issue, Dr Jakobovits issued a further statement asserting that 'the religious community and its organisations can only benefit from the increased participation of our womenfolk in their deliberations and activities. At present, neither at local nor at communal level are sufficient opportunities afforded for women to make their full contribution, thus recognising the role of our womenfolk within the organised structure of our community and its effort to give a more dynamic response to current challenges.

'It is important for the very flourishing women's organisations already active and playing a notable part in the wider community to be more closely linked with our synagogal life. However, the halachic ruling on women's participation states that women members may not be elected as honorary officers or appointed as officiants; and that they have the active, but not the passive, elective right – that is, they may elect to office but may not themselves be elected. They may be appointed or nominated to synagogue boards and councils (either by women of the congregation or by the local ladies' guild or other local women's organisations) and they may exercise full membership rights.'

Some weeks later, a demand that women be allowed to serve on the boards of management and councils of Orthodox synagogues was carried, by an overwhelming majority, at the annual meeting of the League of Jewish Women. With only four opposing votes among more than 200 women present, the meeting approved a resolution that 'urges the United Synagogue and other Orthodox synagogal bodies to allow those women who are full members in their own right and wish to play a fuller part in the life of the synagogue to serve on boards of management and councils.'

In the course of a lengthy debate, Mrs Jakobovits emphasised that acceptance was 'largely a matter of individual relationship between male and female members of congregations'. In many congregations outside the United Synagogue – in Leeds, for example – women could become members of boards of management. She urged the League to be patient and 'sit through this fight until you succeed.'

In the event, nothing more was heard for two years, but when he did speak again on the subject, the Chief Rabbi was to dash the campaigners' hopes, with a declaration that 'women cannot be elected to serve on boards of management of synagogues under the aegis of the United Synagogue, nor on the council of the US'. The president of the United Synagogue, Salmond Levin, told a meeting of its council that he had received a letter from the Chief Rabbi forbidding the amendment of a clause (41b) in the Scheme of the Charity Commissioners for the US which laid down the organisation's working constitution.

The Chief Rabbi's letter stated: 'I reaffirm that, in accordance with the ruling given by my predecessor [Chief Rabbi Dr Israel Brodie] on 9 January 1951, Clause 41b cannot be amended.' The clause noted that 'a female member shall not be eligible for election or hold office as an honorary officer of the US or serve as a member of the council or of the executive committee of the US, or of the finance committee, or as an honorary officer of any synagogue of the US, or serve on the board of management of such synagogue'.

Seeking to clarify the position, the Chief Rabbi's Office issued the following statement in December 1977:

> The Chief Rabbi has frequently urged that women should be encouraged and enabled to participate more fully in the life and activities of our congregations. To this end, he discussed a proposal which would enable women to serve on synagogue boards of management (as they presently do in many congregations), subject to halachic requirements being met. These requirements exclude the participation of women in anything directly affecting the conduct of the religious services and impose certain provisos on their election or co-option.
>
> An alternative proposal was put forward [designated by the United Synagogue council as Clause 41c], namely to transfer the general functions of a community in the spheres of education, youth, cultural and other activities from boards of management to new synagogue councils. On these synagogue councils, both male and female members would be eligible to serve.
>
> Regarding this proposal, the Chief Rabbi wrote: 'I would not regard the election of women to the proposed new councils of synagogues as infringing the halachah. Accordingly, while I myself feel that, in the relationship between the proposed new council and the board of management, their respective jurisdictions and control over finances are not yet defined with sufficient clarity, I have no objection to the proposal on religious grounds.'
>
> As the functions of the boards of management would thus be limited to deal with matters affecting synagogue services, the Chief Rabbi reaffirmed the ruling of his predecessor, Sir Israel Brodie, on the ineligibility of women to be elected to boards of management. But he did this only on the understanding that the decision to set up the new councils would be passed. He certainly hopes that 'this far-reaching innovation, when ratified and effectively operated, will go a long way towards the intensification of our communal life and the enlistment of our finest human resources to strengthen and enrich the United Synagogue and its constituents'.
>
> In these terms, the Chief Rabbi has endorsed the new proposals, which have also been welcomed by the Association of United Synagogue Ladies' Guilds.

Clause 41c, however, never saw the light of day. It was rejected by the United Synagogue council on the grounds that such lower councils 'would prejudice the present functions of boards of management, which, in any case, are free to set up committees covering the subjects with which the proposed councils would deal'.

Little more was heard on the issue until 1986, when the Chief Rabbi and Beth Din were warned by United Synagogue president Victor Lucas that 'the search for a formula to enable women to play a more active role in Orthodox Judaism cannot be postponed indefinitely'. Mr Lucas assured the Association of United Synagogue Ladies' Guilds that 'a route must be found within the halachah for what will undoubtedly prove, when resolved, a boon to the traditional community'.

Lady Jakobovits, president of the association, told her members that while she had never been treated with anything but equality, 'I know that, as long as we as an association continue to press for what we want, then a formula will be found – perhaps even within the next few weeks or months – which will satisfy everyone.'

In response to Mr Lucas' call, the Chief Rabbi issued the following statement:

'Realising the urgent need to strengthen the fabric of our communal life and leadership by harnessing the enormous talents and energies of our women, I share together with the Beth Din the concern to promote their active involvement in all areas of religious, educational, cultural and social activities, compatible with halachic requirements.

These requirements exclude only eligibility to serve as honorary officers (which is neither sought nor constitutionally admissible) and a formal role in decision-making as congregational representatives. To this end, several options are open:

1. To restrict their membership of synagogue-sponsored governing bodies to consultative or observer status.
2. To set up councils of management in each individual congregation to discuss all relevant matters and to decide, by vote if necessary, on recommendations to be put to boards of management.
3. To devise technical safeguards which will ensure their full participation short of vesting formal decision-making in women representatives, in whatever way they are elected or appointed. This can be made operative by limiting the proportion of female members on any board or committee to a specific number or percentage, and then on insisting on separate male and female block votes (in the rare cases when decisions require formal votes), with the result that women will have a full and equal say in the conduct of communal affairs, without any disenfranchisement, and yet leave formal decision-making to a male majority. This method will also enable specific interests of and by women to be ascertained and pursued collectively.

In all communal matters requiring endorsement or decision by the general membership, women have equal voting rights.'

Ann Harris, chairman of the Association of United Synagogue Ladies' Guilds, described this statement as 'disappointing and tortuous'. The women's campaign, she said, 'is by no means a bid for a takeover, or even equality, since no religious rights were requested, just parity in non-religious decision-making. I ask the following question to US council members: "Are you happy that your own synagogues work so well that you can afford to disenfranchise half the work force?"'

The Chief Rabbi responded with a further clarification:

Some reactions to my recent statement on the place of women in the Jewish community have grossly distorted what I stated, in tone as well as in substance. Thus, I am reported to have 'formally rejected a plea by women for a more active role in running the United Synagogue'. The exact opposite is true. My statement was specifically calculated to promote 'their active involvement in all areas of religious, educational, cultural and social activities, compatible with halachic requirements'. This is what the women (and many others) demanded and this is what they have now obtained.

It is no good asking for halachic guidance and then, when it is received, arguing: 'Yes, but we cannot accept it, unless we know the sources,' or 'We need a

41. Presentation of a painting to join portraits of other college presidents displayed on the walls of Jews' College in North-West London.

42. With Rabbi Alan Plancey at the consecration of a Sefer Torah at the Borehamwood and Elstree Synagogue.

43. With Prime Minister Margaret Thatcher, the local MP, at the induction of Rabbi Geoffrey Hyman (left) as minister of the Woodside Park Synagogue, 1986.

44. With United Synagogue honorary officers at the induction of Rabbi Ivan Binstock (second from right) as minister of the Golders Green Synagogue.

45. Open day with toddlers around the Shabbat table at Cockfosters and North Southgate's Yavneh nursery.

46. With the Mayor of Barnet at the Harry and Abe Sherman Rosh Pinah Jewish Primary School in Edgware.

47. Left to right: Stanley Kalms, Henry Knobil, Lord Jakobovits and Gerald Ronson at the official opening of Immanuel College – the Charles Kalms, Henry Ronson Immanuel College – on 2 June 1991.

48. The Chief Rabbi explaining the Ark at London's Jewish Museum to a group of Manchester schoolchildren.

49. A discussion on Succot traditions with pupils and staff at the JFS Comprehensive School in London.

50. In conversation with Chief Rabbi Moses Rosen of Romania at a 1982 education conference in London.

This Rosh Hashanah....
Safeguard the future
of Jewish education

51. With United Synagogue honorary officers at the launch of the Year of Jewish Education in 1987.

52. Lighting the menorah on the fifth night of Chanukah for MPs and peers in the crypt of the House of Commons.

change in traditional attitudes to the halachah.' If the halachah is to be our guide, then we need to change *our* attitudes to conform to it.

As has been made clear, it is perfectly compatible with the halachah for women to 'have an *influence* on decision-making' (as demanded by the Association of United Synagogue Ladies' Guilds), and the manner in which this can operate has now been spelt out in some detail. This advance should be acknowledged as well as encouraged, and any attempt to belittle or negate its significance can only prove counter-productive, increasing resistance, scepticism and resentment.

If what the women want is full participation, they can and will have everything. If what they want is equal rights in a spurious quest for 'women's liberty', they will have nothing. This distinction is all-important. The contribution of our women to enriching and intensifying our communal life can be invaluable. The anaemia so widespread in our community badly needs the injection of their energy and their vision.

Most of our women's organisations are far more active and enterprising than their male counterparts, and it is their extra dimension of practical sense, enthusiasm and dedication which could make an enormous difference to the vitality of all our communal enterprises. But their role must be played as women, and not as worshippers of a popular fad.

The opportunities for participation which already exist, and as now further extended, are practically limitless. Any woman who wants to assert her influence in the community is free to do so, without let or hindrance. One has only to look at the names of honorary officers listed on the association's note-paper to be convinced that women acting strictly within the parameters of the halachah are not exactly denied their rightful place in making themselves and their influence felt in the community's affairs.

What the halachah requires even more urgently than circumscribing the role of women on boards and committees is to insist on retaining the uniqueness of the services rendered to Judaism and the Jewish people by men and women, respectively. If by opening up our institutional leadership ranks to women we would lose or weaken their primary commitment to securing stable marriages, building happy homes and raising intensely Jewish children, the sacrifice of further eroding the strength of Jewish family life would not be worth the gain in improving the management of communal affairs.

No one in this day and age argues that the woman's place should be exclusively in the home (any more than the rabbi's is in the pulpit). But we must be realistic and keep our perspectives right. If we are alarmed about increasing intermarriage and dropout rates, about shrinking numbers and growing alienation among our youth, the root cause lies not merely in the manner we run our institutions. We can hardly ignore the decline of the Jewish home, the catastrophic divorce rates, and the host of Jewish children raised in a spiritual no man's land, deprived of the warmth and inspiration which only a truly Jewish mother can provide.

Therefore, if women will now have more opportunities to influence our policies, their own priority should be to press for greater urgency in properly preparing young Jews for marriage and in consolidating Jewish homes so that our heritage will be passed on to future generations. Once the primacy of the Jewish home and education is safeguarded, by all means should we mobilise for community service the enormous resources of our women, now enjoying far more spare time from domestic drudgery than in the past and therefore more easily able to cope with a dual role inside and outside the home.

But let there be no illusion: the real impediment to women's participation lies not so much in constitutional or halachic constraints as in the sparsity of women prepared to come forward and offer their services. The recruitment of capable men, as well as women, as competent community workers will be a far more critical factor in determining the quality of community service and leadership than any structural revisions. I hope our policy-makers and the thousands of congregations they represent will not lose sight of these supreme priorities and realities.

The halachic sources governing my recent statement are, of course, readily available and easily accessible. I am quite willing to give a properly documented lecture on the subject. But it is neither practical nor traditional to annotate statements or directives of this nature with references to sources or proof-texts. To seek instruction is one thing, and perfectly commendable; but to demand corroboration is another, and quite inadmissible if meant to validate a rabbinic pronouncement.

CHAPTER THIRTEEN

Spiritual Defences

'Enhancing the status of the Anglo-Jewish ministry'

'Today, by and large, ministers are a frustrated and often even aggrieved group of people, as proved by the fact that we have virtually no recruitment of first-class men coming forward to enter into the ministry. Just ask yourselves how many of you would wish your sons to take up the ministry. How many of you as Jewish parents would see it as the fulfilment of your greatest ambition if your sons came and told you they wanted to become spiritual leaders of our people? I would not like to take a show of hands to prove my point.

Until we reach a situation in which that will be your ambition and you feel that the ministry is 'good enough for a Jewish boy', until you will be convinced that they will derive as much satisfaction, gratification and material reward out of dedicating themselves to the highest service to our people – until then the ministry will not be able effectively to perform its tasks, nor will it attract adequate recruits to man our spiritual defences.

We have within our ministry, certainly within the United Synagogue's ministry, some excellent material. There are some wonderful men who potentially possess all the energy and the vision, and all the initiative, we expect of them. But we crush this initiative before we give it a chance to unfold. Naturally, if these men are being subjected to a barrage of instructions from the Chief Rabbi, and another barrage of instructions from the United Synagogue head office, or from their own honorary officers, what kind of leadership can be expected of them?

Many of these men have been frustrated, have given up the struggle, long before they come to grips with their real task in earnest; and, if I may say so, some of them may have prematurely gone to seed for lack of opportunities to unfold their potential.

Let the successful minister who establishes a school, or creates a youth club, or lectures in a university, or in any other shape or form does more than his routine duties, let that man feel that there is a reward for this extra action, as a bonus, or whatever you like to call it, which will reflect this success or its effort. And those who are sluggish, uninterested, who do not constantly go out to work day and night to promote the welfare of the community, to sow the seeds of education, and to win the interest of their members, will know that they will remain at a standstill in regard to their material rewards.

I often feel that our ministers enjoy what you might call over-security. The moment they get a major appointment, it is automatically a life appointment; whether they succeed or not, they are going to remain there for the rest of their lives.

As a result, after the first few years, they get accustomed to what they see around them, they resign themselves to the situation as they find it, and they fail to grow and develop themselves later on.

Ministers are entitled to security. After training for years, they should not have to fear they will not be able to sustain themselves and their families. But having said this, I believe you ought to consider introducing a system whereby you can, in consultation with the ministry, every ten years or so, change a minister's position from one synagogue to another.

I can tell you from my own ministerial experience that ten years is normally about as long as you can be creative in a congregation. After that, you begin to stagnate. But if you switch to another community and have to start all over again, grapple with new problems, meet new challenges and see new faces, you become young again and you begin once more to tap resources which otherwise lie buried within you.

Today, rabbis ought to be 'running the show'. They ought to determine congregational policies and seek your partnership in putting them into effect. They ought to seize the initiative in expanding classes, making appointments, deciding that there should be a youth centre at the synagogue, or arousing enthusiasm for any other new enterprise. They ought to enjoy sufficient confidence to assume the driver's seats in the congregation.'

Chief Rabbi Jakobovits, 'Looking Ahead'
United Synagogue Council, London, 26 November 1967

Having addressed the United Synagogue's lay leaders on the subject, the Chief Rabbi proceeded to face his ministerial colleagues, using as his platform the sixteenth Conference of Anglo-Jewish Preachers, held in Manchester in May 1968:

'The Anglo-Jewish ministry [he said] has often been afflicted with a feeling of futility. Limited in the exercise of local authority by a centralised Chief Rabbinate and Beth Din, on the one side, and in the display of effective leadership by the constitutional powers of lay officers, on the other, ministers frequently sensed that they were dispensable in the government of the community. In really important matters, they were made to feel that the community could well do without them.

Worse still, some ministers were quite prepared to resign themselves to this role of impotence. With an altogether false modesty, they surrendered all ambition to assert themselves as leaders inside and outside their congregations, contenting themselves with playing a merely functional part in the conduct of religious services and some other routine activities. I believe this is an altogether wrong attitude, pernicious to personal as well as communal advancement. Far from saying that our congregations can run without us, the ideals of Jewish ethics challenge us to assert 'For our sake were they created'.

For my part, I am doing my utmost to enhance the role of the minister in the community, both by inviting my colleagues to share some of the responsibilities of my office with me and by constantly urging the lay leaders of our congregations and of the community at large to increase the scope and authority of their spiritual leaders. But, ultimately, the success of these efforts to achieve this far-reaching evolution will depend on the ministers' own determination to seek and discharge wider responsibilities and to find the correct balance between humility and ambition.'

In 'Moving Ahead: A Review and a Preview', Dr Jakobovits gave a progress report later that year:

'In accordance with my plans for the reorganisation of the Chief Rabbinate, a 'Chief Rabbi's Cabinet' has now been set up. By assigning specific departments to some of our leading rabbis and ministers, and by constituting an advisory plenum meeting regularly to take counsel on the major challenges confronting religious leadership in the community, this innovation, which has already proved extremely helpful and effective, is to serve a threefold purpose: to diffuse the authority and scope of the Chief Rabbinate; to create a sense of partnership and opportunities of advancement for the ministry; and to bring rabbinic influence and guidance to bear on areas of communal, educational, charitable and national Jewish concern hitherto often more or less divorced from the rabbinate or even from the religious Jewish community.

In addition to the 'Cabinet', various other steps have been taken to cement the bonds of partnership and communications between my office and my colleagues. Thus, conferences of ministers from all parts of the country have been held with greater frequency than before, culminating in the very successful Conference of Anglo-Jewish Preachers, held last May in Manchester, the first such meeting ever held in the provinces, and the first to involve the lay community as well. A regular newsletter is being published to maintain more intimate contacts with my colleagues.

Altogether, I have tried to encourage ministers to play a more commanding role in their communities and congregations, just as I have urged the lay leaders and members of our congregations to assign greater responsibilities to their spiritual leaders, at least by expecting them to participate in, if not actually to initiate, all congregational activities, projects and policy-making decisions. For my part, too, I have endeavoured to treat my colleagues as partners and not as subordinates, preferring consultation to instruction, and guidance to edicts, and favouring the judicious growth of some local autonomy and diversity within the limits of halachic flexibility.'

Some 18 months later, the Chief Rabbi submitted his 'New Charter for the Ministry' – a memorandum on ministers' status, functions and conditions – to the honorary officers of the United Synagogue. Its main proposals included the following:

1. Provision should be made for the participation of ministers in the direction of all United Synagogue affairs and policy-making decisions, from the highest levels down.

   (a) A representative of the ministry, selected by the United Synagogue Council of Ministers for a period not exceeding two years at a time, should be co-opted as an honorary officer of the United Synagogue, and be invited to all meetings other than those dealing exclusively with purely financial matters.

   (b) Ministerial representatives should likewise be added to the executive committees and councils of the United Synagogue, as well as to all its subsidiary bodies and committees, such as visitation, welfare and the burial society.

   (c) On a local level, the minister of the congregation should be invited to all meetings of the board of management, exercising his own discretion to attend in the light of the agenda.

   (d) Co-option and participation in all these cases should be without voting rights.

   (e) Wherever possible, and without regard to the nature of the agenda, the attending minister should open or close the proceedings of all meetings by a few minutes' religious discourse or study session, or at least a short prayer, so as to give all meetings concerned with synagogue affairs a distinctly religious flavour.

2. In the placement of ministers, synagogue appointments should be broadly divided into four principal categories: A – smaller peripheral congregations, or as an assistant/junior minister in a major congregation; B – larger static congregations; C – larger congregations in the process of dynamic development; and D – 'prestige' congregations among constituent synagogues. Appropriate steps should be taken to ensure that every minister, as he moves from apprenticeship to retirement, would normally pass successively through all these categories.

   In order to promote the appointment and periodic movement of ministers in accordance with these principles, a ministerial appointments committee, consisting of ministerial and lay representatives in equal numbers, should be set up to initiate consultation and action on filling vacancies as they arise, based on the following guidelines:

   (a) No full-time position should ever be offered to an unqualified candidate (that is, one who has not pursued a course of study at a recognised rabbinical academy of learning), nor should a candidate seeking his first appointment be assigned to a congregation other than type A, or type B in exceptional cases. For vacancies in congregations of type C and type D, high priority should be given to candidates with at least ten and 20 years' experience, respectively.

   (b) Whenever possible, appointments should await or anticipate a number of vacancies so that the appointments committee can consider these in the wider context of the above principles to ensure that

(i) ministers will serve congregations for which they are best fitted; and

(ii) ministers will generally advance from lower-type to higher-type positions during their ministerial careers.

(c) Consideration should be given to the eventual expansion of the ministerial appointments committee to cover Orthodox synagogues throughout the country, so as to rationalise the distribution of ministerial resources on community-wide basis.

3. The emoluments for ministers should be thoroughly revised to approximate the income scales of other comparable professionals by budgetary projections aimed at such parity within the next five years.

About 60 per cent of the maximum projected income should be covered by a basic salary, payable equally to all full-time ministers irrespective of the size or situation of their synagogue. To this basic salary should be added extra specified emoluments in respect of each of the following entitlements:

(a) for every 500 members of the minister's congregation in excess of the first 500;

(b) for every ten years of ministerial service;

(c) for the holders of a rabbinical diploma and/or postgraduate university degree;

(d) for literary or lecturing activities or other regular services to the community in the spheres of education, youth, students, smaller communities, etc.

These payments should be determined and assessed by a special board.

4. The minister's agreement of service should be revised to bring it more closely in line with the new status of the minister and to provide for the proposed alterations in the conditions of service.

5. In order to make Jewish spiritual leadership more effective, more attractive and more widely available, official encouragement should also be given to

(a) more regular exchanges of pulpits;

(b) periodic visits, including weekends, to smaller communities;

(c) a sabbatical leave of absence every seven years, extending to at least three months, for study, research or literary purposes, preferably to be spent in Israel, or for foreign exchange visits;

(d) the relief of ministers engaging in more creative work from routine visitation duties, such duties to be taken over by other ministers, chazanim, and lay visitation committees to be set up in all major congregations;

(e) the relief of ministers engaged in teaching or superintending of Hebrew classes from attendance at tombstone consecrations on Sunday mornings; and

(f) the initiative of ministers in pioneering the establishment of new day-schools, youth clubs and other communal projects.

6. The council of the United Synagogue should set up a working party on a New Charter for the Ministry, consisting of eight laymen (including two under

age of 30 years), two representatives of the Council of Ministers, and two nominees of the Chief Rabbi, to study these proposals and to submit to the council of the United Synagogue, within six months, a practical scheme to implement them.

Besides his ministers' charter, the Chief Rabbi was also working on a programme to enhance the appeal of synagogue services. Addressing the first national conference of the Association of Ministers-Chazanim of Great Britain, attended by more than 80 readers from all over Britain and Ireland, he said that Shabbat services should never be longer than two and a half hours, and that no more than seven people should be called up to the reading of the Law. On those rare occasions when the number had to be exceeded, it should never be more than ten. A maximum of 30 minutes should be allocated to the minister, including the delivery of his sermon.

In every synagogue, there should be appointed a ritual committee under the leadership of the reader, so that the conduct of the service was constantly under review and more congregational involvement encouraged.

Higher salary scales for religious and lay officials of the United Synagogue were approved by the United Synagogue council at a meeting in February 1975. The salary increases, which also affected the dayanim of the London Beth Din but not the Chief Rabbi (whose emoluments were set by the Chief Rabbinate Council), took effect from the beginning of March.

The proposals were advanced by George Gee, a vice-president, who chaired the committee of inquiry which called for increased salaries as part of a new deal for ministers and officials. He said that 'the whole future of the services provided by the US depends on its ability to attract personnel of the right calibre'. The proposed salary scales, he added, were 'not only essential but also minimal'.

Commending the scheme, the president, Alfred Woolf, said: 'We are conscious that council members have complained that our ministers are underpaid and that we offer no incentive for young men to study for the ministry. We have endeavoured to put this right.'

The secretary of the United Synagogue, Nathan Rubin, said in 1977 that vacancies for rabbis at Hampstead Garden Suburb Synagogue and Edgware Synagogue, and for readers at St John's Wood Synagogue and Finchley Synagogue, were 'symptomatic' of a national shortage.

Full-time ministers had been sought for over a year to replace incumbent ministers at Ilford and Hendon who had reached retirement age. Ten major synagogue posts remained vacant, and there was a five per cent shortage in the 200 synagogues in Britain under the Chief Rabbi's jurisdiction, including vacancies at Brighton, Southend, Glasgow, Bradford, Nottingham, Dublin and Birmingham.

Commenting on the problem, the Chief Rabbi said that he had submitted a plan to the United Synagogue for a ministerial placements bureau as a means of filling vacancies. 'We must work on a rational community basis to ensure that our resources are effectively deployed. Congregations are not making the career attractive enough for young men in terms of remuneration, scope and status. More scholarships should be available for people to enter the ministry, because it involves seven or eight years' study. And families should give more encouragement to their sons to enter the ministry.'

Following consultations between the Chief Rabbi, the United Synagogue honorary officers and its Council of Ministers, agreement was reached to revise the method of ministerial appointments. In a letter to ministers, Rabbi Jakobovits stated that the principal objects of the scheme were 'to initiate, expedite and rationalise steps to fill the increasing number of ministerial vacancies; to deploy resources more effectively by considering the requirements of the community as a whole rather than each congregation in isolation; and to protect the dignity of candidates in the selection process'.

The scheme was also designed to encourage ministers seeking or willing to change their positions, but not prepared to go through the present selection procedure and the risks involved; to provide a basis for a proper career structure, whereby ministers could expect gradual promotion from junior to senior or more rewarding positions; and to encourage recruitment by improving placement and promotion prospects. Initially, the Chief Rabbi stated, the scheme would be limited to the United Synagogue in London, but it was hoped eventually to extend it to the provinces and perhaps even to other countries.

The proposals were approved at a meeting of the United Synagogue council in September 1980, more than a year after they were first proposed.

MIDDLE-OF-THE-ROAD RABBIS

The difficulty in recruiting middle-of-the-road Orthodox rabbis was highlighted, in 1985, by the chairman of Jews' College, Stanley Kalms. Speaking at a college council meeting, he asserted that 'the vast majority of the middle-road Orthodox insists on the right to enjoy both an intense Jewish life and the full benefit of a secular culture, and equally that their children should achieve a higher education, preferably university, often with an Israeli experience – yeshivah or whatever – as a bonus.

'Their attitude is that Torah and Shakespeare are not in conflict. To savour a traditional and soulful *nusach* [mode of service] does not exclude Mozart or, indeed, the Beatles. Yet we seem to have a major problem in recruiting and employing spiritual leaders who will totally accept this philosophy. It seems to me an inviolable principle that whomever one elects or employs should accept without equivocation the conditions and attitudes of the appointment.

'Yet increasingly there is a substantial drift, whether it be on accepting our own kashrut, how to relate to the women of the community, or even a 100 per cent commitment to the State of Israel. It is into this loosely disciplined leadership role that we are endeavouring to recruit suitable candidates, and I have to say that it is an increasingly hard task during this contemporary phase of ambivalence and uncertainty. Unless we fight with greater eloquence for our love of our way of life and emphasise that middle-way Orthodoxy is a meaningful and complete Jewish experience, with an unbounded commitment to Israel and a haven of tradition and Yiddishkeit, unless we profoundly proclaim this from the platforms as well as from the pulpits, I fear for Anglo-Jewry in the next decade.'

The 'rather limited perspective' of some of those seeking to enter the rabbinate was also criticised by the president of the United Synagogue, Victor Lucas, at a meeting of the US council. Supporting Mr Kalms, he said that the 'narrow *hashkafah* [outlook] of these rabbis does not seem to meet the needs of the spectrum of our membership'.

Nor did he limit his comments to rabbis. 'This critique', he added, 'applies just as strongly to many of our lay leaders, local honorary officers and members of boards of management, whose limited vision of their roles and responsibilities proves to be a rather negative and unhelpful factor.'

The problem of finding the right kind of rabbi, he said, could not be ignored. 'We must address ourselves seriously to this especially tough challenge and find ways and means of broadening the outlook of our religious and lay leaders.'

Interviewed by the *Jewish Chronicle*, the Chief Rabbi disputed the statements made by Mr Kalms and Mr Lucas about the kind of rabbis needed in United Synagogue congregations. And when the issue was discussed at a meeting of his Cabinet, its members were 'sharply divided. Some felt affronted, while others felt the remarks justified'.

The Chief Rabbi said that Mr Kalms and Mr Lucas 'expressed their own views and did not pretend to speak on my behalf. Their opinions, however, are legitimate, even if they do not reflect my own. I believe the diversity among congregations must be matched by a diversity among the rabbinate.' He added that he himself was the product of a 'middle-road philosophy' – a combination of Jewish and secular culture, as identified with the school of Samson Raphael Hirsch – and had pursued secular studies. Yet he recognised that times had changed and that his own children – 'and, even more so, my grandchildren' – were 'more fastidious in their demands of Jewish life'.

Mr Kalms and Mr Lucas' remarks, said the Chief Rabbi, reflected the fact that they were 'troubled by the increasing polarisation within the traditional community. The lay leadership senses that the distance between some rabbis and their congregations is widening'. The debate, however, was entirely unrelated to compromising the halachah, as had been alleged in some quarters. 'It is of no halachic significance, since all the rabbis and lay leaders insist that the halachah is sovereign and not negotiable. The debate is about relationships, attitudes. It concerns tolerance and a willingness to count in those sections of the community, or those individuals, who are not fully observant. It is about whether we should be inward-looking or outward-looking, about whether we should encourage secular degrees among rabbinic qualifications.'

The Chief Rabbi said that, in the community of today, 'we will have to allow for diversity of opinion, so long as it is within the parameters of the halachah. Some rabbis may insist that we should be inward-looking, with no communications with the outside world, while others believe in greater contact with the secular world. There is room for both within the United Synagogue.' It was wrong to say that rabbis who had only a yeshivah training were not suitable for US pulpits. Some were highly successful, though he conceded that they had exceptional ability. There were 'three or four' currently occupying US pulpits who had encountered problems because of their perspective, which was conditioned by the 'limitations' of their education and training.

Most congregations wanted rabbis who had been trained at Jews' College. But because the community had failed to invest sufficiently to recruit such rabbis, not enough had been produced, and so others had come in 'by default'. For the United Synagogue, the ideal combination was a Jews' College experience after a yeshivah education, and a number of yeshivah-educated students were now attending special courses at the college to acquire 'the professional skills' demanded by modern congregations.

Describing the controversy as 'healthy', the Chief Rabbi said that the process of polarisation in modern society was 'a fact of life. The United Synagogue can still retain the loyalty of the bulk of our community, as it has done during the 18 years I have been Chief Rabbi, despite all the forecasts to the contrary. I believe this solid strength of the traditional community will be maintained for the foreseeable future.'

CHAPTER FOURTEEN

Jewish Education

*'Assuring the inalienable birthright of every Jew to an
adequate Jewish education. On this I stake the success of my
ministry, for on this will depend Jewish survival'*

'Pursuant to a resolution passed by the council of the United Synagogue, and
to promote my own plans for the intensification and expansion of Jewish education under communal auspices, I am now setting up a commission of inquiry,
and I have much pleasure in inviting you to serve on this important body. This
commission is to inquire into the adequacy of Jewish religious education
for children of school age in the Greater London metropolitan area, with
special reference to the operations of the London Board of Jewish Religious
Education.

The investigations should cover the structure, administration, finances and
policies of our educational institutions, the recruitment, training and present
availability of competent Hebrew teachers, and the involvement of our synagogues, especially the United Synagogue, in helping to provide these facilities
and resources on an ever-increasing scale.

The commission is to be joined by two or more educational experts from
abroad who are to help in the preparation of a comprehensive Jewish educational reconstruction plan, designed to modernise, intensify and expand our
educational services in order to secure the rise of a highly knowledgeable and
profoundly committed generation of Jews and Jewesses able to assert their
Judaism against the intellectual, moral, social and secularist pressures of our
times.

In particular, I shall look for the formulation of plans to make Jewish education
the primary concern of the leaders and members of our congregations; to at least
double the number of Jewish children, especially in the post-barmitzvah age
group, receiving regular Jewish instruction; to launch a major fund-raising
campaign for capital expansion and improvements; to shift the emphasis
gradually from Hebrew classes to Jewish day-schools, in terms of both communal support and popular enrolment; to facilitate the introduction of Ivrit as
the exclusive language of instruction in all Hebrew classes and day-schools from
kindergarten upwards; and to raise the status of Hebrew teachers.'

*Letter from the Chief Rabbi to communal leaders
and educationalists, 28 May 1968*

Six months later, the Chief Rabbi invited two American educationalists to help solve the problems of Jewish education in Britain. They were Dr Joseph Kaminetsky, head of Torah Umesorah, and Rabbi Simcha Teitelbaum, dean of Yeshiva High School, Queens, New York. Both were well known in the sphere of American Jewish education, and Dr Jakobovits had worked with them while ministering in New York.

Following the circulation of his May letter, a panel of experts with a first-class knowledge of education was set up under the chairmanship of Professor Cyril Domb, of King's College, University of London (and later of Bar-Ilan University). Their ideas would be put to a second panel, comprising professional educationalists.

At the same time, adult education throughout the community was given a boost. The Chief Rabbi announced that a director was to be appointed to take charge of educational programmes for adults, and that the United Synagogue had pledged financial support.

A £3 million Jewish education plan for the next five years, to come into effect immediately, was recommended by the American rabbis following their visit. In the first part of their report, they declared: 'We feel that the entire system must be given a shot in the arm and be dramatically revamped'. What was need was 'a grand strategy', an overall plan. The key to their recommendations lay in the belief that 'there must be established within the Office of the Chief Rabbi a special educational department, with an education officer directly responsible to him'. It would serve as his executive arm in implementing the five-year plan and in running a development campaign, also suggested by the Americans. While controlling Jewish education throughout Britain, it would not replace any existing organisations.

Following the report, the Chief Rabbi approached a number of prominent members of the community to support a major appeal aimed at raising the £3 million needed. One-third of the proceeds, he said, would be invested to provide a recurrent annual budget.

JEWISH EDUCATION: IS THE ALARM JUSTIFIED?

'We are advised that we will require no less than £3 million to be spent over the next five years on our most urgent educational requirements – on more schools, on better instruction, on higher salaries, on teacher-training and on numerous other needs. To raise this kind of money, I will have to expect some members of a congregation such as this [the Marble Arch Synagogue] to come forward enthusiastically with donations not in the £100 or £1,000 range, but in denominations of £10,000 or more in order to give the proper impetus to the campaign. These are exacting demands, and I will have to justify them if the community is to rally to my support.

If, as the many empty seats at today's Yizkor service have so eloquently testified, respect for parents is no longer powerful enough to make children honour them by a single visit to the synagogue, then how much less can we rely on such respect to make them act as loyal Jews all the year round, outside the synagogue as well as inside? We might as well resign ourselves to the grim new fact of Jewish life: either we intelligently teach our youth what Judaism means, or else Anglo-Jewry is going to become one of the lost tribes of Israel. Either we will educate them to proclaim 'This is my God', or they will have no God at all.

On my success in persuading you and other congregations in this country to take Jewish education far more seriously, and to adopt imaginative and expensive programmes of educational expansion, may depend the survival of Anglo-Jewry. We should be under no illusion about it: only a thorough and profound understanding of Judaism, of Jewish ethics and philosophy, of Jewish law and theology, of Jewish literature and history, can counter the rebellion, distractions or apathy generated so profusely in the intellectual and social climate of the restless society around us.

Without such understanding through education, especially at the post-barmitzvah level, many of our youth will be left defenceless against the allurements of defection and intermarriage; they will opt out of the community. If we are not going to embark immediately on a massive campaign of educational reconstruction, there will be little left to salvage in ten years' time. If nothing drastic gets done in the meantime, we shall by then have to close scores of synagogues for lack of enough regular worshippers to sustain them.

Worse still, we shall have no spiritual leaders to guide our congregations. The recruitment situation, already more precarious than is generally realised – with ever-more important vacancies we are unable to fill adequately – will be nothing short of disastrous in ten years from now, unless an altogether new attitude to Jewish education and scholarship will again begin to attract some of our most promising young men to dedicate themselves to rabbinical and teaching careers in the supreme service of our community.'

From a sermon delivered by the Chief Rabbi
on Pesach 5729, 10 April 1969

Re-elected unopposed as president of the United Synagogue, Sir Isaac Wolfson pledged a substantial personal contribution towards the £3 million fund which the Chief Rabbi required to implement his educational programme. Addressing a meeting of the US council, Sir Isaac said that the US had to find a way of assisting the Chief Rabbi in his efforts not only to extend the educational work in the part-time classes and in the day-schools but also to intensify Hebrew and religious studies. It was therefore his intention to recommend to the Chief Rabbi that he convene a working conference of a small number of representatives from the US, Jews' College, the London Board of Jewish Religious Education and other educational bodies in London and the provinces.

'It will be the duty of this conference to work out a blueprint of what is required in the immediate years ahead and to cost it in terms of capital and revenue requirements. When this is done, we shall take steps to see that the appropriate finances are made available and, at the same time, proceed to implement the decisions taken.'

Sir Isaac told the meeting that he intended 'to support the Chief Rabbi's schemes in a very substantial manner. Jewish education is very near to my heart and I would like to put it on a sound and solid basis before I retire.'

A major breakthrough in training State-recognised teachers of Jewish studies was made six months later with the establishment of a three-year course at Trent Park College of Education, Cockfosters. The course, in the college's divinity department, was arranged in conjunction with the Faculty for the Training of Teachers, run under the joint auspices of Jews' College, the Jewish Agency Torah department, and the London Board of Jewish Religious Education.

Formal approval was given at a meeting of Trent Park's standing committee in divinity. Students would take Jewish studies as their main subject – the first time this had been accepted at a secular college of education – while participating in the educational course of the college, enabling them to qualify as certificated teachers recognised by the Department of Education and Science.

The new syllabus was drawn up in consultation with the Chief Rabbi; compulsory sections included biblical and modern Hebrew and Jewish history. In the vacation period between the first and second years, students were expected to spend some time in Israel, possibly gathering material for their special projects.

Yaacov Lehman, a senior official of the Israeli Ministry of Education, arrived in London in September 1970 to take up his appointment as the Chief Rabbi's executive officer for education. The appointment was a key recommendation in the report of Rabbis Kaminetsky and Teitelbaum.

With more than £1 million already pledged, the Chief Rabbi launched his £6.5 million education programme – 'Let My People Know' – in November 1971. It was to be implemented in two phases over the ensuing ten to 15 years, with the funds being administered by a Jewish Educational Development Trust [JEDT] headed by Dr Jakobovits. Leading supporters included Sir Isaac, who pledged £350,000; the family of the late Charles Wolfson (£100,000); the Sieff-Sacher family (£100,000); and a score of others who each promised five- or six-figure amounts. Trustees of the fund, which was recognised as a charity by the Department of Education and Science, were – in addition to the Chief Rabbi – the Haham, Rabbi Solomon Gaon; Sir Isaac; Roland Franklin; and Harry Landy. Trevor Chinn and Leo Graham were joint treasurers.

The target figure for the first phase of the programme, to be completed in five years, was £2,610,000. Dr Jakobovits stated that plans to raise the rest of the money were well in hand and that 'that is the least of our worries'. Phase I provided for the establishment of two secondary schools – one with six-form entry in North-West London (£800,000) and the other with five-form entry in the Ilford-Wanstead area (£700,000), plus Hebrew departments costing an additional £150,000. The first of these schools, proposed for the Wembley–Kenton–Kingsbury area, would initially provide for 180 pupils, with a further 150 accommodated at the Ilford school.

The programme also sought the establishment of a two-form-entry primary school in North-West London (probably Kingsbury) and a one-form-entry school in Enfield, which together with Hebrew departments would cost a total of more than £500,000. Other expenditure included £100,000 on teacher-training schemes; £30,000 on special courses for teachers; and £50,000 on withdrawal classes and study groups.

It was intended to grant bursaries of £1,500 to £2,000 per annum to train suitable educationalists to fill an expected 25 to 30 senior positions – headmasters, directors, inspectors and heads of departments – due to become vacant by 1980. This aspect of the programme was budgeted at £70,000. A further £30,000 was being set aside for one-year postgraduate courses in Hebrew and Jewish studies for qualified teachers from Britain, tenable at colleges in Jerusalem. Sixth-form colleges, using the facilities of Jews' College, the Montefiore College and the Sir Israel and Lady Brodie Hall of Residence, would account for £65,000.

Launching the Trust, the Chief Rabbi stated that he was redeeming 'a long-standing personal commitment to concentrate the major part of my energies on the expansion and intensification of Jewish education. We believe that a new scale of communal priorities, which recognises the primacy of education in securing the survival and regeneration of Anglo-Jewry, will create enough confidence in the stability of Jewish education to attract ever-more of our finest young Jewish men and women.'

Grants totalling £10,000 were made by the JEDT early the following year to enable nine educationalists to engage in postgraduate studies for between one and three years; these were tenable at universities in Britain, Israel and the USA. While in Israel for a conference, the Chief Rabbi met Yigal Allon, the Minister of Education, for a discussion on Jewish educational issues in Britain, among them the supply of teachers and exchange schemes for pupils. Dr Jakobovits also met Hebrew University educationalists to discuss teacher-training schemes and pre-college courses.

After major cutbacks in the Government's spending plans on education, JEDT leaders announced in June 1977 that the Trust was being 'completely revamped'. A programme of Jewish educational development, including teacher-training at various levels, had been made possible following a decision by the leadership of the Joint Israel Appeal and other communal leaders to pledge their personal support for the 'considerable funding' that would be necessary. JIA funds would not be involved, but the organisation would lend its expertise in the administrative sphere.

No price tag had been attached to the cost of helping existing schools and classes to expand their Jewish educational facilities or for the provision of new ones, though it was anticipated that some £750,000 would be required in the first year alone for the support and extension of existing facilities. Similar sums would be needed in each of the following years for such purposes. Major developments in school building envisaged in the plan – including school expansion in London and Leeds and the building of a new school in Kingsbury – were expected to require over £2 million in capital costs over the ensuing five years.

A BLUEPRINT FOR SURVIVAL

National education scheme

The JEDT's plans to build new schools cannot at present proceed because of Government cutbacks resulting from the economic situation. At the same time, the deteriorating financial situation of schools in the private sector has created concern for their ability to maintain existing places. The Jewish community will therefore have to bear the whole of the cost of establishing new schools.

Over the next seven to ten years, the JEDT will promote and finance those development schemes which will attract State aid immediately on completion or which will increase the number of places at existing schools. It recognises the need to assist schools and attached kindergartens with their running costs. This aid will not be forthcoming automatically and will be allocated specifically for Jewish and Hebrew studies.

Excellence is the aim

We want pupils to know why they are Jewish and how their Jewishness can be expressed. We want them to have a knowledge and appreciation of Jewish history and culture, and an understanding of Jewish values. We would like to produce pupils who speak Hebrew. We want our young people to be aware of contemporary Jewry ... and to feel a direct and personal link with Israel.

While we will not seek to impose conditions in making grants to schools and synagogue classes, we will strongly endeavour to encourage higher standards of Jewish education, leading not simply to greater academic achievement but also to personal involvement, identification and commitment.

The quality of education is not merely a reflection of an adequate syllabus. It derives from dedicated, committed and trained teachers, from a real concern of teachers for pupils, from free, two-way communication, and from the general *ruach* of the schools.

We will seek to encourage standards of excellence and in this connection will involve ourselves closely in those schools which have already achieved high standards and which serve as an example to others.

Development plans

At Ilford, planning permission has been received for the existing Jewish primary school to be extended to take an additional 140 pupils.

A school will be built in Kingsbury–Kenton as a replacement for the present Solomon Wolfson School. There will be no State participation in any of the land, building or equipment costs, but plans have been approved for the new school to receive State-aided status immediately it opens. Work could be completed by September 1980.

Within the next five years, it is hoped to purchase from the local authority at Ilford a primary school which is being phased out as a county school and will continue as a denominational school with State aid. This will provide places for an additional 280 pupils.

Also within a five-year period, it is hoped to expand the Brodetsky School in Leeds and the Hasmonean Girls' School in North-West London.

Other desirable projects which it is hoped will be started with a five-to-12-year span include a secondary comprehensive school in Ilford, on land at present owned by the JEDT; and a primary school in Southgate, the building of which already has London Education Authority approval and which will be accepted for State-aided status on completion.

Completed projects

Special development projects completed by the JEDT include

- the building of a sixth-form college for the JFS Comprehensive School in Camden Town. This is now the largest sixth-form college of any comprehensive school in the country (increase in number of pupils, 150);
- extra classrooms at the Mathilda Marks-Kennedy School, Golders Green, and participation in the erection of the Leeds Middle School and the Simon Marks Primary School (increase, over 250 – these two projects in conjunction with the Zionist Federation Education Trust);

- building of sixth-form accommodation for the Lubavitch School (increase, 100);
- assistance to purchase premises for the Yesodey Hatorah Girls' Primary School, North London (increase, 150);
- new building for the Hasmonean Girls' School (increase, 200), plus a loan of £82,000.

The Trust has given assistance to the following schools which have experienced financial difficulty in maintaining their existing programmes of Jewish and Hebrew studies: King David Schools, Manchester; Hasmonean Grammar School for Boys; Yavneh Primary School, Wembley; Menorah School, Sunderland; North-West London Jewish Day School; Brighton and Hove Jewish Day School; Delial Didsbury School, Manchester; Kisharon School for handicapped children; Lubavitch Schools.

The Trust has purchased ten acres of land at Ilford, where a primary school and a comprehensive school can be built.

Revised prospectus of the Jewish Educational Development Trust, 1977

The Chief Rabbi's Office announced in August of that year that a JEDT plan to treat requests for Jewish schools as a 'global problem' was under 'very active consideration' by the Education Secretary, Shirley Williams.

Moshe Davis, director of the Chief Rabbi's Office and a senior negotiator for Jewish day-schools with the Department of Education, said that discussions had been taking place with Mrs Williams on the pooling of minorities from different boroughs, so that one school could be used to service the needs of Jewish communities in several linked areas.

He added that the acquisition of a secular school that was defunct and turning it into a Jewish school was also being considered. Mrs Williams had asked local authorities to ascertain whether there were any schools surplus to their requirements, since such schools could be utilised by the JEDT. Mr Davis said that his negotiations with Mrs Williams had been 'very friendly and very positive'.

Concurrently, the JEDT had been investigating ways to improve teacher-training and encourage recruitment. Its recommendations, published in June 1979, included the following (asterisk denotes priory):

1. Financial assistance should be provided for the purchase and maintenance of a mobile resources centre which could visit schools and part-time classes in the metropolis and the provinces.
2. Financial assistance should be given to the more impoverished schools in the independent sector so that they can purchase essential educational equipment and teaching resources, and also effect essential minor building improvements.
3. *The opportunity to take at least a one-year course in an approved Israeli institute of higher education should be made available to all students who are training to become teachers.
4. Financial support should be given to all Jewish schools to enable them to offer financial incentives to all teachers who acquire approved qualifications in some sphere of Jewish studies so that this sector of the profession receives due recognition.

5. Jewish teachers who are employed in non-Jewish schools which attract Jewish pupils should be encouraged to attend courses, and suitable recognition should be given to them if they involve themselves with the Jewish pupils in their school.

6. *Teachers and students-in-training who are unable to spend a year of study in Israel should be encouraged to take part in Israel in suitably structured vacation courses, so that they return to England appropriately informed and inspired.

7. *Israel-based courses, in themselves, are inadequate to deal with teaching situations in England. In addition to these courses, it is essential that there should be organised in this country the following categories of in-service courses:

- Preparatory and follow-up courses linked to the Israel-based courses and, if possible, conducted in association with appropriate Israeli universities and teachers' seminaries;
- Courses which cater for the specific needs of individual schools or of groups of schools which have common needs: there is need for a provincial centre for teachers' courses;
- Courses or conferences which would deal with general educational topics.

8. Financial support should be given to educational bodies which organise in-service courses in this country.

9. Approaches should be made to local education authorities and to institutes of higher education in Israel to mount suitably structured courses, to meet the needs of teachers, in this country.

10. Israel-based courses should be mounted in vacation-time; courses based in this country should be held during term-time. Financial assistance should be given to independent schools to engage temporary staff who might be required to replace the teachers attending the courses held in term-time.

11. *The different educational bodies should be encouraged to make the participation in a one-year course of teacher-training in Israel a high priority in the list of qualifications for employment for all newly qualified teachers.

12. Financial recognition should be given to teachers who regularly and effectively attend approved short courses.

13. In Jewish schools, every teacher must be encouraged to regard himself/herself as a custodian of Jewish heritage and should be suitably rewarded for specifically undertaking this responsibility.

14. Financial support should be given to ensure that schools in the independent sector are able to give to suitably qualified teachers an adequate salary and are able to employ full-time rather than part-time staff.

In 'Jewish Education 1983–1984', the chairman of the JEDT's education committee, Stanley Kalms, reported that 'the past two years have been extremely busy for the Trust in its now familiar and traditional front-line role on behalf of Jewish education. We continued to help to fund new schools, to extend existing ones, and generally involve ourselves in all the complexities that make up a Jewish educational programme.

'Yet I will not dazzle readers with statistics, tempting and impressive as they may be, but rather reflect on the other area of real development emerging from within the ranks of the JEDT: our efforts to improve the quality and range of *limmudei kodesh*. We are now strangers to the world of platitudes and have passed the luxury of believing in the numbers game. No longer do we, for example, take comfort in the fact that the cheder system is being taught three hours on a Sunday morning to many thousands of children. We know to our spiritual cost how misleading are cold numbers.

'Today, we believe only in hard facts, the reality of the end-product, the pupil we seek to educate. We are totally objective in our analysis. In some areas, we have made great strides forward, in others we ought honestly to say that we can and must do considerably better.

'This means a better understanding of demography and the true future needs of changing communities. It means a clearer concept of the changing role of Jewish Diaspora life in relation to Israel. Our thinking has to continually reflect the strains within our own communities, and the insidious effects of pluralism, as Israel develops from our unquestioned Utopia into a mature State, with all the attendant conflicts. Our children must have the issues explained.

'Alas, it also means that occasionally we have to be exceedingly critical and unsupportive of narrow and parochial efforts by unskilled or old fashioned "well-meaners." It further sometimes necessitates our refusal to co-operate with high-sounding but often unnecessary, uneconomical or egotistical projects.'

Fulfilling a 'long-held dream', the Chief Rabbi launched the United Synagogue's Year of Jewish Education in September 1986. He called on 'every member of the community to realise that without our support of Jewish education as the focus of our priorities, without our Jewish knowledge and commitment, every other phase of our activities would simply disappear. There would in future be no Jews and no Zionists; no kashrut in our homes, and no congregations in our synagogues; no supporters of Israel; no defenders against anti-Semitism; and no resistance to the erosion by assimilation and intermarriage.'

The Year of Jewish Education, said the Chief Rabbi, 'offers an exciting opportunity to Anglo-Jewry at all levels and ages to become involved in the revival of Jewish learning and in the enhancement of Jewish life. There will be widespread publicity and the promotion of the programmes and activities, as well as urgent fund-raising appeals in order to meet the growing needs of Jewish education within our community.'

Leaders of the JEDT announced in July 1989 that its new independent Jewish secondary school in Bushey, Hertfordshire, would be called Immanuel College, after the Chief Rabbi.

The first head teacher of the school, due to open in September 1990, would be Denis Felsenstein, deputy head of the JFS Comprehensive School from 1959 until 1970, who would see it through its launch stage. 'Within two or three years, he will retire and another head will be appointed', said Simon Caplan, the Trust's director.

At the turn of the year, after some doubt as to whether the school would open on time, the JEDT issued a challenge to the local community to raise £3 million to guarantee its completion. The Trust, which had bought the site for the school, pledged £9 million – 75 per cent of the start-up costs – provided that the community found the rest. The challenge was quickly taken up and a further £3 million pledged, one-third of it within the month.

In another development, in what the Chief Rabbi hailed as 'one of the most momentous weeks in the history of Anglo-Jewish education', the United Synagogue's plans for a State-aided Jewish comprehensive for Redbridge, East London, in 1991 were approved by the local council's education committee.

THE QUEST FOR EXCELLENCE

The new Jewish Independent College in Bushey is an independent Jewish secondary school whose aim is to provide an ambitious and exciting educational programme which will develop each pupil's gifts to the highest possible levels of excellence. The quest for excellence in all aspects of school life will be through a curriculum which integrates Jewish and secular studies, through a close partnership with parents, and through a committed and highly professional teaching and non-teaching staff.

There will be a strong emphasis on the importance of service to and participation in the full life of the school community, of the Jewish and general community, and of the State of Israel. The organisation, curriculum and atmosphere of the school will encourage pupils to develop their own personalities, to learn and develop good relations with tolerance for others, so that they will leave the school not only academically well-qualified, but proud of their Jewish heritage and its values, and ready and anxious to accept leadership roles in the Jewish and wider communities.

A particular feature of the school will be the integration into the school day of what are often considered as 'extra-curricular' activities, whereby the formal curriculum will be reinforced by half-termly option choices that pupils will make in areas such as further Jewish studies and Ivrit, the arts, physical activities, technology, communication, and environmental studies.

From the Prospectus of Immanuel College
September 1989

Early in 1990, the Bushey school appointed its head of Jewish studies, and the chairman of the board of governors, Henry Knobil, declared: 'It's all stations go!' The official title of the school, he announced, would be the Charles Kalms Henry Ronson Immanuel College, but it was likely to be known simply as Immanuel College, in honour of the Chief Rabbi. The new head of Jewish studies would be Paul Shaviv, sharing the deputy headship with Myrna Jacobs.

The school – also known as the New Jewish Independent College in Bushey – opened on 4 September 1990. Apart from the Chief Rabbi's name, its full title incorporated the names of the fathers of two of its main benefactors, Stanley Kalms and Gerald Ronson.

The school was launched with 40 first-year pupils – 23 boys and 17 girls. Twenty-nine came from Jewish primary schools – ten from Sinai, four from Kerem, four from Hasmonean Preparatory, three from North-West, three from Jewish Preparatory, three from Independent, one from Rosh Pinah, and one from Israel.

The initial two-form entry was due to increase to four-form entry the following year, when the designated annual intake was expected to reach 90–100. The ultimate size of the school would be 650–700 within six years. No class would comprise more than 25 pupils.

While Immanuel College was organised as a mixed school, and the boys and girls mixed freely for breaks, lunch and extra-curricular activities, they were taught for formal lessons in separate classes, though following an identical curriculum. From 1991, each year comprised two classes of boys and two of girls.

Of the nine full-time and four part-time teachers employed at the time, only three – one an Ivrit teacher – came from other Jewish schools. Some were heads of department at non-Jewish schools.

A MODEL SCHOOL FOR MODEL JEWS

'I am immensely proud that my final contribution, while still in office, to the institutional structure and life of Anglo-Jewry is the legacy of Immanuel College, upon which so many hopes for the enrichment of the cultural and religious attainment of our young are reposed. It is, I believe, the single most ambitious enterprise ever undertaken in the history of Anglo-Jewry, and I am delighted that it bears my name in association with the names of two invaluable partners.

Most significantly, the College will pioneer an altogether new dimension of Jewish education in this country. Guided by the motto *Torah im derech eretz* – Torah in harmony with worldly culture – the College is dedicated not only to excellence in Jewish and secular studies alike, but to their benign interaction, so that our children will grow up free from spiritual schizophrenia and from becoming victims of tension and conflict.

By underrating the intellectual capacity of our children, we often tend to demand far too little from them. Jewish schools are really successful only when they generate a passion for learning. We pray for 'the love of Torah' rather than merely the knowledge of Torah. The splendid team of headmaster and teachers, chairman and governors, rabbinical adviser and consultants holds out every promise of matching ambition with fulfilment.

I hope that out of this model school will emerge a new generation of model Jews – building consecrated homes, leading communal enterprises, solidarity with Israel as a sanctuary and not only as a refuge, caring for other Jews – now notably in the Soviet Union – and contributing to Britain's moral excellence in the finest exemplification of *kiddush hashem*.'

Lord Jakobovits
Jewish Chronicle, *7 September 1990*

CHAPTER FIFTEEN

Bridges of Understanding

*'Doing all within my power and authority to close
the gaps within our people'*

Emulating the enlightened example set by his father in Germany in his approach to
the Progressive community, 37-year-old Rabbi Immanuel Jakobovits posed the following questions at the first Conference of European Rabbis, held in Amsterdam in
November 1957: 'What ails Orthodoxy? Why have we lost our hold on the masses?'
He continued:

'The Reform movement, it seems to me, is not our chief problem. It is merely a
symptom, not the cause, of the general malaise. Reform has not drawn its ranks
from the Orthodox camp, but from those already lost to us. The State of Israel
has virtually no organised Reform, yet the religious problems there are much
the same as they are here.

Our main enemy, I submit therefore, is not Reform but the secularisation of
Jewish life. The real challenge before us is not the low proportion of strictly
observant Jews – for which there are ample precedents in our history – but the
widespread refusal to recognise our spiritual leaders as the true custodians of
our national destiny – for which there are only few precedents … Perhaps
more imagination is required in our public enlightenment drives … I can see no
reason why we should not follow the example of the prophets and personally
enter the Reform strongholds to preach our message on their own platform.
There are surely also ample precedents for rabbinical disputations with the
sectarians of earlier generations; why should we shy away from such direct
contests between truth and falsehood? And, after all, the Torah was not given
for Orthodox Jews only.

We cannot win the battle of the minds unless we are prepared to fight it …

I believe we have to decide whether to write off the Reform movement and
its followers as a dead loss, and try to insulate it completely from the adherents
of Orthodoxy, or go all out to retrieve what can be salvaged even at the cost of
some formal compromise with them. In the havoc wrought by these dissenters,
we must distinguish between irreparable damage, which will leave sores festering on the body of our people for generations to come, and purely temporary
infractions of the sanctities of Jewish life, causing wounds which can be healed
by individual acts of repentance.

Into the former category belong notably the Reform's arbitrary incursions into the spheres of marriage and proselytisation in complete disregard of Jewish law, leading to untold personal tragedies and, above all, to the increase of persons who cannot be recognised either as legitimate or as Jewish by the law-abiding majority of our people. To eliminate this appalling evil, gnawing at the very roots of Jewish existence, must be our foremost aim. It might be worthwhile, therefore, to explore the possibility of offering the Reformers, as an earnest of our anxiety for the preservation of Jewish unity, some kind of truce based on their acceptance of our exclusive jurisdiction in all matters affecting marriage and conversion, even if this meant closing our eyes to their forms of synagogue services and religious education for the time being.

Their agreement to this suggestion would, to my mind, constitute an invaluable gain and possibly pave the way to their eventual return to our fold. On the other hand, if they rejected the offer, we would at least win a substantial moral victory. Their refusal would publicly reveal more clearly than ever before who are the real disruptive influences in Jewish life today. The true causes for disunity and strife would be exposed for all to see. I still maintain that our chief enemy today is the secularisation of our national and even communal life. By our rift with the Reform, we are dissipating our vital energies and deflecting our attention from the most crucial struggle ahead of us.'

Recollections of this address could not have been far from his thoughts when the Chief Rabbi-elect was asked, in a BBC interview some nine years later, to define his thinking 'on religious matters as between the Liberals, the Orthodox and the very Orthodox groups'. He replied: 'I believe in the unity of the Jewish people, cemented by our common allegiance to our religious faith.

'We have lost six million Jews by violence, and another three million behind the Iron Curtain through spiritual attrition. I am not prepared to write off any Jew from the Jewish community. I will seek to build bridges of understanding, or at least of constructive dialogue. I certainly prefer to enlighten and attract rather than to denounce or ostracise, and I am hopeful for a form of union and common endeavour among all sections of Anglo-Jewry.

'My efforts, I hope, will be directed to focusing attention on the positive aspects rather than the negative and destructive ones of inter-communal rivalries and rifts. I hope that by getting the bulk of the community to think on these positive lines, those other institutional problems will gradually take care of themselves.'

In the run-up to his installation in London, Rabbi Jakobovits was invited to respond to a leading article in *Pointer*, the journal of the Union of Liberal and Progressive Synagogues, which had discussed his declared desire to 'build bridges of understanding across factional differences'. Accepting the challenge – 'unprecedented as my action may be' – he reiterated that 'I will recognise all Jews, whether Orthodox or not, as cherished members of our people; I will value and encourage their contributions, as Jews, to the welfare of our community and the enrichment of Jewish life,' and continued:

'Deeply pained though I am at the abandonment of much of the Jewish tradition by Progressive Jews, I realise that they have served to prevent many Jews from being lost altogether to our people, and I also realise the far greater danger to

Jewish religious survival stemming from the scourges of indifference and secularism – the paganism of our day. But for the very reason that I believe in the Torah as 'our common heritage … not given for Orthodox Jews only', the rejection of a large part of it by Progressive Judaism cannot be a matter of equanimity to me. You cannot expect me to acknowledge as a 'different, and legitimate, interpretation of Judaism' (to use your leader's words) a system which grievously violates many of the fundamental sanctities that are the essence of the Torah to me.

It would be idle and utterly inconsistent to pretend that to require the traditional observance of the Sabbath and kashrut laws *and* not to require it, or to have the same persons regarded as Jews or married by some *and* as non-Jews or divorced by others, can be equally legitimate. The same God surely cannot demand of me that I worship Him three times daily and after every meal (as I believe) *and* not care if you don't (as you believe). It lies in the nature of our dispute that there cannot be complete reciprocity in our relations. While you can eat in my home and worship in my synagogue without qualms, I cannot eat or worship in yours without offending my religious dictates. You can approve of my religious conduct and yet remain true to Progressive Judaism; I cannot endorse yours if I am to be loyal to Orthodox teachings. This obvious distinction, surely, you must and will understand.

Now, what can we build together on these premises? First and foremost, we can forswear intolerance and personal acrimony in our relations. I can oppose 'heresy-hunts' looking for a deviant in every cupboard, and you can oppose 'heresy-hunts' in reverse, whereby every little incident of Orthodox zeal is inflated into a *cause célèbre* or a public scandal. We can generate goodwill and banish despondency by confounding the prophets of doom who hold out, and preach, nothing but strife and disintegration for the community. We can jointly fight all attempts to sow subversion and secession breeding further disunity within Anglo-Jewry.

Next, we can intelligently debate our differences, using light instead of heat in our arguments. In this way, we can raise from the dregs the intellectual level and public image of our community, and at the same time test our convictions by mature discussion rather than by the exchange of irrelevant abuse. We can work together in Jewish and general causes upon which our religious differences do not impinge, such as Jewish defence, Zionism, philanthropy and Jewish–Christian relations. We can also join with our fellow-citizens in the moral crusade against rampant evils. We can participate together in communal and national events, so long as they are not of a specifically religious character in form or locale, implying a mutual endorsement where there can be no mutual endorsement.

Most importantly, we can explore ways and means to narrow our religious gap. I can make my synagogue services more attractive to the unfamiliar, and you can make yours more traditional. We can search for formulae to put an end to the fearful havoc wrought by our conflicting definitions of divorce and conversion, whereby tragic marriage barriers are being raised between Jew and Jew, and whereby thousands of people are considered Jewish by some Jews and Gentile by all others. These, and eventually other, bridges of understanding and co-operation can rise over the wide gulf at present separating us. But let me add this word of caution to prevent them from collapsing before they are even built.

Do not force the pace of this historic evolution by looking for issues, challenges or head-on collisions. These developments must grow organically from the seeds of goodwill fertilised by time. Any act of provocation only leads to a reaction of antagonism and drives us further apart. Also, never press or expect me to give rulings or opinions which would make me a fugitive from the law I am sworn to defend by conviction and by the terms of my appointment.

On these lines we should all look forward to playing our due part in building a great community and in uniting the House of Israel through our common heritage.'

In an interview with the *Sunday Times*, in March 1967, Dr Jakobovits spoke about the possibility of a 'reconciliation' with Rabbi Dr Louis Jacobs. 'If he [Dr Jacobs] can see his way clear to accept the jurisdiction of the Chief Rabbinate, the path to a reconciliation would be wide open,' said Dr Jakobovits. Invited by the *Jewish Chronicle* to enlarge on the statement, he replied that he did not wish to do so then, as he intended to deal with 'the broader issues involved in communal relationships' in his address after his induction as Chief Rabbi.

Dr Jacobs, however, responded in a letter to the *JC* the following week:

> Rabbi Jakobovits, in a statement to the *Sunday Times*, which you reprinted in your last week's issue, has suggested that the path of reconciliation is open were I but to accept the authority of the Chief Rabbinate. Acceptance by the New London Synagogue of the authority of the Chief Rabbi ought to be seen clearly as irrelevant to the question of 'reconciliation'. I was brought up, by pious rabbis of the old school, to believe that the Chief Rabbinate, of very recent origin, is an example of *hukkot ha-goy*, and further experience and study have convinced me that in this they were right.
>
> It is not only that the idea of a superior rabbi is unknown in Judaism and involves the abdication by the subordinate rabbi of the responsibilities conferred on him by his semichah. The office of chief rabbi in Anglo-Jewry is modelled on that of bishop and archbishop in the Christian Church, which, in turn, is based on belief in the apostolic succession. Thus, unlike the wearing of the clerical collar and canonicals, the institution has strong doctrinal overtones. It is not for us to cast stones at those who see fit to recognise the office, but for ourselves we prefer to abide by Jewish tradition.
>
> What can 'reconciliation' mean in this context? If it means that our group will engage in friendly dialogue with other groups in Anglo-Jewry and work together with them for the many aims we all have in common, this is already happening; and where it is not, the remedy lies with Rabbi Jakobovits and his colleagues.

FACE TO FACE WITH REFORM

A few days after his installation, Dr Jakobovits met with Rabbi Dow Marmur, editor of *Living Judaism*, the journal of the Reform Synagogues of Great Britain. During the course of a lively discussion, the Chief Rabbi was asked how he assessed the Reform movement:

On the one hand, Reform Judaism is for me, as an Orthodox Jew, an extreme tragedy, because it is organising a defection from Jewish law not merely for individuals – that has happened before in Jewish history – but for entire communities. It is, as I see it, an organised movement which legalises the breach of the Law. This is a source of unending grief to me, because I look upon every fellow Jew as being a party to the Covenant at Sinai with God to maintain the supremacy and the sovereignty of the Torah. Therefore, he who does not agree with the creedal and practical demands of the Torah is not helping to carry out our historic mission.

Moreover, Reform is, of course, causing an enormous amount of personal tragedy in family relationships whereby there is now the grave prospect of having two peoples that cannot marry with one another. This is, to my mind, a major disaster, the full dimensions of which can be assessed only in the course of time.

On the other hand, I am quite ready to admit that there are many Jews who, had it not been for the Reform movement, would have been far more complete casualties to Judaism and entirely lost to us. For them, the Reform movement has helped to stem the drift from Judaism. But I will go further than that: the Karaite heresy was in its day an exceedingly sad phenomenon, but it did also have many very important constructive features in that it triggered a vast outpouring of creative thinking in the traditionalist camp. We would not have had the contributions of a Saadya, an Ibn Ezra, a Maimonides without that challenge.

In the same way, the Reform movement could provide a challenge to traditional Jewish thought. Unfortunately, however, this has not yet happened. Instead of becoming creative and dynamic as a result of the dispute, we have involved ourselves in petty strife and in organisational quarrels. We must find a way to use the situation for constructive aims. The very fact that our beliefs are being challenged should force us to articulate these beliefs so that they become persuasive and attractive. So far, very little of that has taken place. Therefore, I will do my utmost to encourage such a development and to try to turn into a blessing that which otherwise, to my mind, is a blight on current Jewish history.

Seeing that you refer to Reform Judaism as 'a blight', compare it to 'the Karaite heresy', and regard it merely as a sparring partner for Orthodoxy, do you think that there is any theological common ground between us?
This question should be answered by you rather than by me. For my theological tenets are very clearly and distinctly defined. The question is: How far do you subscribe to them? As for me, I accept all the Thirteen Articles of Faith as formulated by Maimonides, including those about reward and punishment, messianism, physical resurrection, and the immutability of the Law of God as revealed on Sinai.

If we go through these articles one by one, we might find ourselves on common ground as far as the first few are concerned – about the concept of the Deity, the eternity of God, the creativity of God in relation to man, and, perhaps a little more vaguely, the inspiration of the Prophets. But, when it comes to practical definitions, I think that we would find ourselves poles apart. For me, every law of the Torah is divine, and thereby God becomes sovereign. It is He who dictates to me what is divine. You, on the other hand, use a system of discretion and discrimination in which you become the arbiter as to what is divine and what is not; you use God merely as a rubber-stamp to confirm your conscience. It is in this that our fundamental difference lies.

There can be, then, no question of a theological dialogue?
I don't think that you can have dialogues in theology. That is why we do not encourage theological dialogues with the Church. We can explain ourselves to each other, but if a dialogue is to mean 'give and take', it is not possible in theology, as I understand it. In the same way as I would not entertain any argument that questions the paternity of my father, I cannot concede the basis of any challenge implying that my beliefs may not be true.

There are Freudians who, when you challenge their views, dismiss you with the assertion that you need an analysis, and Orthodox Jews who analogously will tell you that you are an am ha'aretz when you argue with them. Do you, too, distrust the integrity and knowledge of those who disagree with you?
I don't distrust their integrity, but I have reason to distrust their knowledge. I believe that what divides us is education. I am convinced that had the bulk of the members of Reform congregations had the kind of intensive religious education I believe to be essential, they would share my views.

But there are Reform Jews who have had the type of education that you advocate!
There are exceptions to every rule. There are strictly Orthodox people who suddenly fall by the wayside. Knowledge in itself may not be a guarantee for the acceptance of traditional tenets, but without knowledge, Orthodox Judaism is not possible.

The way you speak of Progressive Judaism leaves one with a certain feeling that you are patronising us.
To patronise is the very last thing I wish to do, but it may be in the nature of things that if you yourself are so convinced of something, you want to convince others, too. That is bound to sound patronising, but I don't see how I can act differently and yet present my firm convictions.

You have spoken of bridges. What exactly do you have in mind?
First of all, we must establish personal contacts. That is the most important bridge. The next thing is to promote such joint efforts as do not involve controversy or religious divisions. And then there is an even more important factor: if, every time a little concession is made here or there, a little breach in the rigid walls that have separated us until now, there is going to be a public issue over it, we shall not be able to afford to take such steps. For, through such publicity, I am bound to arouse opposition and indignation in my own quarters. However,

if we can learn to work quietly and discreetly, we could not only build bridges, but walk on them, too.

We need a common-sense approach to things. I don't have to tell you that there are enough hotheads on all sides who are only waiting for a chance to pounce on us. I want to keep them at bay.

On the one hand, you repudiate Reform Judaism both theologically and halachically, but on the other hand, you wish to build bridges and introduce concessions?
Concessions of method – not of principle! I am not going to modify any law, for it is within neither my power nor my conviction to do so. When I speak of concessions, I have in mind steps that would break down the ostracism, the abuse and the impregnable wall of separation. One day, we may understand each other better and so come closer together. For this purpose, I am eager to encourage and promote the mood of reconciliation.

In May 1968, the Chief Rabbi delivered a lecture to students at the Leo Baeck College, which trains candidates for the Progressive ministry. Also present were members of the college staff and a number of Reform and Liberal rabbis; the president of the college, Rabbi Dr Werner Van der Zyl, was in the chair. Dr Jakobovits spoke on 'Halachah as the expression of Jewish thought and ethics' and later answered questions from the students. He let it be known that he had given the lecture 'despite certain obstacles' put in his way.

Later that year, he and Rabbi Louis Jacobs shared the platform at a Hampstead Synagogue meeting of the B'nai B'rith First Lodge, of which both were members. Rabbi Jakobovits was speaking on Jewish medical ethics. In his opening remarks, Dr Jacobs, who presided, said that anyone expecting 'the flashing of knives' would be disappointed, for the meeting was to be in accord with B'nai B'rith's motto of 'benevolence, brotherly love and harmony'. But while he subscribed to the first two, he added, he was 'not certain about the third'.

The Chief Rabbi recalled the biblical story of two brothers who, after many arguments, made a public reconciliation by shaking hands and kissing each other. The most important aspect, he said, was not the reconciliation but the fact that one of the brothers, Jacob, had successfully struggled on his own to overcome his ill feelings towards his opponent. Dr Jakobovits hoped that everyone could go through such struggles with themselves when ideas assailed them and become ultimately successful in carrying out the ideas behind the teachings of Judaism.

Rabbi Jacobs responded by asking if he should regard himself as the Esau of that biblical story. The Chief Rabbi replied that he had on purpose mentioned only Jacob, whose name was incorporated in both their names.

The verbal exchange took a more serious turn when a questioner from the floor expressed the hope that their appearance on the same platform would signal 'a new phase in communal unity'. Rabbi Jakobovits replied that the platform could be shared when the subject would not impinge on religious differences. Otherwise, they must go their separate ways.

Early in 1971, a controversy erupted both within Orthodox circles and between them and the Progressives over a proposal – supported by the Chief Rabbi – to amend Clause 43 of the Board of Deputies' constitution, aimed at according consultative status to the ecclesiastical heads of religious groups not under his jurisdiction or that of the Haham. Rabbi Jakobovits referred to the dispute in an article in the *Jewish Chronicle*:

'Initially there was broad agreement on granting the Progressive congregations their request to be consulted on religious matters concerning them, and the Haham and I acknowledged the president's assurance that the proposed change, formalising an existing practice, would in no way affect the Board's ecclesiastical authorities. But when the Progressives subsequently revealed that what they really intended was communal recognition for their 'religious authorities' rather than mere consultative status, the Orthodox opposition hardened. It became evident that communal unity would be gained at one end of the spectrum only by sacrificing it at the other. We then decided not to support any amendment, unless it proved its purpose by commanding the agreement of all parties.

The issue transcends the offices of the Haham and myself. By constitutionally acknowledging us as the Board's sole religious advisers, the Orthodox character of Anglo-Jewry is officially affirmed and maintained. With 90 per cent of all synagogue-affiliated Jews belonging to Orthodox congregations (according to the Board's own count), we continue to be, institutionally at least, an Orthodox community. I see no cause or reason for surrendering this traditional hegemony, unless representational functions affecting Orthodox interests were to be completely transferred from the Board to some new lay body acting for the traditional community only.

Hence, Progressive Jews are certainly entitled and welcome, through the deputies of their congregations, to play their full part in all the Board's affairs. They constitute an important section of the Jewish community, and they can and should make a valuable contribution to its welfare and interests. Their views may certainly be consulted on religious matters concerning them. But if they seek to exploit the Board as an instrument to destroy the Orthodox complexion of the organised community, they can hardly expect support from the Orthodox majority.'

It was eventually agreed to place before the Board a compromise amendment, which defined the powers of its ecclesiastical authorities. The new clause, while reaffirming that the Board would be guided on religious matters by its ecclesiastical authorities – the Chief Rabbi and the Haham – also established for the first time the right of the Progressive religious leaders to be consulted on all religious issues concerning them. The Chief Rabbi and the Haham had withheld their consent from the formula unless it was accompanied by a declaration that their ultimate authority in religious matters would remain binding. Their acceptance of the amendment, which was adopted by the Board in October 1971 (with schismatic consequences), followed an assurance from its honorary officers that in no circumstances would they make any announcement or take any action that was contrary to the advice offered by the Chief Rabbi or the Haham as the Board's ecclesiastical authorities.

Rabbi Jakobovits and Rabbi Gaon urged the Board's Orthodox group, led by Dr Bernard Homa, to accept the amendment both for the sake of communal unity and in the light of the assurances obtained from the honorary officers. Dr Homa, however, together with representatives of the Federation of Synagogues and of the Union of

Orthodox Hebrew Congregations (the Adath), refused to do so and resigned from the Board. Subsequent talks between the parties had mixed results: the Federation rejoined the Board in 1973, but to this day the Adath has declined to do so.

Orthodox and Progressive religious leaders agreed in March 1974 to establish a 'consultative committee on Jewish–Christian relations'. Its members were the Chief Rabbi; the Haham; Rabbi Dr Solomon Goldman, minister of the St John's Wood Synagogue; Rabbi Sidney Brichto, chairman of the rabbinic conference of the Union of Liberal and Progressive Synagogues; Harold Langdon, a vice-president of the Reform Synagogues of Great Britain (RSGB); and Alfred Woolf and Victor Lucas, president and joint-treasurer, respectively, of the United Synagogue. The convenor was Rabbi Hugo Gryn, chairman of the Council of Reform and Liberal Rabbis. Agreement to form the committee came at a meeting held at the Chief Rabbi's Office.

Months later, a joint Progressive and Orthodox approach to conversions was advocated by Rabbi Dow Marmur, vice-chairman of the Council of Reform and Liberal Rabbis and minister of the North-Western Reform Synagogue. Writing in the newsletter of the RSGB, he cited the opinion of two leading American rabbis – Dr Eliezer Berkovits (Orthodox) and Rabbi Theodore Friedman (a past president of the Conservative Rabbinical Assembly of America) – that non-Orthodox conversion procedures could be acceptable to Orthodox Jews since 'differences in interpretation of the halachah are not permitted to rupture the unity of the Jewish people'.

Rabbi Marmur declared: 'We appeal to the leaders of British Orthodoxy to heed this principle, lest the unity of our people be ruptured'. He added that, in view of the recent conciliatory and 'eminently sensible' comments about the separation of politics and religion made by the Chief Rabbi, 'is it not reasonable to expect Dr Jakobovits to take a leaf out of Dr Berkovits' book and give a lead to Anglo-Jewry?'

Commenting on Rabbi Marmur's suggestion, the Chief Rabbi's Office stated: 'At a time like this, far from accentuating and perpetuating our differences, we ought to be making a supreme effort to narrow and eliminate them. If only to find strength and comfort through unity, can we not now draw closer to our common heritage and repair the tragic rifts in our ranks whereby we cannot worship together, we cannot eat in each other's homes, and sometimes not even marry each other's children?

'Whether the arguments advanced by Dr Berkovits are tenable, and whether they bear the construction placed upon them, is open to debate. The Chief Rabbi has always favoured continued research and consultation on all matters concerned with conversion, including sociological and contemporary aspects, as well as historical and religious implications. He has been particularly concerned to avoid family tragedies resulting from the present divisions and the estrangement from traditional practices.'

The Reform and Liberal rabbinical authorities followed Rabbi Marmur's lead by approving a dialogue with their Orthodox counterparts, 'in an attempt to heal the sectarian schism within Anglo-Jewry, especially in the field of conversion, marriage and divorce'. Their initiative was positively received by Chief Rabbi Jakobovits.

Acting in his capacity as chairman of the Council of Reform and Liberal Rabbis, Rabbi Sidney Brichto invited the Chief Rabbi, the Haham and the acting Rav Rashi for 'immediate and joint discussions'. His move followed exploratory talks the Chief Rabbi had had some weeks earlier with him and representatives of the Reform movement, concerned mainly with matters of personal status in Jewish law and the effects of sectarian divisions on communal unity.

In attempting to formulate a joint approach to conversion, however, the Chief Rabbi faced considerable opposition from his own Beth Din to his talks with the Progressives. Dayan Morris Swift stated that, 'in my view, there can be no possibility of any discussions with the Reform on the question of conversion. The Reform and, in many ways, the Conservatives have rejected the divine revelation of the Torah, the Written and the Oral Law. The admission into the Jewish faith of a convert by religious procedure, even if it includes *tevilah* (ritual immersion), is not sufficient. The convert must accept completely that the Torah was divinely revealed.'

Dayan Swift was supported by the acting Rav Rashi, Dayan Michael Fisher. The Haham, on the other hand, supported the talks, which eventually came to nothing.

Asked in 1979 to join the Beth Din of the Union of Orthodox Hebrew Congregations and a group of roshei yeshivah and rabbis of independent Orthodox congregations in a blanket denunciation of Reform and Liberal Jews, the Chief Rabbi refused to comply. In a statement, he declared:

'I cannot exclude non-observant Jews from my concern and co-operation. This would gravely damage Orthodox interests, as well as communal unity and the endeavours based on it, notably in the support of Jewish education. My experience convinces me that what drives waverers to Reform is Orthodox intolerance and divisive agitation, rather than any 'legitimacy' allegedly conferred by sharing secular platforms with its leaders.

All Jews are authentic Jews, but neither Judaism nor rabbis can be authentic, in the Orthodox view, unless they embrace the totality of Jewish belief, law and tradition. Therefore, my own policies have consistently been guided by the principle I clearly spelled out in my installation address 12 years ago: 'I cannot join with Reformers in areas affected by dissent from our traditions, but I will work with them on matters on which we are united, such as Israel, Soviet Jewry, welfare and Jewish defence.' In this, I follow the example set by my father, my predecessors and even such a distinguished pioneer of 'Independent Orthodoxy' as Rabbi Ezra Munk, of Berlin, who collaborated with Dr Leo Baeck, the Reform leader of German Jewry. I believe that these policies are overwhelmingly understood and supported and have resulted in the intensified loyalty of our community to the values we cherish.'

Despite this declaration – and, indeed, because of it, depending on their individual viewpoints – the various Orthodox and Progressive authorities continued to tread an uneasy path in their relations with each other, prompting the Chief Rabbi to assert at a meeting of the Board of Deputies in 1984:

'In the face of the likely trends of polarisation followed by the renewed ascendancy of the most committed elements in the community, our communal statesmanship will have to be exercised to preserve the essential cohesion of Anglo-Jewry by preventing a form of confrontation in which a single section will make demands upon the rest of the community such as it cannot as a matter of conscience meet.

If the community is not to be riven by irreconcilable communal conflicts spilling over into areas at present at peace, we must uphold a form of tolerance which extends to recognising the fact of dissent, deems every Jew an infinitely precious brother whom we will always join in defending common Jewish interests, and encourages goodwill and solidarity, but which retains the right of traditional Jews refusing to accept, and rejecting, the claim that the beliefs of other segments are equally authentic.

To demand equal legitimacy for all in a predominantly traditional community would brand those making the demand as intolerant, and those ready to grant it as hypocritical – since fulfilment and non-fulfilment of religious conscience can never enjoy equal status.'

Some months later, Reform and Liberal leaders attacked new guidelines on intra-communal relations issued by the Chief Rabbi to his ministers. In a private memorandum, he had urged them 'not to allow their presence or their name to be used for promoting or sanctioning any activities which could be construed as according legitimacy to non-traditional Judaism'. He explained the reasons for his guidelines in an interview with the *Jewish Chronicle*:

'When I advised my colleagues not to engage in any activity that could be construed as conferring legitimacy on Reform Judaism, I did not tell them not to appear on a platform with Reform ministers. Indeed, I appear on such platforms, at JIA meetings and on numerous other occasions. Because of certain events which had taken place, what I did was intended to prevent their presence at, and participation in, Reform activities which might be interpreted by leaders of Reform as indicating that their activities enjoy the endorsement of the Orthodox community.

The moment this abuse of an Orthodox presence takes place and is constructed as giving the event a *hechsher*, a formal stamp of approval, and the organisers go on to claim that they do not represent just Progressive Judaism but the totality of Judaism, then I have to tell my colleagues that they are being exploited, that their presence is being misrepresented and, therefore, 'be careful'. But I have never said they should not appear together on a platform where no such misconstruction can take place.

I believe the religious stability of the community will determine the future of the community more than our unity. Unity is a precious thing, an important thing. But even more important than a façade of unity where none exists is that we should convey to our children, and our children's children, loyalties and allegiances, beliefs and practices, which are the sole *raison d'être* of Jewish existence. I cannot compromise on that.

We had reached a gentleman's agreement with the Progressives, which has worked splendidly over these nearly 18 years that I have been in office, whereby it was understood that, while I would make statements on behalf of the Jewish community where they represented a consensus of opinion, if these statements were on Judaism I would not look for a consensus.

On Judaism, I am the spokesman not for the majority (even if I speak of Sabbath observance, I recognise that I do not speak for the majority), but I speak for authentic Judaism as I see it. It has always been understood that this would

53. The Chief Rabbi at an intra-communal gathering with (left to right) Eric Moonman, MP, Professor Emil Fackenheim, Greville Janner, QC, MP, and Rabbi Sidney Brichto.

54. Watched by Rabbi Hugo Gryn (centre), Sir Sigmund Sternberg presents the Chief Rabbi with a 'Peace Through Dialogue' award for his contribution to inter-faith co-operation.

55. Chief Rabbi Jakobovits welcomes the Queen to the 1971 centenary celebrations of the United Synagogue. With them are Board of Deputies president Michael Fidler, MP, and US president Sir Isaac Wolfson.

56. Accompanied by his wife, Chief Rabbi Sir Immanuel Jakobovits displays the insignia of his knighthood conferred in the 1981 Queen's Birthday Honours.

57 and 58. With Lady Jakobovits after receiving the freedom of the City of London in 1983; and with chairman Norman Tebbit, MP, at the 1991 'Men of the Year' awards.

59. In the Chinese Room at Buckingham Palace with the Duke of Edinburgh following the 1991 award of the Templeton Prize for Progress in Religion.

60. In the Moses Room of the House of Lords on 9 February 1988, before being introduced by Baron Mishcon of Lambeth (left) and Baron Young of Graffham, the Secretary of State for Trade and Industry.

61. Guest speaker Margaret Thatcher, MP, with Lord and Lady Jakobovits and Chief Rabbi-elect Dr Jonathan Sacks at a Jewish Educational Development Trust dinner in March 1991 to mark the Chief Rabbi's retirement.

62 and 63. Chief Rabbi Jakobovits with Israeli Chief Rabbi Shlomo Goren following the inauguration of the Immanuel Jakobovits Chair in Jewish Law at Bar-Ilan University, Ramat Gan, in 1974; and in the company of fellow recipient Mikhail Gorbachev (seated), Lord Jakobovits receives the honorary degree of Doctor of Philosophy at a ceremony at Bar-Ilan in 1992.

not compromise my ability to be a spokesman in the tradition of the Chief Rabbinate of this country. I think that if we were to continue with this mutual understanding, we should concentrate, as I have pleaded throughout my incumbency, on our constructive work, putting our own houses in order, strengthening our education and our synagogues, without abusing one another, without throwing mud at one another.

But the community should know that if there is any threat of stirring up communal disunity beyond the truly internal religious confines, such a threat comes solely from the Progressives. They have recently published in the national press articles and letters grossly offensive to the Orthodox community; some of their leaders have called for breaking up such co-operation as has for years existed; and in utter disregard for the well-being and reputation of Anglo-Jewry, they now warn that they may carry the battle into the public arena and into areas on which we have been, and continue to be, united as Jews.

We have avoided a collision for nearly 18 years. I don't say we have lived happily together. I was never happy about the divisions between us. But we have had a *modus vivendi*, a working relationship. We didn't abuse one another. I never went out of my way to denounce those who did not subscribe to my innermost beliefs.

If, occasionally, I have to tell my congregants or my colleagues that they should not do anything which will blur the distinctions, then I am only doing my duties as a rabbi, which means teacher. If the Progressives choose to disagree, then we have to agree to disagree, as we have done in the past. But if they are to take every assertion of Orthodox belief which conflicts with their teaching as a *casus belli*, then I am afraid there is bound to be friction leading to a great deal of communal heartbreak.'

EIGHT-YEAR SECRET UNVEILED

A closed-door 'liaison committee' of prominent Orthodox and Progressive Jews this week decided to shed an eight-year-old veil of secrecy in a bid to encourage 'respect and tolerance' across doctrinal divides. A co-founder of the group – Rabbi Maurice Unterman, rabbi emeritus of the Marble Arch (United) Synagogue – said that wider communication was essential. 'Human beings who don't speak will always quarrel,' he declared. 'There is too much collective position-taking in Anglo-Jewry, and not enough respect, sympathy and communication among individuals.'

The committee, which also includes prominent members of the Masorti, Reform and Liberal movements, was set up with the aim of 'agreeing to disagree amicably' on differences of doctrine, while trying to work for compromise solutions to other problems. 'We are present in individual, not organisational, capacities,' said Jonathan Lew, the United Synagogue's chief executive. 'What has made the arrangement work is the honesty and trust that exist among all of us.'

The main focus of the group – which began in 1985 as an informal response to a series of perceived attacks by a Progressive rabbi on the then Chief Rabbi, Sir

Immanuel Jakobovits [alluded to in the above interview] – has been to take the 'personal sting' out of relations between the various religious groups, one member said. 'We've had successes, partial successes, and failures', said Rabbi Tony Bayfield, the chief executive-designate of the Reform movement. 'But the attempt has always been to address the real issues without posturing.'

The nine-member group, whose other founder was Liberal Rabbi John Rayner, is chaired by Lionel Swift, QC, of the United Synagogue, and also includes Progressive Rabbis Hugo Gryn and Charles Middleburgh; Reform movement executive director Raymond Goldman; former Union of Liberal and Progressive Synagogues chairman David Lipman; and Mrs Eleanor Lind, of the New London (Masorti) Synagogue.

Jewish Chronicle, *19 March 1993*

Reflecting, in 1992 – a year after his retirement – on the vicissitudes of his Chief Rabbinate, Lord Jakobovits wrote of his efforts to close the gaps within Anglo-Jewry:

'I realise all too painfully that I had my great disappointments and setbacks. But my own assessment of crisis and failure does not necessarily correspond to public or press perceptions. For instance, I deeply regretted my inability to move the community to greater self-esteem, away from its proneness to self-denigration. How much more could be achieved, and how many more talented younger people could be recruited to leadership, if Anglo-Jewry were more confident in its future and took greater pride in its enormous achievements, with less inclination to highlight petty squabbles and passing scandals?

I was also unsuccessful in two particular sets of negotiations I initiated. The first was conducted and initially concluded while I was still in New York – with Sir Isaac Wolfson, then president of the United Synagogue, and Rabbi Dr Eliezer Kirzner, the newly appointed Rav Rashi of the Federation of Synagogues. The signed agreement provided for a working arrangement with the Chief Rabbi and the London Beth Din to obviate rivalry and duplication; unfortunately, petty interests invalidated the accord. I was never unduly concerned with whether there were one, two or three kosher stamps on our products, except that it would involve an enormous extra cost to the community. The Federation could have contributed something invaluable to the community had they chosen fields like schools, adult education or leadership training. But by providing services adequately taken care of without them, they proved a vociferous and expensive anachronism.

Also futile was an effort to secure some real Jewish unity when I convened, and engaged in, intensive parleys with Progressive leaders, seeking an agreement on marriage, divorce and conversion to which all sections could subscribe. Such an agreement would have removed the calamitous rift whereby members of one community could not marry those of another, and whereby persons deemed non-Jewish by some were accepted as Jews by others. This sad rupture distressed me endlessly.

Another objective which eluded me was to help eliminate, or reduce, the polarisation of our people into ever-more extremist groups, widening the gap between the religious and the secular, the Orthodox and the 'ultra-Orthodox', and even the political divide. The trend is global, and less pronounced in Britain, with its more mellow tradition, than in Israel and America. But for me, committed as I am by nurture and conviction to *Torah im derech eretz,* in a setting of tolerance and moderation without sacrifice of principle, the process was, and remains, profoundly disturbing.

I was far less ruffled by the several scurrilous campaigns against me, some on an international scale and including the picketing or cancellation of lectures I was to deliver abroad, following statements on Israel I had made – or, more often, falsely attributed to me by those who did not want my views aired. There were occasions when even our Board of Deputies publicly dissociated itself from my views – as if I had ever claimed to speak in its name. I do not relish public controversies, but I must be at peace with my conscience, and as a spiritual leader I cannot suppress it. On Israel, my foremost commitment has always been to peace with security rather than territory with violence, and to appreciate Arab as well as Jewish fears and aspirations. I have never had any sympathy for the political radicalism so prevalent among Orthodoxy under American influence *à la* Kahane, Gush Emunim or even Lubavitch. Israel's recent election seems to vindicate me as less out of step with opinion there than my detractors claimed or would have wished.

On communal and public policies, I have always tried to be guided by my sainted father's motto: 'One enemy is too many, a hundred friends are too few.' My efforts to cultivate friendships have, I believe, proved rewarding to the community and to the Jewish people no less than to me. I have never yielded to the temptation to resort to mere gimmicks. In public utterances, I avoided expressing views with which all would agree – the convinced need no persuasion from anyone. After all, the task of a rabbi is to speak for Judaism and not necessarily for Jews.'

Five years later, reverting to his efforts to build bridges of understanding and co-operation, Lord Jakobovits admitted that he had never supported the view that 'the unity theme will determine the future strength of the Orthodoxy community – or, indeed, of any part of the Jewish people'. He added:

'Our capacity to survive as Jews will not depend on whether we sit round the same table, or publicly debate our differences, or pursue a search for common ideals where none exist. Promoting goodwill within the community – however desirable – was never my top priority. I had no illusions that, simply by talking with the dissidents, we would heal the rift of their defection; or save a single Jew from the prospect of marrying out; or make our youth more observant, our university students more committed to Jewish values, and our professionals more Jewish in the practice of their vocation.

For those objectives we need not tolerance but learning and commitment. I was, and remain, convinced that the key to the religious stability and growth of Anglo-Jewry lies in intensive Jewish education, not in debating chambers and declarations of goodwill. Indeed, we are now beginning to reap the benefits of greatly expanded and intensified Jewish day-schools, into which such enormous efforts have been invested over the past 20 years.

The obsession with communal unity is a peculiarly Anglo-Jewish trait. It does not feature in such a form among American or European Jews – and certainly not in Israel. It is time we shifted our concern from form to substance: how to live as fuller and better Jews, rather than how to gloss over differences and proclaim a unity which turns out to be a mirage.'

CHAPTER SIXTEEN

Success and Succession

'THIS REMARKABLE MAN'

Sir Immanuel Jakobovits was presented with a *festschrift* – a collection of essays – at a celebration at Jews' College last week to mark his 20 years as Chief Rabbi. Communal dignitaries and friends praised 'this remarkable man', as Sir Zelman Cowan – the provost of Oriel College, Oxford, and former Governor-General of Australia – called him. The Chief Rabbi was 'a man of deeply civilised mind and feeling, unswerving integrity and, above all, moving faith and exemplary courage', Sir Zelman said.

The venue was significant, for the Chief Rabbi helped to secure a future for the college, of which he is president, when it faced desperate uncertainty a few years ago. Also housed in the college complex is the office of the Jewish Educational Development Trust, set up on Sir Immanuel's prompting 15 years ago.

'Jewish education has flourished during the past 20 years, due largely to his determined and unceasing effort,' said United Synagogue president Victor Lucas. Another achievement of the Chief Rabbi was that 'harmony within Anglo-Jewry, despite one or two hiccups here and there, has been preserved … and sustained'.

Sir Immanuel, who was 66 on Sunday, said he was grateful that he had experienced none of the symptoms of rabbinical burn-out so far. He gave no hints about his retirement, due in four years' time.

Speakers paid tribute to Lady Jakobovits' communal efforts. There was laughter when Rabbi Jonathan Sacks turned to her and suggested that 'when Sir Immanuel retires', she should be the next Chief Rabbi.

Jewish Chronicle, *13 February 1987*

The first move in the search for a new Chief Rabbi for British Jewry was made in October 1988, when the United Synagogue council set in motion the complex election machinery. Sidney Frosh, newly elected president of the US and of the Chief Rabbinate Council, said: 'We are starting with an empty piece of paper. We have no particular candidate in mind.' Asked what kind of person he would be looking for, he replied: 'He has to be a man of learning and of stature, and a man for this day.'

Three former presidents of the United Synagogue, as well as Mr Frosh, were among the 36 men nominated to choose the next Chief Rabbi. They were George Gee and Victor Lucas, who were among the 15 US representatives on the Chief Rabbinate Conference committee, and Salmond Levin, president of the National Council of Shechitah Boards.

On the advice of its rabbis, the Federation of Synagogues pulled out of the election. 'The Federation wishes to keep its independence and could not work under a constitution where it would have to accept the authority of the Chief Rabbi,' its president, Arnold Cohen, declared.

Chief Rabbi Jakobovits, meanwhile, called for his successor to be a 'man who is in tune with the times'. Speaking on Greater London Radio's 'Jewish World', he said: 'I am not looking for a repeat performance of my 22 years. Every age needs its own unique response.' He avoided naming names, but laid down some guidelines for his successor. They included giving priority to Jewish education, strengthening the bonds between Israel and the Diaspora, and searching for issues that united the Jewish people, transcending 'what are, alas, and to our bitter distress, major religious divisions'.

A STEP CLOSER

Rabbi Dr Jonathan Sacks, 41, principal of Jews' College, London, and rabbi of the Marble Arch Synagogue, last night moved a step closer to succeeding Lord Jakobovits as Britain's Chief Rabbi. A committee appointed by the Chief Rabbinate Conference to consider a successor unanimously endorsed the recommendation of its chairman, Sidney Frosh, president of the United Synagogue.

Mr Frosh had proposed that Rabbi Sacks' name be placed before the 200 members of the Chief Rabbinate Conference on 1 April for a 'call' to be made to him to take up the role. It would be unprecedented if the recommendation were overturned.

A statement issued last night by the Chief Rabbinate Council quoted Rabbi Sacks as saying he would be honoured to accept the 'call' and the high responsibilities of leadership that went with it. It said that Rabbi Sacks, who has been chosen to deliver this year's Reith lectures, had indicated that he would wish to take up office in September next year. Mr Frosh said: 'Rabbi Sacks has a great intellect. He is one of the young group of modern philosophers in the Jewish community.'

Rabbi Sacks was born in Britain and educated at Gonville and Caius College, Cambridge, and New College, Oxford.

Daily Telegraph, *26 February 1990*

Days later, Rabbi Sacks, selected to be the next Chief Rabbi, announced that he would spend a year of study in Israel before taking up office in September 1991. 'I want to come to the position having immersed myself in the atmosphere of Torah learning,' he said.

In an official statement, the selection committee, headed by Mr Frosh, said that Dr Sacks had asked to take up the appointment in September 1991 in order to disengage himself from commitments. It also praised Lord Jakobovits, who had agreed to waive his right to retire in February 1991.

Lord Jakobovits, in turn, paid tribute to his successor after Rabbi Sacks' appointment was approved by the 200-member Chief Rabbinate Conference. 'I greet his election with particular delight,' said Lord Jakobovits, who added that Dr Sacks' record of leadership and scholarship provided 'every promise of a richly blessed incumbency'.

OF JAKOBOVITES AND THATCHERITES

In her first formal speaking engagement since resigning three months earlier, former Prime Minister Margaret Thatcher told a JEDT fund-raising dinner in February 1991 – held to mark Lord Jakobovits' impending retirement – that 'no other Chief Rabbi has had so profound an effect on the life of this nation'. She continued:

'The Office of the Chief Rabbi is by British standards a relatively recent one, dating back only to the mid-nineteenth century. But among the holders of that office there have been some formidable figures. No more than the office of Prime Minister does that of Chief Rabbi suit characters of the wilting kind. Yet amid this pantheon, no one will easily challenge the unique position which Lord Jakobovits has secured during his 24 years of office.

I can certainly let his friends here tonight into one of the nation's worst-kept secrets – that he has had, through his thinking and writing, a deep effect on me, though whether this makes me a Jakobovite or him a Thatcherite I would not like to say.

Chief Rabbis retire nowadays at 70, though Lord Jakobovits is standing in for his successor for a month or two. I know that he has just celebrated his seventieth birthday, and that he and Lady Jakobovits have spent it in the company of his six children and a representative sample of his 36 grandchildren. As one grandparent to another, may I wish you a belated but affectionate birthday greeting.

Many of us know, full well, that it is private life which makes public life tolerable – above all, the private life of our family. Lord Jakobovits has never made a secret of how much he owes to Amélie. Theirs has been that kind of partnership in which the qualities of each complement the other, the personality of each enhances the other, and the love of each strengthens the other.

Not, of course, that such a life is *always* easy. I believe, Lady Jakobovits, that you once remarked that 'a girl should always think twice before marrying a rabbi'. I am glad not to have heard Denis' advice on those minded to marry politicians.

As Chief Rabbi, Lord Jakobovits leaves to his already distinguished successor, Rabbi Jonathan Sacks, a Jewish community in Britain whose standing and confidence have never been higher. The marks of Lord Jakobovits' leadership have been an unbending commitment to principle, a refusal to seek easy popularity at the expense of integrity, and a fearless statement of values symbolised not just in the life of the Jewish people but of lasting relevance and general application to the modern world.

Lord Jakobovits and I first met when I was Secretary of State for Education. He impressed me with a remark which I shall long remember. 'You are really the Minister of Defence', he told me. And he meant, of course, that it is ultimately what is taught and learned at school which keeps the nation whole and strong. This has always had a particular significance to Jews, who are, as the Chief Rabbi has put it, 'a tiny faith-community, counting only some one dozen million people altogether, widely dispersed throughout the world, for whom education has become the principal instrument of national defence. Where others relied on prudent statecraft and military skill to preserve their integrity, Jews relied mainly on learning as the supreme condition for survival.'

Lord Jakobovits' actions have spoken in this regard even more eloquently than his sermons. As founder and president of the Jewish Educational Development Trust, he has helped inspire an unprecedented increase and improvement in Jewish education here. To provide a distinctively Jewish education for a higher percentage of Jewish children, the Trust has continued to build, to extend and to modernise schools, making grants to some to help with essential work or expand Jewish studies; stepping in to ensure the viability of others; providing teacher-training scholarships. Last year saw the opening of Immanuel College in Bushey, a worthy tribute to the Jewish community's generosity, to the work of many here tonight, and to the Chief Rabbi's determination.

The great tradition of Jewish charitable concern in Britain reaches well back into the nineteenth century with the foundation of Jewish charitable schools, benevolent and friendly societies, relief work, help for new immigrants, and many other activities as well. But the Chief Rabbi has helped write an inspiring further chapter in that story of noble achievement.

Lord Jakobovits has never lost sight of the fact that what makes a man, a family, a community or a nation are the values by which they live. For values not only inspire policies: they inspire people. The story of the Jewish community's success in providing so many of this country's most brilliant talents and dynamic leaders in our professions, business and charitable service bears witness to what motivated people can achieve.

Lord Jakobovits has spoken movingly of how Jewish families struggled to give their children the best possible education; how they discouraged idleness and rooted out crime; how they emphasised duties as well as rights; how they respected hard and honest work, thrift and moral probity. Nor are these just Jewish values – though the Jewish community has practised them in an exemplary manner. And they are not just Victorian values – though I wish that those who criticise our Victorian predecessors for their undoubted failures were able or willing to emulate their achievements. These are, in truth, the values which are part of that legacy of Judaeo–Christian tradition which underpins the free society and without which so much of what we treasure would perish.

One of the most arrogant claims of Marxism was to know the future course of history. And now it is the Marxists – not us – who are being swept up into its famous dustbin. A salutary lesson, you may think, to politicians who aspire to prophesy. But *my* confidence about the future – the future of the Jewish people and the British people, and of the Jewish faith and the Christian faith – is of a different kind. Fallen, man definitely is. Foolish, he often is. Evil, he can be. But nourished on truth and taught by freedom, ours and future generations have now a fairer prospect than ever before to create a better world.

You, Lord Jakobovits, are one of those few who, in every generation, speak out for enduring truths and traditional beliefs; who first are criticised, mocked and even slandered; and who, then, as the years go by, are ever-more intently heard, admired and ultimately followed. Leadership of any kind, in any age, is a lonely virtue. But today you are not alone. For among those of all faiths and of none, you have secured this nation's esteem, affection and respect.'

Responding to Mrs Thatcher's tribute, the Chief Rabbi declared:

'Were I to emulate the biblical Preacher of old, I would say with him: 'Better is the end of the matter than its beginning.' Indeed, I feel very much better today than at my installation 24 years ago. The risks were greater then. Now, at worst, they can give me six months' notice to quit. As I survey my great good fortune, the words that leap to my lips are those of the Psalmist: 'How can I return unto the Lord all the kindnesses He has bestowed upon me?' How few rabbis or spiritual leaders, past or present, could exclaim this as passionately and as unreservedly as I can!

If we look back in our chequered history, Moses, traditionally our first and greatest rabbi, despaired of his community and cried to the Lord: 'What shall I do unto this people? They seem about to stone me.' Did the Hebrew prophets fare any better? Were they not denounced and persecuted by kings and potentates, hunted by the powerful and the wealthy? Over 100 years ago, the famous Rabbi Israel Salant, founder of the moralist Mussar movement, was wont to say: 'A rabbi whom they don't want to drive out of town isn't a rabbi, and a rabbi whom they actually drive out isn't a man.' My more immediate predecessors were no better off. Some of you will remember the bitter quarrel between Chief Rabbi Hertz and his president of the United Synagogue, Sir Robert Waley Cohen, who flagrantly challenged Hertz's support of Zionism. More recently, Chief Rabbi Brodie was locked in a painful communal conflict which caused him and his wife so much distress.

Yet, here am I, far beyond my deserts, saying with the Psalmist: 'The lots of my fortunes have fallen in pleasant places.' Especially in the present illustrious company, I can literally say, in the words of the Psalmist in an outpouring of gratitude to my Maker: '... who raises up the lowly out of the dust, Who lifts up the needy from the dunghill.' Were it not for His Divine protection, I should have been but another speck of dust on the dunghills of Auschwitz or Belsen, along with six million of my European brothers and sisters. But by the willing hospitality of this country and, during my Chief Rabbinate, by the favour of our special guest, I was uplifted: '... to be seated among princes, among the noblemen of his country', as the next verse in the psalm has it.

May I say that we have here this evening princes of our national and communal leadership, princes of scholarship, princes of industry, and princes of the professions.

In the almost infinite catalogue of my indebtedness to those who have helped make me what I am, there stand out, of course, first and supreme, my sainted parents. Although my revered father passed away some 44 years ago, he is still with me and instructs me daily, as I seek to model myself by his teachings. Every day I remember his motto, which he constantly repeated to me: 'One enemy is too many, a hundred friends are too few.' Tonight I reap the harvest of this legacy.

But my parents fashioned only one half of me; the other half is Amélie. Some call her 'Lady J'; to me she is 'Lady Joy' – and a lot else besides. You have no idea how many friends I would not have had, how many sick people I would never have visited, how many of my speeches and sermons would have been unintelligible and far too long, and how much commonsense I would have lacked, without her inspiration, her constant encouragement, sometimes her nagging to do better, and certainly her extraordinary example of boundless energy, cheerfulness and devoutness, in public as well as in private, in the kitchen as in royal palaces, and in her love of people as in the fervour of her daily prayers.

We are also uniquely blessed with children and grandchildren who exemplify everything we stand for, dedicating their all to the service of God and man – professionally, communally and domestically.

I am enormously proud of my rabbinical colleagues. I have been exceptionally privileged to preside over a Beth Din of dayanim, led by Dayan Chanoch Ehrentreu, whose learning and authority are respected the world over as the leading Jewish religious court in the Diaspora.

Among the many hundreds of my colleagues here, in Europe and in the Commonwealth, as well as elsewhere in the Jewish world, with whom I have worked closely, I must single out two who have helped me enormously and with whom I join in congregational prayer every morning: my own rabbi of the St John's Wood Synagogue and seated every day right next to me, Rabbi Maurice Unterman, whose great gifts of speech and pen he has so freely placed at my disposal; and, of course, I greet with special fondness Rabbi Jonathan Sacks, my designated successor, who has recently so greatly enriched the British literary scene with his widely acclaimed Reith lectures. No one can pray with greater fervour for his success than I, for whatever he builds will consolidate the foundations laid in earlier generations of the high office I am bequeathing to him.

A debt I discharge with particular delight is owed to my office staff. Their efficiency, loyalty and even cheerfulness under often trying conditions were truly invaluable, as well as indispensable, to me.

Among leading laymen, no rabbi could ever wish for better friends and more agreeable partners. How much I rejoice this evening in the company of specially cherished associates co-sponsoring this dinner, both of them by virtue of their enthusiastic involvement in the promotion of Jewish education, so close to my heart, and both responsible now for helping to raise thousands of our precious children as proud and knowledgeable Jews. I refer to Michael Phillips, chairman of the Jewish Educational Development Trust, which has transformed the educational landscape of our community; and to Sidney Frosh, president of the United Synagogue, now directly responsible for the Jewish training of more infants, children, students, adults and teachers than any other organisation in the community. Also precious beyond words are the wonderful friendship and invaluable support of Henry Knobil, chairman of Immanuel College, so graciously named in my honour.

To them, and indeed many other supporters, I owe whatever made my 24-year ministry in your midst really worthwhile.

And now, our dear and distinguished guest of honour, Mrs Margaret Thatcher, I come to the most joyful and the most difficult words of my career.

I was delighted to read the White House announcement that you are to be accorded the highest civil order, the Medal of Freedom, as a token of esteem for your world leadership. If we had the right to confer honours, we would reach way back in history to King Solomon, who established the highest honour for those who make a special mark in life, and we would say to you, Margaret Thatcher: 'Woman of Valour, whose worth is far above rubies', to quote the Book of Proverbs. Every verse in that marvellous chapter can be applied to your leadership, not least the words: 'Many daughters have done valiantly, but you excel them all.'

How can words ever match my personal debt? Let me merely allude to it by bracketing you together with my parents. For next to them, in a sense, I owe you my name, which you have changed twice, though not without some loss. When I was knighted, I lost my doctorate; worse still, I lost my Mrs. And when I was elevated to the peerage, I even lost my first name.

Having travelled in three continents since your resignation, I can testify that no name is more universally hailed and respected than yours. Long after the erratic gyrations in the ups and downs of economic indicators and political popularity polls will be forgotten, your achievement will be saluted in history not just as the longest-serving British Prime Minister this century, but as having transformed the ethos of this country, and, by dint of your vision and unyielding resolution, as having contributed, I believe, more than anyone else outside Eastern Europe to the collapse of Communism, perhaps the most momentous single event this century.

We know that your unrivalled statesmanship will continue to be in demand the world over, especially in tumultuous times like ours, when steady hands and steadfast minds alone can guide us to the safe haven of a better world – a world in which your name will always be honoured. And by none more so than our community and our people.

We live in brittle times, when history itself is no longer the record of the truth, but often manipulated to impose present ideologies on past facts. In no part of the fabric of history have these revisionists sought to wreak greater havoc and more cruel damage than in the efforts to expunge the Holocaust from history books and instruction. As I conclude a jubilee of years in my own little encounter with the makers of history, I am most anxious that teaching about the Holocaust will feature in the national curriculum of our schools. In these grim days of renewed murderous attempts to inflict tyranny and brutal oppression on an entire region and beyond, nothing can serve as a more assured deterrent than the certainty that history will never betray the innocent, and that the perpetrators of evil will be pursued to the ends of the earth and the end of time.

Had the likes of Pol Pot and Idi Amin been apprehended and brought to justice for their monstrous crimes, we might not now have had to invest so much blood and treasure in the defeat of Saddam Hussein. No one will have contributed more to this prospect that evil and appeasement will never again be allowed to prevail than our very special guest. Had her determined resistance to appeasement governed the 1930s, we might have been spared the horrors and the tens of millions of victims of the Second World War.

More broadly, no section of society will do more to assure the triumph of truth, decency and moral progress than those raised and steeped in immutable values which transcend the vagaries of time, fulfilling the promise of Isaiah: 'And all your children will be learned of the Lord, and great will be the peace of your children.' To this vision we rededicate ourselves tonight, and for this vision we acclaim you, Mrs Margaret Thatcher, as we laud the help of all our friends, who tonight and every night will cause the night to pass until, quoting Isaiah again: 'Your light will break forth like the morning, and your healing will sprout forth speedily.'

PLANTING SEEDS FOR THE FUTURE

An era is drawing to a close. On Sunday, Rabbi Immanuel Jakobovits will end nearly a quarter-century as British Jewry's most prominent religious leader, and Dr Jonathan Sacks will assume the office of Chief Rabbi. When Lord Jakobovits assumed office, he inherited deep divisions within mainstream Orthodoxy. He can rightly claim to have helped narrow that rift; to have helped the religious centre to hold; and, despite an overall shrinkage of the identifying Jewish community, to have planted seeds for the future through his unflagging commitment to Jewish education. At least as important, he has exercised the prerogative – indeed, the duty – of a Chief Rabbi in raising his voice on issues of compelling social, and moral, concern. If he has erred on occasion – and what leader worthy of the title, during 24 years at the centre of influence, decision and controversy, would not have? – it is perhaps in a tendency to overstep the blurry boundary between moral and temporal power; between the political and the partisan. Far better this, however, than to have made of his pulpit an ivory tower, or to have shied away from issues because they were not explicitly 'Jewish', much less strictly Judaic. His successor inherits new challenges. Although he will be called upon to turn his own erudition and leadership skills to many of the same national and international issues as Lord Jakobovits, the communal imperatives have changed. Far more pressing than the halachic debate that gripped United Synagogue Orthodoxy in the 1960s is the divide between it and the more strictly Orthodox on the one hand, and the degree to which increasing numbers of Jews, especially the young and the secular, feel little or no sense of communal involvement, on the other. Chief Rabbi Sacks may be tested less by what he says about the inner city, Israeli politics, or even the inherited question of Paula Cohen's conversion, than about the recent stain of mob intimidation in Stamford Hill. Among the young or secular, he will be challenged less by the tendency to marry out than to opt out altogether. He will have to listen as often as preach, and to apply his Orthodox Judaism to unorthodox questions. It is a tall order – but one to which Rabbi Sacks' background and talents seem especially well suited, as were Lord Jakobovits' to the challenges he inherited 24 years ago.

Leading article, Jewish Chronicle, *30 August 1991*

'LET US BE STRONG TOGETHER'

Rabbi Sacks was inducted into office as the sixth Chief Rabbi of the United Hebrew Congregations of the Commonwealth at a service at the St John's Wood Synagogue, London, on 1 September 1991, before an invited congregation of 1,300 guests. In his valedictory sermon, Lord Jakobovits urged his successor to resist pressure to bend 'in matters of principle and conviction' and called on him to 'assert your freedom of action and of speech'. He went on:

'Be strong, be strong, and let us be strong together.' This call reverberates with emotion within our synagogues everywhere whenever we conclude the reading of one of the Five Books of Moses. The words are a reference to the first installation charge in history when Moses told Joshua, his successor, *chazak ve'ematz* – 'Be strong and of good courage'. It was both the end and the beginning of a new era. For me, too, this is a double event.

At this momentous hour in my life, when I conclude twenty-four and a half years in the highest office this community or, indeed, any community can confer, and inaugurate the new epoch by installing my successor, my heart is filled to overflowing with the three essential constituents of prayer:

First, *shevach* – praise to the Almighty for the infinite blessings of life, for myself and my family, and for His divine deliverance from all undue trouble and sorrow; second, *hoda'ya* – thanksgiving for a wonderful community which has given me loyalty, affection and opportunities enjoyed by few other rabbis; and third, *bakasha* – 'petition', pleading that my distinguished successor, too, may enjoy these blessings at least in equal measure; that he likewise may in due course look back without regrets, echoing the words recorded in the Yom Kippur machzor on the High Priest emerging safely from his supreme service in the Temple on the holiest day of the year: 'And the High Priest would make a feast for his friends, as he entered in peace and came out in peace, without mishap', after making atonement for his people in the Holy of Holies.

As I fleetingly reflect on the experiences of my four illustrious predecessors over the past century and a half, I have particular cause to render thanks. For they faced greater internal strife and tribulations than I ever had to endure. Under Dr Hertz, lasting communal splits occurred with the foundation of the Adath and, at the opposite pole, of the Liberal congregations. Moreover, he was locked in bitter conflicts with his lay leaders, when, in a letter to *The Times*, he denounced their opposition to the Balfour Declaration, and later, when the president of the United Synagogue countermanded the Chief Rabbi's instructions to his ministers to protest against the British White Paper on Palestine. His successor, Rabbi Israel Brodie, faced a major rebellion which threatened to break up his office as well as the cohesion of the community altogether.

As this year happens to be the 100th anniversary of the installation of Chief Rabbi Hermann Adler, it is appropriate to recall that already the Adlers witnessed major challenges to communal unity, with the break away to the Right of the Federation and the Machzike Hadath, and of the Reform to the Left. By comparison, I can say of myself that I went in and I went out without hurt, and I have reason to turn this day into a feast, a yomtov of very special thanksgiving.

The thanksgiving is increased by a particular joy. During this final year in office, concluding today, two new Jewish day-schools have been approved, while another opened earlier this year, already operating with such singular success. I refer to Immanuel College, so magnanimously named in my honour. These three schools will almost exactly complete the educational development programme for new schools announced some 20 years ago. Much remains to be done, but for much we have reason to rejoice and be profoundly thankful.

As I now address you for the last time as 'my community', I want you to share these feelings with me. Together, we have gone through some of the most convulsive times in history – the Six-Day War, with the exultant return of Jerusalem undivided to Jewish sovereignty; the Yom Kippur War and the thrilling exodus of Soviet and Ethiopian Jews to Israel; the collapse of Communism; the reunification of Germany; and the Gulf War – all events of cataclysmic proportions from which we have emerged, by the grace of God, as a stronger community, a better educated community, a more committed community than has ever inhabited these shores, since Jews resettled here in 1656.

I now turn with affection to my dear and revered successor. If you were to pose the questions, 'How can I, as the newly installed Chief Rabbi, triumph over the lurking dangers, pitfalls and challenges, how can I assert myself to leave the distinctive mark of my leadership upon this great community, and how can I be certain that I will enter *b'li pega*, without mishap, and emerge without mishap, to celebrate a yomtov at the end of my career?', then the two words *chazak ve'ematz*, addressed to Joshua, say it all: 'Be strong and of good courage.'

Our sages in the Talmud interpreted this phrase to have two distinct meanings: *chazak batorah ve'ematz bema'asim tovim*, 'Be strong in Torah, and courageous in good deeds.' In your new exalted office, your first task will be to preserve the Torah, to keep intact our traditions, to interpret Jewish teachings as you find and understand them. *Chazak* – for this 'be strong!' If you will sometimes encounter enormous pressures, to bend a little here, to modify there; if some will seek to subject you to their dictates, telling you what you may say and what you may do, then 'be strong'. In matters of principle and conviction, resist at all costs, assert your freedom of action and of speech to ensure that you are never deflected from what you deem to be right. Thus you will be respected. Your task will be, above all, to become, as our illustrious predecessor, Chief Rabbi Hertz, said of his charge in his installation address in 1913, 'Defender of the Faith'. His biography, written some 30 years later by Philip Paneth to mark his seventieth birthday, was entitled 'Guardian of the Law'.

Secondly, *ve'ematz*, 'be of good courage', *bema'asim tovim*, regarding good deeds in the community. Anglo-Jewry has a peculiar penchant for self-denigration. It delights in running itself down, stressing failings, magnifying scandals, while ignoring or belittling successes and achievements. A community that does not believe in itself cannot flourish. It will not attract its best sons and daughters to community service – for who wants to invest in failure?

Ve'ematz – 'be of good courage'. Highlight *ma'asim tovim*, the many wonderful good deeds to be found in the community, and confound the prophets of doom. Generate courage through self-esteem, and success through confidence. Through such good courage, Joshua managed to conquer the Promised Land, and through such indomitable courage, this great community under your leadership will prosper spiritually.

I recall that on one of my last visits in Jerusalem to Rabbi Abramsky, of sainted memory – one of the greatest Torah sages ever to have graced our shores – he showed me the passage in the first chapter of Joshua: 'Be strong and of good courage, for you shall cause this people to inherit the Land which I swore to their fathers to give to them.' Then it states: 'Only be strong and very courageous to observe, and to do according to all the law which Moses My servant commanded you.' You see, commented Dayan Abramsky, 'for the conquest of the Land, you need to be "strong and of good courage"; but for the conquest of the Torah, you require to be "strong and very courageous".'

After 2,000 years of exile, and the catastrophe of the Holocaust, our generation has two supreme priorities: to consolidate our national rebirth in the Land of Israel given to our fathers; and to restore our people to its timeless assignment given at Sinai. Of these two, said the dayan, the second is the more difficult and demands even greater courage.

This is indeed manifest in our time. Harder still than to generate concern to advance peace with security is the even greater challenge to excite Jews the world over to resume our destiny as a 'light unto the nations', as spiritual pathfinders and moral pioneers, fulfilling the purpose for which we wondrously survived all our tribulations over the millennia. We, the rabbis, must help to restore the balance between the yearning for our physical homeland and the commitment to our spiritual heritage, as commanded to Joshua.

My dear colleague, you enter this venerable office with a higher public profile than any of your predecessors. Your notable achievements, in reviving the fortunes of Jews' College, in blazing new trails through your Traditional Alternatives, and in winning fame and acclaim through your outstanding Reith lectures – all these testify to the exceptional endowments you bring to this high office, and the goodwill within and beyond the community on which you can count for support and response to your leadership.

Sustained by your wife, your parents and family, and your many friends, may you be blessed with robust health and the gift of wisdom to write a new volume, a *shirah chadashah*, to the glory of our community and our people, earning the reverence for our faith by this promise of Moses when he laid down his office: 'And all the peoples of the earth shall see that the Name of the Lord is called upon you, and they shall have respect for you.'

Chapter Seventeen

House of Lords

In the spring of 1975, Chief Rabbi and Mrs Jakobovits were invited by the Queen to dinner and an overnight stay at Windsor Castle, in the company of the Duke and Duchess of Norfolk, the Earl and Countess of Antrim, Lord and Lady Nugent of Guildford, and Home Secretary Roy Jenkins and his wife. Rabbi Jakobovits was to meet Her Majesty many times thereafter, most notably on receiving a knighthood in the 1981 Queen's Birthday Honours.

But greater recognition was yet to come. In the 1988 New Year Honours, he became the first Chief Rabbi to be elevated to the peerage – a unique tribute, said the *Jewish Chronicle*, to his 'spiritual leadership of the overwhelming majority of Anglo-Jewry, and particularly to his personal contribution to the national debates on the great moral and ethical issues of the day'. He was not, the paper added, 'the first Jewish refugee from Nazism to become a peer, but he is the first for whom a Jewish inheritance has been the vehicle that carries him into the House of Lords'.

Commenting on his elevation, the new peer said that he had been honoured 'for being true to my faith, for teaching Judaism in an unadulterated form, for not having made compromises, and for remaining loyal to my convictions'. It was living proof, he added, of a cherished belief – that Jews could play their part in society by standing firm for traditional Jewish values and virtues, 'a rebuttal of the kind of reformist views that gained currency among Jews in the last century'.

YARMULKAS IN THE LORDS

The question for Shimon Cohen today was this: when had there been so many yarmulkas in the Peers' Lobby at the House of Lords? 'Never before,' said Mr Cohen. Then, gesturing towards the blue-carpeted chamber, he added: 'And what I can safely say is there have never been any yarmulkas in there until the Chief Rabbi walks in.'

Moments later, Immanuel Jakobovits, the Chief Rabbi of the United Hebrew Congregations of the Commonwealth, entered the House of Lords, watched by many, including Mr Cohen, his aide; the six Jakobovits children; and 30 grand-children. Wearing a red robe trimmed with white fur, he swore his oath of loyalty to the Queen under his new title, Baron Jakobovits of Regent's Park, an area near his home in St John's Wood.

It was a moving moment for many of the elderly Jews watching from the galleries for the reasons of history cited earlier by the Chief Rabbi in an inter-view. 'I will be the first rabbi ever to sit in the House of Lords, and, I would imagine, the first rabbi in Jewish history to be ennobled since medieval times,' said Lord Jakobovits.

Britain's two Anglican Archbishops – Canterbury and York – and its 24 bishops also sit in the House of Lords, but only so long as they hold ecclesiastical office.

For students of Thatcherism, the introduction of the 67-year-old rabbi to the House of Lords was striking for reasons beyond history. Lord Jakobovits is widely regarded as Prime Minister Margaret Thatcher's favourite religious leader. His formal elevation today underscored the estrangement between Mrs Thatcher and the Church of England, and her clear affinity for the moral precepts of Orthodox Judaism as enunciated by Lord Jakobovits.

His firm pronouncements on the values of work, thrift, family solidarity and personal morality fit nicely with Mrs Thatcher's campaign to popularise what she thinks of as Victorian values. Mrs Thatcher is known to regard the English bishops as a collection of soggy liberals, and the Chief Rabbi as the country's most authoritative spokesman for traditional values.

His elevation marks a continuation of her policy of placing Jews in positions of prominence. Lord Young, the Employment Secretary and one of three Jews in the Cabinet, was among the Chief Rabbi's official escorts in the House of Lords today. Altogether, there are 45 Jews in the House of Lords, and 28 in the House of Commons. The British Cabinet numbers 22, the Commons has 635 members overall, and the House of Lords about 1,100.

Despite his ties to the Prime Minister, Lord Jakobovits will go into the House of Lords as an independent rather than a Conservative, and he does not move in political lockstep with the leader who put him on the New Year's Honours List. For example, the rabbi's total opposition to homosexuality and premarital sex has led him to condemn the Thatcher Government's advertising campaign to encourage the use of condoms.

'All this propaganda around the condom has introduced into millions of homes of young people who had never heard of extramarital or premarital sex notions that are utterly alien to them, and I think are demoralising to them,' he maintained.

But the alliance between the two was firmly cemented in 1986 when the Chief Rabbi criticised a Church of England report, *Faith in the City*, that accused Mrs Thatcher of being indifferent to the plight of black and Asian immigrants. The Chief Rabbi's response, *From Doom to Hope*, urged blacks to emulate Jews who arrived in Britain when 'there was no Welfare State and we could not fall back on State help' and attained success.

'We had the patience, the perseverance, the willpower and the addiction to education and so on to achieve it,' the Chief Rabbi said in an interview. 'We therefore want to serve as a beacon of hope to the current generation of new immigrants who find themselves in such despair.'

Some Jews regard the rabbi's stand as insensitive to the special problems of blacks. His comments on this and other issues such as the role of women have caused strains within Britain's 330,000–350,000 Jewish community.

By tradition, the Chief Rabbi of the country's 200 Orthodox synagogues is regarded as the spokesman for all British Jews. But Lord Jakobovits' hard-line stands on social issues and his clear identification with Thatcherism troubles some non-Orthodox Jews.

Indeed, critics say that Lord Jakobovits' unbending traditionalism has contributed to the polarisation of Britain's Jews and to the declining numbers caused by emigration and assimilation. The Jewish population has fallen from 450,000 in a quarter-century, but the Chief Rabbi says that his example will help reverse the trend.

'Nobody today thinks that, by dropping their Jewishness, they will find it easier to be accepted in society,' he said. 'My elevation is the best example of that. I have been elevated not because I renounced my Jewish beliefs or modified them or made concessions, but, on the contrary, because I held strictly to them and proclaimed them without adulteration and without concessions.'

The New York Times, 10 February 1988

'I, Immanuel, Baron Jakobovits, do solemnly, sincerely and truly declare and affirm that I will be faithful and bear true allegiance to Her Majesty Queen Elizabeth, her heirs and successors, according to law.' With these words, uttered while kneeling on one knee, the Chief Rabbi was introduced in the House of Lords on Tuesday as Lord Jakobovits of Regent's Park in Greater London.

In a ceremony dating from 1621, he was led into the chamber by his two supporters, Lord Young and Lord Mishcon, all wearing red robes with ermine collars. In his right hand, the Chief Rabbi clutched his Writ of Summons. The three were steered around the chamber by the Gentleman Usher of the Black Rod and the Garter King of Arms.

Before a chamber packed with senior peers and a Stranger's Gallery bristling with members of the Chief Rabbi's family from London, America, Israel and Switzerland, Lord Jakobovits took his seat as an independent peer. Among others in the gallery were Yehuda Avner, the Israeli Ambassador, and Dr Lionel Kopelowitz, president of the Board of Deputies. Before the ceremony, there was a kosher lunch in the Lords for the family and guests.

In the evening, the Chief Rabbinate Council hosted a reception for some 600 communal leaders, ranging from the Liberals to the Adath. Sidney Frosh, president of the Council – and of the United Synagogue – said that the elevation 'provided one of those splendid occasions when we can all rejoice together'. The other speakers were Dayan Chanoch Ehrentreu, head of the London Beth Din, and Dr Kopelowitz. All paid particular tribute to Lady Jakobovits.

The most moving speech, addressed to 'Mummy and Daddy', came from Esther Pearlman. An illuminated address, designed by another daughter, Shoshana Turner, was presented to her father. [It is reproduced as the endpapers to this book.]

Jewish Chronicle, 12 February 1988

A PEER WITHOUT PEERS

In his historic maiden speech as the only rabbi to address the House of Lords, the Chief Rabbi told of his experiences as a refugee from Nazi extermination. He was speaking during a second-reading debate on the Immigration Bill:

My Lords, several reasons prompt me to ask for your Lordships' indulgence today. I am deeply touched by the warm and gracious welcome extended to me by the noble Earl [Ferrers], which has been supported by the other speakers.

Notwithstanding the reassuring words that I heard from the noble Earl about maiden speeches, I can assure him and other noble Lords that I share with every new Peer, whatever his or her past experience in public life, some trepidation in speaking for the first time within earshot of these venerable walls that have listened and still often listen to some of Britain's finest minds and most eloquent orators. In fact, I feel somewhat like my ancestor and namesake, the patriarch Jacob, who slept on a stone which, by legend, is not unconnected with the early history of this House. He awoke in the morning and exclaimed, 'How full of awe is this place. This is none other than the House of the Lord.'

My awe is all the greater because, unlike most other noble Lords who have been elevated to this upper House from the ground floor of common citizenship, I was lifted from the basement of refugeedom – indeed, from the even lower sewers of Nazi oppression and humiliation. I am ever conscious that but for the grace of God and the compassionate haven of this great country, I should today be an anonymous speck among the ashes of millions defiling the soil of Europe.

A third factor daunts me. As the only rabbi ever to take a seat in this House, I am, as it were, a Peer without peers, and I feared that I should be a little lonely. However, that fear was dispelled at my introduction by my most distinguished supporters – and I should like to say how privileged I feel at seeing both in the Chamber at the present time – as well as by the extraordinary warmth with which I have been received by so many noble Lords and illustrious friends, most notable among them being the most reverend Primates the Archbishops of Canterbury and York. Perhaps I may say at this point that I join countless other citizens in wishing to see their primacy preserved among the nation's religious and moral leaders.

Moments before my introduction, I began to feel at home when I was robed in the Moses Room with its painting of Moses, the law-giver, holding the Decalogue – presumably as the foundation of laws enacted in this Mother of Parliaments. And since Jews traditionally regard Moses as the first rabbi, I am clearly here as the second rabbi, still upholding the same Ten Commandments.

My experiences as both a refugee and a rabbi have a bearing on immigration policies. The conventions attaching to maiden speeches prevent my saying anything provocative or controversial on this occasion. I can assure the noble Lord, Lord Bonham-Carter, that my temptation is great to break those conventions. But I am occupationally committed to overcoming temptation. Nevertheless, I hope that I am qualified to draw a lesson on the philosophy of life applicable to both hosts and immigrants.

An ancient saying in the Talmud has it, 'According to the hardship is the reward.'

When one climbs from below the ground floor, one has to work harder. What one gets for nothing is worth nothing. People who have everything usually enjoy nothing. Having too much can be as debilitating as having too little. Too many of our children no longer know what it means to struggle, nor have they ever tasted the thrill of triumph over adversity through some special effort. The experience of treasuring freedom is often alien to them.

Our youth might learn from minorities who are fighting for equality that one should never take anything for granted. And the newer arrivals might feel encouraged that by rising the hard way, they are making a special contribution to the moral dynamic, as well as the cultural richness, of the nation. Hosts and immigrants alike, I am convinced, are bound to be beneficiaries of benevolent policies.

However, there is also an obverse side. Even more important than liberal immigration laws is the prevention of oppression which causes the dislocation of refugees in the first place. All involuntary migrations from one country to another testify to some human failure, and every political refugee dramatically epitomises some violation of human rights in his native land. Welcoming strangers is not enough. The supreme effort must be to ensure that no one will need to leave his country, fleeing from intolerable conditions of discrimination, persecution or alien conquest.

I am acutely aware that the most poignant contrast on the fate of refugees is today provided in the State of Israel. There are Jewish refugees who arrived from lands under oppression by the hundreds of thousands in a miracle of absorption and integration; and there are about the same number of Arab refugees who have suffered under different regimes and who still languish in wretched refugee camps – an unspeakable tragedy of rejection and human indignity. What started as a conflict between two rights – between two peoples claiming the same land – has now become a conflict between two wrongs, with Israel still being denied the right to exist under the threat of war and terror, and with Palestinians still widely denied their national aspirations and subject to conditions that they are not prepared to accept without hope of amelioration.

In the context of our debate on immigrants and refugees, what are the lessons, individually, nationally and internationally? Perhaps I may suggest that they include the following: to accommodate opposing rights before they become opposing wrongs; to befriend newcomers before they become hostile aliens; to secure decent conditions for citizens in the lands in which they live before they become frustrated minorities in places to which they are driven; and, above all, to remember that we are all, each one of us, temporary residents on this planet where we have to learn the art of living together in harmony before our visa expires and we are called to migrate to another world.

Parliamentary Debates (Hansard*):*
House of Lords Official Report, 4 March 1988

EDUCATION REFORM BILL

Lord Jakobovits: The last speech [by Lord St John of Fawsley, who referred to his having opened an exhibition of Jewish art and having been presented with a mezuzah], which was for me the most heart-warming, has made it easier for me to say a few words in the debate, despite the fact that I rise with consider-able diffidence because I face a double dilemma. One is purely pragmatic, in that my public and communal commitments are such that, unfortunately, I was unable to attend the entire debate on the Second Reading. However, I made up for that by reading through the massive proceedings – the 80-odd speeches recorded in *Hansard*. Because of another urgent engagement which was set many months ago, I shall be unable to stay for the whole of the debate this evening.

My second predicament is that we are touching on delicate ground. It is obviously thin ice on which Christian angels fear to tread and Jewish rabbis may sink and drown if they are not careful. Therefore I crave the Committee's indulgence in taking advantage of these precious minutes to address myself in wholehearted support of the amendment tabled by the right reverend Prelate, and perhaps to anticipate debates which will follow in respect of other amendments, as other speakers have so anticipated.

I should like also to share a few general reflections on the place of religious education in the raising of tomorrow's citizens. Earlier in the debate, the noble Lord, Lord Callaghan, told those on the Benches opposite that they should not betray what they have been saying for the past 40 years. I must be careful not to betray what has been said for the past 4,000 years. It will not be easy to compress my comments into the few minutes at my disposal.

I am the product and the spokesman of a tradition which has cultivated a passion for education. It is a tradition which places the precept of parents teaching their children, as we have been reminded, and teaching them religion, in a scroll called a mezuzah, which is placed at every doorpost of a Jewish home before you enter. It states: 'And thou shall teach these words diligently to your children.' It is a tradition which ranks the sanctity of a house of religious learning higher than a house of worship. We believe that a house of learning is holier than a house of worship. It is a religion which some 2,000 years ago made provision for communal schools for religious instruction mandatory.

As heir to that tradition, I welcome with enormous delight the new Bill's striving for educational excellence in general and its enhanced emphasis on the paramount importance of religious education in particular. I am sure that Members of the Committee will not expect me to mediate or to take sides in an internal argument concerning the role of teaching a faith other than my own. However, some observations may be relevant both to the national scene and to the effect on my community and other religious minorities.

Obviously, I particularly welcome a provision which would require non-denominational maintained schools to provide religious education for minority groups at the request of parents and where the number would warrant it. Also particularly welcome for the burgeoning network of Jewish-maintained schools would be the requirement for the State or the local authority to assume responsibility for providing for religious education to be included in the school curriculum.

However, as regards the main thrust of the amendment, I should like to say this. The principal enemy of all religion is no longer heresy or apostasy; it is simple paganism. It is the refusal to believe in any faith or in any accountability before our Creator. That leads to the moral anarchy which is now so rampant and pernicious. Therefore, religious education must be the transmission of a commitment even more than of mere knowledge. A religiously indifferent teacher can hardly instil religious convictions and sensitivities.

Moreover, if we consider religious faith and precept as the spiritual lifeblood of the nation and all its citizens, then effective religious instruction can no more be administered by and to persons of a different faith than can a blood transfusion be safely given without first ensuring blood-group compatibility. Indiscriminate mixing of blood can prove dangerous, and so can the mixing of faiths in education.

I should like to apply that in practice from a Jewish perspective. I shall do so by quoting from a 'Thought for the Day' talk on Radio 4 given last Thursday by my learned colleague, Rabbi Jonathan Sacks, principal of Jews' College. He described how he was raised at a primary school which was devoutly C of E and where Jewish boys had their separate Jewish assemblies. He said: 'The effect of this schooling on our Jewish identity was curious. It made us, of course, acutely aware that we were different. But because those around us were taking their religion seriously, it made us consider our Judaism seriously too.' Then he added: 'So it isn't so strange that all this produced a rabbi. From living with those who valued their traditions, I learned to cherish my own.' Continuing, he said: 'What brought this to mind was the report … called "Crisis in Religious Education", in which two Newcastle teachers complained that children in today's schools are losing the chance to grow up as practising Christians. They might, I think, have gone further still; for if Christianity suffers, so, in a curious way, does every other faith as well.' He continued: 'It happens with the best of intentions. How else, in a multi-cultural society, should we promote tolerance than by teaching children something about every religious group with which they are likely to come into contact; a touch of Christianity; a dash of Judaism; a slice of Islam; and so on through a fruit cocktail of world faiths. But the whole that emerges can be less than the sum of its parts. For it misses out on the most crucial element of all: the fact that, for each of us, there is usually only one faith that resonates with personal meaning: the faith of our community, our culture, our family, our past. In trying to teach all faiths, it's possible that we succeed in teaching none.' Finally, he concluded: 'From schools that had confidence in their Christianity, I learned an answering pride in my Jewishness; and I discovered that those who best appreciate other faiths are those who treasure their own. Might not teaching children their own traditions do more for tolerance, and for faith, than teaching them everyone else's?'

Of course, I want to see included in religious instruction not only what distinguishes us, what separates one faith from another, reflecting the dominant ethos for the majority and the particular beliefs and observances for the minorities, but also what we have in common. I believe that particular attention should be given to the moral dimension in preparing the rising generation for responsible marriage and responsible citizenship. For example, these days youngsters receive little if any guidance on dating, courtship, the choice of a partner and the expectations within marriage. Instead, they simply rely on momentary infatuation and snap decisions, with the result that so many unions contracted in this casual manner soon founder, with catastrophic results for the stability of society. Broken homes cost the nation far more, socially and economically, than Aids.

Altogether, because formal education has become largely a system of career training rather than the nurture of the total personality and its harmonious interplay with the rest of society, we develop and exploit only a small fraction of the child's mind, with much of the brain remaining unused, going to waste and often to mischief. To me, religious education in the widest sense should embrace efforts to excite the intellect with the wonders of nature; to inspire the awe of the human genius as expressed in art and literature. It should cultivate an insatiable appetite for learning and a thrill in the pursuit of knowledge through reading and study for its own sake, until killing time becomes as reprehensible as killing life, because time is our most precious commodity next to life itself.

In such a philosophy of education, moulding the parent is just as important as teaching the child, never forgetting that the true education of a child begins 24 years before it is born. Likewise, decisions made now, at this late end of the twentieth century, will determine the quality of life and the moral fibre of our citizens in the twenty-first century. In this spirit, I commend the advice of the Preacher in the twenty-second chapter of the biblical book of Proverbs: 'Educate a youth in the way he should go, so that even in his old age he will not depart from it.'

Hansard, 4 May 1988

WAR CRIMES INQUIRY REPORT

Lord Jakobovits: My Lords, rarely, I dare say, have the walls of this Chamber listened to a debate more sombre than this, discussing as we do the continued culpability or the remission of a crime so horrendous and so unprecedented that a new term had to be invented and coined – namely, the term 'genocide' – to describe it, as the *Oxford English Dictionary* informs us.

Let me at once declare my interest. I have an interest, but it is not as a Jew, not as a rabbi, and not even as a refugee from Nazi persecution who lost numerous close relatives in the Holocaust. Rather, I move to speak simply as a member of the human race. The monstrous crimes perpetrated in our lifetime have diminished my own humanity and that of all my contemporaries.

It is a welcome new feature of the post-war period that civilised people every-where feel involved in the ordeals – be it famine, oppression or discrimination – suffered by others many thousands of miles away. In this new spirit of col-lective responsibility, it is now also widely acknowledged that those who allowed Nazi barbarities to happen, standing by as silent witnesses without protest, must share the guilt of the perpetrators. Silence, indifference and inaction were Hitler's principal allies. If we were, by our own default, to let his hench-men go unpunished, we would be handing the tyrant a posthumous victory. We would make it easier for the dominion of evil to assert itself once again at an incalculable cost in human suffering and degradation. The risks are not diminished by the present turmoil and uncertainties in Europe.

At the same time, I am acutely aware of the danger that, if we are not careful, this debate itself may aggravate tensions and divisions, leading to bitterness and strife within the nation, instead of strengthening our human fellowship to ward off any future threat to man's humanity on such a staggering scale. I sincerely hope that this debate will narrow differences and perhaps even promote a consensus of practical conclusions to which we can all subscribe.

I know that there are some very plausible arguments against the proposed legislation. I believe that they are all questionable and open to refutation. First, the action is seen by many as vengeful. Jews in particular are often charged with feelings of vengeance. This attitude, like many other falsifications which have led to so much persecution and bloodshed over the centuries, is attributed to the Old Testament. Let me once and for all lay the ghost of this vicious canard.

My faith abhors vengeance. The Law of Moses denounces as a grave moral offence the bearing of a grudge or the taking of revenge, as will be found in the Bible in the Book of Leviticus. There is all the difference in the world between justice and vengeance. Vengeance, by definition, is when an aggrieved party takes the law into his own hands, circumventing the due process of the law. Justice is when guilt and punishment of a transgressor are determined by an independent agency, by a judiciary. That is what the recommended legislation seeks.

Again, it is argued that, after all these years, the trials of Nazi criminals cannot be fair, that the witnesses may not be reliable, and that there is therefore likely to be a miscarriage of justice. I have enough confidence in British justice and in the judiciary to dismiss these fears as groundless. Whether witnesses and their evidence are acceptable and trustworthy is for the DPP, or in Scotland the Crown Agent, and then for the courts to judge, not for the legislators. Our charge is to establish that the arm of the law is neither withered nor too short to apprehend and punish some of history's worst offenders if there are sufficient grounds to arraign them, as has been established in the Hetherington inquiry.

For my part, I am less interested in securing criminal convictions than in demonstrating our moral convictions. It would be a devastating travesty of justice if the legislation itself were to exonerate such arch-criminals and expunge their guilt. Indeed, it is a cruel irony that the Nazi mass-murderers were much more successful in hunting down their innocent victims than were the Allied Powers in rounding up the major perpetrators of these crimes. I am reliably informed that the Nazis succeeded in herding together, transporting and eventually liquidating 90 per cent of all Jews in occupied Europe, whereas the Allies managed to bring to trial only some 35 per cent of Nazis suspected of war crimes or crimes against humanity. That is a shocking indictment of the civilised world.

Of course, it is urged that, after all these years, we ought to forget and forgive. I believe that that would be a supreme betrayal both of the past and of the future. We have no mandate from the victims to pardon the crimes committed against them. And as for the passage of time, that in itself can surely neither condone nor expiate these offences. But worse still, we would betray the future were we to allow potential arch-offenders against humanity to believe that they will eventually be forgiven and forgotten. In fact, far from these crimes being mitigated by the passage of time, they are in a sense worse today than they were

40 years ago. For added to their heinous offences at the time is the further guilt of having escaped from justice all these years: hiding from the law and evading justice is itself an unconscionable crime.

Finally, it seems fallacious, as has been so impressively argued by both the opening speakers to the debate, to call this retroactive legislation, and therefore alien to British law and perhaps even without a relevant precedent. After all, the conduct was criminal in international and in British law at the time of its perpetration. Moreover, the crimes under discussion were infinitely more unprecedented and rather more alien to the British tradition than the proposed legislation.

I see in *The Times* today that the noble and learned Lord, Lord Shawcross, who regrettably cannot be with us this afternoon, argues, as he has done before, against the proposed legislation on the grounds – to quote him – that the major trials at Nuremberg seem, alas, to have done nothing to deter the odious crimes of Idi Amin, of Pol Pot, of the Khmer Rouge, and so on. I would reach the opposite conclusion. The fact that they no longer had to fear that the civilised world would not tolerate them getting away with such crimes, and that they were no longer convinced that we would one day apprehend them, try them and punish them, in itself encouraged them and made their crimes possible. Who knows how many innocent lives – thousands of innocent lives – might have been spared had they known that the law would always hunt them down, wherever they were.

Until the perpetrators of crimes against humanity know that they will never be allowed to find a safe refuge from justice, humanity will not be safe, and justice will never be vindicated. We now have an historic opportunity to affirm the ceaseless fight against evil, by the unrelenting pursuit of mass-murderers, so as to ensure the triumph of justice, as both a warning to potential criminals and as a reassurance to future generations that never again will rivers of innocent blood be allowed to pollute the world with impunity. The more unsafe the world becomes for the guilty, the safer it will become for the guiltless.

Hansard, *4 December 1989*

WAR CRIMES BILL

Lord Jakobovits: My Lords, one of the delightful fringe benefits in speaking in this otherwise grave and what I am sure to all of us is a painful debate is that I can wholeheartedly join the previous speaker in congratulating the noble Lord [Swaythling] who bears such a distinguished name in the annals of our people and our community. He made a beautiful maiden speech. In it, he gave so much heart as well as thought to a problem of utter perplexity. I have the added benefit which the noble Lord, Lord Hutchinson, who followed him, did not have: of being able to agree with him as well. Therefore, I thank him for the encouragement that he has given me. Perhaps I may say for the two of us that, belonging as we do to a people described in the Bible as the smallest of all peoples, we are not exactly unaccustomed to being in a minority. I appreciate the trend of view so powerfully and often logically expressed by speakers before me and no doubt will be again by many of those who are to come afterwards.

Frankly, I hesitated before adding my name to the list of speakers on this occasion. I had already spoken in an earlier debate and my views are known. I face a dilemma. I wear my uniform on my head and my vocation in the title of my office. Therefore, I cannot speak as anything but as a spokesman of my faith and my people. Yet I do not want this discussion to be regarded as a Jewish issue, which it is not.

I hope that a commitment to bring criminals to justice and to fight evil wherever and whenever – and, I stress, wherever and whenever – it is to be found unites all decent men and women irrespective of belief. Conversely, I fully accept that opposing the proposed legislation need have nothing whatever to do with anti-Semitism. I was deeply heartened by the truly noble words expressed by the noble Lord, Lord Callaghan, which were enforced by other noble Lords, in condemnation of this evil that has wrought such unspeakable suffering on my people and many others. In fact, I know that some opponents of the Bill – indeed, many who are speaking here today – are among the staunchest friends of the Jewish people. But I am bound to add that so were some of those who were appeasers of the Nazis in the 1930s.

Since our last debate took place, some new circumstances have arisen, and there are some new arguments. Our vote in this House will be carefully scrutinised throughout the world as an indicator of moral sensitivities in contemporary Britain. As we have been reminded by several speakers, quite recently the civilised world has been shaken by the hideous desecration of the dead in Carpentras and elsewhere in outrages of anti-Semitic frenzy and vulgar inhumanity which were unknown even at the height of the worst medieval persecutions of our people.

But more important than these isolated acts of a few sick and sickening minds was the quite unprecedented world reaction to what was seen as threatening a recrudescence of racism. In Paris alone, some 200,000 demonstrators marched in protest, led by the President of the Republic and other national, political and religious leaders from every party, every faith and every segment of society. Indeed, the fear of new outbreaks of race hatred has lately swept Europe, both East and West.

A negative vote now in this House, preventing the prosecution of suspected arch-criminals who succeeded in our lifetime in turning foul teachings of racism into rivers and lakes of innocent blood, would give a wrong signal to a world seeking reassurance that civilised governments and legislatures would never again allow such evil to triumph with impunity. After Carpentras, we cannot afford a collective act of exoneration of the most monstrous acts of brutality, acts which, as we have also been reminded lately, are either being denied altogether or being belittled as not even worthy of deterrence.

It was argued in our last debate by my noble friend the right reverend Prelate the Bishop of St Albans – and we heard it said again this afternoon – that it might be better for the Jewish people if the legislation were not introduced lest it intensify anti-Semitism. Let me assure him, and others holding this view with every sincerity, that it is not shared by the great majority of my community.

Finally, I note with deep concern bordering on disbelief that in his amendment the noble Lord, Lord Campbell of Alloway – and, indeed, he is supported in this view by others – again doubts whether there is a 'reasonable assumption of a fair trial.' In other words, he assumes that the trials will not or cannot be fair. That casts an unwarranted slur on our judiciary. It questions and prejudges the fairness of both our judicial system and of those appointed to administer it. It also overlooks the fact that the legislation is only permissive or enabling and not mandatory.

To my mind, there are three options before us. If we are reasonably confident that our Law Officers and our courts will ensure fair trials or else dismiss the charge, we should vote for the legislation. If we are quite certain that the trials cannot and will not be fair, we should support the amendment. If we are in any doubt whether they will or can be fair, we should abstain.

Voting against the Bill forecloses even the possibility that the evidence might conceivably be conclusive. The amendment is therefore prejudicial to the outcome of any trial. It is tantamount to a dismissal of all charges before they have even been heard in court. An abstention reserves judgement; a vote for the amendment passes judgement: it denies the chance of the evidence ever being heard and tried.

The proposed legislation might at least make it possible for a few of history's most horrendous criminals to be brought to justice. A vote against the legislation will unfortunately make it certain that for millions of victims there can be and there will be no justice, not even in theory or symbolically. Should it be said that we cared more for mass murderers who were allowed to get old in peace than for their victims whose innocent lives were brutally cut short?

I quite agree, as has been argued, that the Bill is 40 years too late. But 40 years of moral negligence is no excuse for persisting in it after it has been brought to light. If it were discovered that some water supply is contaminated and that it has been contaminated for 40 years, does that justify not purifying the water after the discovery? Such an injustice surely cannot accord with the moral traditions of our country and the noble record of this venerable palace of justice and of humanity.

Hansard, 4 June 1990

SLAUGHTER OF POULTRY REGULATIONS 1990

Lord Jakobovits: My Lords, as the religious head of the community that has been singled out for the special attention of the noble Lord, Lord Houghton of Sowerby, in the Prayer that he has put before us, I shall presumably be expected by your Lordships to say a few words to explain that we shall under no circumstances ever accept the charge that our method of slaughter is in any way inferior in terms of animal welfare to any other yet devised or in practice anywhere.

I am gratified to hear that the noble Lord is satisfied with some of the improvements effected by the new regulations. I am also able to assure him that any cut made in a sawing fashion, as he described it, is invalid in Jewish law. Therefore, we would disqualify a religious slaughterer who resorted to that method. The noble Lord need not suspect that it is our intention to inflict any such discomfort on the animal being slaughtered.

Since the declared object of his Prayer, as the noble Lord has stated in a newspaper interview, is the eventual abolition of the Jewish religious method of slaughter, or for that matter the Muslim method of slaughter, and not merely the contents of the regulations placed before Parliament by the Minister, perhaps I may be permitted a few words of explanation. Perhaps I may also say a few words in rebuttal of the implied charge that we are guilty, through our long tradition, of applying a method in the preparation of animal food that inflicts unnecessary suffering upon brute creation. My remarks will therefore deal not so much with the new regulations, which we have broadly accepted – we certainly accept them as they stand now – as with the principle of allowing Jews and Muslims their religious freedom to prepare meat foods according to our millennial tradition.

The matter was last raised in this House in a debate on the Slaughter of Animals Bill, a Private Member's Bill presented by the noble Lord, Lord Somers, in December 1962. That Bill was later withdrawn. In the debate, the late Lord Cohen of Birkenhead, one of the most eminent physicians ever to grace this House, eloquently and with rare erudition refuted the charge that the Jewish method was cruel. After quoting and examining leading scientific opinion, in addition to his own expert judgement, he stated that 'the available scientific evidence supports [the] conclusion, which is the most recent of those who have gone into the matter with great care, that the method is humane and will almost immediately render the animal unconscious'. [*Official Report*, 3/12/62; col. 46.]

As have numerous other leading veterinary and medical authorities since then, Lord Cohen asserted quite categorically: 'Shechitah' – which is the technical name for the Jewish method of slaughter – 'is as humane a method as any.' I need not weary your Lordships with all the technical evidence for that view. Two further quotations from Lord Cohen's speech at the time will suffice:

'What are the scientific data? When you cut the throat of an animal … the blood pressure falls off very rapidly. Within four seconds, the blood pressure drops in the femoral artery to half what it was before the cut, and that rate of fall means unconsciousness must have occurred earlier.' [*Official Report*, 3/12/62; col. 43.] He declared further, on the cut itself: 'The cut, as made by the shochet' – that is, the highly trained religious slaughterer – is somewhat similar to the experience of having been 'cut by a razor blade and knows of it only when the blood flows; [this] is almost certainly painless'. Then he added: 'I would say that it is certainly painless.' [*Official Report*, 3/12/62; col. 44.]

Jews need hardly be lectured on the prevention of cruelty to animals. They introduced the whole concept long before any other civilisation or any other faith cared about animal welfare. To inflict any suffering on animals is a religious offence in the Mosaic legislation enshrined in such laws as the obligation to assist an overloaded animal or not to remove chicks or eggs from a nest in the presence of the mother bird, and – better known still – to include domestic animals ('your ox and your ass') among the beneficiaries of the duty to rest from work on the Sabbath, as expressly declared in the Ten Commandments. No wonder that the pioneer of the first Society for the Prevention of Cruelty to Animals was a Jew, by the name of Lewis Gompertz, in 1824 in London.

However, there is something strangely inconsistent in the agitation against the Jewish method of slaughter and the allegation of cruelty. We have never deemed animal welfare more important than human welfare. The Hebrew prophet Hosea denounced the perversity of placing the loving care of animals above the care for humans in the immortal words, 'They who slaughter men kiss the calves'.

Let us look at a brief history of this sordid inconsistency. At the dawn of man's history, there were the first two brothers: Cain and Abel. Abel was a herdsman and brought of the firstlings of his flock as an offering to the Lord. Cain was a vegetarian. He would not touch an animal. He offered of his fruits instead. Yet the same Cain who cared so much for animals did not shrink from killing his own brother in cold blood in history's first recorded murder. Later, at the end of the Book of Genesis, there are the ancient Egyptians who worshipped animals and forced Jacob and his sons to live in the land of Goshen away from the rest of the population because, as is stated, 'all shepherds of flocks are an abomination of Egypt'. Yet those same Egyptians had no compunction in brutally drowning Hebrew babies at birth and building huge pyramids with slave labour tortured without pity.

In modern times, one of the first pieces of legislation introduced by the Nazis in Germany after assuming power in early 1933 was to prohibit the Jewish method of slaughter, for they cared deeply about animals. However, that did not prevent them from gassing and incinerating human beings by the million in history's supreme orgy of inhumanity.

Lately, that perversity has begun to blemish society in our own country when supporters of animal liberation, as they call themselves, out of concern for animal welfare laid bombs to kill human researchers seeking to bring healing to suffering humans by carefully controlled experiments on anaesthetised animals.

I seem to recall that, in our recent debates on embryo experimentation and abortion, the noble Lord, Lord Houghton, expressed little concern for embryonic or foetal human life in relation to the expression of concern by many others. I detected a similar indifference to human victims of mass murder and mass torture when the noble Lord referred to the perpetrators of those unspeakable crimes as 'a few miserable old men over the age of 70 who are probably hard of hearing, have failing sight and are ill'.

Shall we have a new ethic in which the care of mice and guinea pigs counts for more than the life and health of humans, and in which the pity for arch-criminals is greater than the pity for their victims? We as Jews care profoundly to prevent causing pain to animals, but not to the point of absurdity in which human welfare is ignored or violated. A society which still tolerates the cruelty of battery farming or blood sports, with the agony of the chase and the often slow, writhing death of misfired shots, should have more important concerns than the few seconds' interval between a painless cut and the cessation of consciousness from the brain in the Jewish religious method of slaughter.

We did not seek the regulations, but we understand their intent. As of two days ago, all leading rabbis supervising Jewish religious slaughter operations in this country unanimously agreed to accept the new regulations as compatible with our religious requirements. On behalf of the entire Jewish community, I must express appreciation to three successive Ministers of Agriculture and their officials for the understanding that they have shown for our religious requirements throughout the long period of negotiations leading to the issuance of the new regulations. The regulations will combine every reasonable care for animal welfare with the freedom to practise our ancestral faith as a heritage which has preserved our people and has helped to bring inspiration to other peoples the world over.

Hansard, 13 July 1990

SUNDAY TRADING BILL

Lord Jakobovits: My Lords, I join in the tribute to the noble Earl, Lord Ferrers, for the immaculate skill and judicious impartiality with which he opened this notable debate. If I have any quarrel with his arguments, it is only with the suggestion that because a law has been broken, it should be abolished. As mentioned by the noble Lord, Lord McIntosh, the logic of that argument would lead to our opening up all the prisons because the law has clearly been broken.

I listened with particular gratification to the reflection of some of my own thinking in the notable speeches of the noble Baronesses, Lady Young and Lady Nicol, and above all that of my dear friend the right reverend Prelate the Bishop of Liverpool, who delivered a speech which was spiritually elevating and, to me, of particular value.

It may be argued that I have enough unfinished business trying to prevail upon Jews to observe the Jewish Sabbath on Saturdays without adding the Christian Sunday to my commitments. I do so because, born as I was to a people that gave the world its weekly day of rest, enshrined in the Ten Commandments, I have a sense of almost proprietary or at least hereditary interest in the continued existence of this weekly day of rest.

A nineteenth-century American economist, Henry George, wrote: 'That there is one day in the week that the working man may call his own, one day in the week on which hammer is silent and loom stands idle, is due, through Christianity, to Judaism.' The preservation of that unique spiritual and social treasure cannot be a matter of indifference to any citizen of this land, least of all to Jews.

In history, two attempts have been made to eliminate the weekly day of rest: one after the French Revolution, when a ten-day week was tried, and the other in the 1920s by the Communists in the Soviet Union, who wanted a five-day week. In both cases, the avowed aim was to destroy Christianity and religion in general. Both attempts failed. The seven-day cycle is almost innate in man. In fact, an early Jewish source suggests that the cycle is reflected in nature itself. In the height of man, six-sevenths is made up of the body while one-seventh is the head, crowning and controlling the body – one elevated part to six more mundane parts.

The loss of the Sabbath would deprive Britain of the last visible vestige of national spirituality and sanctification. For most citizens, regular worship every week was given up long ago and is now a dim memory of former generations. The sanctification of the family through lifelong marital faithfulness also endures in ever-fewer homes. But at least on Sundays even the streets proclaim that man does not live by bread alone, that the material quest for profit can be interrupted, and that there is more to human happiness than the pursuit of wealth and of power over others.

Representing, as it were, the originators of the Sabbath, perhaps I may say a few words on its special significance to us in the modern world. By closing our shops and workplaces, we proclaim the equality of all men. The rich do not earn more than the poor. For once we do not measure all values in life by their material price or rewards.

Of course, I recognise that what the Bill demands in keeping Sunday different is still a far cry from the severe Jewish impositions to sanctify the Sabbath. For us, the Sabbath requires that for one day a week we suspend the exploitation of the powers of nature, that we become creatures instead of rivalling the Creator.

Perhaps I may explain. Under our relatively rigid laws, on the Sabbath we have to abstain not only from physical toil and hard labour but also from creative work. We must not switch on the light, nor use the radio or television, nor drive by car or use the telephone. For one day, we are to be liberated from the tyranny of the machine. And what a tyranny the television and the telephone can be! Nature is to be emancipated from, and remain untrammelled by, man's domination. We are to demonstrate once every seven days that we are not the ultimate masters of the universe after all, that there is a Master above us, and that greater than the capacity to harness the infinite forces of nature is the capacity of man to know when to stop. For the Sabbath celebrates not the six days of creation – they are not holy days – but the seventh day, on which God ceased creating in order to control what he had created.

Perhaps there is no lesson that we need to learn more urgently in our time of the ceaseless drive for technological and scientific conquest than knowing when to stop. The supreme lesson of the Sabbath is to teach us that greater than the God who called the heavens and the earth and all their infinite powers into existence is the God who knew when to stop and when to call a halt in order to control what He had created.

It may be that the entire future of man will depend on our capacity to learn when to call a halt, at least occasionally, to what man's inventiveness has created, whether in scientific or medical research, in the exploitation of atomic energy, or in the disposal of waste material without polluting the air we breathe, our soil, the rivers and the seas on which human life depends. On that capacity to keep what we create in check and to stop occasionally in order to survey where we are and where we are going, on such a Sabbath periodically suspending our work, human survival may depend.

Reinforced as I am by three-and-a-half-thousand years of uninterrupted Sabbath observance, I therefore plead with your Lordships not to abandon this priceless national and human asset and not to allow the creeping secularisation of life to make further inroads into the last remaining bastion of spirituality.

Of the Sabbath in relation to the Jewish people, it has been said that more than we kept the Sabbath has the Sabbath kept us. Likewise, I can assert, so long as we keep the Sabbath special, it will keep us safe from moral decay and self-destruction.

Hansard, *8 March 1994*

DEBATE ON THE ADDRESS [QUEEN'S SPEECH – FOREIGN AFFAIRS]

Lord Jakobovits: My Lords, the gracious Speech, as has just been mentioned in a splendid contribution, pledged the Government's continuing support for the Middle East peace process. Reference has been made to this in several contributions this afternoon, most notably the speech to which we have just listened. That dealt primarily with foreign policy elements on which I do not claim to be anything like equally competent to comment. Therefore, I speak on the same subject overall but without overlapping what has just been communicated to us.

Unfortunately, I was unable to add a few words to the moving tributes paid in your Lordships' House and in another place to the memory of Prime Minister Rabin on the day of his funeral a week ago on Monday. As president of the Conference of European Rabbis, I had to conduct an urgent meeting of the conference in Zurich that day. Allow me, therefore, to take this opportunity to speak of this awesome tragedy and its traumatic after-effects. In the Jewish tradition, anything that disgraces Jews or Judaism is called a desecration of the Name of God. Anything which does honour is called a sanctification of the Name of God. The assassination of Yitzhak Rabin, particularly because the crime was perpetrated by a Jew claiming to act out of religious motives, was perhaps the greatest desecration of God's Name in Jewish annals. Conversely, the unprecedented honours shown to the bereaved family, the stricken Government and people of Israel at the funeral, attended and addressed by scores of world leaders, constituted an unparalleled sanctification of the Divine Name. The presence of the Prince of Wales, the Prime Minister, the leaders of the opposition parties, the President of the United States, the leaders of virtually all the European countries, and also King Hussein of Jordan, President Mubarak of Egypt and other Arab leaders, was profoundly appreciated and offered real comfort to a nation still stunned by shock, grief and anxiety.

As happens so often with perpetrators of evil, in the long run they achieve the opposite of what they intend. For the maintenance of civilised life, it is vital that terrorism and acts of violence must never succeed. There are indications that the peace process, far from having been sabotaged, will be given new momentum by Prime Minister Peres, co-architect with Mr Rabin of the historic agreements so far reached. Very recent visitors to Israel have reported Israeli taxi drivers – usually the best barometers of public opinion – saying that they have been adamantly opposed to the peace process out of fear that the Arabs can never be trusted, but now that they have seen the sincerity of the sympathy expressed at the funeral by some Arab leaders, perhaps past attitudes will have to be revised. For no section of the Jewish people has the blow been more devastating than for the religious community. At the same time, no fanaticism is more irrational and more deadly than religious fanaticism.

There is little comfort in the knowledge that other great faiths, too, have manifested murderous fanaticism. In the name of Christianity, the Crusaders in the Middle Ages carried out their campaigns of massacre and pillage against scores of Jewish communities, and religion proved the ultimate source of implacable and bloodstained hostility in Northern Ireland. Among Muslims, the very term 'Jihad' or 'Holy War' points to the ingredient of religion in the cocktail of war and violence.

Religious Jews had thought themselves immune until the dreadful massacre of Arab worshippers in Hebron early last year, now followed by that black day ten days ago. Once again, we are warned how easily even people who until recently were held up as the finest examples of idealism, selflessness and moral virtue can be seduced by a few extremists. I speak not only of the events of comparatively recent times but also of those who have in one form or another condoned the crime. For them, the unity of the land of Israel under Jewish control became a supreme article of faith, obscuring the most fundamental teachings of Judaism. The inflammatory attacks on the peacemakers turned into virulent and irresponsible charges of treason, construed by some fanatics as a licence to kill. What fearful power attaches to words when uttered by purveyors of extremism of any kind.

Of course, as in most human conflicts, this is not a black and white situation, with the onus only on one side. The apparent official unconcern with the fate of the settlers certainly generated much resentment. More importantly, the fiercely secularist policies pursued by members of the Israeli Government increasingly alienated wide sections of the Israeli public from all traditional Jewish values. It widened the cultural gulf and accentuated the bitterness within the land.

These ominous tensions might have been reduced had spiritual leaders of the more radical groups not turned to ultra-nationalist politics but instead demonstrated, by precept and example, the splendour of truly Jewish life; how it could have cemented the unity of the Jewish State by common ideals, reducing the curse of crime, vice and broken homes, thus helping to create a model society of Judaism in action. Such pristine ideals once inspired these pioneers, and one hopes the present tribulations will restore that vision. There can be no Jews without Judaism, any more than Judaism without Jews.

The challenge to Jewish spiritual leaders is now grave indeed. My successor, Chief Rabbi Dr [Jonathan] Sacks, in his resolute Albert Hall address on Sunday, spoke of hanging his head in shame. For my part, the resolution which I drafted and which was adopted unanimously at our European rabbis' conference in Zurich proclaimed:

'We call upon Jewish religious leaders and teachers not to tolerate fanaticism and blind intolerance … More important than an undivided Land of Israel is an undivided People of Israel. We appeal to all responsible leaders in Israel and in the Diaspora to maintain the spiritual and moral values of Judaism as the indispensable link binding the Jewish people together and justifying our claim to continued national survival.'

In an agonised burst of soul-searching and contrition, some disciples of the very teachers who began to worship the Land of Israel even more than the God of Israel have turned to me, as to other rabbis, in a quest for atonement. They realise they have been misled on the true priorities of Judaism. Some are even considering a public fast to demonstrate their striving for a faith of which the Book of Proverbs states: 'Its ways are ways of pleasantness, and all its paths are peace.' Let this be a warning to all religious fanatics on how easily unguarded speech and inflammatory teachings can lead to the worst sacrilege, turning even the most pious idealists into murderers.

Jews have prevailed over immense adversity in the past. Sustained by our faith and encouraged by our friends, I am confident the present grave crisis will be overcome to bring stability and moral strength to Israel, and to inaugurate an era of enduring peace with all her neighbours through moral rectitude and a passion for justice.

Hansard, 16 November 1995

FAMILY LAW BILL

Lord Jakobovits: [This] Bill contains some valuable provisions which merit support. More important, it helps to bring one of the most depressing problems besetting the country to national attention. It places it at or near the top of our parliamentary agenda … I should like to make a final point on [its] Jewish ramifications, particularly the hardship bar. A special difficulty arises out of a divorce. While dissolving the civil contract of the parties, it leaves the religious bond – equally recognised by the State as valid in parliamentary legislation – still intact, thus leading to a 'limping marriage' liable to cause immense hardship. The noble and learned Lord the Lord Chancellor has been most helpful and has indicated that if I table an amendment to the hardship bar, designed to alleviate the hardship, the Government will look seriously at it in Committee. I repeat that I am most grateful to the noble and learned Lord for his understanding.

As heirs to the Judaeo-Christian heritage, most of us appreciate that the biblical story of the Creation starts with marriage as the first human institution. In their togetherness, man and woman were told by their Maker to be fruitful and to multiply; to fill the earth and to conquer it; and to have dominion over nature. It is no good reaching the outer spaces of the heavens, ruling over the mysteries down here on earth through the conquest of nature and being dominant outside if the inner space of the home collapses, and the hallowed bond between man and wife is allowed to snap. I hope that the Bill, with amendments, will help millions of homes to be built or rebuilt as secure havens of love, virtue and joy.

The Lord Chancellor: As I indicated at the outset of the debate, and again a moment or two ago, I certainly believe that the issues here are ones which will require to be carefully considered in Committee. All the amendments that may be suggested will be, certainly on my part, very carefully looked at, including the amendment which the noble Lord, Lord Jakobovits, said he wished to propose in relation to the particular problem that he referred to at the end of his remarks.

Hansard, *30 November 1995*

[The amendment, dealing with the problem of agunot *– 'chained wives' – is discussed below and on pages 41–3.]*

FAMILY LAW BILL

Lord Meston moved Amendment No. 11:
Page 6, line 10, at end insert –
('(2A) If the parties –
(a) were married to each other in accordance with usages of a kind mentioned in section 26(1) of the Marriage Act 1949 (marriages which may be solemnised on authority of superintendent registrar's certificate), and
(b) are required to co-operate if the marriage is to be dissolved in accordance with those usages,
the court may, on the application of either party, direct that there must also be produced to the court a declaration by both parties that they have taken such steps as are required to dissolve the marriage in accordance with those usages.
(2B) A direction under subsection (2A) –
(a) may be given only if the court is satisfied that in all the circumstances of the case it is just and reasonable to give it; and
(b) may be revoked by the court at any time.') …

Lord Jakobovits: My Lords, there is no need to rehearse once again the considerations leading to the presentation of this amendment which was so splendidly put before us by the noble Lord, Lord Meston. I would merely want to add two remarks on the significance of this amendment, which I hope will be accepted.

First, I dare say that of all the new clauses and new amendments now introduced into this Bill, none will have more immediate significance as a source of relief to those affected than this particular amendment. It would mean, possibly, that they would not have to remain in a state of suspension, neither married under the previous marriage which has ended in a civil divorce, nor being able to contract a new one because of the commitments entered into at the time of the original bond between them. Therefore, the amendment will come as an enormous relief to those in our community, and far beyond. In many foreign countries, people have constantly watched the progress of this amendment with a view, possibly, to adopting it to resolve what has proved to be an agonising problem caused by the exploitation of one party. Usually it is the wife who is held to ransom by the husband, but this can occur the opposite way around. I hail with profound appreciation, on behalf of a grateful community, all those who have contributed to this historic amendment. I hope that it will be passed and will be confirmed in another place.

Secondly, on most matters of policy there are deep divisions within the Jewish community. This is the one item on which all sections of our community are united, whether they be Reform, Liberal, Orthodox or Conservative. They are all united in supporting this measure. If there has been a degree of opposition or questioning, it was solely by individuals who spoke for themselves – and said so – and who were concerned partly with matters of principle to them, but in greater measure with presentation of the problem which did not always reflect the complete realities of the situation.

Therefore, I join the noble Lord, Lord Meston, in expressing profound and abiding appreciation, above all to the noble and learned Lord the Lord Chancellor for his immense help and counsel in making the presentation of the amendment possible, and to the noble Lord, Lord Mishcon, who has been uniquely helpful. To use the Hebrew phrase, last but not least, I should like to thank the presenter of the amendment, the noble Lord, Lord Meston.

Hansard, *11 March 1996*

MARRIAGE

Lord Jakobovits: My Lords, before contributing to this important debate, perhaps I may be allowed to say a word in tribute to that great personality whom we lost overnight. I refer to Lord Beloff, who so greatly enriched our debates, our thinking and the literary riches of our country. If we are seeking one simple phrase that epitomised his life, it would be the title of one of his early books, one of the most popular of the many that he wrote, *The Intellectual in Politics*. He was that intellectual *par excellence*. We shall profoundly miss his erudition, wit, perspicacity and friendliness and the insights which have helped to make our House into what it is and which will make his name immortal in the annals of this House and of our country.

We are once again grateful to the noble Lord, Lord Northbourne, for raising the supremely urgent subject of marriage. I make no apology for having agreed to take part in this debate. We are given an average of six minutes for each contribution. That is soon going to be the average time for each marriage if we are not careful. Our job in those six minutes is to make some contribution to ensuring that the period for a marriage is greatly extended.

Now that we are a multicultural society, with many strands making up the diversity of our citizens, we ought to try to collect from each constituent something of enduring value which can contribute to our debate, and eventually towards the solution to one of the gravest problems besetting contemporary society.

We are not helped by some of the statements made by Ministers of the Crown, two of whom have already been referred to. In a recent television interview, the Home Secretary argued that the Government, now representing a secular State, should altogether withdraw from moral judgements affecting marriage. The stability of the home is clearly no longer the charge of the Home Secretary. Likewise, the example of the Foreign Secretary in relation to the durability and sanctity of marriage, or the action of the Chancellor in withdrawing the last financial props that encourage the preference for marriage, do not augur well.

We have already paid an extortionately high price as a nation for our indifference to marriage. The People's Princess would still be alive today, and so would her lover, if they had observed the laws on the sanctity of the marital bond. Let us consult each strand of our multicultural society to see whether we can enucleate from them something that can help each one of us to contribute towards solving the massive problem that now engages our nation.

Perhaps I may say a word or two drawn from the faith and family tradition which gave birth to me. I wish to mention just two items. A 2,000-year-old saying in the Talmud has it that: 'He who divorces the wife of his youth, even the altar sheds tears over him.' Why the altar? The altar is the instrument of sacrifice. If a marriage fails, it is a sign that the two spouses were not prepared to make enough sacrifices for each other and thought first of their own happiness before the happiness of their partner and spouse. The altar has failed to teach that lesson, and weeps for its failure.

Perhaps I may give a second, more personal illustration. I heard with pleasure the personal references by previous speakers. My wife often told me that, when she left her parental home to be married to me, in a Paris synagogue where her father was the rabbi, her mother told her: 'You'd better make a success of your marriage because, if you don't, I won't take you back home.' Today, far too many think that if they do not succeed in their new home, there will be an open door when they return to their parents or elsewhere.

The alternatives to success are far too easy today. Every marriage encounters its occasional problems and disappointments. But if the alternatives were too simple and the escape too easy, few would make enough effort to make their marriage succeed. The more precious it becomes by dint of the effort put into it, the less dispensable it turns out to be.

I speak as the father of six happily married children and eight happily married grandchildren. I am asked, 'What is the recipe?' I answer that, in addition to the careful choice of carefully nurtured genes in the partners to be chosen, it is to close the door of your home to smut and indecency and to open it to the healthy whiff of social engineering to create a Rolls Royce of a home which is indestructible and full of comfort and security …

We believe that the education for marriage starts long before birth, and is never finished. We are bidden to go into marriage preparation, which is so widely neglected today, by making sure that we do not allow children to be born and raised without some form of preparation and training in the most delicate art of human relations. If we succeed, the rewards will be infinite and the rejoicing in countless thousands and millions of homes will be immense.

Hansard, *24 March 1999*

HUMAN EMBRYOS AND CLONING

Lord Jakobovits: My Lords, we are once again indebted to the noble Lord, Lord Alton of Liverpool, for giving us the opportunity to delve into this perhaps most vital – literally, most vital – of all subjects that we could ever hope to discuss.

When the Warnock Committee considered the whole issue of human reproduction in the light of modern scientific and technological advances, it wisely recommended a complete ban on the cloning of human beings. That is the law to the present day, as it was enshrined in the Human Fertilisation and Embryology Act.

Let me say at once that I am not impressed by the argument so frequently advanced that we are playing God by delving into these mysteries of creation itself. On the contrary, I believe that we as human beings, endowed with a divine soul and intelligence, are meant to use that endowment in the service of mankind, medically or otherwise; and every time we bring human ingenuity to bear on alleviating human suffering, bringing solutions to problems of human reproduction, not only do we not play God; we perform an essential basic duty of man – that is, to be Godlike, *imitatio dei*.

The specific reference to human cloning may call for some fresh consideration and elucidation, especially in the light of the latest scientific and medical developments. In the debate in 1989, when the Bill was passing through your Lordships' House, I suggested that the line drawn between embryos under and over two weeks old – as was mentioned in two contributions here this afternoon – seemed entirely arbitrary. Because the first signs of the so-called 'primitive streak' were not apparent before that, it was suggested that, up to two weeks, one should be able to carry out experiments, and that thereafter such experiments should cease. Rather, I suggested then that a distinction ought to be made between embryos generated for experimental purposes, which ought never to be sanctioned, and between embryos that were potentially viable and others which were in any event destined to die.

Let me explain. There was no reason why an excess of embryos which had to be generated in *in vitro* fertilisation procedures in order to produce the one or two possible viable births, and which could not afterwards be re-inserted in the mother because it might lead to multiple births and thereby either endanger the mother or the developing foetuses, should not be used for experiments, so long as those experiments were designed to lead to possibly life-saving ends. That seems to make a much more logical division that would not infringe or impinge on the dignity and value of human life, potential or otherwise. The whole subject calls for careful re-examination to ensure that human life is adequately protected as well as promoted and that human intelligence is used to remove, as far as we can, human suffering and deprivation.

Let me conclude with one important observation that exercises me constantly as a recipient of an age-old tradition in the pioneering of the moral law and the tremendous infinite esteem for human life that we cherish and wish to share with the rest of the human family. These are subjects that are still far too delicate and weighty and, as we have seen in this debate already, too contro-versial to warrant a definitive ruling, decision or vote at this early stage – early both scientifically and morally.

Therefore, what is called for is a further moratorium, as President Clinton advocated not so long ago, before we take steps that cannot be reversed which could lead to incalculable disaster. If we make one slight miscalculation, we may produce monsters over the generations that cannot be undone. Therefore, caution is the order of the day. But let us not forget that our ultimate assignment is to bring healing, on the one hand, and the supreme dignity of man and his repro-duction, on the other, to bear on us as humans in maintaining a divine order; a human order that will preserve the distinctiveness and uniqueness of our task as men and women made in the image of our Creator.

Hansard, *28 April 1999*

[This was Lord Jakobovits' final speech in the House of Lords, one of 29 he made during his 11 years on the cross-benches. His last appearance in the House was on 20 October 1999 – 11 days before his death – when he voted in two divisions on amend-ments to the Immigration and Asylum Bill.]

A ROCK OF CERTITUDE

On a battlefield, fixed points and strong positions are enviable possessions. If it is true that there is a general search for a moral universe within which to locate our fragmented lives, then those who are discovered to be occupying firm rocks already – preferably rocks of ages – will benefit.

Sir Immanuel Jakobovits, Chief Rabbi of the British Commonwealth, ennobled in the New Year's Honours List and the first rabbi to have been so, stands on such a rock. The vigour and certitude with which he gives voice to moral concerns is contrasted by many with the bitter internal wrangles within the Christian churches on, above all, matters of sex: in particular, women priests, homosexuality, and Aids.

His moral positions are not adopted – not consciously, at least – by reference to points fixed by contemporary debate, but wholly by reliance on scripture, on the law and the prophets. His social reflexes derive from the position of a Diaspora Jew of the late twentieth century drawing on a tradition, a history and a tragedy which are far more consciously realised in every Jew than their equivalents (where they exist) in most Christians.

By creating him a peer, the Prime Minister has put into Parliament the most authoritative spokesman for 'traditional' virtues in the country: it is an irony, but not in these times strange, that he should be an immigrant and that his values are those of a community which is determined to maintain its separateness.

To maintain separateness, Jews must maintain their very existence; and that at different times and in different countries has been in doubt. Jakobovits is not in doubt as to how that has been achieved: 'The whole art of Jewish survival lies in the fact that we have managed to triumph over nature.' And his own affinities with the Government are expressed in the congruity of its values to Jewish ones: 'I think [the Government] has created a veritable revolution of attitudes, perhaps even more important than the economic advances which have occurred …'

People, he believes, are seeking stable truths in a febrile age and, in his belief in that, he recognises, unwillingly and conditionally, a parallel with the current traditional versus liberal travails in Anglicanism: he took public issue, earlier this year, with the Very Reverend David Edwards, Canon of Southwark Cathedral, for calling the Bible 'fables'.

'I do not rely on the fickle human conscience to guide me on what is right and wrong. I rely on external revelation and on the law. And so I wouldn't call that fables: that is a denigration of something I hold dear, precious, more than life itself. It is for the sake of this that all our martyrs gave their lives – to maintain the primacy of a teaching which gave meaning to our very existence.

'I do not think that modernity in itself, coming to terms with the moral world and what it has to offer, is in any way in conflict with believing that my moral norms are governed by factors which are immutable, beyond time, as true today as it was 3,000 years ago and will be 3,000 years from now.

'The very value of religious truth I see as being its not changing: it is beyond the freak ups and downs of fashions and fads; and therefore, as I once put it, I am a salesman of antiques: and the value of what I sell is that it has lasted, it has endured.'

John Lloyd, Financial Times, *4 January 1988*

Part Two

LEGACY

CHAPTER EIGHTEEN

'A Prince Has Fallen'

Chief Rabbi Dr Jonathan Sacks called him 'a prince of God'. Lady Thatcher lauded him as one of the century's 'most remarkable spiritual leaders'. The Queen and Prince Charles said he would be 'greatly missed'.

Tributes poured in this week from across the nation and from all sections of British Jewry for Emeritus Chief Rabbi Lord Jakobovits – the first rabbi to be ennobled – who died, from a brain haemorrhage, in the early hours of Sunday morning, aged 78.

Lord Jakobovits, who retired as Chief Rabbi in 1991 after 24 years in office, was laid to rest on the Mount of Olives in Jerusalem on Monday morning. His body had been flown from London, where the previous day the crowded streets of mourners attending a pre-funeral service at Hendon Synagogue testified to the wide communal respect in which he was held.

In a message read out at the service by Lord Levy, Prime Minister Tony Blair paid tribute to 'a man deeply respected and admired throughout the country'.

Lord Jakobovits had been due in Paris on Sunday to head a delegation seeking French President Jacques Chirac's intervention on behalf of the 13 Iranian Jews accused of spying for Israel. On Tuesday, he was to have been one of 300 high-achieving Britons honoured at a millennium lunch by the Lord Mayor of London, Lord Levene.

But on Saturday, having performed the havdalah ceremony, he complained of feeling unwell and was rushed to hospital. Early on Sunday morning, as he had appeared to be weakening, family members assembled a minyan at his bedside. As they recited the Shema, Lord Jakobovits moved his head, in apparent recognition, for the first time in several hours. Shortly afterwards, according to family members, he passed away peacefully.

Thousands of people crowded into Hendon Synagogue to pay tribute to Lord Jakobovits before his body was flown to Israel. The shadows cast by the unrelieved black of the men's hats and coats created a scene suggestive of a Rembrandt painting. In the ladies' gallery, Lady Jakobovits – supported by two of her four daughters and seven granddaughters – walked down to the front row, while a dozen yeshivah students brought in the black-draped coffin to rest on two plain trestles, adorned only by a yahrzeit candle.

In Jerusalem, hundreds of Israelis gathered to bid a final farewell to Lord Jakobovits as he was buried. Church bells tolled in the distance as rabbis circled the grave several times, reciting psalms – an old Jerusalem tradition – overlooking the Temple Mount. Among the mourners were Chief Rabbi Dr Jonathan

Sacks, Haifa Chief Rabbi Shear Yashuv Cohen, Rehovot Chief Rabbi Simcha Hacohen Kook, Israeli Religious Affairs Minister Rabbi Yitzhak Cohen, and former Finance Minister Yaacov Neeman. Also present were dozens of British Jews who have made Israel their home, as well as Bnei Akiva members on year-off courses who travelled to the funeral from yeshivot and seminaries across Israel.

The British Government was represented by its Ambassador, Francis Cornish, who said later: 'I have come to pay tribute to a great Chief Rabbi, a courageous yet humble man who made an enormous impact on Jewry in England and across the world'.

Jewish Chronicle, 5 November 1999

NOBLE LEGACY

The extraordinary life of the Emeritus Chief Rabbi, Lord Jakobovits, came to an end on Sunday, prompting a no less extraordinary array of tributes from Jewish and non-Jewish Britain, and from abroad. Lord Jakobovits was in many ways a man of paradoxes. He grew up in the shadow of the Holocaust, yet ultimately embraced a vision of Judaism and Jewishness rooted not so much in that tragic past as in the search for a self-confident Jewish future. He was at first a reluctant rabbi, but became a hugely influential one. He was a quiet man, shy, sometimes politically naïve – naturally more comfortable in personal conversation than as an orator. Yet he would leave a lasting mark not only as a religious leader, but on the national political stage as well. He had an instinctive talent for speaking in a Jewish voice which resonated far more widely (a talent perhaps with no recent equal in British Jewry, ironically, except the late Reform rabbi, Hugo Gryn). On Judaic, communal and domestic political issues, Lord Jakobovits' views and instincts were deeply traditional and conservative – frequently frustrating or angering some on the Left of British Jewry. On Israel, Rabbi Jakobovits was outspoken in his criticism of Orthodox involvement in national politics, and of what he saw as many Israelis' inability or unwillingness to grasp the pain and to meet the aspirations of the Palestinians – views which angered those on the religious and political Right.

Yet no one who met, knew or worked with Lord Jakobovits could doubt the sincerity and immutability of his core beliefs, nor his instinct for seeing the good in even – perhaps, especially – those fellow men and women with whom he ostensibly had the least in common. He was, in every sense of the phrase, a deeply thoughtful man. The praise which was lavished on him this week, and the crowds who descended on the memorial service hastily arranged at Hendon Synagogue just hours after his death, conveyed the depth and breadth of the respect in which he was held by a community whose constituent groups and leaders had sometimes fiercely disagreed with his views on particular issues. It is hard to imagine a greater accolade, or a more fitting tribute to his life and leadership. Lord Jakobovits' achievements should also stand as a timely reminder to all in our community that strongly held views, honestly and forcefully expressed, need not preclude respect for, and by, fellow Jews with differing traditions, backgrounds or outlooks.

Leading article, Jewish Chronicle, 5 November 1999

Among obituary notices in the national and religious press came the following tributes:

The Times: Immanuel Jakobovits had a powerful influence on British spiritual life – and, indeed, political life – far beyond his own faith. He was a staunch upholder of conservative values who provided an extra dimension to the reaction against what was in many quarters perceived as the permissive society of the 1960s and 1970s.

Indeed, he related strongly to Margaret Thatcher when she was Prime Minister, and she in turn regarded him very much as 'her archbishop', having little sympathy with the Church of England of the time.

To the end, he remained loyal to the German Jewish tradition in which he was reared, which owed much of its ideology to the nineteenth-century Frankfurt rabbi, Samson Raphael Hirsch. He stuck to the Hirsch line of strict observance, combined with an open engagement with the society and culture round about ...

Family tradition and influence directed him to the rabbinate, where he finally gave the British Chief Rabbinate a higher standing, inside and outside the Jewish community, than it had ever enjoyed before ...

In his induction sermon in April 1967, he made clear his unyielding adherence to the old traditions. He would uphold the belief in the divine origin of the whole corpus of Jewish law and tradition (the issue in the Jacobs affair) but at the same time would 'do all within my power to close the gaps within our people'.

To a considerable extent, he succeeded in both these tasks. While employing a more liberal vocabulary than his predecessors or the Orthodox rabbinate generally, he never departed from the strict attachment to traditional beliefs and observances and opposed all efforts directed at change. Concurrently, he established and maintained friendly relationships with the non-Orthodox sections of the Jewish community without accepting the authenticity of their interpretations of Judaism ...

Jakobovits regarded the conferment of a life peerage in 1988 very much as a personal honour. And so it was. He was the first Chief Rabbi in more than a century and a half of the office to get a peerage. He was to an extent a working peer, seen frequently around the House of Lords even when he was not speaking. But he did speak regularly on any topic with a moral or religious angle.

In appearance, he was tall and impressive, relaxed in his manner and always an agreeable companion. He was a fluent and amiably diffident conversationalist, avoiding subjects on which his rigidly orthodox views might have provoked argument. He never entirely lost his German accent but nevertheless became an eloquent speaker in the English language, his text often enlivened by the apt quotation, anecdote or telling phrase ...

The Daily Telegraph: Lord Jakobovits would not, perhaps, have claimed that God was a Thatcherite; he was, however, one religious leader whose preaching did not, in Mrs Thatcher's view, give God a bad name.

It would, though, be a mistake to view his 24 years as Chief Rabbi merely through the filter of national politics. Though he advocated hard work and civic responsibility, his first concerns were the commandments of God, which he plainly stated should be applied to the ethics of the nation.

He sought the moral regeneration of society, denouncing abortion, sex outside marriage, easy divorce, and slackness in the instruction of children. 'When Government propaganda', he said, 'promotes something that comes to terms with evil without saying so, then that is inherently unacceptable ...'

Though Orthodox in outlook, he was refreshingly unorthodox in approach and could at times startle even his own followers with the vigour of his advocacy. He did not waver in expressing views that attracted hostility, either in defence of the Palestinian minority in Israel or against campaigners for a homosexual way of life.

If he provoked controversy, he also excited admiration, both within his community and without. His social and economic views in particular appealed to Anglicans unhappy with the direction many in their own Church were taking ...

The Guardian: Immanuel Jakobovits was perhaps the most unusual rabbi ever to have practised his calling in this country ... From the moment he took his seat in the Lords in 1988, Jakobovits' dark-blue skullcap – the only one ever seen in the chamber – was as familiar a sight as the Lord Chancellor's wig.

He could fit comfortably around the banqueting tables of Buckingham Palace or 10 Downing Street – always eating specially provided, strictly kosher food. Equally, the Chief Rabbi of the United Hebrew Congregations of the Commonwealth was a familiar figure at functions for obscure Jewish organisations, stooping slightly to discuss the problems of, say, an unemployed man, or a woman who was having trouble getting a religious divorce – difficulties that would be taken up almost immediately ...

[He became] the most active and effective Chief Rabbi in decades ... His influence – and his activities – spread far beyond the congregations where his writ ran, from Hackney to Hong Kong, from Manchester to Melbourne. He had the highest profile of any Chief Rabbi, matched only by that of his successor, Jonathan Sacks ...

Jewish Chronicle (Chaim Bermant): It is difficult to know what qualities raise one rabbi above another, but if simple goodness is any criterion, then Immanuel Jakobovits was far and away the greatest Chief Rabbi Britain has had. It was evident in his attitudes, his actions, his very appearance.

He had a spiritual quality which, with the possible exception of Nathan Adler, was not shared by any of his predecessors, and exemplified the belief that Jews were *rachamonim uvenei rachamonim* – merciful, and the sons of the merciful. His natural sense of compassion led him into serious controversy, as, for example, when he touched on 'the unspeakable misery' of the Palestinian refugees, and suggested that the Arabs, too, had some claims to the Holy Land.

All of which might suggest that he was a good but naïve and unworldly man, which in some ways he was. Yet he was also a man of action who found the Chief Rabbinate in tatters and gave it a standing and prestige among Jews and non-Jews it had not previously enjoyed …

He was – as he readily admitted – lucky both in his private and public life. Where his predecessors presided over periods of unbroken religious decline, he witnessed a religious revival. He did not claim to be responsible for it, but he did much to enhance it. He not only widened the appeal of Judaism to the Jew, but made it seem relevant to the life of the nation …

[In 1948] he was invited to become Chief Rabbi of Ireland. But more importantly, he found a wife in the person of Amélie Munk. It was a singularly happy choice, for, with all his qualities, it is unlikely that he would have got half as far as he did without her.

Amélie, although of German origin, was almost ostentatiously French, exuberant, uninhibited, coquettish. She also had great charm, and knew how to use it. 'She'll never make a lady', observed her future mother-in-law, who had serious misgivings about what sort of a rebbetzin she might make. In fact, she made an ideal one, for with her light-heartedness she was shrewd, serious, devout, with a stern sense of duty.

Her husband soon discovered that everything he had preached about the joys of Jewish family life was abundantly confirmed by his own experience. He became a new man. For all his youth, he had a gravity and earnestness about him which was almost oppressive. He became more genial, relaxed, self-assured, and while never adept at small talk, his conversation became less ponderous …

[In sum] he had his failings, but they were trivial compared to his virtues – and his failures, but they were insignificant compared to his achievements.

[Chaim Bermant wrote his tribute – from which the above is excerpted – some months before his own sudden death in January 1998. It appeared for the first time the week the Emeritus Chief Rabbi died.]

IN MEMORY OF HARAV LORD JAKOBOVITS

A memorial service for Lord Jakobovits was held by the United Synagogue at the St John's Wood Synagogue, London, on 16 December 1999 (Tevet 8, 5760), attended by members of the family, private individuals and representatives of organisations and institutions from across the national and communal spectrum. The main speakers were Chief Rabbi Jonathan Sacks; Dayan Chanoch Ehrentreu, Rosh Beth Din; Norman Turner, a son-in-law; Lord Mackay of Clashfern, former Lord Chancellor; and Peter Sheldon, president of the United Synagogue. The service was introduced by Dayan Ivan Binstock, of the London Beth Din.

In his opening address, Chief Rabbi Sacks described HaRav Lord Jakobovits as 'one of the truly great Anglo-Jewish leaders, a man who raised the standing of Judaism and made us walk taller as Jews.' He continued:

A Prime Minister of this country called him 'a giant among men', and we knew him as *moreh moreinu,* a teacher of teachers, a rabbis' rabbi, an inspiration, a role model, and a guide.

When he passed away, I quoted the words of King David: 'A prince and a great man have fallen this day in Israel.' In Jerusalem, at his funeral, those words were taken up and amplified very beautifully by Rav Shear Yashuv Cohen, the Chief Rabbi of Haifa. He asked: 'What is the difference between a *sar* and a *gadol,* a prince and a great man?' And he said: 'A prince is one who is outstanding by virtue of his office; a great man is one who is outstanding in and of himself. There can be a prince who is not a great man, and there can be a great man who is not a prince; and rare it is to find both of them together.'

And that is what Lord Jakobovits was. His personal gifts were immense – as a teacher, a preacher, a Torah scholar, a pioneer, the virtual founder of Jewish medical ethics, a man you could never meet without learning something new. Truly he was a *gadol.* But he was also a *sar,* a man utterly undaunted by the challenges of office, fearless in all he said and did, a man of peace at times of conflict, a man of moderation in an age of extremes, never afraid to speak when others were silent, never afraid to say no when every other voice was saying yes. In him, high office and great character were combined, he was truly a *sar v'gadol.* His Hebrew name was Israel. And surely his epitaph will be *oteh yisrael betifarah* – in him God crowned Israel with glory.

How shall we remember him? Tonight, as we light the candle of memory, let me do so in terms of the three other candles in the Jewish faith – *ner Shabbat,* the lights of Shabbat, *ner Chanukah,* the Chanukah lights, and *ner havdalah,* the havdalah candle. What is the difference between them?

Ner Shabbat have always symbolised the light within, the light in the Jewish home, the inner light. Lord Jakobovits knew with unshakeable conviction that the strength of a Jewish community is measured not by outward success but by its inner spiritual dynamic. Its strength, always, is the strength of the great three institutions of Jewish life – the home, the school and the shul – and how passionately he fought for all three.

He founded the Jewish Marriage Council and constantly fought for the sanctity of the family and of marriage. To build schools, he instituted the Jewish Educational Development Trust, with its slogan 'Let my People Know'; and how moved I am that our youngest daughter should attend the school that bears his name – Immanuel College. And when it came to synagogue life, he never tired of reminding us, his rabbinical colleagues, *mon malki? rabbanan* – who are the kings? Answer: the rabbis. He challenged us to lead, and to lead the way. He led by action and by example.

Let me share with you one very personal memory of that example, which took place 31 years ago. Rabbi Jakobovits was new to his office. I was just a student, president of the Jewish Society at Cambridge, and another young man, Philip Skelker – today one of our leading educators – was president of the Jewish Society in Oxford. We were full of the chutzpah of youth. We phoned the Chief Rabbi and demanded an audience, which he graciously agreed to. We went round to Hamilton Terrace and told him that the Jewish students needed a rabbinical presence on campus. He listened and, instead of reprimanding us for our impetuosity, he agreed. He not only agreed but he acted – and it was then that Jewish university chaplaincy was born. That was one small example of the kind of man he was – one who did what he said and led by what he did, and it left a deep impression on us. In all aspects of our communal life, he lit the Shabbat candle and strengthened Anglo-Jewry from within.

The Chanukah candle is exactly the opposite of the Shabbat candle. It is not meant to light from within but to send light to the outside, to publicise the miracle, to light up the public domain. And I do not think that any Chief Rabbi before felt more deeply than he did the imperative of bringing the light of our Jewish teachings to the wider society, to light up the public domain. He was the first Chief Rabbi to become a national figure, and he was held in great respect, immense respect, way beyond the borders of our community. When he spoke on ethical and social issues, his was a voice of clarity in an age of confusion; he was a man of conviction in an age of doubt. He never forgot his thankfulness to this country which had let him in, taken him in as a young man fleeing from Nazi Germany, and which later ennobled him as the first Chief Rabbi to sit in the House of Lords. He repaid that debt generously through his moral leadership, which he painted across the broadest of canvases with immense dignity and power.

And, of course, I have left to last the *ner havdalah*, the havdalah candle, and you surely know why. Because lighting the havdalah candle, making havdalah, was the last mitzvah Lord Jakobovits performed in his life. And in a sense it summarised his life. We make havdalah on the borderline between *kodesh* and *chol*, between the sacred time of Shabbat and the secular time of the week; it is the border between the world of home and the world of work. And the havdalah candle is unique because it is a single flame embracing many lights, one candle woven out of many strands, to teach that the light by which we live in all our many contexts – whether at home or in the street – should always be one and the same.

And that was Lord Jakobovits – the same in private as in public. Never once would he be different at home from what he was on the platform. He never changed his words or deeds: what he was on the outside he was on the inside. And that is why he was held in such high respect by everyone – by supporters and opponents alike.

The Torah says a remarkable thing in explaining why Abraham was chosen. It says that he was chosen so that he would teach his children after him to keep the way of God. More even than Abraham was chosen to be a leader and a prophet, he was chosen to be a husband and a father.

And what strength Lord Jakobovits gave to, and was given by, his family! Words are inadequate to say how much he owed to his beloved wife, Amélie: always there, always supportive, his constant companion, his continuous *ezer kenegdo*. It was a unique partnership. And tonight we say to you, Lady Amélie, knowing how much of what he gave us you gave him – we say: may the Almighty grant you health and comfort and blessing for many years to come. And to his remarkable sons and daughters, his sons-in-law and daughters-in-law, his many grandchildren and great-grandchildren, all of them continuing the path that he began, we say: may he live on in your lives as he will live on in our hearts.

Dayan Chanoch Ehrentreu: I stand here tonight among a distinguished gathering who have come to pay respect and tribute to the memory of a prince of Torah, an outstanding and remarkable spiritual leader of our community, an ambassador of our people.

The Gemara cites the source for the requirement to rend one's garment on the death of one's father, mother or teacher. Of the departure of Eliahu the prophet on the chariot of fire, it is written that Elisha – who was watching – exclaimed: '*Avi, avi, my father, my father, the chariot of Israel and the horsemen thereof!*' And he saw him no more. And he took hold of his clothes, and rent them in two pieces. The repetition of 'My father, my father', says the Gemara, is an allusion to the passing of one's father and one's mother; 'the chariot of Israel' to a teacher who taught one Torah.

HaRav Yisroel was to me, and to many of my colleagues in the Beth Din and the rabbinate, a father figure whose guidance, teaching and advice were those of a father to a son. Whenever a problem arose, however difficult and involved, we could turn to him for guidance. For 15 years, while here in London, I had the privilege to be within the ken of his personality. His dignity, nobility and the countless hours we spent together will remain with me as deeply cherished memories. As *avi*, my father, and also as *imi*, my mother – a mother figure – he was one who was sensitive to the feelings of others, who constantly gave encouragement in times of difficulty and distress, who shared and empathised with our problems and concerns as if they were his own.

'The chariot of Israel and the horsemen thereof.' As Chief Rabbi, he was Anglo-Jewry's spiritual power, whose impact went far wider – through his unwavering loyalty to Torah and to his faith, through his consistency, his modesty, his humility, the courage of his convictions and the nobility of his character, and through his concern for the spiritual, moral and religious welfare of every Jew. He raised the honour and glory of the Torah, brought honour and dignity to our community, and was highly respected and recognised by all as a great leader, with the courage to stand up and express the relevance of traditional morals and attitudes to society's current problems …

HaRav Yisroel commanded our respect by his quiet, unassuming and dignified manner, by his modesty and humility, and by his inner strength of character. Greatness and humility go together: they are, indeed, a true reflection and characteristic of divine leadership.

Norman Turner: Over the past six weeks, thousands upon thousands of letters have been received by the family from around the globe, and certain words keep appearing: 'inspirational', 'rabbi of rabbis', 'spiritual giant', 'beacon of light', 'perfect role model', coupled with such words as 'humility' and 'sensitivity'. But there is another group of words that keep appearing – 'integrity', 'sincerity', 'being genuine'.

The first time the Torah mentions Yaacov, our patriarch Jacob – Yaacov, of course, being the basis of the name Jakobovits – it says: *veyaakov ish tom*, 'Jacob was a wholesome and a perfect man'. Rashi adds three words: *kilibo kein piv*, 'what was in his heart, that was on his lips'. There were no ulterior motives; he was totally sincere. And this was the hallmark of Papi as we knew him through the family and beyond.

In one of his articles, Papi wrote that every human being should regard himself or herself as unique, destined to be responsible for some incomparable enrichment of society. We just have the difficult task of selecting, seeking and finding that particular niche where perhaps we can excel. But there is a constant reminder of this ideal which we say in the morning prayers, in the words 'Let me sing praises to Hashem with those unique characteristics that I and each one of us possesses so that we can honour Hashem'.

I conclude with words again taken from our daily prayers: '*shomer yisroel*, Guardian of the people of Israel, *shmor she'eiris yisroel*, guard the remnants of the people of Israel'.

Perhaps one can say *shomer yisroel*, guardian of HaRav Yisroel, now looking after that beloved soul, the *neshomoh*, in the next world, *shmor she'eiris yisroel*, guard the shattered remnants of HaRav Yisroel – those people worldwide, Jew and non-Jew alike, who feel this vast void since he departed six weeks ago, the people of this country, the people of Israel, Anglo-Jewry, his close friends and close family.

Lord Mackay of Clashfern: Lord Jakobovits was the author of the major work, *Jewish Medical Ethics*, and it was in this area that he first made his mark as an acknowledged expert, outside the ordinary vast range of his rabbinical work. He spoke on this subject with great authority. But it was on the family, above all, that he gave us some of his most eloquent addresses. They were not only beautiful in themselves; they are evidence of the careful preparation and hard work our dear friend put into every utterance he made in the House of Lords.

He came to see me often, and, although we had a profound difference in our faiths, we had a great deal in common. His deep study and reverence of the Scriptures made him, for me, a very congenial visitor, and I was greatly encouraged and guided by his remarks on biblical passages with which I was familiar and sought to treasure.

He was very understanding of my faith. When I was invited to Israel, after my appointment as Lord Chancellor, I was anxious at reports of the possibility of legislation being passed by the Knesset which would make unlawful my possessing my New Testament in that land. I wrote explaining my concerns to Lord Jakobovits and, after looking into the matter, he replied that I could go to Israel with my New Testament with every confidence that what I was doing would not be unlawful there.

He had a profound respect for the faiths of others and often expressed to me – and publicly – his appreciation of the Christian witness in this country, in which he had found his home and which had given him much happiness throughout his long and distinguished time here.

I warmly salute his memory as a cherished friend and outstanding public figure.

Following his address, Lord Mackay read this message from Prime Minister Tony Blair:

I am sorry that Cherie and I are unable to be with you this evening at the memorial service to Lord Jakobovits. His passing has left a great gap in the British Jewish community and all of British society.

May I take this opportunity to send my personal condolences to the family and to the community. In particular, I should like to make mention of Amélie. Can there be anyone in your community whose life has not been touched by an act of her kindness? A true 'woman of valour'. We share your personal loss at this time.

Since that sad day six weeks ago, I have reflected on the life of this extraordinary man: an inspirational Chief Rabbi who transformed the face of British Jewry; a dignified peer of the realm who ensured that the values of Judaism have universal relevance; a stirring prophet for peace and co-existence in the Middle East. But, above all else, Lord Jakobovits was a man of unshakeable faith – a man who, in the words of the Jewish teaching, 'knows where he comes from, where he is going, and to whom he is accountable'.

Yet Lord Jakobovits was determined to translate faith into action, and throughout the Commonwealth one sees his work – schools, communities, rabbis, teachers – inspired by his challenge to live a full Jewish life within the modern world, and to make a personal contribution to both. That vision lives on and now becomes his legacy.

May Lord Jakobovits' memory be a blessing to his family, to the Jewish community, and to all of Britain.

Before commencing his tribute, United Synagogue president Peter Sheldon read the following message from Baroness Thatcher:

It is an honour to pay tribute to Lord Jakobovits, as one of the most remarkable spiritual leaders of the twentieth century. No Chief Rabbi has had such an enormous and beneficial influence on our country. He was a wise and fearless guide to his own flock, and an inspiring example to the rest of us. Immanuel Jakobovits has left behind him a reputation which will last for as long as integrity is honoured – truly a man for our times.

Mr Sheldon then continued:

Two days before his untimely death, I received a typically generous and moving letter from HaRav Lord Jakobovits, in which he wrote: 'I remain convinced that the United Synagogue is the key to the future of Orthodoxy in Anglo-Jewry.' The deep belief and conviction that lay behind those few words epitomised Lord Jakobovits' relationship with the United Synagogue, whose members he referred to as 'my family'.

In an era of unparalleled decline both in moral values and in the status of the family unit as the central pillar of a stable society, his was the often-lone clarion call for the preservation of those timeless Torah values that are the ethos of the organisation he served – the organisation which now I serve with such pride, but which he served with such distinction.

Yet even as we mourn for him, we are mindful that, for all his great achievements, he would not have felt that his work was done. In a speech to our council, made 32 years ago, his first as Chief Rabbi – a speech that is as relevant today as it was then – he said: 'There is a spark of Jewish religious feeling in every Jewish heart. However much our youth may protest, however defiantly they may reject our beliefs and observances, no one is beyond the pale of redemption, provided we are persistent enough and keep on trying, whatever our disappointment. If we work hard enough and never take "No" for an answer, we will find that nothing is impossible in reclaiming those lost to the service of our people and our imperishable ideals.'

As a well-known columnist said, in a most moving tribute published a day or two after his death, Lord Jakobovits was one of those rare individuals who led not by rhetoric but by example. He never took 'No' for an answer. I believe that that, above all, is the legacy he has left us, and the example he would have wished us to follow.

We, the members of his chosen family, mourn the loss of this great man, this prince among men – as our Chief Rabbi has described him.

Lady Jakobovits – Amélie – on behalf of the whole family of the United Synagogue, I want you to know that we shall treasure his memory; we shall continue to be motivated by his example; and, in our quest to bring our community ever closer to the Almighty, we, too, will never take 'No' for an answer.

Bar-Ilan and the Future

In April 1974, two chairs were inaugurated at Bar-Ilan University in honour of Chief Rabbi Immanuel Jakobovits and the Haham, Rabbi Dr Solomon Gaon. Among those present at the ceremony, on the university campus in Ramat Gan, were the Minister of Health, Victor Shemtov, representing the Israeli Government; the British Ambassador, Bernard Ledwidge; and a 60-strong delegation of British Friends of Bar-Ilan University, under the chairmanship of Henry Knobil, who sponsored the project. The holder of the chair in Sephardi studies was Professor Ezra Zion Melamed, while Professor Shalom Albeck occupied that in Jewish law. Following the inauguration ceremony, Chief Rabbi Jakobovits addressed the gathering on 'Conformity and Diversity in Jewish Historical Tradition':

Of all the enduring ideals inspiring Western civilisation, there is only one which is not Jewish in origin or orientation. Monotheism, the brotherhood of man, social justice, neighbourly love, the quest for universal peace and the hope for man's redemption are all part of our biblical heritage. They reflect cardinal Jewish teachings throughout the ages. The only exception is the ideal of democracy, much as we value it as the best system of government so far devised.

This notion of the rule of the people, as determined by the majority, is of Greek origin, as is the term itself. Judaism never vested the exercise of power or the arbitration between right and wrong through legislation in the consensus of superior numbers. On the contrary, in opposition to this view, the Book of Job declared (32:9): 'The many are not wise.'

Wisdom is not necessarily the prerogative of the majority. The opinion of the majority prevails only among equally qualified experts, for, as the *Sefer HaChinuch* puts it (Mitzvah 78): 'It would be improper to say that a small group of sages should not outweigh a large group of ignoramuses, even if they were as numerous as the participants in the Exodus from Egypt.' Otherwise, Judaism always upheld minority rights rather than subjecting all to the absolute will of the majority.

This is how the Jewish people – chosen for its historic assignment of moral leadership 'because you were the smallest of all peoples' (Deuteronomy 7:7) – became the great nonconformists of history. Conditioned from the start to accept minority status, Jews at all times swam against the stream of conformity and spurned public opinion. The Hebrew prophets in their days were the loneliest and most unpopular leaders of all times: yet, today, they are immortal, and through the impact of their teachings, the mighty flood of paganism which engulfed them has been contained and pushed back.

The Maccabees represented a tiny band of idealists pitted against the massive strength of the Greek Empire and its Hellenistic culture. Through their victory, and because of their triumph, the great monotheistic faiths survived or came into existence, determining ever since the advance of civilisation and social justice on a global scale. And need we be reminded that, throughout the Middle Ages, right up to our own time, our people defied the blandishments of the dominant faith and the cruel blows of our persecutors, persevering as an insignificant minority, ever ready to pay a fearful price for being out of step with our contemporaries?

The firm commitment of Judaism to nonconformity and diversity also finds striking expression in its attitude to proselytisation. In contrast to the other monotheistic faiths, Judaism never went out of its way to encourage conversions, nor did it aspire to become a universal religion. It emphatically rejects the belief that it is, or will ever be, the sole portal to human salvation, holding instead, in the words of the prophet Micah (4:5), that 'all the peoples shall walk each one in the name of its god'.

A uniform human society in which all groups and individuals strive to be identical would be as stagnant and unworkable as a machine constructed of equal parts only, or as an orchestra in which all instruments are the same. Once the common fundamental imperatives of the moral order are accepted, we do not advocate a merger of man's diverse religions or races or national characteristics and cultures. Any blurring of these distinctions can only have blighting effects on human progress.

Lately, or at least until Yom Kippur, we were in some danger of losing the distinctiveness of the Jewish national character, of shedding the pride in being different. Altogether, we live in an age of rigid conformity, an age in which nothing is harder than to defy the pressures of uniformity. Through instant global communications, through the all-pervasive indoctrination of the mass media, through the growth of international organisations and combines, national and individual features are being levelled out to produce an amorphous homogeneity of opinions, fashions, tastes, eating habits, social forms and even moral, or immoral, norms all over the world.

For the Jewish people, for whom the refusal to join the majority is an indispensable condition of national survival and fulfilment, this headlong drive towards nondescript uniformity presents a particularly deadly peril. For some centuries past, in the long struggle for Jewish emancipation, we have fought for the right to be equal. Having gained our emancipation, at any rate in the Western world, we now find it hard to fight for the right to be different, or indeed to assert the wish to be different, with the result that the gravest internal Jewish challenge we now face is the crisis of identity.

Paradoxically, the emergence of the Jewish State, founded as a bulwark against assimilation to fulfil the Jewish national purpose, has aggravated the tendency towards national assimilation through the quest for equality. Notwithstanding its immense contribution to the consolidation of Jewish pride and identification inside and outside the Land, Israel has increased rather than weakened the pressure of conformity.

The emphasis in our national Jewish stance is largely on becoming and being like everyone else. Corporately, we take more pride in what we have in common with the nations of the world than in what distinguishes us from them. We boast of a parliamentary system, universities, industrial enterprises, not to mention armed forces, like unto others; but we show less pride in what sets us apart from others, in possessing a religious system, academies of Jewish learning, spiritual values and moral attributes which are uniquely Jewish and unlike any other people's national treasures.

As I recently told communal leaders in London in a lecture on 'The Spiritual Challenges of the Yom Kippur War': 'The benefits of equality escaped us, as the nations still do not treat us as equals, while the liabilities of equality afflict us, as we now sadly experience, like all other peoples, rising rates of delinquency, divorce, illegitimacy, social inequality, if not downright discrimination, and many other evils which erode society at large.'

The utter loneliness which we have experienced so dramatically with the desertion of our fair-weather friends since the Yom Kippur War, and the double standards applied to Israel by the international community, have demonstrated that if we do not freely accept the uniqueness of Israel, it is providentially imposed on us against our will. As is now evident, individually many Jews may opt out, but nationally we cannot escape from our destiny of being 'a people that dwells alone'.

BAR-ILAN TO BUILD BEIT HARAV JAKOBOVITS

Israel's Bar-Ilan University is to build a £4.9 million centre in honour of the Emeritus Chief Rabbi, Lord Jakobovits, who died in October. It will house the department of Jewish and general philosophy and, according to the British Friends of the University – which is sponsoring it – will be the only one of its kind in the country to combine a Jewish and Western programme.

The five-storey, state-of-the-art marble and glass building will be erected in the new northern campus extension, due to be completed by 2004. It will be called Beit HaRav Jakobovits for the Study of Philosophy, Ethics and Jewish Thought.

The department – part of the faculty of humanities – will also be home to the interdisciplinary centre for Jewish social ethics and morality. The centre will address ethical problems and dilemmas in modern society.

Bar-Ilan president Professor Moshe Kaveh said: 'HaRav Jakobovits worked strenuously to foster Jewish unity and cohesiveness. His great contribution to British society and the Jewish people in this regard was recognised by world leadership at all levels.'

In a letter to Professor Kaveh, Lord Jakobovits' widow, Amélie, wrote of the 'wonderful prospectus of Beit HaRav Jakobovits and its future programme'. She added: 'Our children and I feel humbled by, and infinitely proud of, your magnificent vision in honour of my husband. On reading the prospectus, we can sense how very well you and your colleagues knew him and knew what were his priorities in life, and the Jewish values which clearly guided him through life.'

Jewish Chronicle, *24 March 2000*

HARAV LORD JAKOBOVITS AND BAR-ILAN

With the passing of HaRav Immanuel Jakobovits, Bar-Ilan University lost a staunch advocate and loyal friend. The relationship between him and Bar-Ilan was one of shared values and ideology. Despite the numerous demands on his time, and his full involvement in the affairs of Anglo-Jewry and in national life, he served for some 30 years as a trustee of the university and was a long-time supporter of its British Friends.

With the help of funds from the Immanuel Jakobovits Chair in Jewish Law, four volumes by its incumbent, Professor Shalom Albeck, were published by Bar-Ilan University Press: *Foundations of Criminal Law in the Talmud* (1974); *Introduction to Mishpat Ivri in the Times of the Talmud* (1976); *The Courts in the Time of the Talmud* (1996); and *Foundations of Financial Law in the Talmud* (1999).

In 1992, together with former Soviet President Mikhail Gorbachev and 14 other dignitaries, Lord Jakobovits received the degree of Doctor of Philosophy *honoris causa* at a conferment ceremony at Bar-Ilan University.

HaRav Jakobovits' association with Bar-Ilan saw it grow into the second largest institution of higher education in Israel. When the university was founded in 1955, its enrolment numbered some 55 students. Today, more than 26,000 students are registered in its highly regarded academic programmes in the faculties of the social sciences, humanities, Jewish studies, law, and the life and exact sciences.

Beit HaRav Jakobovits for the Study of Philosophy, Ethics and Jewish Thought will be a dynamic monument of learning to HaRav Jakobovits' life and legacy. Located there will be the university's department of Jewish and general philosophy, including its related programmes and research centres.

The department is the only one of its kind in Israel to combine an entire programme of Western and Jewish philosophy. Teaching and research cover all aspects of the field, from the philosophy of ancient Greece to medieval religious philosophy and contemporary issues, from moral and political philosophy, linguistics, aesthetics and existentialism to Jewish mysticism and the philosophy of halachah and the halachic process. The unique structure of the department nurtures a challenging synthesis of Western and Jewish philosophical traditions.

A master's programme in the philosophy of law, for law-school graduates, examines from a philosophical perspective the complex relationship between individual rights and obligations in the context of society and the State. Teachers of Jewish philosophy in secular high schools are encouraged to participate in another master's programme designed to deepen their understanding of Jewish thought and to raise the level of the subject as taught in schools. The department is also home to Israel's first graduate programme in bioethics, a subject of profound interest to HaRav Jakobovits.

Motivating the creation of Beit HaRav Jakobovits are the unprecedented moral challenges facing contemporary society, due not only to ever-expanding technological innovations but to the social and cultural upheavals of modern times. In the realm of values, traditional sources of authority are frequently being re-examined and sometimes undermined. The blessings of spiritual freedom are mixed with deep uncertainty over the ways individuals and society may meet their personal and collective responsibilities. Confronting the moral challenges of today – and tomorrow – requires an amalgam of creativity and rootedness.

Scholars steeped in religious traditions are often too secluded or reluctant to address the issues of the day boldly and open-mindedly. Conversely, scholars committed to social and technological advance are often unable or unwilling to be inspired by time-hallowed tradition. HaRav Jakobovits, however, combined the best of both worlds. His life's work encompassed the fertile and meaningful combination of Jewish tradition with contemporary ethical and moral issues.

Beit HaRav Jakobovits will address many such issues, including values in politics and public policy, ethics in business and finance, morality in the military and in law-enforcement, and ethical dilemmas in medicine and the life sciences.

While its primary academic base will be in the faculty of humanities – home to the department of philosophy – the Centre will be thoroughly inter-disciplinary. Scholars versed in moral philosophy and in the philosophy of halachah will engage with colleagues in the faculty of Jewish studies and the faculty of law (including *mishpat ivri*, Jewish law), as well as with members of Bar-Ilan's various schools and departments – social work, political science, education, life sciences, and others – as dictated by particular issues. Each subject will feature traditional Jewish perspectives as a central component of the discussion.

A forum of selected scholars in various fields, distinguished thinkers and *talmidei chachamim*, will form a central think-tank. This forum will set the agenda for the Centre's efforts, defining the issues of highest priority and relevance to Israeli society and to Jews in democratic countries worldwide.

To address each issue thus defined, the Centre's leadership will identify appropriate scholars within the Bar-Ilan community and bring them together to form either dedicated research teams or ad hoc discussion groups. To share their findings with a broader audience, as well as to enjoy input from external sources, occasional conferences will be held on defined topics.

Beit HaRav Jakobovits will foster research and creative thinking by Bar-Ilan's senior faculty members and their graduate students in the forefront of contemporary social ethics in interaction with Jewish tradition. It aims to become a vibrant resource for influential and inspiring analysis and guidance for decision-making institutions throughout society.

Designed by the renowned Israeli architects Zalman and Ruth Enav –

responsible for several other buildings on the Bar-Ilan campus – Beit HaRav Jakobovits, while standing distinctively on its own, fits harmoniously into the context of the new faculty of humanities complex. Its five levels are divided, in ascending order, into classrooms and administrative offices; library and faculty offices; the Centre for Excellence in Bioethics, with its own library, lecture and seminar rooms and faculty and administration offices; eight faculty offices; and classrooms, archives and offices for the department of philosophy publications, *Philosophia* and *Da'at*.

Beit HaRav Jakobovits is a stunning physical and tangible tribute to the life of one of the great Jewish leaders of the twentieth century. The Talmud teaches that words spoken in the tradition of a departed master animate the memory and legacy of that teacher. Bar-Ilan is proud to be associated with the Jakobovits family and the British Friends of the University in establishing a permanent living legacy dedicated to Jewish learning in the tradition of the teacher himself, one from which future generations in Israel and throughout the Jewish world will continue to benefit.

Bar-Ilan University, Ramat Gan, Israel

Bibliography

In addition to the publications listed in the Preface, the following are recommended reading: Chaim Bermant: *Lord Jakobovits: The Authorised Biography of the Chief Rabbi* (Weidenfeld & Nicolson, 1990); Michael Shashar: *Lord Jakobovits in Conversation* (Vallentine Mitchell, 2000); Gloria Tessler: *Amélie: The Story of Lady Jakobovits* (Vallentine Mitchell, 1999); Immanuel Jakobovits: *Jewish Medical Ethics* (Bloch Publishing Company, 1959, 1975), *Jewish Law Faces Modern Problems* (Yeshiva University, 1965), *Journal of a Rabbi* (Living Books, 1966), *The Timely and the Timeless: Jews, Judaism and Society in a Storm-tossed Decade* (Vallentine Mitchell, 1977), *If Only My People: Zionism in My Life* (Weidenfeld & Nicolson, 1984); Jeffrey M. Cohen (editor): *Dear Chief Rabbi: From the Correspondence of Chief Rabbi Immanuel Jakobovits on Matters of Jewish Law, Ethics and Contemporary Issues, 1980–1990* (Ktav Publishing House, 1995); Jonathan Sacks (editor): *Tradition and Transition: Essays Presented to Chief Rabbi Sir Immanuel Jakobovits to Celebrate Twenty Years in Office* (Jews' College Publications, 1986). This last title includes a 60-page bibliography of HaRav Jakobovits' writings from 1940 to 1986.

Index

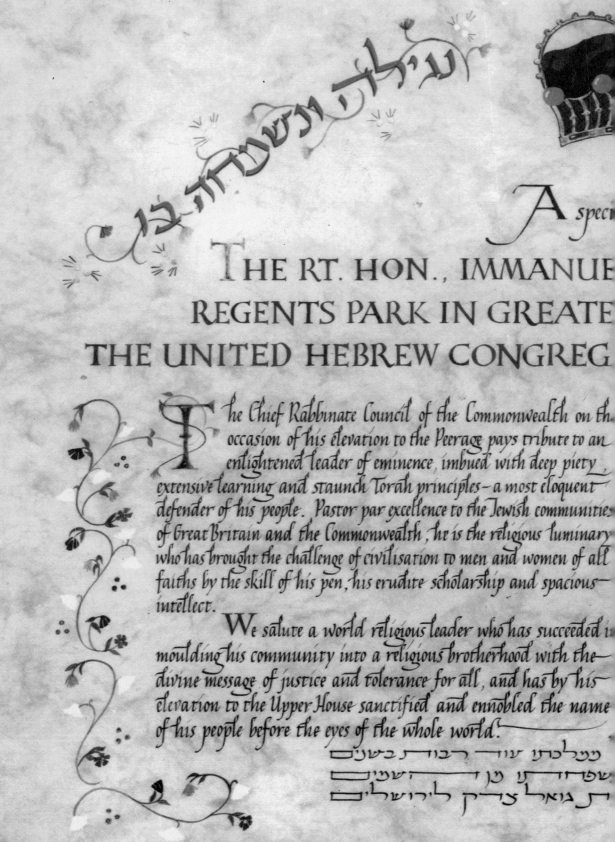

עירו וירושלם

A speci

THE RT. HON., IMMANUE
REGENTS PARK IN GREATE
THE UNITED HEBREW CONGREG

The Chief Rabbinate Council of the Commonwealth on th. occasion of his elevation to the Peerage pays tribute to an enlightened leader of eminence, imbued with deep piety, extensive learning and staunch Torah principles – a most eloquent defender of his people. Pastor par excellence to the Jewish communities of Great Britain and the Commonwealth, he is the religious luminary who has brought the challenge of civilisation to men and women of all faiths by the skill of his pen, his erudite scholarship and spacious intellect.

We salute a world religious leader who has succeeded i moulding his community into a religious brotherhood with the divine message of justice and tolerance for all, and has by his elevation to the Upper House sanctified and ennobled the name of his people before the eyes of the whole world.

מעלתו עוד רבות בשנים
שיחיה ויזכה ויראה
גאולת ציון לירושלים